THEODOR ADORNO
AND THE CENTURY OF NEGATIVE IDENTITY

Cultural Memory
in
the
Present

Hent de Vries, Editor

THEODOR ADORNO AND THE CENTURY OF NEGATIVE IDENTITY

Eric Oberle

STANFORD UNIVERSITY PRESS
STANFORD, CALIFORNIA

Stanford University Press
Stanford, California

© 2018 by the Board of Trustees of the Leland Stanford Junior University. All rights reserved.

"Jazz, the Wound: Negative Identity, Culture, and the Problem of Weak Subjectivity in Theodor Adorno's Twentieth Century" was originally published in *Modern Intellectual History* © 2016, University of Cambridge Press. Reprinted with permission.

No part of this book may be reproduced or transmitted in any form or by any means, electronic or mechanical, including photocopying and recording, or in any information storage or retrieval system without the prior written permission of Stanford University Press.

Printed in the United States of America on acid-free, archival-quality paper

Library of Congress Cataloging-in-Publication Data

Names: Oberle, Eric, 1968- author.
Title: Theodor Adorno and the century of negative identity / Eric Oberle.
Other titles: Cultural memory in the present.
Description: Stanford, California : Stanford University Press, 2018. | Series: Cultural memory in the present | Includes bibliographical references and index.
Identifiers: LCCN 2017052516 | ISBN 9780804799249 (cloth : alk. paper) | ISBN 9781503606067 (pbk. : alk. paper) | ISBN 9781503606074 (epub)
Subjects: LCSH: Adorno, Theodor W., 1903-1969. | Identity (Philosophical concept)—History. | Critical theory—United States—History.
Classification: LCC B3199.A34 O24 2018 | DDC 193—dc23
LC record available at https://lccn.loc.gov/2017052516

Typeset by Bruce Lundquist in 11/13.5 Adobe Garamond

Contents

Acknowledgments		ix
	Introduction	1
1.	"Jazz, the Wound": Negative Identity, Culture, and the Shadow of Race	29
2.	America; or, the Stranger	71
3.	Negative Identities of the Subject in Wartime America	115
4.	Critical Theory Goes to War: The Critique of Positive Identity and Positive Science	131
5.	Negative Modeling: Objectivity, Normativity, and the Refusal of the Universal	207
6.	Subject/Object and Disciplinarity	241
	Conclusion	289
Abbreviations		295
Notes		299
Index		317

Acknowledgments

This book was long in the making, and it is suffused with obligation. My sense of indebtedness makes it a privilege and a pleasure to thank everyone who supported and sustained me through many years of struggle and discovery. I thank Stanford professors Keith Baker, Kurt Mueller-Vollmer, Paul Robinson, and James Sheehan, who advised the research out of which this book grew. To Detlev Claussen and Axel Honneth, who mentored me and provided feedback on much earlier stages of this project, I am particularly obliged. To Ken Moss, I owe a deep debt of dialogue and friendship. Christine Holbo's conceptual clarity and tough love for the truth make her my ideal reader. Without Gerald Izenberg this book would not exist; he provided lively and incisive commentary on multiple drafts. This book is dedicated to my parents, Wayne and DeEdra Oberle. I also thank Naomi Andrews, Celia Applegate, Marc Caplan, Charly Coleman, Dan Coleman, Bradin Cormack, Cora Fox, Malachi Hacohen, Espen Hammer, Robert Hullot-Kentor, Jack Jacobs, Martin Jay, Peter-Erwin Jansen, Emily Levine, Thomas Martin, Ian Moulton, Sam Moyn, Anca Parvulescu, Devin Pendas, Ramsey Eric Ramsey, Amy Randall, Noah Strote, K. Stephen Vincent, Michael Werz, and Steven Zwicker. I am grateful as well for the brilliant guidance of Emily-Jane Cohen at Stanford University Press for long support of this project and for the assistance of Jessica Ling, Cynthia Lindlof, and Faith Wilson Stein. I thank Rolf Tiedemann at the Theodor W. Adorno Archive and Jochen Stollberg at the Universitätsbibliothek in Frankfurt. I am grateful to the Stanford Humanities Center and its Fellows for a year of support and discussion. Finally, I express my appreciation to the anonymous readers at *Modern Intellectual History*, who provided insightful commentary on my "Jazz, the Wound," published in volume 13, issue 2 (2016), pp. 357–86. Portions of that article have been revised and reproduced here in Chapter 1, with permission from Cambridge University Press. Arizona State University's Institute for Humanities Research and College of Integrated Sciences and Arts graciously supported publishing this work.

THEODOR ADORNO
AND THE CENTURY OF NEGATIVE IDENTITY

Introduction

Identity: Theory and Praxis

In 1966, when the German-Jewish philosopher and sociologist Theodor Adorno published *Negative Dialectics*, the volume was chiefly understood as a provocation. The book's opening lines, proclaiming that philosophy "lived on because the moment of its actualization was missed," invoked Marx's *Theses on Feuerbach* in a way that seemed intended to aggravate. Conservatives read it as the confession of an unrepentant Communist. Radicals were perplexed by the inversion of the young Marx: if Marx's original thesis had said "hitherto philosophy has merely interpreted the world, but the point is to change it," Adorno the old Marxist seemed to insist that the day of revolutionary action was over, that nothing could be done but retreat into the academic fastnesses of philosophical abstraction.[1]

During the next three years, the Frankfurt student body interposed itself between Adorno's words and his text, positing a different version of Marx's *Theses* by seeking to transform critical theory into a mode of action. As protests against the Vietnam War and the social role of universities grew pitched, attendance in Adorno's lectures became standing room only. His books came into high demand; his lectures on Kantian ethics, ontology, and the principles of sociology became meeting points for student radicals—and targets for student protests. The ironies compounded as the Institute for Social Research, rebuilt after the war adjacent to Frankfurt's Goethe University with the help of American occupation funds, was occupied by protesters demanding a return to the Institute's Marxian origins. Adorno, protective of the Institute yet sympathetic toward the students, continued to take the double stance suggested in *Negative Dialectics*, sharpening his criticism of the contemporary situation while denouncing the actionistic "Leather Jacket" wing of the student movement that favored direct—even blind—protest actions (and police provocations) over theoretical discussion.

Words became flesh during the spring semester of 1969, when Adorno's lectures were regularly disrupted by protests. On April 22, two groups interrupted "The Introduction to the Dialectic." The first group demanded that the lecture be converted to a teach-in. Calling on Adorno to submit a self-critique on the university's (and his own) relation to authoritarian governance, they wrote on the chalkboard: "Whoever allows Adorno's words to govern will live their whole lives under capitalism." After Adorno assured this group that a lecture on dialectics might prove relevant, he resumed speaking, only to be interrupted again. This time, three leather-jacket-clad women stepped to the podium and, baring their breasts, showered him with rose petals and kisses. This "happening" proved to be Adorno's last lecture. The rest of the semester was canceled; Adorno died of a heart attack a few months later.[2]

Left behind for publication was Adorno's "Marginalia on Theory and Practice," which, though replete with sympathetic gestures toward the student movement, was adamant about what he referred to as the *non-identity* of theory and practice. The *Theses on Feuerbach*, argued Adorno, did not teach the immediacy of action; rather, they showed that the desire for rebellion must never collapse meaningful politico-philosophical distinctions. The attempt to turn the celebrated "unity of theory and praxis" into a "simple identity" threatened, he argued, to turn dialectic into its opposite—authoritarian dogma, reactionary behavior, subjective self-contentment.[3] To underscore the concrete political dangers of such false identities, "Marginalia" pointed to press reports that compared the action and protest doctrines of the extraparliamentary opposition (which later formed the kernel of the Green Party) to the (neo-Nazi) German Nationalist Party. To equate these movements was itself a form of reaction; yet students, their right-wing critics, and the liberal press were converging on actionism. Theories of action must not exploit or coerce identity, argued Adorno. They must heed differences among principles and contexts—among modes of activity, agency, and knowledge—and in this sense they were always in need of the work of theoretical reflection.

This book is the first part of a two-volume study reexamining Adorno's life and theory in terms of the history of a central but neglected contribution of critical theory: the critique of the identity concept that Adorno articulated in the middle decades of the twentieth century but sought to refine up through the 1968–69 crisis. The concept of identity embraced by the students in the late 1960s was not Adorno's starting point, yet he was far more engaged with the challenge of identity than the students understood. The notion that personal identity, action, and philosophy could become identical in politics, that self-making could be action and theory in one, crystallized in a new form in the 1960s. But it emerged out of a broad and loose discourse articulated from a host of sources reaching back to the origin of the modern period, and it was first explicitly theorized by Frankfurt philosophers and social thinkers in exile in America in the 1940s. The idea that every action in society is either an act of cooperation or one of protest emerged from a logical notion of identity rooted in philosophy; the idea that the baring of breasts could bring a halt to capitalist accumulation or the machinery of war had grown out of a vitalistic concept of personal identity and its ties to a notion of political culture. Together these notions were contributing to a new way of thinking about politics and the ideals of emancipation it strives for: the idea that "the personal is political," and vice versa. Adorno was, during his American years, present at the creation of this new idea of personal identity, and he would develop it *ex negativo* in the course of the next twenty years, into the concept of non-identity at the center of *Negative Dialectics*.

If Adorno was, by the end of his life, in many respects thinking along with the protesters, he came at the concept of identity with a longer history and a different perspective. Adorno and the student protesters of the New Left agreed that identity posed a challenge to the politics of social structures and rational interests. Where Adorno differed with the students was in his insistence that identity, if it was to become an expansive concept, must also be a negative one. Throughout "Marginalia," Adorno invoked the idea of identity in a logical sense to show that the collapsing of categorical differences is the first move in a brutalization of the intellect. He also, however, acknowledged the importance of identity in the subjective sense, speaking of how violence accompanies the formation of group identities.

Positing a parallel between thinking about alterity and respecting the rights of others, Adorno argued that deep within the tradition of modern selfhood there exists a desire toward having a self—an identity. This desire liberates. But its other side—negative identity, rooted in loss and woundedness that emerge from the trauma of alienation and self-consciousness—is not only always present but is *prior*: people first experience identity negatively. And identity has a history of actively willing the dissolution of the self into a collective identity, an unmediated relation in which thought is action, theory is practice, and violence is done to others to make them conform with the uncertain and weak self. If the twentieth century's vision of achieving identity hoped to extend and radicalize the tradition of universal rights, Adorno sought to describe the shadow of this tradition, the weak link in its claim to self-grounding. Adorno's proposition was that though identities of self and deed must be taken seriously, they must also be criticized and reconceptualized in terms of their history of truth and falsity. No identity is born pure; identities are always the result of a negation, a recoil from an unreconciled, unemancipated state. To think about non-identity is to think against the subject's myth of self-creation and to consider the subject in a force field of negations, borrowings, and displacements. Doing so, ironically, might strengthen the subject. One could not understand nationalism or terrorism, liberation or domination, fascism or liberalism without addressing identity and negative identity together. Arguing dialectically, Adorno insisted that the negative side of identity—which looks like a side effect—is antecedent to every form of identity. Adorno came to think, however, that it was possible to work through identity as a form of retrograde self-consciousness and thus liberate identity from the fear that drives it.

This book offers a reconsideration of Adorno's argument for the logical priority and emancipatory potential of negative identity. Taking seriously the possibility that Adorno's negative approach to theorizing identity, though cut short by his early death, represented not only a challenge to the developing discourses of identity but also an important clarification and extension of them, this book seeks to accomplish two goals. First, by engaging with the history of Adorno's intellectual development as a theorist of subjectivity, this book inquires into the historical and theoretical meaning of identity as a concept that has shaped the experience and interpretation of modern life since World War I. Second, it suggests that the language of negative identity, though only partly articulated at the time of Adorno's death, offers a significant addition and refinement to the possibilities of theorizing identity. The history of positive identity is entwined with negative forms of identity: identity as racism, prejudice, ontologized conflict, and victim blaming in a world of mass-mediated subjectivities. Arguing that the dual-sided nature of identity has been latent within the concept, this book suggests that if one comes to terms with this history—if one learns to address identity in both its positive and negative forms—it is possible not only to develop a better analytical language of social subjectivity but also to imagine a new interdisciplinary social phenomenology based on a reinvigorated concept of objectivity.

Identity and Modern Freedom

The concept of identity has become so prevalent in contemporary discourse that it is difficult to measure its bounds. Historically, "identity" enjoyed its first success as an analytical term starting in the late 1950s, when Erik Erikson used it to describe the central *psychological* product of the process of maturation and self-development: subjects become subjects as they achieve a stable identity, and vice versa. This usage spread first gradually and then rapidly beyond the bounds of psychology and psychoanalysis, and "identity" became a political, philosophical, and cultural keyword that has reshaped the analysis of every social topic that touches on either the constative or performative dimensions of expression.[4] A distillate of the modern logics of radical self-making, the language of subjective identity contains elements of the existentialist concept of authenticity; the psychoanalytic concept of egoity; the Romantic ideal of the expressive, infinite self; and nationalist and collectivist notions of self-making through cultural self-definition. Though a complex historical and sociotheoretical inheritance, the concept of identity has become so common, so deeply embedded in the discourse of politics, culture, and society, that it has become, at once, a universal answer and a universal problem. In the daily news, in the writing of historians, journalists, political theorists, philosophers, self-help therapists and security experts, it appears with such frequency that its usage attests simultaneously to its clarity and precision and to its impossible vagueness and imprecision.

Undoubtedly, identity's ever-expanding usage is linked to changes in the concept of selfhood, attesting to a broadly held sense that the self is the only truly foundational concept in contemporary life. Identity plays an important role in answering the question "who am I?"—and not just as a matter of introspection but as a matter of professional or political self-understanding. When one speaks in the language of "as an X, I believe Y," one is drawing on the fact that identity's implied ontology reaches into fields of ethical and epistemological deliberation. Positive identity means, in broad strokes, that the question "who am I?" precedes and never fully leaves the discussion of questions of truth or obligation. Establishing a connection between a subjective ontology (who am I?) and questions of ethics (what should I do?) and knowledge (how do I know what I know?), identity presents itself at once as an organizing concept in an interdisciplinary discourse and as a postdisciplinary concept, a new master term that often preempts the need to negotiate the perspectives of different disciplines and different sources of authority. Embedded within this interlocking understanding is a logic of emancipation. In its ideal self-conception, to *have* an identity means to be awakened to *who* one is, and this awakening shapes subsequent questions of *what one must do* and of *how one sees and knows the world*. This emphatic form of subjective identity reveals its relation to the existentialist concept of authenticity, itself a secularized religious concept of faith directed at the self. To become aware of one's identity is to become aware of the power of self-making, and this awareness divides the world into those who are authentic—who embrace their own identity—and those who seek or accept conformity.

The ethicist Christine Korsgaard offers an example of how the languages of identity have transformed the terms of political thought. Korsgaard uses the language of identity to solve an old dilemma in ethics that pitted Aristotle's notion of public action against Kant's notion of autonomy. For Korsgaard, to distinguish between "theoretical" and "practical" identity is to develop a postmetaphysical vocabulary of freedom, selfhood, and action that frames a much broader understanding of politics and personhood than was possible in either the Kantian or Aristotelian frameworks. Indeed, in many usages where Kant would have spoken of practical and theoretical reason, and thus an absolute divide between knowledge of the self and knowledge of the world, Korsgaard speaks of "practical identity" as a continuously unfolding chain of acts of meaningful self-constitution that includes

such things as roles and relationships, citizenship, memberships in ethnic or religious groups, causes, vocations, professions, and offices. It may be important to you that you are a human being, a woman or a man, a member of a certain profession, someone's lover or friend, a citizen or an officer of the court, a feminist or an environmentalist, or whatever.[5]

Even in this short passage, one can sense how closely Korsgaard—for example, with her use of the pronoun "you" or the flippant existentialia of "or whatever"—wishes to cleave to the everyday language of self-determination and action. This is a hallmark of subjective identity, encapsulating the way the language of identity breaks down philosophy's more strict (Kantian) divide between knowing and doing, between practical and theoretical knowledge. In this regard, Korsgaard reflects the absorption of a multivalent existentialism into the everyday language of identity, typifying the way that the modern synthesis of practical and theoretical "identity" implicitly expands the classical categories of citizenship to include many once-excluded dimensions of experience, including sexuality and gender, professional and interpersonal ethics, ethnic and religious affiliation. Offering a provocative synthesis of Kant and Aristotle, Korsgaard argues that human beings constitute themselves through actions that they understand to be self-making and world making at once. Human beings "deliberately decide what sorts of effects they wish to bring about in the world"; in so doing, each individual is "also deliberately deciding what sort of a cause [he or she] will be."[6]

Though the identity concept's articulation in the field of psychology and its roots in existentialism lead it to emphasize the individual, questions of *being* in identity have always been linked to questions of *becoming*, and the individual's identity has been complexly linked to collective identities. The simple way to put this is that identity is seen as something *given* but also as something *earned*, accompanied by a (weaker) sense of obligation to recognize and foster identity in others. Erikson, whose concept of identity subsumed Freud's notion of ego along with the entire domain of culture, saw identity not just as the product of the Oedipal drama—the logic of "identification with" the mother or father—but also as an ongoing series of struggles with conformity or rebellion, with science or religion, with one's own industry or sense of inferiority. And this processual dimension of identity attests to the further fact that Erikson's way of speaking about identity incorporated a deep—half-sociological, half-anthropological—sense of the psychological necessity of social affiliation. No one has an identity alone; the pursuit of identity is always already a kind of group or collective effort toward individuality. There is implied in Erikson's thought—and in the language of identity as it has developed in the last decades—a productive struggle between individuality and group affiliation. At the outer edge, identity is the sui generis and it is a social law. On the one hand, individuals are imagined as needing to belong—to have group affiliations beyond themselves. On the other hand, individuals are imagined as creating unique identities out of these affiliations and personal judgments—as making necessary choices for determining their fidelity to themselves and, through that, gaining perspective on how to acknowledge the necessary difference in others as well. The coexistence of necessity and freedom points to a widely felt tension among exclusionary and exilic, uncoerced and free notions of identity and belonging.

The origins of the mereological (individual/group) tension in the concept of identity go back to the mid-twentieth century, and they map onto the twentieth century's disciplinary unclarity about the relation between science, liberation, and progress. Midcentury discourses on identity, strongly informed by anthropological assumptions, typically attempted to resolve the question of why the supposedly universal need for identity had become so pressing in modernity by arguing that identity, though passively part of traditional societies, became an explicitly necessary goal of the individual only in modern societies. A little bit of Émile Durkheim's mechanical solidarity trailed along, adding the suggestion that traditional societies tend to suppress individuality and foster collective responsibility and group solidarity, whereas modern societies tend to require individual autonomy while undercutting the communal resources that would make it possible.[7] Yet typically such attempts at a historical anthropology of identity, far from overcoming this dilemma, only underscore the fact that the tension between the individual and collective forms of identity has been constitutive of the identity concept's rise. Both Erikson and Korsgaard's use of the term suggests that one *creates* a unique, individual identity largely by participating in and identifying with some larger community of shared meaning. Echoing the Tocquevillean logic of "liberal" or "free association," identity language tends to imply a kind of pride of ownership: as one acquires an identity, one acquires a world of meaning along with the sorts of positive liberties that come with participation in a group. The triumph of this linguistic paradigm in the age of neoliberalism is itself remarkable. In Erikson's psychological or Korsgaard's moral-ethical version of identity, the notion that the individual needs to have an identity, and that society should do what it can to foster the emergence and expression of such an identity, indeed represents a kind of multicultural supplement to a whiggish-liberal conception of history and rational choice theory. The assumption that everything is getting gradually better, that individuals are becoming gradually more free, is reinforced by the idea that identity and culture represent new areas of expanding emancipation in a hierarchy of liberations. Just as the emergence of cultures (in the plural) signifies the liberation of groups otherwise suppressed by the power of the majority, so individuals gradually overcome oppression through the articulation of identities.

Part of the reason for the rising correlation between freedom and identity comes from the way the concept of identity has expanded the liberal language of rights by defining otherwise unpolitical—cultural—activity as political. Personal identity gains a public dimension as the effects of self-making are seen as extending outward from the individual into the larger culture.

The language of identity allows for an ethics of self-creation and for an ethics of recognition of others, but it also allows for a politics of the demonstrative refusal of recognition. If every act of identity making is potentially a political act, then the question of affiliation and the meaning of struggles for recognition can become richly complex, overlaying the expectation of a "thick" recognition of difference onto a "thin," formal notion of legal equality. As the post–World War II world engaged in a successful struggle to remove forms of caste, racial, and sexual discrimination from de jure legal codes, the movement of history tended toward demands for recognition of otherwise marginalized forms of subjectivity. Redefining liberty in terms of expressive subjectivity, these new identity formations have not only broadened the meaning of liberation; they have also exposed the complexities within the discourses of freedom in ways that have made freedom seem incomplete, identity a more desirable solution.

The lexical graph from Google's n-gram corroborates the conceptual story:[8] identity has risen alongside the rise of culture, and the two together appear to be gradually absorbing the language of freedom as a means of expressing the meaning of individual liberation and of explaining the dynamics of group formation and social causality. The raw semantic drift toward the language of culture and identity correlates to a conscious post–World War II movement, one that intensified greatly in the 1960s, toward conceiving of a layer of freedom that unfolds according to individuals' access to cultural particularity, their consciousness of and ability to participate in collective modes of identity.

Identity in the Shadow of Domination

The confrontation between Adorno and the students in the late 1960s prefigured the historical-conceptual expansion of identity. The students' utopian anticipation of a transformation of the meaning of politics itself would be, at least in part, confirmed by the remarkable changes that occurred when identity entered into the public sphere in the form of movements for recognition of sexual, gender, ethnic, or racial identities. But though Adorno's death in the middle of this confrontation cut short the full discussion, it is clear that Adorno identified not only the tension between individual and collective that would increasingly characterize discourses on identity in the last half century but also the challenges that would arise from this essential tension. In emphasizing the importance of a *non-identity* between the personal and collective forms of liberation—as well as among personal authority, professional or scientific authority, and state authority—Adorno was pointing to many of the problems involving the relation between group and individual identity that have become increasingly evident to theorists of the last decades. The mereology of identity includes the fact that sometimes the very thing that is liberating for the group is a burden for the individual, and vice versa; that personal and collective responsibility is often a shared burden; and that agreement on what defines a group often subtly exacerbates tensions within the group or the individual that fuel reactionary patterns of exclusion or conflict. As the concepts of personal and group identity have become routine ingredients of public life and discourse, these tensions have not disappeared but create problems whenever attempts to articulate matters of public responsibility have encountered the individual/collective divide.

A recent example of the problems that arise when identity is invoked as a principle of collective responsibility can be found in a speech given on February 2, 2015, by Joachim Gauck, president of the Federal Republic of Germany. Commemorating the seventieth anniversary of the Red Army's liberation of Auschwitz, Gauck spoke to the Reichstag about the question of historical memory in post-reunification Germany. His assessment begins on an Adornian theme—with the idea that the "majority of Germans would like to forget about the Nazi past"—and unfolds into a discussion of how powerful the will to forget is in modern society. This part of Gauck's speech is in fact a nod at the Institute for Social Research's *Gruppenexperiment*, which studied German attitudes in 1955, a time when the perpetrators of the Holocaust were still alive. The study showed Germans seeking to deflect not just responsibility but memory, and not just memory but self-identification with the perpetrating group. As the speech builds, and Gauck connects the question of collective memory to problems of national self-consciousness, the references to the Institute's work become more clear. Germans in the 1950s, Gauck argues, indeed thought of themselves as Germans almost *exactly* to the extent that they practiced the art of shifting blame for the Holocaust onto some external historical force or foreign group, whether by imagining themselves as powerless to influence public life, by fostering the myth that Germany was attacked first, by insisting that National Socialism "seized power" from without, or by denying that they or their fellows ever held fantasies of domination, revenge, or racial supremacy. Extending the 1955 argument that willful amnesia is an extension of the crime, Gauck insisted that the imperative to remember applied not just to those directly guilty, but also to those who became Germans with the so-called grace of late birth or those who, because they lived or were born in East Germany, imagined themselves to be antifascist by definition and thus to be free of guilt. Summarizing the duty of all Germans—even those born post-reunification—to reflect continuously on their national past, Gauck uttered the quotable subclause that inspired dozens of headlines: "there is no German identity without Auschwitz."[9]

Gauck's speech is sober, reflective, and responsible—and also not fully in control of its governing concept. His speech represents the best of what a head of state has said about how the experience of World War II must continue to shape the collective consciousness of globally engaged citizens regarding the problems of mass murder and genocide. Nonetheless, the statement comes across as strange and jarring. The reason for this is rooted deep in the logic of identity and its historical residues. The positive valence of the concept of identity—with all its unavoidable connotations of self-discovery, self-mastery, and futurity—sits oddly with the exhortation to take responsibility for the brutal objectification of selves in the Nazi era.

The positivity of identity logic tends, as a principle of its own health and strength, to promulgate myths of self-making, to cultivate forgetfulness—and it tends to view notions of duty or weakness as useless or even harmful. Modern identity consciousness aligns with nationalism in wanting self-making without self-incrimination. Thus, though it was clearly the opposite of Gauck's intention to characterize Auschwitz as an "achievement" of the Germans, his representation of Auschwitz as the foundation of German identity carries with it echoes of barbarians crowing over the corpses of their victims. The victims of Nazi mass murder surely did not die so that a coherent Germanness could thrive; yet the logic of the "making of identity" implies this, tending to define victims reductively as objects for the forging of the oppressor's collective subjectivity. Lacking a language for the negativity of identity—for the ways selves are shaped through injuries to others that redound on the self—Gauck's invocation of identity struggles not to reify mass murder into a life-or-death confrontation between dominant and subaltern groups. In the case of Nazism, this risks at the very least positing an essentiality to Germanness and Jewishness that reinforces the racially purified and historically falsified image of Germanness advanced by the Nazis themselves and that effaces the instrumental role that aggression played in the assertion of that identity. In drawing on the language of identity to articulate the ongoing responsibility of contemporary Germans for the crimes of their grandfathers, Gauck unintentionally demonstrates how weak and unstable identity in its national mode is at commemorating victims and taking responsibility for collective crimes.

It is ironic, here, that Gauck not only meant no harm in invoking identity—that he was seeking to be a responsible statesman—but that, in doing so, he was also invoking one of Adorno's most celebrated lines, the pronouncement that "there can be no poetry after Auschwitz." Yet the fact that an attempt to use Adorno as a resource for twenty-first-century political discourse produced this awkward result is itself telling, on multiple levels. In shifting Adorno's argument from poetry to identity, Gauck was seeking to ground an ethical negative historical consciousness in something that seems more proximal to the psyche than the expressive products of a national culture: "identity" seemed to modernize Adorno's strictures for a generation less invested in verse. But Gauck unfortunately failed to see the relevance of the rest of Adorno's sentence: "to engage in a cultural critique of the barbarity of culture [and point to poetry's impossibility] . . . erodes even the insight and intelligence that pronounces it as such."[10] Adorno believed that lyric poetry had non-identity in its identity: it is—*but also is not*—a mode of collective expression. Cultures express—cultures create—themselves through their poetry; yet the power of lyric poetry derives from the fact that what is expressed is not the wholeness of the culture but the woundedness and woundability of the individual self, the fact that the relation between individual and collective always involves a dimension of injury. Adorno was therefore arguing that insofar as the connection between poetry and culture could be addressed, this must be done immanently and historically. In attempting to translate Adorno into the twenty-first century by addressing identity rather than culture, Gauck was making precisely the reduction Adorno sought to warn against. Adorno, at the end of his life, was exploring ways of countering the students' vernacular language of identity with a *negative* approach to identity and philosophical non-identity. Gauck's misunderstanding of how to apply Adorno's ideas—and the distortion of the point he was attempting to make—indicates at once the need for just such a negative concept of identity as Adorno was exploring, and for a more precise vocabulary for this negativity and the social substance of non-identity.

This need is, perhaps, all the more palpable for the fact that Gauck's attempt to deploy a critical construction of identity reverberates not only with the old action logic of the "cult of the deed," the fascist obsession with unity and purity, but also with the more recent languages of "European identity" advanced by a new generation of right-wing activists explicitly opposed to the mandate of critical, historical self-examination. Already in the 1960s, Adorno worried that identity thinking favored the cultivation of social antipathies without objective responsibilities. By the twenty-first century this concern had proven predictive. Despite identity's long-standing association with progressive causes, identity has become a favorite tool of right-wing and reactionary discourses. On both sides of the Atlantic, there have emerged religio- and ethno-nationalist identity movements that declare themselves spontaneous countermovements to left-wing identity politics. There is a Christian Identity movement in the United States that cultivates an "anti-Semitic and racist theology" designed to hasten an "end times" prophecy by (forcibly) returning the Jews to Israel, among other antigovernmental fantasies.[11] In Europe, the *Génération Identitaire* movement seeks to purge the European Union member nations of foreign immigrants and their cultures and to reassert the ethnic roots of nationality. The leaders of these movements draw on the languages of identity and culture as wedge issues for mobilizing ressentiment, and they have become quite savvy at amplifying identitarian rage through social media and sensationalized news.[12] When the language of existential danger is reinjected into identity discourse, a whole set of reactionary notions of encirclement, dilution, and "corruption from within" are reincorporated into languages of identity and culture that had been articulated as permanent replacements for the concept of race. When Geert Wilders and Renaud Camus, practitioners of this new right-wing identity discourse in Europe, speak the language of identity, they do so to stoke fears that the "white" race and its culture are "being replaced" by immigrants with a strong "settler mentality," self-aware of their identity in a way that supposedly weak liberals have forgotten.[13]

One can observe that identity language is increasingly being used as a reactionary counterdiscourse espousing nationalist identity without accusing Gauck or other progressive advocates of culture and identity of being "essentially" reactionary. It is, however, clear that identity has become a treacherous and contested terrain. The discourse of identity as subjective liberation is shadowed by its vitiation of the language of objective historical reflection; identity's utility in imagining new possibilities for freedom is complicated by its instrumentalization for the purposes of identifying enemies and inventing collective antagonisms. For this reason, it is useful to pay attention to Adorno's original complaint, his insistence that it is incumbent on theory to distinguish more clearly among positive and negative, subjective and objective uses of identity within the non-identical fields of culture, society, psychology and law. Just as in 1958 Isaiah Berlin found it necessary to distinguish between "two types of liberty," positive and negative, in order to understand the relation of liberty to concepts of law and the state, so it seems increasingly important to distinguish positive from negative identity in order to analyze its subjective and objective dynamics.[14] Identity, far from being self-identical, is not one.

Positive and Negative Identity: Subject Becomes Object

This book argues that identity was born to be a more dialectical, interdisciplinary, and objective concept than what it has become. It argues furthermore that one can see the lineaments of an alternative history of identity in the critique of subjectivity, alterity, and racism articulated in the exile writings of Theodor Adorno. Adorno's approach to psychology and sociology, epistemology and ontology, law and politics, an approach based on an understanding of the conflicted non-identities within all assertions of identity, holds untapped promise not just for the theory of domination and emancipation but for our understanding of the relation between individuality and public life, science and expression.

The narrow historical and linguistic claim for this argument has to do with the history of the word "identity" itself. Though Erik Erikson became the most celebrated promoter of the concept of identity, he had himself adopted the term "identity" from Erich Fromm's 1941 international best-seller *Escape from Freedom*. This book was also an important starting point for Adorno. Having been Fromm's junior colleague and rival at the Frankfurt Institute for Social Research, Adorno objected to what he saw as Fromm's romanticization of unalienated subjectivity in the figure of the "Renaissance Man." Rejecting this notion of identity, Adorno built his core critical ideas around a negative articulation of Fromm's hopeful invocation of a self strong enough to resist the crushing power of capitalism and fascism. Starting with the assertion that investigation of the "I" needed to be accompanied by an investigation of the "not-I," Adorno began to explore the implications of the idea that modern philosophy and social thought had ascribed too much power to the subject and to subjectivity and had not devoted enough effort to saying what subjectivity is not. Though Adorno's engagement with this question began with—and crucially, never lost sight of—the political problem of how capitalism nurtures fascism within itself, Adorno's analysis quickly went beyond the areas Fromm addressed. Adorno criticized *all* invocations of essential and pure origins, and he carried this critique over from the realm of political analysis to philosophy and the theory of science—to approaches to perspectival disciplinarity and logical non-identity. Startlingly, Adorno warned not only against the reactionary possibility of political arguments based in identity but also against *any* judgment grounded in the self rather than in the object:

There is a moment of content to the form itself, seen in the transcendent critique that sympathizes with authority before expressing any content. The expression "as a . . . , I . . . ," in which one can insert any orientation, from dialectical materialism to Protestantism, is here symptomatic. Anyone who judges . . . by presuppositions that do not hold within that which is being judged behaves in a reactionary manner, even when he swears by progressive slogans.[15]

Rejecting the assumption that the subjective position from which an individual views an object grants a special authority, Adorno also discerned a similarly damaged relationship to the object in scientific discourses that claimed to produce objectivity by imposing the perspective of the discipline on the object of study. Out of this observation arose an interdisciplinary dialectic of the *not-I* that refused to take selfhood or objectivity for granted but saw the negation of selfhood as the beginning of both subjectivity and objectivity. Adorno, I argue, devoted his mature thought to understanding how sociological and psychological ideas of the self as actor had been grafted onto the core notions of epistemology and ontology, and his exploration of the fault lines and possibilities of this graft led Adorno to make his "negative" turn as a philosopher. This negative turn injected the language of the non-identical (*Nichtidentität*) into the analysis of every form of positivity—the assertoric and apodeictic, the constative and performative modes of identity assertion—while expanding the phenomenology of experience so that it could account for every element of objective coercion, from the categorical reduction of agency through instrumentality to the ascription of negatively binding labels of social roles and hierarchies.

The crucial term for the insights Adorno sought to achieve through his negative philosophy was "non-identity." Cutting across his late work in logic, epistemology, sociology, and psychology, non-identity spoke in each case to a problem: the concept never exhausted its object; the clean lines of language and thought were always insufficient to the totalities and particularities of reality. Allegories and analogies, typologies and symbols, the categories and concepts of law and the sciences, failed to express their relation to things, and they concealed the failures in their naming. For Adorno, non-identity was at once a fundamental epistemological problem and a sweeping social and historical one: the rift between concept and object was always a scar, a remnant of the social histories of domination and instrumentalization that allowed the subject to make itself by forming its object. To read for non-identity was to trace out this history of injury and to become aware of the possibility of reversal: subject could become object, object could become subject—the dominant, the victim. Yet Adorno also believed that a full knowledge might take account of this insufficiency in the concept of self-sufficient subjectivity, that it might recover substantive knowledge through the analysis of apparent contradiction. If nature and art, according to Kant, open a window into the sublime by mapping out the limits of our understanding, so Adorno believed that the non-identical allows us to confront the conflict of the faculties and the social substance of the subject constituted by the forms of reason. To read along the cicatrix of non-identity was to discover epistemological value in the dialectical application of objective reason to constitutive subjectivity, and vice versa.

Non-identity is to Adorno's philosophy what *spirit* was to G. W. F. Hegel's philosophy or *being* was to Heidegger's: a keyword positioned at the center of a philosophical system, drawing together the central ideas of a lifetime of philosophical inquiry. Adorno's *non-identity* has, however, received far less attention than these other concepts, either in terms of its unifying role in Adorno's thought or in terms of its utility in relation to broader strains of twentieth- and twenty-first-century thought. Though a small but growing number of scholars have, for instance, recognized the relevance of the critique of non-identity to the concept of nature within the project of environmental studies, the possibility of developing an interdisciplinary inquiry connecting the problem of nature to the construction of the object in other disciplines or to problems of negativity in subjective identity has not been explored.[16] There are several reasons for this relative neglect. One is that previous scholarship has misread Adorno's interest in negativity as a form of psychological or historical pessimism. Another is that the term "non-identity" became dominant late in Adorno's career, summarizing decades of work in which Adorno explored this idea in the languages of a range of disciplines, and that its function as a kind of keystone in the architecture of his thought was less clearly established than it might have been at the time of his death. The importance of this concept for developing a science of negativity—of negativity expressed in real human suffering and mastery—remains to be explored.

Drawing on the distinction between positive and negative liberty that first appeared not in Berlin's essay but in Fromm's *Escape from Freedom*, this book advances the distinction between positive and negative identity as a heuristic to elucidate how Adorno's philosophical critique of non-identity emerged from his American years—from his work on defining the relation between authoritarian politics and racism. Just as the distinction between positive and negative liberty served Fromm and Berlin by providing a clarifying paraphrase of the Hegelian problem of political liberty from a subjective point of view, so the distinction between positive and negative identity can illuminate Adorno's Hegelian approach to identity and its consequences for philosophy and sociology, for the idea of subjectivity and the history of domination. Hegel was a thinker of systems (social and logical) and of the subject as an expressive, autonomous being; he was also a theorist of liberty, slavery, and legitimate and illegitimate authority. Adorno, more than any previous Marxist thinker, was interested in defining how modern subjectivity—in both its positive and negative dimensions—was simultaneously autonomous, a creator of meaning, and dependent, enmeshed in a sphere of social reproduction. Adorno studied how forms of subjectivity mediate the broader systems of social domination, and vice versa, looking at how selves have their own inner dynamics that partly mediate and define social relations but also at how the bourgeois obsession with selfhood can occlude the ability to understand the social systems and forms of domination in which we live. Carrying on what Peter Gordon has called a "contestatory dialogue with the philosophers of bourgeois interiority," Adorno developed a wide variety of terms for his project, whether through his calls for a "critique of identity," his critique of the "jargon of authenticity," or his interest in the "dialectics of the individual and the particular," the "nonidentity of thinking and being."[17] In proposing a distinction between positive and negative identity, this book seeks to show, first, how a concern for the negative dimensions of identity constituted a red thread in Adorno's thought, and second, how Adorno's approach to the negativity of identity can help resolve the kinds of problems that, as we have seen with the example of Gauck, increasingly present themselves when identity is invoked to mediate questions of knowledge and ethics, individual and collective responsibility, majority and minority rights.

To consider Adorno's philosophical work in terms of the concept of negative identity is to recognize a challenge to the existing scholarship on the Frankfurt School. The literature on Adorno, still burdened by misunderstandings dating from the 1968–69 moment, has largely taken for granted that Adorno was hostile to the new philosophical concerns and social movements of the 1960s and has failed to connect Adorno's critique of personality and identity to his exploration of logical and social negativity or to his understanding of the nature of social abstraction. The story is both more complicated and more interesting than that.

As I seek to show, recognizing that Adorno's later critical theory shared a common starting point with the identity discourses that proliferated in the later twentieth century not only clarifies what remains at stake in an Adornian critique of identity, but also shows how Adorno's work points toward the relevance of a critique of subjective identity for the theorization of interdisciplinary objectivity. Far from simply opposing identity, Adorno's work can help us understand how the analysis of identity—as *negative* identity—needs to be extended into a theory of objectivity. The key to this exposition will be to pursue the origins of non-identity historically, in terms of its emergence from the methodological problems that a universalist encountered in studying the phantasms of *racism* as objective false consciousness. If Adorno did not live to articulate the full dimensions of what he called "non-identity," the story of how experiences of negative identity compelled Adorno to address identity as a central problem of the twentieth century can help make clear how Adorno's critique of fascism, anti-Semitism, and racism's inverted constructions of the Other, developed in America, were not only integral to, but also the foundation of, his later, post-exile philosophical engagements.

A Century of Wounded Universality

If one approaches identity not as a subjective notion of freedom but as an objective fact, encoded in passports and identity cards as much as in the minds of the civil majority, positive identity shares a horrifying history with the modern state's modes of exclusion. The Nuremberg Laws of 1935, modeled on the Jim Crow laws of segregated post–Civil War America, outstripped their model by setting the stage for mass deportation and mass murder; but both of these racial laws imposed a binding negative identity upon their citizens. The aftermath of World War I and the attempt to develop new territorial nation-states out of old empires created millions of stateless and semi-stateless people whose only purchase on a universal identity took the form of a negation of their past. Depending on which side of the bayonet, machine gun, or barbed wire one stood, identity could appear in the twentieth century either as a kind of privilege or an unobtainable goal: such is the conclusion that one must draw if one views subjective non-identity in a coldly objective way. Though one can speculate as to whether expanded subjectivity itself fueled an expansion of alterity, the historical record reflects that in the twentieth century, forms of identity proliferated not just as part of liberation but as outgrowths of a century of violence and upheaval. From the growth of coercive group membership to the proliferation of forms of globalized collective subjectivity (involuntary and voluntary), identity expanded objectively and must be enumerated as one of the tools of authoritarian mass movements. It is an inescapable fact that millions of people were murdered in the twentieth century for "having identities" that were in fact imposed from without, and as many (perhaps more) identities were forged, ascribed, and coerced as were freely given, received, or embraced. Objectively speaking, the twentieth century made identities—made them optional and obligatory at once. Though the twentieth century did not invent the situation in which having the "right identity" could win one political or economic rights, it made negative identity as ubiquitous as identity itself.

When one thinks along with Adorno's experience of the twentieth century, it is clear that he initially perceived these objective problems of negative identity as belonging to the historical past. Like many observers of European social democracy after the war, Adorno came of age with the expectation that as empires were dissolved by nation-states, and nation-states were absorbed by global capital, the role of economic, global forces in determining the shape of life would expand while the need to define one's national or group identity would fade. One needed to define oneself as an individual, but not as a member of a group per se. It took hard experience to unseat this bias toward the global and teach Adorno's generation that small details of heritage or historical experience could matter in relation to the forces of modernization. Born in Wilhelmine Germany in 1903 to a Jewish father and a Catholic-Italian mother, Adorno had a mixed identity: he was neither not Jewish nor not *not*-Jewish, and he was culturally and legally a German citizen until that citizenship was stripped from him by the Nazi government. During his middle years—from 1933 to the mid-1950s—Adorno lived in the United States, employed first as a researcher on music and mass media in the age of radio, later as a social scientist researching how anti-Semitism and racism developed in reaction to changes in both the economy and the personality structure of the individual. This process of research and emigration, which led to the publication in 1950 of the landmark *Authoritarian Personality* and culminated in Adorno's return to Germany to teach philosophy and sociology in the mid-1950s, brought about a philosophical reevaluation amounting to a profound reversal in his thought.

Before coming to the United States in 1937, Adorno had a substantially complete theory of social causality, culture, and individual knowledge that one might describe as an Enlightenment universalism buttressed, at its crumbling edges, by a kind of modernist Jacobinism. He was an avant-garde aesthete, a Marxian system theorist, and a heterodox Kantian who stood opposed to subjectivistic and psychologistic theories of culture. Like other Marxists—and most Kantians—of Adorno's generation, he did not accept the idea that people's self-conceptions are pivotal for how history is made or how politics unfolds. Both of these traditions of universalism emphasized objectivity and law in a way that stood in stark contrast to the idea that individual subjective identifications with nationalities or groups are worthy of significant study because they can shape daily praxis. To take subjective identification seriously—even in a negative way—would require a significant reassessment of the philosophical and political traditions represented not just by the Frankfurt School but also by almost every movement associated broadly with the Left, with liberation. Instead, Adorno's Kantian Marxism sought to advance the notion of "the rights of man" by riding out the tide of modernist self-consciousness as it unfolded alongside advancing production methods and an advancing division of labor. Marxian materialism intermingled with a Kantian belief in science and universal subjectivity, and with a Nietzschean and avant-garde belief that each individual needed to cultivate a critical intelligence capable of inverting the stupidities of mass culture and *des idées reçues*. In this mixture of philosophical values, two competing visions of a universalist relation between self and world stood in creative tension. The Marxian theory of human universality addressed the real-world difficulties of being an autonomous subject in the ideal Kantian sense, while the Nietzschean avant-gardism allowed Kantianism to be upheld as a negative utopia. Once one recognized the delusional quality of modern culture as an imposed master morality, one could preserve, philosophically, a model of how an ethical and rational self, undamaged by the world, might behave *if only* he or she were allowed to do so. Adorno's Marxism of the 1930s combined utopian and avant-gardist moments, yielding a kind of aestheticized radicalism in which the imperative to repair the world struggled against a sense of the impossibility of doing so. This view of damaged universalism imagined a productive community of cultural as well as material production, in which all individuals might someday receive as much cultural investment in them as they placed in the production of goods.

America challenged and changed this antisubjective universalism, and in the most interesting way: Adorno pushed subjectivism back upon itself, becoming an innovative theorist of identity's roots in alterity and Otherness, prejudice and racism. To understand how this happened is to understand how Adorno accepted, with modifications, not just one idea but a host of interconnected concepts to whose implications he was deeply opposed. If Adorno arrived in America believing that his goal was to develop an objective, Marxian social science, his understanding both of objectivity and of his role as a researcher ran headlong into America's culture and academic research system. Inside and outside the university, Adorno encountered variations on the themes of cultural relativism and social adaptation. Grateful as he was, as an émigré, to the nation that figured on the world stage as the last bastion of freedom, Adorno could not understand how the Americans, with their narrowly instrumental approach to objectivity and their Pragmatist tendency to equate truth with success, could mount any successful defense against the fascist ideologies from which Adorno had fled. The conflict between Adorno's idealist and social universality and the American celebration of relativism and cultural particularity would shape not only his experience of exile but also the approach to philosophy and the social sciences with which he would return to Germany. His first and dominant reaction to American social science was to seek to defend universality (both in its subjective and objective dimensions) against all attempts at relativist definition. This seemed to Adorno the only theoretically rigorous way to fend off attempts to legitimize race and national particularity as objects of scientific inquiry. It was in Adorno's *second* reaction that the experience of exile began to reshape theory. Instead of viewing historical and scientific knowledge as a matter of aligning the subjectivity of the inquirer with the universality within the object of inquiry, Adorno began to ask what happened when that objectivity or subjectivity had already been distorted by relations of domination. Just as exile turned subjects into objects and distorted the category of subjectivity, so, too, domination could distort science and perception in ways that only a self-reflexive and reciprocally self-conscious science—a dialectical science—could address. Once Adorno came to see things this way, his heterodox Marxianism and Kantianism entered a new phase, in which he theorized how modern society necessarily "produced" victims and tyrants, how it created narratives of domination and control in order to deflect insight into exploitation and inequality.

The key discovery in the history of negative identity came about at a moment of confluence of different research agendas and historical circumstances. This was in the 1944–45 moment, in which Adorno and Max Horkheimer realized that twentieth-century anti-Semitism was far more than hatred of the Jews or even just a peculiar European hybrid of garden-variety racism. Anti-Semitism—particularly the generative *anti* or negative part of it—was in fact a new "populist metaphysics" that sought nothing less than the reorganization of selfhood and religion, nations and states. Independent of the presence of actual Jews, modern mass-mediated anti-Semitism was an attack on political rationality and its narratives of emancipation and redemption. The key logic to anti-Semitism involved displacing the idea of the universal onto a polarized field of negative and positive subjectivity on which complex maneuvers of victim identification and victim blaming could be carried out. The importance of Jews, within this logic, was largely symbolic. Jews could be used to stand in for the decreasing social control individuals felt over their lives. Historical reasons of course made the propagandistic imagery of the Jews particularly well suited for creating, in a moment of world economic crisis, an inverted image of the world spirit out of the negative identity of Jews. The Jewish historical "double nature" as weak and strong, pariah and parvenu, was congruent with the need to personify the historical forces that were mandating an ever-more-advanced division of labor, an ever-more-forceful separation of mental and manual labor within the individual, and an ever-more-distanced relation between individuals and the forces that governed them.

Dialectic of Enlightenment's stunning 1945 pronouncement that true "anti-Semites no longer exist" emerged out of this analysis of the objective power of negative identity in the bourgeois past and neoliberal future. Anti-Semitism was the prototypic, European form of a more general anti-subjectivist pseudo-subjectivism—a scaffold of projection that could be recast into any kind of racism, sexism, or negative identity as needed by circumstance. More importantly, the pure negative construction of identity—based on victim blaming, projection, and ascription of secret control—could find fertile ground anywhere in the modern world, because the prevalent demand of capitalist consumption and production had embedded within itself a kind of impossible individualism—one that places no limits on demands of self-redefinition. Every consumer good, every quantum of labor is stamped with the ideology that the self made it, formed it, and can enjoy it in its entirety: this subjectivism masks the objective domination of labor and nature. This redefinition of selfhood was not without its emancipatory dimension; but the point, for Adorno and Horkheimer, was that the inverted Kantianism of modernity had become an invisible factor of production. To survive and thrive, individuals were expected to distinguish themselves as autonomous, as *laws unto themselves* in a world governed by forces beyond their control. And everyone knew that if they failed to achieve autonomy, they would be devoured by the "antagonistic whole," with only themselves to blame. This internalized set of expectations drives the inward desire for identity—the ontological need—as well as its outward expansion: the impulse to assign a name to some subjectivity, some entity or group of people who, lurking in the margins of the infernal system, are secretly directing it, controlling it, taking advantage of it. Adorno came to regard this systematically distorted phenomenology of social perception as highly dynamic—capable of shifting to accommodate the needs of its subjects and designate new victims according to the historical situation. As he did so, his theoretical concern expanded from the problem of anti-Semitism to racism more generally, and to the problems of the divided self and the dialectics of identity. Adorno believed one had to be interested in the particulars of social projection of positive and negative identity—why the Germans, why the Jews, but also why gender and sexual orientation, why students and why immigrants?—and yet theory also had to rise above mere advocacy. One needed to work through the interaction between the liberating and degenerative forms of identity, and to articulate how negative identity offered a new, false metaphysics, while still being able to address questions of a universal character. This meant thinking against identity as well as with it, being aware that an obsession with the particularities of identity, even by those sworn to defuse its horrors and seek liberation in it, could undercut one's insight into the objective and the universal.[18]

This is not only a book about Adorno but an inquiry into the subjective and objective meaning of identity and its politics. As an attempt to recuperate an analytics of identity's negative side and to restore a missing chapter in the story of social thought, this book is not an attack on the idea of identity but a kind of double history. It presents, at once, a reinterpretation of the intellectual history of the Frankfurt School in the context of American and European social thought and an inquiry into the philosophical-historical tension between concepts of universalist liberation and particularist meaning or being. Implicitly, the two histories meet in that both involve a rethinking of the residue of Hegelianism that is still part of narrative historical explanation and theories of social causation based on metaphors of the subjective. Recognizing that identity has become the contemporary guise of the concept of world spirit should make us wonder about the gain or loss in analytical power that comes from dropping (left) Hegelian distinctions between *an sich* and *für sich* dimensions of ontology, between objective and subjective analytical perspectives, immediate and reflected self-consciousness, abstract and concrete historical conceptuality. The Hegelian questions of how historical subjectivity can be used in a universal mode, and how one can consider universality in a subjective mode, remain crucial for law and ethics in a neoliberal age. Adorno's belief that human universalism must be defended, but that any form of universalism could be turned against its claimant, is a post-Hegelian thought of concern to every human science that would give counsel to modern individuals or states. This core idea of reflexive subject/object universality—the notion of a "dialectic of enlightenment" in our speech about the universal and the particular—was central to Adorno's innovative investigation of racism, and it was crucial to his attempts to understand how the historical transformation of ideas of subjectivity, governance, and domination made such a possibility of reversal not just possible but quite likely under modern conditions. Understanding the negative element of identity is just the beginning of understanding its dialectic. A dialectical theory of positive and negative identity aims to describe the objectivity of subjectivity and the subjectivity of objectivity, and thus makes possible an analysis of identity as both a false and true consciousness of individual emancipation and oppression.

In the sequel volume, we will investigate how Adorno's concepts of woundedness, objectification, and alterity always contemplated a second reversal—the possibility that false consciousness could become the material for self-reflection, that consciousness of negative identity could be turned into a principled self-consciousness. Non-identity, the dominant concern of Adorno's postwar work, frames not only the discussion here but, I would argue, should frame our understanding of what social theory and identity mean today. It is the argument of this book, however, that this later critique of non-identity and the metaphysics of the subjective develop out of a critique of authoritarianism and prejudice, and that the fuller contours of Adorno's unfinished philosophical system are best understood not in terms of its systematic closure and self-identity but in terms of the wounds that went into its making, the experience of damaged life that compelled Adorno to grapple with the subjective as negative identity.

Chapter Overview

Chapter 1 offers a revised interpretation of the infamous jazz controversy and Adorno's first confrontation with the idea of race and the American concept of culture. Chronicling Adorno's missteps in applying a theory of the commodification of musical universalism developed in Weimar Germany to the substantially different conditions of American society of the 1930s, this chapter reconstructs the political and cultural situations in which Adorno's jazz essays were written and published. By examining the history of critical theory through the story of Adorno's understanding—and misunderstandings—of jazz, this chapter explores Adorno's intellectual development in relation to the historical trajectory of twentieth-century attitudes toward culture between the worlds of ethnicity and the avant-garde.

Chapter 2 looks at Adorno's contretemps with American sociology, exploring how his American experience shaped his commitment to a Kantian vision of science, ethics, and human universalism. Drawing its title from Georg Simmel's image for the alienated nature of sociological insight, and from Adorno's extended discussion of Simmel in an important American lecture, this portrait explores how Adorno responded to the daily pressure toward cultural assimilation, and to American academic sociology's emphasis on assimilation and adaptation as the essence of truth and progress, by considering more deeply the importance of difference for American democracy and culture. For the Stranger in America, personal alienation contributed to theoretical innovation, a realization concerning how a commitment to rationalism and universalism might reinforce a commitment to understanding the power of social irrationality. Exploring what it meant for Adorno to be a Kantian Marxist and Nietzschean universalist, this chapter argues that during his early years as an émigré in America Adorno engaged with the relation between universalism and particularity in a way that laid the grounds for his turn toward studying racism and authoritarian politics, the social dynamics of subjective identity, and the interaction between public and private life.

Chapters 3 through 6 constitute a single argument, exploring the relations among the private, philosophical work of *Dialectic of Enlightenment* and *Minima Moralia*, the groundbreaking social-psychological empirical work on prejudice in *Authoritarian Personality*, and Horkheimer's important public lecture series *Eclipse of Reason* (prepared with the assistance of Adorno and Leo Lowenthal). In examining these works together, these chapters challenge several persistent scholarly assumptions about Adorno's intellectual biography: that the war years marked a "retreat" from practice to theory; that the esoteric philosophical speculation of *Dialectic of Enlightenment* and *Minima Moralia* represented the "true" Adorno; that Adorno and Horkheimer were "pessimists" or "nihilists" during this period; that the empirical study of *Authoritarian Personality* was a distraction from Adorno's real concerns. Countering this narrative, these chapters argue that the work of the 1940s must be read in terms of an ongoing attempt, at a moment in which Adorno had become Horkheimer's closest intellectual interlocutor, to realize the work envisioned by Horkheimer's 1931 inaugural address and expanded in his 1937 essay "Traditional and Critical Theory": that of creating a social-psychological model of interdisciplinary inquiry that devolved neither into positivism nor social Darwinism. Arguing not for the unity of theory and practice but for a dynamic interplay between private theorization and publicly engaged practical science, these chapters show that the continuity of collective purpose during these years eventuated in a number of striking intellectual innovations. Demonstrating how the language of identity was articulated by the Frankfurt School as a language of unalienated subjectivity and then was almost immediately set aside for being Romantic and uncritical, these chapters argue that the struggle over the identity concept led Adorno and Horkheimer to a quite different understanding of the Institute's interdisciplinary project than they had started with, and this allowed them to articulate a new notion of social objectivity, reason, and legitimate authority that was explicitly understood as a negation of theories of subjective identity. In pure theoretical terms, I argue that Horkheimer and Adorno came to see themselves as defending an "orthodox" Freud and Marx and a "heterodox" Kant and Weber. Politically speaking, the critical attitude toward the human sciences contained in these orthodoxies and heterodoxies positioned Adorno particularly well to contribute to the reconstruction of postwar German culture.

1

"Jazz, the Wound"

Negative Identity, Culture, and the Shadow of Race

In 1956, a year after Theodor Adorno had returned to Germany definitively, he published an essay, "Heine, the Wound," which asked why the name "Heine" caused such irritation in Germany. Adorno knew the simple answer to his own question. Heinrich Heine, whose name had once been admired, only to be redacted out of the public squares and schoolbooks—whose name was removed from his poetry when the poetry itself could not be dislodged from the national literature—had long been a cultural symbol for the Jewish heritage that a "purified Germany" had tried to erase. While Adorno acknowledged the depth of German anti-Semitism, he argued that the hatred of Heine could not be understood as simple hatred of Jews. Germans hated Heine for the same reason they loved him: because his version of the lyric captured and preserved the trauma as well as the promise of a German nation. The prospect of Heine's lyrical line looked out upon Germany's rivers and countryside; his language had mixed the idioms of the *Volk* with those of commerce and the newspaper; and it did so in a way that did not falsify the complex and ambivalent relation of the individual to the state and its violence. Any German reaction against the "Jew" in Heine was in fact an expression of hatred against a past that was alive in the present and was thus, Adorno argued, a failure to come to terms with the complex questions of German integration through language, commerce, and the often-violent powers of the state. Hatred of Heine was German self-hatred, identity only subconsciously aware of its non-identity.[1] Heine was wounded German self-identity.

Adorno, who had consistently found all language of identity problematic, was of course doing more than simply inverting the valences of identity, showing how sadism was in fact rooted in masochism, how Germanness mutilated itself in trying to separate itself from supposedly "foreign" impulses: he was making a broader point about the relation between art, identity, and suffering as dimensions of historical experience. For Adorno, it was no accident that the Nazis, for all their brutality, could not expunge a poem like "Die Lorelei" from the national memory. The nonidentical was the secret of art. Nineteenth-century nations needed impossible anthems; the greatness of Heine's folk songs was defined by the fact that they incorporated the impossibility of purity within them. They drew the reader to the realities that created the "wound" within the self and the work in a way that drove the violently minded to do to Heine's name what they could not do to his poetry. The name could be hated, but the suffering that animated the art was shared. The wound that Heine's name represented was a mark of the injuries inflicted by a real historical process; thus, its sensitivity not only pointed to the historical and social nature of the lyrical self, but also opened up possibilities for better understanding the material and social dynamics—of nationalism and commerce, power and secularization—out of which the lyrical self had grown.

For the sake of understanding the history of critical theory, it is significant that the composition of "Heine, the Wound" coincided with Adorno's return to Germany. It thus serves as a marker of the beginning of Adorno's late phase, a period when Adorno worked to reclaim the elements of a tradition in which he had been born, a violently disrupted tradition that he found himself reimporting to Germany as a kind of foreigner. This experience of exile and return became central to Adorno's understanding of history, and he came to see the cultural idea of exile as a philosophical problem. Violence forces non-identity upon identity and requires the nonidentical to make that which is supposed to be ever-identical to itself—tradition—seem like it is everything if it wishes to be anything at all.[2] This historical fact and situation, moreover, must be understood and expressed philosophically without fetishizing the so-called poetic power of violence as that which "creates" history. Adorno remained a student of the Enlightenment in this way, believing that the only way to come to terms with this problem was to strip identity of its cultural or collective lie. In fact, only individuals—not cultures, nations, religion, or ethnicities—could ultimately emancipate themselves from the past.

The metaphor of Heine as wound was for Adorno a symbol not only of exile and of negative identity but also of the modern processes of alienation and the production of homelessness. Pointing out that Heine's mother was not entirely fluent in German, Adorno argued that Heine was estranged from his language in a way that caused his lyric alternately to mock the language and to embrace the idioms of folk songs, populism, and collective spirit with the mimetic zeal of a foreigner or a salesman. Heine's lyricism was the necessary complement to Charles Baudelaire's, in that Heine invested the languages of selfhood with a self-reflexivity and negativity parallel to Baudelaire's challenge to the doctrines of aesthetic formalism. In Adorno's view, aestheticism and lyrical irony, both forms of non-identity, served Enlightenment by drawing attention to the excesses of Romanticism. But unlike Baudelaire, who would be sainted by the modernist movement, Heine was misunderstood and even reviled, especially among the Germans. His appeal to "the people," couched as unrequited love, became a vulnerability for which he was held in contempt, and the dislike of Heine was cultivated by aristocratic circles who viewed his work as commercialized and lowbrow. The Nazis fed on these misperceptions of Heine, but, argued Adorno, they could not undo the fact that the German folk tradition indeed existed as a strange mixture of enlightenment and homelessness, commercialism and longing for transcendence: Heine's sensibilities were most penetrating in describing his hatred for the Germany he loved. Few Germans, Adorno observed, understood the full force of Heine's wounded doubleness or the negative identity in his lyric line until the beginning of the twentieth century, when composers like Gustav Mahler transformed the relation of lyricism and nationalism in a way that revealed the divergence between the existential longing for home and the nationalist notions of lyrical identity and common feeling.[3] Arguing that "the power of one who mocks impotently transcends his impotence," Adorno asserted that Heine's ability to mock the manipulators of authenticity survived the Romantic period and spoke again in the age of imperialism and world war. The wound of Heine's poetry carried a truth value that did not become widely sharable until the dynamic between power, subjectivity, and the suffering of others had realigned to disclose it.

In this incorporation of Walter Benjamin's theory of the "temporal kernel" (*Zeitkern*) of works of art, Adorno proposed that Germans needed to become more sophisticated in the way they considered the relation between aesthetic and historical analysis. Truth is temporally bounded, concealed in the social core of objects. This approach made it possible for Adorno to use aesthetic interpretation as a means of thinking about subjectivity and historicity in general. The idea of the wound and its association with emigration became in the Heine essay part of a general theory of how critical thinking begins with failures of assimilation to the group: just as "assimilatory language is the language of unsuccessful identification," so Heine's "stereotypical theme of unrequited love" is an "image for [the] homelessness that has become everyone's homelessness, as all human beings have been as badly injured in their beings and their language as Heine the outcast was."[4] Describing the Holocaust as an event that generalized homelessness, Adorno argued that Heine's words stood in for the general uprootedness that must seek out an "emancipated humanity" that requires no other homeland than "a world that produces no outcasts." The way to seek this "reconciliation," however, is not in trying to achieve a unity of being and language but in understanding the dissonance inside the self and its fraught relation to the world that wounds it.[5]

Adorno's idea of "wounded subjectivity" acknowledged the Lukácsian theory of alienation and homelessness, as well as the Heideggerian notion of "language as a house of Being," but rejected the possibility of a prior wholeness or unalienated state and remained conscious of the violence those two approaches entailed.[6] "Heine, the Wound" shows that Adorno's philosophical logic grew out of a theory of historical subjectivity and that the idea of non-identity as a logical property developed according to social theory's need to explain the repulsion-attraction of individuals to group identities. The notion that knowledge itself is a wound, a form of alienation developed under particular historical conditions, is grounded by the idea that though each wound is particular, each process of healing is, like enlightenment itself, an individual undertaking that establishes a relation to universality. This concept of identity fits the twentieth century, a century of negative identity like no other, and its conceptual origins are worth understanding.

Adorno's theorization of wounded subjectivity developed over the course of a decade, beginning with the Heine essay and culminating in the 1966 publication of *Negative Dialectics*. As he worked with this metaphor, it became a means of synthesizing his theoretical commitments to the Kantian and Freudian traditions as well as of addressing their limitations. The notion of wounded subjectivity is grounded in a view, half-Kantian and half-Freudian, that although only rational individualism and criticism could emancipate individuals from irrationality, subjective rationality in itself contained no positive, substantive goal. The neo-Hegelian paraphrase of this relation was that subjectivity always existed in relation to the "objectivity which, as suffering, weighs upon the subject"—an objectivity which came from its historical unfreedom and, *pace* Kant, from its inherent incompleteness.[7] This dialectical defense of the emancipatory dimension of reason and identity was rooted in Adorno's understanding of mimesis as the propensity of human beings to imitate the nature that they fear. In the mimetic process, Adorno had argued, human beings sought to overcome their fear of a hostile world in two ways: on the one hand, by imagining themselves to possess the powerful attributes of nature sublime; on the other hand, by dividing the hostile world into concepts that limited and partitioned its perceived power, transforming it into a mythico-conceptual world over which they can assert control. In Adorno's understanding, the mimetic process produced both damage and knowledge, and the violence that knowledge does to the world is also violence to the self. Mimesis is not, in the Fichtean or Heideggerian sense, a simple self-assertion but a dialectical matter.[8]

The woundedness of subjectivity means that the self, fragile and vulnerable at its core, becomes something only in its negativity and is therefore stripped of the Promethean self making and self positing celebrated by the Idealist tradition. Kant's neoclassical subject possessed the forms of knowledge a priori; the Fichtean subject posited knowledge in her self-creation. Adorno, by contrast, conceived of the knowing subject as developing through a series of wounds and disappointments modeled on a mimetic reinterpretation of Sigmund Freud's description of the rupture of primary narcissism. In his interpretation of Freud, however, Adorno emphasized the idea that primary narcissism could only be used as a concrete, social concept in retrospect, as a negative concept. Just as neither the self nor knowledge exists until the individual person is wounded and broken from nature, so questions of psychic mechanics—signification, language, meaning, and conceptuality—grow out of a mimesis of the social-material world.[9] Without a negative, non-identical understanding of the origin of the self emergent from a threatening outside world, Adorno reasoned, one could not square Freud's theory of narcissism with his observation that the hostility to civilization precedes any and all intellectual comprehension thereof. The truth, thought Adorno, was that culture, conceptuality, and experience all began as mimetic imprints of the desire to separate oneself from the wound and thereby grow out of it.[10]

As the metaphor of the wound was transformed into a theory of subjective rationality and irrationality, it changed the relation of philosophy and history and, in particular, called into question the tendency to equate universality and lawfulness with truth. For Freud as much as for Kant, the subject was a universal, to be understood according to formal laws of individual development. The defining achievement of civilization, according to this Enlightenment tradition, was its cultivation of the autonomous individual; yet the tradition also posited abstract individualism as something outside any tradition, as the normal state of humanity. Deeply influenced by this Enlightenment tradition, Adorno had, through much of his earlier career, spent a good part of his intellectual energy criticizing appeals to particularity or to false universals, especially the use and abuse of collectivist categories such as culture, nation, and the masses alongside their philosophical correlates of authenticity, being, purity, and unity. In his essay on Heine, however, one sees a wider revalorization of sociocultural particularity, a recognition that the autonomous individual could not exist without the particular experience—the wound—that had made him or her an individual.

There were situational reasons for this turn in Adorno's thought. In addressing Heine, Adorno was addressing (auto)biographical particularity—his own return to Germany, the formative and inescapable relationship to Germany he acknowledged with this return, the Jewishness the Nazi Germans had forced upon him, the Jewishness he would henceforth define by accepting the work of "education after Auschwitz." In the decade after the war, Germany had by and large examined its national socialist past only in narrowly political terms, rather than having addressed genocide as a matter of cultural and social identity and continuity. Adorno would work in the 1950s and 1960s to demonstrate how the German intellectual, philosophical, and cultural traditions were entwined with the Holocaust, while putting the finger in his own wound, underscoring how his own role as a cultural expert implicated him in the very culture that had wounded him and humanity. But Adorno's new interest in problems of identity was also retrospective, a reflection on the particularity of the American culture he had encountered in exile. For if Adorno had long rejected German appeals to the category of national culture, in America he had found himself resisting a very different configuration of particularity and authenticity—one constellated around the problem of American race relations and the promise of an expressive multiculturalism. This too had been formative for Adorno, formative in the quite different sense that Adorno did not understand America until he began to leave, and formative in that the German concepts of race and culture were incongruent with those emergent in America. If we are to understand how Adorno turned from Enlightenment traditions of philosophy to theorizing identity and non-identity, we must start with the non-identity between the two traditions of culture he addressed as a cultural critic.

This chapter analyzes several early moments in Adorno's confrontation with the concept of personal identity as negative identity, and it examines how Adorno's encounter with the real dangers of the world-historical power of racism and violence in the 1930s, 1940s, and 1950s changed his understanding of the meaning and purpose of critical theory. Looking at how this engagement with Heine refigured Adorno's return to post-Holocaust Germany, I show how his attempts to come to terms with the pasts of German culture and his own ambivalent Jewish heritage brought about a new philosophical emphasis on the negative and vulnerable dimensions of subjectivity. As this concept of subjectivity became central to his philosophy, I argue, it regrounded Adorno's idea of cultural critique, transformed his aversion to biographical and culturalist explanation, created a framework upon which he could construct a sociological understanding of collective individualism, clarified the application of the dialectic between enlightenment and barbarism to cultural and political events, and reconfigured his critique of commodity fetishism and class consciousness. Retrospectively, this late interest in a philosophical analysis of identity and negative identity casts light on Adorno's most notorious failure as a cultural critic—his earlier writings on jazz—and on his early convictions concerning the necessary austerity that a Hegelian-Marxist-Kantian framework of analysis needed to have toward ethno-national and culturally particularist concepts of identity. Adorno's own late work, in other words, becomes one of the best tools for analyzing the limitations of his pre-identity phase. This critique is pursued while arguing that Adorno's writings on jazz offer an incisive means of understanding how his early intellectual development—in the course of which he translated a theory of economic and cultural production into a self-reflexive practice of cultural criticism—was rooted in his experience in the Weimar Republic, wartime America, and postwar Germany, and specifically in the tension between the process of coming to terms with his own Jewishness and the way the categories of race and national culture were being articulated in contemporary America and Germany. Finally, by examining how Adorno's confrontation with the concept of culture and the problems of class and group consciousness in the jazz essays contained not only discernible flaws but the seeds of its own later revision and transformation, this chapter explores the limitations in the prevailing concepts of identity then available to Adorno, thus offering a historical analysis of the career of the identity concept in the twentieth century.

Exile and Jazz

If the value of any cultural theory is defined not just by its rigor but by the quality—good or bad—of its *aperçus*, then the work of Theodor Adorno is undeniably marked by a wound. The word "jazz" names this wound; and like the wound that was Heine, the wound of jazz is defined by problems of race, culture, identity, violence, and discrimination. The mere mention of Adorno's jazz writings serves as an irritant in the world of critical theory, eliciting a disheartened sigh in anyone trying to come to terms with Adorno's thought and prosecutorial glee among those who dislike Adorno and all that his name stands for. All of the cards in this game have been played: Adorno has been accused of racism, of Jewish self-hatred, of Teutonic bigotry, of Eurocentrism, and of personality flaws ranging from manic depression to sadism.[11] And though all of these labels fail to do justice to a person who not only forsook personal comfort to return to Germany after World War II but who counts among the twentieth century's pioneering critics and analysts of racism and cultural bigotry, there is no doubt that the jazz question must be taken seriously as a limitation that reflects much about Adorno, both biographically and as a philosopher, sociologist, and cultural critic. The way to unfold this relation is to look at Adorno the way Adorno looked at Heine: the conceptual issues must be related to the material and social conditions of the world, to the problems they were hoping to solve, and to the way in which those ideas necessarily struck against their limits—limits with which the individual thinker had difficulty and that he could do little else but internalize. If the category of jazz points to an element of Adorno's thought that seems non-identical to itself, a historical reflection on the changing understanding of identity and culture in the twentieth century helps concretize this dynamism in theoretical terms.

Adorno wrote approximately six articles on jazz (depending on how one counts them), all roughly within the period of the greatest immediacy of danger for him as someone who—setting aside his own complex thoughts about the matter—was perceived as a Jew. The first published document of Adorno's using the word "jazz" is from 1932, "Zur gesellschaftlichen Lage der Musik" (On the social situation of music). In 1933 appeared "Abschied vom Jazz" (Farewell to jazz). In 1936, as Adorno was moving between England and France but was contemplating a trip to America, he wrote his first major piece explicitly on jazz, "Über Jazz" (On jazz), which was published in the *Zeitschrift für Sozialforschung* that year. In 1938, shortly after his arrival in the United States and during his work at the Princeton Radio Project, he published "Über den Fetischcharakter der Musik und die Regression des Hörens" (On the fetish character of music and the regression of listening). Shortly afterward, while studying English, he wrote a medium-length review essay of the scholarship in the *Zeitschrift*. By 1941, when Adorno was finally capable of writing a proper academic article in English, he published "On Popular Music," also in the *Zeitschrift* (by that time renamed *Studies in the Social Sciences*), which largely dropped the language of "jazz" and analyzed the various forms of "high and low" radio and "popular" music; and then, in 1946, he wrote a small article titled "Jazz" for a musicological encyclopedia. Finally, in 1953, during the first years in which Adorno could be said to have returned to Germany but before he was definitively there to stay, he pieced together arguments from the earlier essays into "Zeitlose Mode. Zum Jazz" (Timeless fashion: jazz), the essay that is most commonly read today as part of the collection *Prisms*.[12]

The dates of these articles alone have led to the suspicion that there was something "racially charged" in Adorno's writings about jazz. This is undoubtedly true, but saying so raises the question of what combination of context and concept would bring this charge to ground. For the jazz essays mark the point at which the traditions that had shaped the young Adorno and the modes in which Adorno's early work had been done—the nineteenth-century German-Jewish tradition of humanist and universalist culture, the aesthetic politics of the 1920s avant-garde, and the explicitly antiracist mode of Marxian social critique—ran up against the very real and destructive power of racial and identity thinking in the 1930s.

As a public dispute, Adorno's "jazz controversy" began in 1953, when the German critic and impresario Joachim-Ernst Berendt, reviewing the 1953 "Timeless Fashion: jazz," accused Adorno of being a self-hating Jew who turned his musical expertise and his wit to tearing down the great art of American pluralism, an art the Nazis had similarly honored in their attempts to efface it along with Heine's name. Adorno reacted to this charge with horror, expressing shock at the "grotesqueness" of the charge of racism being aimed at someone "who had escaped Hitler" and "who had just published a critically acclaimed study on the problem of racial prejudice in the United States."[13] There is every sense that Adorno's shock at the accusation was genuine. Having made this protest, however—and strongly wishing to bracket any race-inflected culturalist reading of jazz (not without good reason in Germany, circa 1953)—Adorno insisted on carrying forth the debate as a purely technical argument concerning claims that Berendt (among others) had made concerning jazz's superior musical originality relative to the classical or modernist traditions. Somewhat pedantically, Adorno drew on his extensive knowledge of the history of composition to show the baselessness of Berendt's claims. He argued, for example, contra Berendt, that prior to jazz's innovations, improvisation had long been part of organ music, that polyphony had been explored by Richard Wagner and Johannes Brahms, that the innovative neutral thirds and tonal voids that jazz critics proclaimed as jazz's invention had in fact served as entire compositional frameworks for composers such as Béla Bartók, and that the tension between melodic rhythm and fundamental rhythm in the *Lieder* tradition had already been rich and complex in the early Romantic period. Adorno, in other words, worked to disarm Berendt's innuendo of racial or cultural bias by turning the argument into a musicological duel over which tradition "invented what first." By arguing from the universalist framework of technical innovations in musical tonality, Adorno won for himself an easy victory and avoided legitimizing the category of race, but both this victory and the deflection have necessarily come to seem to many later readers hollow and ignominious. A historical investigation of the relation between theory, praxis, and self will reveal that Adorno was still working through the relation of culture to universality and group identity, and that he was doing so at both a personal and practical as well as theoretical level.[14]

And this is a pity—not least because there were more interesting issues at stake for Adorno than the triumphs represented by mere technical "firsts." What *was* at stake becomes clearer when one examines the final jazz essay in the context of the larger pattern of Adorno's writing in the 1950s. The essay collection *Prisms*, in which the "Timeless fashion: jazz" essay attacked by Berendt appeared, was in fact largely organized around a single theme: the problems posed by the affirmative character of culture.[15] Thus, for instance, almost exactly the same set of arguments that Adorno leveled against jazz in the 1953 compilation essay were also present in his polemic against the Bach revival then taking place in Germany: Adorno savaged the way Bach fans fetishized technique; identified music with the ethno-national cultural "belonging" of "small German baroque villages, as if magically untouched" by the war; and enthused over the "paradox" of an old music being extraordinarily contemporary—when in fact what they were worshiping, argued Adorno, was the music's commodification, the way in which it was being placed in the service of regression.[16] Declaring that "Bach needed to be defended against his admirers," Adorno argued that Europeans were exploiting Bach to indulge in wholly detemporalized understandings of musical innovation, improvisation, and creativity, all at the expense of the real truth: the reality of a culture shot through with violence, suffering, dehistoricization, and loss. To make clear that this argument was not just about music or just about paying his disrespects to jazz and J. S. Bach fans, Adorno prefaced *Prisms* with an essay that implicated the cultural critic himself in the whole duplicity of culture. Following a line of argument that would, in a few years' time, be developed into the concept of the wound, Adorno argued that the cultural critic was always caught in a double relation to the culture that he wished to criticize—that he must remain part of culture and nevertheless think himself above it. Adorno thought, however, that there was no choice but to engage at a double level. The critic must engage first with the problem of culture and collective meaning, addressing the task of raising public sensitivities to issues that many would rather avoid, introjecting self-reflexivity into the existing debate, and attempting to raise public awareness of the affirmations and immediacies of modern culture. Only thereafter could the critic work to define a more comprehensive notion of reason that could both diagnose the cause of this blindness and suggest how to overcome it.

This history undercuts the idea that Adorno had a particular animus against jazz any more than he had against Bach; it is more accurate to say that Adorno found much to fault in the "fan" literature of both types of music. Nevertheless, the argument cannot stay at the formal level of the critique of music or consumer culture in general. Musical formalism cannot explain away the real stridency in Adorno's work on jazz—a stridency that extends beyond a general critique of the affirmative character of culture, and that reaches into the history of recognition that has since come to be associated with jazz. The argument for formalist analysis becomes aggravated by the deeper question of trying to define a universality of culture. Adorno was not the first to gravitate toward a Germanocentric notion of musical universality or the first to view innovations in tonality and compositional form as the waymarkers of this "universal history." But the failure to question those assumptions was compounded by a failure to analyze critically the international character of jazz or the particularity of German musical culture. While other topics in *Prisms* were more narrowly German in nature, the discussion of jazz required one to address the full scope of what Adorno would later describe as the challenge that the American concept of "culture" posed to the *Kultur* of "Old Europe."[17]

Without question, the 1937 "On Jazz" was inadequate to its moment. It presented American jazz in a way that bespoke a deep incongruity between Adorno's sociological, cultural, and aesthetic theory and the cultural material he was trying to analyze. Adorno, to be sure, had ample company in advancing his arguments. Many of the criticisms Adorno voiced concerning the repetitive or commercial aspects of jazz, or its relation to a certain commodified clownery, were also advanced by avant-garde musicians in the jazz community not only in the 1950s, 1960s, and 1970s but in many forms going back to the turn of the century.[18] Nonetheless, it is clear that Adorno did not have a sociocultural theory of the avant-garde capable of analyzing how technical innovation and subcultural self-expression related within musical form. Issues of the cultural symbolism of jazz aside, there is something tragic in the fact that Adorno seemed to limit his recognition of the great jazz innovators of his generation—Louis Armstrong and Duke Ellington—to their ability as performers and arrangers rather than composers, and for this reason he seems to have found no equivalent in jazz to defend "against its admirers," as he had in the case of Bach, or as he did the early Arnold Schönberg against the later. Moreover, Adorno clearly applied a far-too-easy typology to the sociology of music, dividing it—at least until the final years of his life—into three parts: a genuine folk or cultural tradition, an experimental avant-garde, and a middle no-man's land of *Gebrauchsmusik* (commercial or purpose-driven background music). And it is further clear that Adorno, especially in his earlier phase, greatly overestimated the radical power of avant-garde art and had a weakness for arguing that high art's "progressive" quality was somehow rooted in the superiority of certain forms of technique over others. This view allowed him, for example, to identify the "revolution" in tonality with the very possibility of cultural transformation itself and to judge anything that did not deploy the absolutely most advanced technique to be a misappropriation of the expressive power of art.

The Heine essay suggests that in 1956 at least, Adorno was beginning to develop a positive idea of how to discuss the problems of race, class, and national historical consciousness in public in a way that did not accelerate the process of dehistoricization and loss accompanying increased subjectivization. Furthermore, there is evidence to suggest that, had he lived a few more years, Adorno might well have come around to addressing the problem of how a sociology that draws on the tension between personal intuition and the alienated power of social structures might be reconciled with a fundamentally anthropological, pluralist, and "cultural" framework of historical analysis.[19] Such a theory would have been able to do justice to the great divide separating the New World experiences of African Americans, transcribed in jazz, from the experiential content of Old World peasants transcribed in the music of Mahler or Bartók. Be that as it may, in the 1930s, he was in neither full theoretical nor material control of the subject matter he wanted to address. As the scholarly literature on Adorno developed during the course of the 1960s to the 1990s—years that corresponded to increasing attention to the ideal of multiculturalism—the controversy concerning jazz gravitated to the center of discussions of his work. And the scholarship has followed the suspicion that if one interprets Adorno through his miscomprehension of jazz, one will find him at his truest and worst. One can acknowledge the validity of such suspicions while also recognizing that such reasoning-by-association itself amounts to trading in cultural stereotypes in a way can impoverish the discourse without getting to the truth. Thinking about how the limitations of Adorno's jazz theory were tied to his early experience shows that the wound is related not only to his thought but also to the social structures to which Adorno was responding. This biographical insight, in turn, renders intelligible the theoretical objections to cultural and biographical analysis.

Musical Universality and the Politics of Early Experience

In discussing Heine and the problem of wounded subjectivity, Adorno emphasized that Heine's early experience intermingled freedom and unfreedom, individual-aesthetic and German-cultural understandings of language. For Adorno, music more than language was the immediate medium of cultural experience. If one reads Adorno's 1933 essay "Vierhändig, noch mal" (Four-handed, once again) with woundedness and immediacy in mind, it is possible to understand something significant about how he came to identify music not only with intellectuality and technical achievement, but also with freedom and expression, and how the question of identity and non-identity emerged from this analysis of experience.

The essay was written as a kind of *adieu* to the world he had known, and the "once again" of the title highlights the fact that no other essay Adorno would write carries quite the same attachment to the sentimental power of the nineteenth century or to the emotional significance of his own musical upbringing. In Adorno's childhood education, music indeed had stood for the full sense of freedom and universality, of bourgeois particularity and domesticity to which nineteenth-century Europe aspired. This understanding of music was central to German life generally, and to German-Jewish life more particularly, given that music's color-blind universality appealed—more strongly than any other branch of the arts—across the divide that separated the ghetto from the city in the age of bourgeois culture. It is perhaps even not too much to detect, in Adorno's thoughts about this relation, a memory of the idea of a sacred text, a reconstruction of the Jewish experience in general, and of Adorno's own Jewish heritage in particular. Much is said in the opening lines of the essay, with its interest in the *dürfen* (being allowed to) attending the relation between text and magic, interpretation and feeling, the sacred and the particular, the good life and the highest ideals:

That form of music that we have become accustomed to labeling the classical was something I learned, as a child, to play four-handed. There was little of the literature of the symphonic or chamber music traditions that was not brought into household life with the help of the large, folio-type books obtained from the bookbinder in uniformly green-colored bindings. They seemed as if they were made to be browsed; and I was allowed [*dürfte*] to do so, even before I had learned to understand the notes, simply following them from memory and by ear-feel. Even Beethoven violin sonatas were subjected to the curious reworking [of four-handed playing]. Some pieces, like Mozart's G minor symphony, so impressed me in this time, that it seems to me, still today, as if the tension within the introductory eighth development can never be so completely reproduced by an orchestra as it can through the dubious poundings of the second player. More so than any other, this music was appropriate for the house. The piano was a piece of household furniture from which music came forth, and those who threw themselves into the music without fear of hesitations or false notes belonged to the family. Playing four-handed seemed to place the geniuses of the bourgeois nineteenth century as a gift at my cradle at the beginning of the twentieth century.[20]

The sense of historical tragedy pursued by the essay inheres in the contrast between its tender depiction of bourgeois life as sentimental inheritance and its emphatic use of the past tense: its descriptions of playing the piano as the second player, while his mother or his aunt played or sang along, are memories of a world eclipsed. And though there might be nothing "more German," in the nineteenth century sense of this identity, than imagining the longing for home as a form of lost universality, by the same token there was something very painfully "Jewish" in transcribing this loss circa 1933 as negative identity. Being allowed (*dürfen*) to read from volumes so similar to those of the Torah was an anticipation of subjective universality, or what philosophical and religious tradition called *Mündigkeit* (rational, legal maturity). Both kinds of lawfulness had been publicly revoked by Adorno's thirtieth birthday. One can argue whether Adorno was then culturally German, Jewish, or the cosmopolitan refusal of both; but after this juncture, he was not-German and much more aware of his Jewishness, even if this awareness was shot through with nostalgia and an inchoate sense of homelessness.[21] Violence splits identity; its negativity registers loss.

These elements of biographical identity are important for understanding Adorno's work. Adorno's musical inheritance came from his mother and aunt, both skilled and trained musicians, who had had to negotiate the complex marginal world of nineteenth-century musical performance—which is to say, who moved uncomfortably between being thought of as "performers" and as "artists." This marginality, sympathetically appreciated by the Jewish Frankfurt wine merchant Oskar Wiesengrund (a man who by trade dispensed an aristocratic pleasure to a bourgeois world), shaped the material-cultural experience of the child who came to identify music not only as a calling and profession, but also as the medium for freedom and universality as such. This identity was never unambiguous. The Wiesengrunds, on account of the "mixed confessional status" of their union, had married in a London civil ceremony, which itself was symbolic of a westward orientation and a desire to assimilate as Europeans—a nonexistent legal category. Though we can recover little of the political views of Adorno's father during these years beyond his Anglophilia and his profession, there is one fact that can help us speculate. It is known that though he was a prosperous bourgeois, he seems to have had no quarrel with his son's socialism. This makes sense if one surmises that the young Teddie Wiesengrund was probably encouraged to think of his relative privilege in terms of that most English of socialist tropes—a Fabian socialism, which did not think of socialism as an alternative culture, antithetical to the bourgeois, but rather conceived of socialism in terms of the ideal of making good on the promise of bourgeois universality contained in culture. If universality, like the home itself, could be experienced at the piano bench as the gift of the nineteenth century—if cultural equality could be law—it only seemed reasonable to imagine that the experience of that universality as culture should not be denied to the laboring masses. Though later theorists of identity would denounce this ideal of universal cultural enjoyment as elitist or insufficiently radical, this vision of an expansive, holy permissiveness was a regulative ideal within many aspects of late nineteenth- and early twentieth-century politics and culture.[22]

Like many Germans in his generation, Adorno was politically radicalized by the inflation of the early 1920s, which destroyed households, undermined plans, and undercut the economic basis of cultural dreams. Germany's growing anti-Semitism probably contributed to this radicalization, but it was not the source of his political convictions. He simply did not think of himself as Jewish in the same way that the Nazis did. Adorno never viewed Judaism racially or religiously, or even as inherited in any objective sense, and in this sense of Jewishness as an elective identity, he largely followed the model of his Frankfurt peers. In Frankfurt—a city long the object of anti-Semitic innuendo (Luther had called the city a "sinful bowl of gold")—it was not until the last years of the Weimar Republic that it became impossible, as someone of Jewish descent, to continue viewing anti-Semitic rhetoric as simply something to be ignored.[23] Caution was cultivated, to be sure. Even as many German Jews in Adorno's situation saw their personal fortunes ruined during the 1920s and watched their civil rights first symbolically and then literally revoked as the idea spread that the inflation was a Jewish conspiracy, Adorno's father was cautious enough to not be consumed by events. Both Adorno's parents and their resources survived the Weimar Republic and escaped Germany before the outbreak of the war. Yet it was to socialism—and particularly Marxism—that Adorno turned to explain why the world was falling apart, why bourgeois experience and its freedoms seemed to be under the threat of extinction. Socialism was as valuable for its *Erkenntnischarakter* (its ability to help one perceive, through the aid of theory, the changing dynamics of the bourgeois, capitalist world) as for its capacity to express political solidarity with the disenfranchised. Though it seems hardly necessary to say so, it is a misconception to think that the only available notion of socialism during this period was one of an authoritarian or conspiratorial sort. Recognizing this helps one understand something further about Adorno's overall intellectual makeup: he assumed, like many others, that the racism of the German fascists was a twisted and inverted form of a theory that might explain what was going on in the world. Racism, at least for those in a relatively sheltered bourgeois existence in Frankfurt, could be perceived as what August Bebel called "the stupid man's socialism."[24]

Music, Social Theory, and the Urgency of Praxis

Written the year of Hitler's ascent, "Four Handed, Once Again" speaks to the proposition that Adorno may not have become a social theorist were it not for the collapse of the bourgeois world under Nazism. Up until the crisis of 1932–33, he was primarily engaged in making a career as a musician and a philosopher of subjectivity. This self-understanding informed his analysis of the artistic, intellectual, and scientific dimensions of bourgeois freedom prior to writing his first Marxian theoretical essay, his 1932 "On the Social Situation of Music," which depicts music as freedom under eclipse.[25] The essay remains impressive. Though organized according to the classic, orthodox Marxian schema of nineteenth-century political economy—the problem of production and consumption—the essay is not, as one might expect, focused on a revolutionary theory of either a proletarian or bourgeois avant-garde. "On the Social Situation of Music" does not seek to create a theory of a people's culture. Rather, it is concerned with the problem of fetishization in music and with the degree to which fixed genre categories have their origin in different nineteenth-century forms of musical production—aristocratic chamber music, proletarian men's choruses, bourgeois sheet music—and different kinds of experience: for example, folk and guild traditions, theater and court performances, private and academic study, military marches, chansons, and aria.

The essay's emphasis on the range and variety of musical expression stood far from the party-line Marxism of the day. "On the Social Situation of Music" can be described as an open-ended historical-diagnostic piece of writing, seeking, as the title suggests, to analyze the social forces acting within music in its moment. It attempted to read genres not so much by identifying them with class formations as by thinking of genres and the work they performed as attempts to achieve universality through art—attempts at universality that were constantly pushed off course by the social pressures acting on art (commodification, technology, etc.) or by the social pressures alive in art (the desire for freedom, the relation to nature, questions of domination, the interplay of overlapping logics of development, etc.). Adorno believed that genre categories were not to be equated with class in a schematic way that called certain types of art "proletarian" and others "bourgeois." Rather, individual works of art should be evaluated both individually and generically and related to class only through the overall relation of society and experience. This task was necessarily a difficult one. That the genres appeared to be in disarray in the era of modernism, argued Adorno, was due not only to the influence of new means of production and new modes of consumption, but also to the fact that the mass-market concentration of these forms of experience in the hands of modern capitalism was altering the way in which art drew on experience and structured expectations concerning it. Untethered from earlier social contexts—each of which possessed its own awareness of history, its own index of social perception—music in the modern world was being transfigured by the commodity form and was thus becoming exploitable both commercially and politically in new ways that escaped easy classification. As a result, Adorno argued, experience itself, and the idea of freedom that accompanied its production and reproduction through music, was being commodified, dehistoricized, ruptured, and distorted.

As a general Marxian theory of a particular form of culture, "On the Social Situation of Music" went well beyond what had been offered either by the *Völkerpsychologie* of the German academy or by the Marxian tradition. Adorno argued that one should not try to reduce the unfolding of artistic impulses within art to social developments, because to do so would equate society with a fully fetishized commodity world and leave no room to theorize emancipation. Since use value and exchange value stood in a complex dialectical relation, the unfolding of this contradiction within the world of industrial production needed to be both sharply differentiated from, and systematically related to, the dialectical-historical unfolding of the tension between the commercial and artistic forms within the musical world. This was not an argument for the "objectivist" conception of art then endorsed in the Soviet Union in either its aesthetic or its theoretical modes; it was a sweeping repudiation of the idea of art as a mere transcription of social circumstances. Central here is the idea that freedom and art are intertwined, just as are freedom and individualism. Adorno defended the reality of the nineteenth-century concept of bourgeois subjectivity even as he tried to read music socially, looking into changing structures of musical expression for the sake of understanding the changing balance between forces and relations of production in the broadest, dialectical material sense: for the sake of understanding how freedom and the possibility for experience were also part of what was "produced" in musical production. Another way of putting this is that Adorno thought that art held out a model, if not of unalienated production, then of a form of object orientation for the individual in which dynamic social forces and the desire for freedom were both visible. And this was retranslatable, thought Adorno, back into the realm of Marxian social theory, into the critique of commodification. Just as the people wanted something different from commodities than what they received, so they wanted something different from music as well; but these very different sorts of alienation (music's use value was simply different from that of a toaster or an automobile) were not to be reduced to one another, but rather used to diagnose the overall historical tendency, the *gesellschaftliche Lage*. The power of Adorno's essay consisted in the idea of sociohistorical "situatedness" as part of the objectivity of the work of art, and thus as something that all studies of the work must take into account. Adorno wished to reinvigorate the concept of the dialectic as the basis for the analysis of experience and society as they stood in relation to one another through the activities of human making and consumption, and he wished to do so in terms of a reading of Marx that addressed the overall dialectic between nature and society, between forces and relations of production. Such a reading would not demonize the relations of production or consumption and worship labor, nor view art as the ideological "dross" of societal production, but would address each of these as constitutive elements of society.

"On the Social Situation of Music" shows the thirty-year-old Adorno at the forefront of Marxian cultural theory. The idea of setting what Leszek Kołokowski called the "Promethean-Faustian" elements of Marxian humanism to work on the problem of aesthetic genre and its material dynamics—the idea that one could develop a theoretically grounded understanding of society out of any genre; the suggestion that there was something liberating about bourgeois art that posed a challenge to the economic-deterministic or revolutionary-conspiratorial strands of Communist politics—was both a brilliant and dangerous move in the climate in which it was proffered. This danger came not just from the Nazis, who were busy waging street battles against Communists in 1932. The idea that international Communism provided a refuge on the Left was disappearing. Adorno, who had followed along with the Institute's own discovery of the young Marx in the 1920s and 1930s, and who had learned the better part of what he knew about Marx through reading Benjamin, Ernst Bloch, and Georg Lukács, entered this field of politico-theoretical activity naïvely, though at an extremely high philosophical level. His inaugural lecture of 1931 had, brilliantly and a bit foolishly, offered a philosophical synthesis of the post–World War I era of Marxian theoretical speculation by wedding Marx to his friend Benjamin's reinterpretation of the concept of nature. Adorno's earlier absorption in Søren Kierkegaard had meant that when he turned to work on Marxian philosophical thought, he was already looking at Marx through the philosophical lens of Lukács's *Soul and Form* (1911) and, above all, Lukács's *Theory of the Novel* (1920). This latter work had offered a broad generic theory based on the concept of the inner tensions inherent within art in various eras of civilization, which Lukács at that point defined in terms of secularization and degeneration of spirit rather than capital. Adorno's interest in genre and its relation to bourgeois life connected with his interest in Kierkegaard via his reception of Benjamin's understanding of art as the "unleashing of human powers."[26] Innovations in artistic form were, following an analogy to the Marxian unleashing of the productive power of nature, machinery, and capital, to be treated as part of a logic of development congruent with the fetishization of commodities and also as moments of sociohistorical particularity in which the "monadic quality" of individual works of art mirrored the reflexive defense of human spontaneity and autonomy.[27] Horkheimer's inaugural address encouraged the development of a social-scientific synthesis of these approaches to genre: this, in a highly ambitious form focused on music, was what Adorno produced in 1932.

The irony is that 1932 was about the last year such work was possible in European society east of the Rhine. The idea of self-consciousness, upon which genre analysis hinged, was to be replaced by Party discipline. Lukács, who, along with Karl Korsch, had pioneered the field of what would later be called "Western Marxism," had found himself, in 1931, "Cominterned," which referred to the bizarre procedure whereby the police of European democracies arrested their more engaged Communist Party activists and deported them to the Soviet Union—with no expectation of a speech at the Finland Station. This was justified partly as a measure to quell the forces of reaction growing across Europe, partly as a revenge for the revolutionary activity of the early 1920s, and partly to "protect" the individuals in question from violent attacks from ultranationalist groups. By 1932, Lukács was by no means an "independent" Marxist: he had already acquiesced to Soviet censure of his *History and Class Consciousness*, a humiliation for which he repaid the Party with redoubled outward loyalty, while they viewed him as a deviationist.

On theoretical matters, the Institute for Social Research, which had started life by laying claim to the Marxian tradition without alignment to the Soviet Union, diverged further from the Soviet line than Lukács ever had. In 1932, Frankfurt (unlike Vienna) was at a sufficient geopolitical remove from Moscow that such "Cominternation" was unlikely for its members. Nevertheless, one cannot deny the independence of mind represented by the Institute in publishing an essay that insisted on the ultrarevisionist and Enlightenment idea that Marx should be interpreted in terms of his ability to address the totalities of bourgeois culture. The Institute was already receiving ominous updates on the Russian situation from David Rjazanov, the director of its Moscow counterpart, the Institute for Marxism-Leninism, who reported that the Russian Thermidor was at hand. He also noted the strange fate of Lukács, who, courtesy of the Viennese police, was "installed" at the Moscow Institute as a theorist whose primary occupation would soon become that of renouncing his early work for the pleasure of the Party. Rjazanov, a more independent thinker, was not amused to watch the Hungarian tack politically toward the authoritarian Andrei Zhdanov, the man who would play the role of Stalin's prosecutor in the Show Trials.[28]

Self-Inflicted Wounds

With a clear understanding of Adorno's attempt to mediate between socialism and sociology in the 1930s, one can reread Adorno's jazz critique of the period in terms of its own "woundedness." Here one further context becomes relevant. Adorno wrote the jazz articles to become an "expert" on American culture so that he could obtain an entry permit: in a literal sense, it was by only writing "on a theme that could pass as characteristically American" that he escaped the prison that Europe was becoming.[29] The changing political situation continually upended the theory that mediated between Adorno's aesthetic-cultural and political-philosophical impulses. Adorno's theoretical goal had been to examine the production and consumption of music both in terms of the total commodification of capitalist society and in terms of an overall dialectic between nature and society, relations and forces of production, bourgeois subjectivity and its constellations within social groups. A scholarly and open-ended analysis of bourgeois society in its transformation conceived as an objective analysis was altered when the subjective freedoms of bourgeois life fell into crisis. A work like "On the Social Situation of Music" becomes non-identical with itself when the world around it changes. And so does its author. As Adorno turned toward the topic of American music, he was pushed to narrow his approach on two accounts: first, to engage in politics; and second, to begin to speak in code. For the purposes of Adorno's politics at the time, this drive led in two directions: the first was to champion Schönberg and his school as the defenders of a truly progressive, non-objectivist avant-garde (which he did, much to the consternation of Lukács, who denounced as decadent the "bourgeois" Marxists of Frankfurt); and the second was to try to write about a musical form that seemed to have a broader audience, such as jazz. The two moves went hand in hand.

Though Adorno's relation to the Schönberg school also came to be simplified in the process of emigration, his urgent need for praxis was inflicted foremost on popular music, and jazz in particular. As the analysis of genre as fetish was turning into the analysis of culture, there was high demand for good theory of how popular music and mass media were changing public life. In his 1932 essay, written in Germany, Adorno had defined jazz as a commercialized combination of various banalized, dehistoricized, decontextualized forms of "light music," which had been overlaid with the nimbus of an avant-garde internationalism for the purposes of marketing a *utility music* to the machine age. Adorno compared jazz's social constellation to other forms of commercially counterfeited "folk" culture, including gimmick tunes such as the faux Bavarian "Wer hat denn den Käse zum Bahnhof gerollt?" (Who rolled the cheese to the train station?) or that undoubtedly reactionary invocation of fraternity life, "Trink, Brüderlein, Trink" (Drink, little brother, drink). The examples he gave for "jazz" music, by this same analysis, were not the recent works of Sidney Bechet but rather such "forgotten classics" as Paul Whiteman's "Valencia," W. C. Polla's "The Dancing Tambourine," and "The Wedding of the Painted Doll" from the MGM musical *The Broadway Melody*—all of which (it seems inoffensive to say) were wretched kitsch. The implied fusion of syncopated orchestral music with a graft of horns and an invocation of a communal tradition was probably representative of what the word "jazz" meant toward the end of the Weimar era in Germany (even if an ambitious critic could have, with effort, purchased some Sidney Bechet). Significantly, Adorno did not single out jazz for his musical-sociological opprobrium, nor did he draw any absolute line between jazz's appropriation of traditions and that practiced by late Romantic or early modernist masters in their dissonant integration of *völkisch* tonal elements into their compositions. Adorno remained interested in analyzing the social situation in terms of the overall processes of consumption and production of music. The questions he asked were how the market was harnessing the extra-market desires of individuals, how the integration of these desires with easily consumable forms was changing music, and how this process was changing the bourgeois self and its ideas of freedom. But he also challenged the one-sided notion that the only legitimate conclusion to be drawn from Marx's "double character of the commodity" pointed to the appropriation of the means of production by a "worker's state."[30] Given that he was interested, therefore, in how mass-produced music became part of the economic system and that his political goal was one of agitating against the anti-jazz agitators, it is hardly surprising that the word "race" is not invoked: Adorno's concern with the social state of music as art internationally suggested a very vague and loose interest in the American "social situation." Instead, the word *Volk* is used, purely descriptively, to speculate about the desires and consumption patterns of the disenfranchised masses. Adorno would have considered it a mistake to valorize the pseudo-scientific concept of "race" in this context; by the same token, he did not consider African American jazz artists to be anything other than a special case of a disenfranchised proletariat exploited by a production system in search of light entertainment.

Shortly after the grotesque 1932 elections, Adorno took several months to draft the two-part article, pausing to make his first attempt to try to render political his overall analysis of the social and historical consciousness embedded in music. This happened in a radio talk with Ernst Krenek, whose jazz opera *Jonny Spielt Auf* (Jonny starts to play) had already been the target of demonstrations by brown-shirted thugs interested in disrupting "degenerate race music."[31] The charge of cultural degeneracy, typical of Nazi racial politics, insinuated a "Jewish-African" racial-cultural axis against whose encroachments the "Aryan race" needed to defend itself in a life-or-death struggle. The psychoanalytically astute Adorno immediately interpreted these attacks as the reaction formation of a weak subjectivity, channeled into German nationalist anxiety about contamination and reactionary fears of being left behind by modernity. Such arguments would appear later in print, but in his 1932 radio conversation with Krenek, Adorno, without mentioning the Nazis, argued that one should not fear jazz, given the fact that jazz, having long been commercialized, had also long since ceased to be threatening. Instead, argued Adorno, it would be better to look behind the jazz controversy and see that fear of modernity could be transcended by an insight into the material, historical, and technical forces that brought it about. To this, Adorno added that an embrace of the modernity of an avant-garde genius such as Arnold Schönberg was far more revolutionary than the commercialized fusion of classicism, *völkisch* and primitivist elements, and allegiance with technology offered by jazz. Repurposing fascist conceptions of revolution and beauty, Aryan mysticism and technological power, Adorno sought to subvert the incipient revolution from the right by pointing people toward a different, cultural left.

This was certainly not brilliant political rhetoric, but it was not so dumb either. The stupidity came a year later, after the Nazis had seized power, when Adorno redoubled his investment in the same strategy of inversion—with ever-fewer opportunities to make his point in an uncompromised manner. Neither he nor Krenek was going to be allowed back on German radio. So Adorno published, in the Parisian *Europäische Revue*, an essay called "Abschied vom Jazz" in which he repeated the same argument but in further dumbed-down terms. Here he argued that the Nazis were merely chasing a ghost in issuing a degree banning *Negermusik*. Jazz had long since ceased to relate to either the "genuine music of blacks" or the supposedly threatening "degeneration" of the big city. Jazz was a form of international musical-economic integration, whose function was to wipe out local, peasant, and lower-class forms of expression and thus to make the lower class forget their "aesthetic claims" on society. By banning jazz, argued Adorno, the Nazis were trying to ban the idea of a commercial music and to promote a pure diet featuring military marches and "every sort of folklore." But, he concluded, perhaps the silence created by a lack of utility music will allow for the "tension between culture and society" to break free.[32]

The regime still stood; Adorno was forced into exile. And so, feeling isolated in Oxford in 1935–36, he decided to be more forceful—to argue more like Benjamin's friend Bertolt Brecht, who reminded himself how to write good agitprop by placing a donkey figurine on his writing desk with a sign that said "even I must understand it!"[33] At the same time, Adorno, frustrated by his isolation at Oxford, was starting to contemplate the possibility of exile in the United States—a possibility becoming more distinct as the Institute second-guessed its plan to maintain offices in Geneva and Paris. The overall climate of appeasement in England, the increasingly palpable threat of war in Europe, made America the safer harbor—and, given the outcome of World War I, a strategic choice for reasons geopolitical and intellectual-cultural. American immigration restrictions were tight, however, even in the wake of Hitler's war drums and massive expulsions, arrests, and murders of Jewish and socialist intellectuals; to escape, he needed a work visa, and to do this, he needed to become an expert.

Adorno achieved his dual goal of playing the agent provocateur and of establishing his bona fides as an expert on American culture by writing, in England—and still in German—a further article, his 1936 "On Jazz," published under the absurd pseudonym Hektor Rottweiler. The name says much about the article's spirit: by taking the name Rottweiler, after the Nazis' favorite dogs, Adorno sought to undermine that viciousness by assuming a voice more German than German; the first name recalled the good son of Troy, the patriot, defender, and critic of his country's policies, but also connoted mockery, the sense that the rules of culture may need to be violated to defend culture against the barbarians. Adorno thought he would kill two birds with one stone, adopting a heroic-subversive strategy that Herbert Marcuse had earlier pursued in trying to transform the German term *Lebensraum* into a left-wing revolutionary idea, a strategy that Walter Benjamin would later adopt in collecting a book of letters that tried to show the strength of German men to be their capacity toward self-doubt, and that Adorno had himself tried in 1934 in giving a tactically subversive review to another ethno-national type of music, the "men's choir" tradition.[34] As clever as this tactic might have seemed at the time, it was not Adorno's finest hour. "On Jazz" introduced virtually nothing new, nor did it defuse racialized thinking when it tried to ridicule the concept of the "threat" of jazz as a manifestation of sexual insecurity.[35] It did, however, go further in "dumbing things down," this time for the Americans as much as for Adorno's benighted countrymen: dropping all vocabulary of social analysis from his earlier pieces, Adorno tried his hand at providing a critique of jazz's social character that dropped the Marxist idioms of domination in favor of purely psychoanalytic ones.

"On Jazz" effaced much of the power of the social-aesthetic analyses of "On the Social Situation of Music," not only by abandoning the overall theoretical framework for analyzing genre-change in terms of the dynamics of commercialization and electro-mechanical reproduction, but also by focusing on one genre as culture rather than conducting the more thorough, comparative social analysis mandated by his own theory. Though not without its insights, "On Jazz" suffered from its attempt to shift the language of analysis from Marx to Freud while submerging theoretical reflection for the sake of popularization. Freudian literalism can be worse, but not much more so. Not only is practically every aspect of jazz read in terms of castration complexes and the fear of premature ejaculations—from the spasms of the jitterbug, to the vigorous sound of trumpets, to the sense of timing suggested by horns "coming in late" to join the band—but even where "Hektor Rottweiler" appears to have restrained himself, the social analysis is drowned out by the chorus. In trying to evade claims of cultural authenticity by mocking them, "On Jazz" so strongly emphasizes the power of commercialization that it all but discounts the ethno-historical roots of jazz, making its social worlds disappear.[36] Both object and subject can be wounded together.

From the standpoint of a refugee trying to rescue German culture—or the idea of culture itself—from Hitler's Germany between 1932 and 1937, it is clear why Adorno would have wanted to downplay the African American dimension of jazz. For the refugee scholar, there was no strategic value in telling the Rockefeller Foundation that there were unresolved racial tensions in America. There *was* value in refining socialist arguments to speak to the threat of right-wing populism, explaining how modern society was shot through with a search for a falsified, cheaply reproducible sense of immediacy; how modernity longed for primitivism as a protest against a world that demanded continuous labor and tried to brand it as fun; how modern life advanced the interest of recorded music and mass-media celebrities over live performance and attention to matters of orchestration, tonality, harmony or expression; how dangerous it was to celebrate technical progress and mass popularity while the world careened toward disaster. Critical theory had to sell to America.

A half century or more later, Adorno's arguments against jazz appear factually mistaken and culturally insensitive. One outcome of the multiculturalism discussion of the 1980s was to create a kind of culturalist parallel to the Kantian imperative of subjective recognition: a demand for cultural recognition and plurality that views the acknowledgment of aesthetic merit among the artworks of an oppressed group as the entry price of cosmopolitan intellectual engagement. In the course of this wave of discovering cultural theory, the dissonance between this imperative and Adorno's condemnation of jazz came to mark the limits not only of Adorno's relevance to the new consensus but also that of the Frankfurt School more broadly: the limits of the critique of affirmative culture. In this negative sense, Adorno's encounter with jazz itself must be understood historically, as part of a general history of identity and cultural studies that continued to unfold after his death.

Theories of Non-Identity

In 1872, Friedrich Nietzsche's *Birth of Tragedy* shocked the serene world of German philo-hellenism and neoclassical aesthetics by asserting that the formally "pure" notion of tragedy as the celebration of the universal and human was inextricably derived from the Dionysian principles of the Greek chorus. Though art retained its connection to the idealism of proportion, harmony, and form labeled the Apollonian principle and was associated with the logic of words, Nietzsche argued that behind all art stood a torrent of suffering expressible only by a *musical* imagination that urged the destruction of harmony and the Bacchanalia's ecstatic devouring of everything divine. Though Nietzsche believed music, tutored by philosophy, poetry, and all the formalisms of language, could indeed incorporate universalism into its very core, he thought that music most deeply expressed the idea of suffering and that it was defined by the fact that all suffering was particular, human, and distinctly ungodlike. Nietzsche's essay, which ushered in many central notions of modernist cultural criticism, exposed something peculiar in the logic of nineteenth-century musical-philosophical discourse: the idea that music expressed simultaneously the most *universal* and the most *particular* dimensions of a culture. Two further contradictions connect to this one. First, *The Birth of Tragedy* suggested that music represented the most logical and formal as well as the most illogical and primitive possibilities of expression. Second, it argued that music was both the furthest removed from the idea of logical thought and also, in the chorus's presaging of the emancipation of man from nature, that which set Western thought on the road to philosophy's most fundamental and most absurd assertion: the idea that with every expression of truth, freedom is anticipated and becomes a force in the world.

Nietzsche's goal in *Birth of Tragedy* was to shatter the illusions of nineteenth-century aesthetic Idealism. Directly connected to Nietzsche's leading thesis that music was simultaneously universal and particular came the assertion in *Beyond Good and Evil* that at the center of art lay a daimonic notion of truth, one that relied not on the correspondence of one's ideas with a universal truth but on the alignment of one's passions with the history of suffering. And if art was not about the achievement of form but about recognizing the experience of belonging to a group, then the central truth value of art was that it could help one achieve a perspective otherwise unknown to the masses. This feeling of the "free spirit" could lead one to feel simultaneously both "inside and outside" the appearance of truth, and it could lead one to separate oneself from the formalism of good opinion or the immediacy of the masses and seek a higher form of emancipated selfhood—one that saw beyond the unfreedoms of particularity as it existed.

Today's theorization of art in terms of negative identity—of art's relation to unwanted or falsified identity—owes a great deal to Nietzsche, but not in the first instance through the influence of Adorno. Rather, it was the American scholar W. E. B. Du Bois who, whether through the direct reading of Nietzsche, Hegel, and Johann Wolfgang von Goethe or through his reading of Georg Simmel's Nietzschean-influenced sociology, created a completely new and distinctly American interpretation of the "second sight" that the experience of race brought to the analysis of society. The career of "negative identity" as the social index of truth begins with the doubled relation between Du Bois's sociohistorical view and his aesthetic views. As the first American theorist to make negative identity his main subject, Du Bois conjoined the topic that Nietzsche and Adorno both pursued—the universality of music—with the topic that they both eschewed: the concept of race. For Du Bois, the negativity of race and the color line was a kind of wound in the fabric of universality, but one that the most educated souls—"the talented tenth"—could see both inside and outside, and thus through and beyond.[37] The scar of race was, in Du Bois's understanding, to be transformed into its opposite: a higher consciousness—first for the wounded, but eventually for all of humanity. The medium for this transformation was the teaching of history. African American history according to Du Bois had deep roots, yet its telling had just begun with the end of the Civil War and the cataclysm of a failed Reconstruction. Only when the narrative of the color line became part of history as such, and thus only when negative identity became part of one's understanding of subjectivity as such, would the reality of citizenship have any relation with its ideal.

The Souls of Black Folk, published in 1903, saw race in sociological terms as something structural that needed to be overcome from within and without. A remnant caste system, race was a form of mental slavery that needed inversion. But until such a reconciliation between narrative and reality occurred, universal culture served as a healing balm: art offered a vision of happiness, a program of refinement, and an outlet for suffering. Art was education freed from the mandates of labor. Singling out music as the most powerful of the arts in this regard, *The Souls of Black Folk* traced a vision in which the "sorrow songs" preserved a memory of slavery and provided an avenue to the "kingdom of culture." The sorrow songs Du Bois cited were neither jazz nor the blues, but spirituals. Their name defined not just their particularity but the alliance between art and the suffering that ultimately creates self-knowledge and emancipation. Each sorrow song for Du Bois formed a chapter in the self-education of the American Negro, and it allowed culture to preserve a memory of dignity in suffering until a full historical emancipation was achieved in society as a whole.[38]

It is an index of modernism's foreignness that Du Bois, however, did not uncritically embrace all forms of African American music in his canon of cultural memory. In 1933, the same year that Adorno started writing on jazz in Germany, Du Bois responded sharply to a review in the *New York Times* that disparaged the Fisk University Choir's performance in favor of a "real religious revival in Harlem," which would reveal the "wildness, melancholy, the intense religious feeling communicated when Negroes sing in the sacred spirit and uncorrupted manner of their race."[39] Having none of it, Du Bois translated this as a demand of a racist society—the demand that "Negroes must not be allowed to attempt anything more than the frenzy of the primitive, religious revival." Espousing a view of art that was classical, cosmopolitan, and cultured rather than expressionist, modernist, or culturalist, Du Bois insisted that "the answer is, Art is not natural nor is it supposed to be natural."[40] True art may incorporate elements of the folk tradition; however, to dissolve the distinction was to embrace a theory of primitive expression and false memory. And this, for Du Bois, not only abrogated the relation between art and nature, but blurred the lines between artistic legitimacy and mere minstrelsy. Du Bois's vision of an African American music was not based on a particularist notion of culture per se but on an idea of creating a true universalism based on a self-consciousness of historical emancipation and suffering. He hoped to realize the promise of a universal, cosmopolitan music, not overturn formalism in an attempt to overcome the color line.[41]

Seen in the context of the early 1930s, Du Bois and Adorno's theories of musical culture have structural similarities, both bearing the marks of a Nietzschean negative universalism. Both theorists recognized that music can mark cultural difference, but both tended to evaluate the expression of cultural difference in terms of the role of a higher art in preserving a memory of how civilization's accomplishments are mixed with horror. Their analysis of formalism and genre required that explorations of particularity, primitivism, and expressivity be measured against a universal history that included domination as well as freedom. Consistent with the combination of Nietzschean ideas and emancipatory universalism, this was an aesthetic cosmopolitanism that wished to compel the "beautiful ideas" of civilization to speak about horror while not surrendering beauty. Both Du Bois and Adorno admired serious music's ability to integrate folk traditions with the universalist appeal and formal sophistication of the symphony, the *Lieder* tradition and the opera. Both were guarded against the use of aesthetic elements that claimed to be "authentic" forms of "primitivism" or that seemed to eschew historical self-awareness for the sake of felt immediacy. Both admired music's ability to communicate the complexity of suffering and the incomplete nature of freedom. Because both Adorno and Du Bois were in 1933 aware that the concepts of primitivism and immediacy in music could be (and for many listeners were) connected to an aggressive logic of race, they were on guard against attempts to valorize a "revolutionary" embrace of primitivism or to equate it with the power of musical expressivity as such.

The difference between what was to become the Frankfurt and Harlem Renaissance theories of race and culture emerged not from aesthetics but from sociological-philosophical ideas about autonomy. Du Bois was an American, and more than a full generation older than Adorno. He had traveled through the Jim Crow South and through much of Wilhelmine Germany. *The Souls of Black Folk*, published a year before Adorno was born, sought in the first instance to address the incompleteness of African American emancipation. It therefore accepted the category of race as a sociological fact and a historical horizon against which any form of freedom must be measured. For Adorno and his fellow Frankfurt theorists, race had not yet been forced on them as an inescapable category of the social analysis of modernity. When race was first addressed by the Frankfurt theorists, it was as *racism*—an example of *a* general civilizational impulse toward embracing irrationality, alongside, for example, violence, religion, or even gambling. It was therefore the case that when Adorno first approached the theory of race, he did not engage the question head-on but addressed it as a negation of universality, asking about the paranoid perception of a "threat" of miscegenation through music. The absurd idea that music could contaminate a culture was for Adorno something that could be accounted for best by analyzing how the siren song of commodity fetishism (and its call to abandon the historical in favor of the *now*) incited the desire for immediacies that the culture industry could market and serve. In the early 1930s, Adorno sought to disparage the meaningfulness of the concept of race, whereas Du Bois in America never enjoyed the luxury of pretending race was not real.

World War II brought about a sea change in critical theory, requiring Adorno and other members of the Institute to accept what Du Bois had always understood: that they were condemned to the study of race; that henceforth, the analysis of cultural identity, prejudice, and race thinking would be central to their research. During the period of their emigration and return, the Frankfurt theorists sought to define society and culture as non-identical categories of historical experience that needed to be treated in dialectical relation to economics and natural science. For Adorno, there were two focal points of this theoretical work up until the 1950s. The first was philosophical, concerned with the rebuttal of the false identities and manufactured authenticities that he saw as sponsored by the right-wing inheritors of Nietzsche: the movements of existentialism, vitalism and *Lebensphilosophie*, and their sponsored nationalisms and group psychologies, all of which sought to exempt their notion of subjectivity from the more fundamental dialectic of civilization and barbarism. The second was psycho-sociological and culminated in the publication of the 1950 *Authoritarian Personality*: it sought to understand the cultural and political production of prejudice and paranoia, how social fear, domination, and exploitation came to be incorporated into the structure of the personality and, in turn, the politics and epistemology of collective forms of identity.

The modest influence of these Frankfurt theories on the postwar imagination was ultimately dwarfed by Harlem's theoretical approach to the idea of culture. Influenced by the rise of the culture paradigm in American social science, thinkers of the Harlem Renaissance shaped the identity theory of art during the course of the 1920s, 1930s, and 1940s. Exemplary of this development was the Du Bois protégé Alain Locke, who developed a culturalist extension of Du Bois's folk music model by addressing the central fact of post-Reconstruction America: race segregation as the domination of social space. Where Du Bois envisioned African Americans contributing to a universal culture, Locke saw them as the avant-garde in forging a new kind of culture. He argued that turning away from America's North/South split and toward the East—toward Harlem as a kind of Mecca or Zion—allowed a creative forgetting of the Negro's agrarian past. Where Du Bois often struggled to purge sociology of the categories of Darwinian determinism or Spencerian functionalism that were expected for a science to be regarded as "scientific," Locke underscored the creative power of culture and pointed to the political power of contesting shared spaces and memories. Locke's vision combined an affirmative notion of folk culture with a historical memory of negative identity and struggle to emphasize a "constructive participation" in shaping the cultural consumptions of urban life through the power of "creative expression."[42] The fact that people wanted to consume "Negro culture" allowed it to serve as an integrative force that could challenge national and international color lines. Explicitly citing the wave of international anti-Semitism in the 1930s, Locke argued for the importance of cultural reassertion in a moment of retrenching social domination. "Persecution is making the Negro international," he argued, but this internationalization offered opportunity for his cultural identity not just to advance individual "race consciousness," but to extend his folk contribution beyond "the protective social mimicry forced upon him by the adverse conditions of dependence" and to let the Negro spirituals freely break the boundaries of the "stereotypes of Wesleyan hymn harmony" in which they were enchained. Locke argued that the advancement of cultural desegregation would lead to mental desegregation, and this, in turn, could transform a history of social domination into an expressive narrative of achieved self-consciousness. Embracing the knowledge hidden in negative identity, whether in musical structures or social spaces, was the secret to becoming self-identical.

In Locke, one can see the potency of a historically rooted politics of identity: it extended politics beyond the formal civil equality of the franchise, beyond the idea of mere cultural recognition and to the concepts, images, and practices that constitute groups and selves. Locke upheld a calculated rupture with universality paired with an acknowledgment that identity is not essence. Traditional liberalism and Marxism, precisely because of their commitment to the ideal of universality, were poor at defining individual freedom—freedom in its particularity—and thus at nurturing the minority position of liberation. The contagious popularity of the language of identity in the culture of modernity came from its affirmative character, the sense of private accomplishment that "identity" bestows in a world of incomplete emancipation—and incomplete theorization of freedom. The language of positive identity can misleadingly assert a simple process whereby cultural self-definition leads inexorably to emancipation; the philosophical and historical account of the negative dimension of identity go hand in hand. The idea of a negative identity recognizes the "uneven developments" of political right and cultural recognition, and it demands that the idea of identity be articulated both in terms of the empirical necessity of "having an identity" and in terms of the fact that identities are nevertheless rooted in domination, in falsity as well as truth. Theory must come to understand the dialectic between identities that are freely chosen and those that are imposed.

Crucially, these questions of twentieth-century identity theory revolve around histories of universality and emancipation that have a dual origin, both in the abstract logic of the Hegelian dialectic and in its real-life referent, the problem of slavery, racial hierarchy, and domination. Embracing a theory of the emancipatory power of expressivist culture is not sufficient for understanding the dialectic of identity, either in social theory or the theory of race. Nor is it adequate to the history of jazz. Scholarship on jazz has long emphasized a correlation between the internal music of jazz as a musical form and the external struggle for African American emancipation. This internal historicity is not, however, self-evident in the works of Ellington, Armstrong, Bechet, Lester Young, Charles Mingus, or Charlie Parker; it requires a kind of double vision, either in the form of an explicit theory of negative identity or a historical narrative that incorporates an awareness of the intertwinement of mimesis with domination. The history of writing on jazz is a history of how these judgments are synthesized. In the 1930s, as we have seen, it was possible for even Du Bois to exclude much current music from a theory of musical emancipation. This attitude was shared by many contemporary African American intellectuals.[43] The conversation on the meaning of jazz would develop in the following decades, and by the 1960s the relation between jazz and civil rights was being theorized in terms of three basic categories of sociocultural explanation. The first is sociological in nature, narrating a story of how the long-standing separation of American music into high and low forms was overcome. It examines how jazz, as the music of the dominated fraction of the dominated class, slowly won acceptance, moving from being the background music of the brothels of New Orleans to prohibition speak-easies to Carnegie Hall, precisely through jazz's ability to cross the color line and challenge antiquated distinctions of "high" and "low." A second category of jazz scholarship is political in nature, emphasizing not the sociology of musical consumption but the intertwinement of jazz with the history of the international civil rights movement: jazz, it is argued, rose to prominence as a space in which African Americans excelled and through whose appeal the struggle for recognition and respect could unfold. The third category of jazz scholarship advances an expressivist aesthetic: it sees jazz as a special and free province of minority expression in the United States, one that was particularly cunning in turning the forms of racial domination and the commodification of culture into a vehicle that uniquely combined mockery and high aesthetic ambition. Though these three modes of interpretation have developed in roughly historical order, all can trace their origins to Du Bois. At the same time, however, their contours are marked by the postwar transformation of liberal (Kantian and Hegelian) theories of freedom.[44]

Thus, if the notion of jazz as the "music of the civil rights movement" traces its lineage back to Du Bois's notion of the sorrow songs, it does so best not by arguing that jazz effected or expressed freedom but that the histories of jazz carry within them an important popularization and expansion of the concept of negative identity: a memory of once being slaves in a foreign land. Just as Alain Locke's embrace of the affirmative notion of culture was predicated on acknowledging the historicity of "[self-] protective social mimicry" enforced by domination, so Adorno came to articulate how aesthetic theory could embrace elements of biographical and cultural expressivity if they were tied to an awareness of the repression of suffering.[45] Negative identity knows the truth of identity, above all in the realm of aesthetics: central to this idea are the notions, first articulated by Nietzsche and expanded by Harlem and Frankfurt theory, that a negative identity can be transformed into a positive one; that the logic of truth is perspectival; that the geography of cultural space is layered; that there is no such thing as a pure origin; that cultural pluralism does nothing to undermine but everything to enhance the practice of self-determination; and that the mixture of cultures, traditions, and personalities defines the joyous impurity of all self-knowledge. Within the story of jazz becoming a form of culture, the outlines of a history of negative identity begin to appear. But this history of course did not start with the first note of jazz but with the formation of opinions about jazz as an expression of race, culture, and freedom or its negation.

Race and the End of the "Gay Science" of Culture

The conclusion to Adorno's essay "Heine, the Wound" points to Heine's great poem of exile, "Die Heimkehr" (The homecoming). Written in the Romantic idiom of unrequited love, it presents what Adorno described as an "intentionally false folk song" in which the return home through the "joyously shining May" is disrupted by an abrupt turn at the very end:

The maidens are bleaching linen—
They skip on the grass and play,
The Mill-wheel scatters diamonds,
Its drone sounds, far away.

A sentry-box is standing
[In] the old grey keep below,
And a lad in a coat of scarlet
Paces there to and fro.

He handles and plays with his musket—
It gleams in the sunset red,
He shoulders and presents it—
I would that he shot me dead![46]

For Adorno, Heine's triumph came through his ability to write a compelling German folk song about returning home that efficiently turned against its too-perfect image of identity. A poem of the radical Heine who could not return from Parisian exile, and a poem of Heine the German Jew who could not fully identify with his homeland, "The Homecoming" pursues a memory of sacrifice and suffering, an image of homelessness that renders objective alienation into a love song. Suggesting that the wound of Heine's homelessness was not fully comprehensible within the Romantic tradition, Adorno points to its resonance with Mahler's ability to "write songs in which the brittleness of the banal and the derivative is used to express what is most real, in the form of a wild, unleashed lament." Mahler's *Lieder* of soldiers flying their flag not out of patriotism but out of homesickness, his symphony that is interrupted by the funeral march, "his folk songs with the harsh alteration of major and minor . . . finally release the full musicality in Heine's verses." The shape of truth here is "aesthetic rupture," and the homelessness felt by the poet and by the songs is now the homelessness felt by everyone. Again, the concluding words to "Heine, the Wound": "All human beings have been as badly injured in their beings and their language as Heine the outcast was. His words stand in for their words: there is no longer any homeland other than a world in which no one would be cast out any more, the world of a genuinely emancipated humanity." The inverted folk song is testimony to negative identity and to wounded subjectivity.[47]

Adorno's work after the mid-1950s analyzed the non-identity within works of art; within cultural, national, and group categories of identity; within the conceptual assertions and logic of all claims to universality. This was not an attempt to map out the nature of unconscious desires or to unmask the hidden social intention of art, but a dialogue between the subjective and objective, positive and negative dimensions of identity. Understood as a doubled form of consciousness that sought both to reveal the limits of these closed systems of signification and yet thereby to affirm them within the bounds of their truth and their relation to emancipation, the concept of non-identity at the heart of Adorno's negative dialectics was articulated in terms of a wounded and vulnerable subjectivity, which, unlike the subject/object models of the Enlightenment or Romantic conception, is not in a situation to "posit" the world out of his or her own self. The sense of universal homelessness and woundability go hand in hand in this post-Enlightenment, post-Holocaust world. For Adorno, the central critical vision of this new historical situation offers a variant of Du Bois's second sight: critical theory must not merely posit new utopias, new ideal subjectivities, but it must learn to perceive the world anew through the very things that terrify the critical mind.

The musical association that Adorno suggested by interpreting "Die Heimkehr" through Mahler is an example of Adorno's theory of negative identity at work. The critique of nationalism, culture, or race as reifications of (subjective) identity writ large was Adorno's starting point. Philosophically speaking, these were errors—overstatements of the power and universality of subjectivity embedded in the logic of Kantian no less than Fichtean, Enlightenment no less than Romantic, liberal no less than socialist Idealism. Mahler's abrupt key changes, his "intentionally false" use of folk material, his plunge into aesthetic ruptures where subjective zeal clashes with the past and future visions of reconciliation all unleash the truth of "intentionally false" lyricism and folkishness of the Romantic age. Works of art can, by imitating and embedding the lies we tell about ourselves, serve as texts through which we can read the dangerous instability of identity and collective subjectivity. Adorno's later aesthetic theory reads texts for the history of subjectivity embedded within them and seeks to show how the embedded claims to subjectivity and mastery are incomplete, partial, and thus non-self-identical.

Adorno's critique of philosophical non-identity—of the (Kantian) rational subject—expands from this historical-aesthetic center. To analyze how Adorno came to believe that the history of aesthetic perception required one to think about political, scientific, or disciplinary subjectivity in its non-identity is the subject of our entire inquiry. As Adorno puts it in *Negative Dialectics*,

> The precondition of all truth is the need to make suffering speak. This is true because suffering is the weight of objectivity upon the subject, and because that which the subject experiences as its most subjective moment—the expression of suffering—is objectively mediated.[48]

The cultural-aesthetic context in which "Heine, the Wound" is written marks a halfway point between Adorno's earlier engagement with jazz and the later development of his notion of negative identity. The Kantian subject, the liberal subject, the universal subject are wounded by the very identity they seek.

Where the jazz essays, written against the horrors of 1933–37, view nationalism and commodification as parallel, fatal vortices for the self-destruction of politics and the intellect, Adorno's essays after his return to Germany were engaged in intellectual reconstruction. They looked for the non-identical element within the commodity or national structures of identity, acknowledged the ubiquity and dominance of these limitations, and argued that it is the role of art and theory to draw upon these falsifications of identity, not just to unmask the lie of identity but to produce knowledge. Knowledge based on the determinate negation of incomplete emancipation points to how a wounded or subaltern subjectivity can be a model for subjectivity and knowledge in general. This negative Kantianism combines Enlightenment and Romanticism in a modernist epistemology, pursuing universalism and the dignity of particularity in a way that rejects the idea of a classical or natural ground to humanity along with the idea that a merely formal definition of art or subjectivity guarantees its universality. Knowledge is ungroundable, individual identity precedes the interest in knowledge, and formalism is an abstraction from the stream of already existing representations that constitute an individual's reality in an exploitative and antagonistic society. In other words, Adorno came to argue that modern identity begins, as Heine began, with the mockery and transformation of lyrical language: by engaging with both the homelessness of the modern world and with the non-identity of what is given. To live in a world of negative identity means that there is no escape from longing for home, nor from the terrifying knowledge that this image of home is unobtainable. There was, for Adorno, only the power to name this horror and recognize the woundedness and homelessness of all subjects and the kinds of needs and knowledge that this homelessness entails.

The comparison of Adorno's first writings of exile—the jazz articles in particular—with the writings of Du Bois or Adorno's articulation of identity theory in Heine is important because it speaks to the theoretical difficulty that even the most sophisticated universalism had in coming to terms with the problem of race. To invoke race as a scientific theory of history or society was, Marx and Engels argued, simply bad theory. But the race concept that disavowed its biological reality, and yet studied racism's effects as an extension of the logic of culture, haunted systematic social theory.[49] Du Bois managed to turn the wretched concept into a powerful sociopolitical theory. The Frankfurt School began with the premise that more work was needed to explain both the significant autonomies of bourgeois education and the ways they informed the identities of social theory: they wanted to know more about how to unblock the natural progression from the bourgeois liberalism of their parents to a rational liberal socialism. Through exile and war the Frankfurt School became dedicated to analyzing how the intertwining of culture, race, prejudice, and irrationality formed a rival system to the Enlightenment ideal.

Critical theory learned much from its emigration. The wound of segregation—and the paradoxes of defending an incomplete Reconstruction—had long required African American theorization of identity to be more sophisticated than the European. The Frankfurt theorists caught up to the African American theorists' discovery of the political importance of negating negative identity only in the terrible years of 1944–47, the years of first understanding the destruction of European Jewry. By this point, the concept of anti-Semitism as the reflex of capitalism was insufficient; it was impossible to avoid analyzing the global power of *racism*. In these years, where one sees the first nondismissive use of the concept of race in Adorno's thought, it appears as a *völkish* delusion aligned with capitalist models of domination: "Today race has become the self-assertion of the bourgeois individual integrated with the barbaric collective. . . . [It is] the [forced] harmony of 'communal' nationalism." Yet in the following sentence one sees a hint of the next turn in Adorno's thought: "Anti-Semitism is not a distorted form of the underlying social order; rather, this social order cannot exist without distorting men."[50] A few pages later in the text, one sees the Freudian restatement of race not as disguised class interest but as a form of damaged subjectivity mimetically projected onto an ontology:

The cry of pain of the victim who first called violence by its name—the bare words used to designate the victims (Frenchman, Negro, or Jew)—gives rise to a sense of despair among the socially downtrodden, compelling a powerful, even violent reaction. The victims are the counterparts of the dread mimesis; they reproduce the instability of the power they fear.[51]

Though Adorno seems not to have known of Du Bois's understanding of race as a form of second sight,[52] before he leaves America, he had already theorized one important consequence of racism as a social fact, translating the problem of racial difference into a theory of a wounded humanity and the mimetic ontologization of the Other.

"Heine, the Wound" is the first postwar essay to invoke the term describing how the attractive power of racism fuses with the beguiling power of art and culture: "dread mimesis." Mimesis for Adorno was the inverse of identity, the process whereby wounded subjectivity incorporates into itself what it fears in order to declare itself independent or to declare its hatred of the Other, the non-identical. But if for Adorno, racism works through identity logic, so does subjectivity, so does art, and so does critical thought—although each with higher levels of self-reflexivity, conceptual clarity, and awareness of one's own vulnerability. In the Heine essay, Adorno speaks of "dread mimesis" as the technique by which Heine sought to address the German culture that scared him, that rejected him, and that he loved enough to wish to civilize. Heine's art, turning imitation into social critique, worked because it was capable of entering into the fetishized logic of German self-adulation and then showing people how to stand outside and beyond it. "Calling violence by its name" was only a first step: genuine critique showed that identity was based on a desire for the Other and thus for a home that never was.

If Adorno's theory of wounded subjectivity could illuminate a history of negative identity in the metamorphosis of the folk song into national anthem, it of course should have been capable of explaining jazz and its place in the American consciousness. Though Adorno did not revise his analysis of jazz after developing his theory of negative identity, it is possible to hypothesize what such a revised account would have looked like. The portion of the analysis of jazz that would have been derived from "On the Social Situation of Music" is clear and is legible in Adorno's articles: jazz did, as Adorno argued, have a plurality of ethnic and social origins, combining nationalist and *völkish* elements of music with the marching band tradition and elements of the performance traditions of Appalachia and black as well as white minstrelsy. How this account of jazz's social "situation" would have benefited from Adorno's later theoretical innovation becomes clear when one looks at the discussion of the "eccentric-clowns" of jazz in "On Jazz." Clowning mimesis is a topic that cultural critics have only recently come to analyze—and with great difficulty and discomfort.[53] What Adorno referred to as "clowning" in jazz is the element of the minstrel and vaudeville traditions that can make jazz seem, at best, a mockery of itself or, at worst, a projection and reproduction of racial stereotypes. To understand American culture well enough to see how jazz frequently incorporates and inverts elements of white racist caricature into its own performances is a high standard; but the theory of negative identity that Adorno later developed to analyze German-Jewish inversions of racial stereotypes would have utterly transformed his jazz articles. The complex ethno-historical emergence of jazz, structured by American pluralism, by the dread mimesis of Jim Crow performance traditions, by the rise of a national market for sheet music and, subsequently, recorded music in an era of cultural, legal, and institutional segregation, remains an element of American identity—and transatlantic identity—that scholars are still laboring to understand. Adorno's theory of negative identity, which emerged from its wounds as much as its strengths, remains both largely unexamined and misunderstood. The idea that behind every claim of identity there rests a negative identity—one that preserves a social and cultural, aesthetic and material history—helps ground the otherwise airy concept of identity and move it beyond the narrow language of culture and self.

Negative Dialectics is at first glance a culturally "German" book, directed at the tradition of German philosophy: Kant, Hegel, Fichte, Marx, Heidegger. However, its critique of falsified universality, which aimed to push the German philosophical tradition beyond the bounds of cultural provincialism, disciplinary narrowness, or historical triumphalism, looked beyond Germany and beyond philosophy as it sought to address those places where the model of rational subjectivity failed or otherwise misrepresented reality. Though articulated in the abstract realm of epistemological and ethical theory, the concept of negative identity grew out of decades of grappling with the concrete sociological and cultural problems of incomplete emancipation in the twentieth century.[54] Though the concept of identity was not *new* in the twentieth century, its racially inflected history amplified the inner contradictions of identity as a lived structure, cultivating the desire for a stable identity, examining its instability, and—more frightfully—enumerating the dangers of having identity imposed by another. From Adorno's starting position as a Kantian in subjective matters and a Marxist in all things objective, the sense of insularity and closure promised by the idea of identity lent too much dignity to the all-too-easily ethnocentric jargon of existential "authenticity." In Adorno's historical understanding, the experience of the 1930s and 1940s was about the collapse of systems. The concept of reason, the notion of progress, the ambition of universalism were all gravely wounded. Completely dead was the ideal of a mass progressive movement that would spontaneously emerge to counter the forces of domination from tipping over into mass destruction. The impulse to denounce all false revolutions in favor of the good one was travestied by events, rendered moot by emigration, and pushed inward by the realities of finding intellectual labor in the world of American consumer culture. It is difficult, perhaps impossible, to sort out the dominant impulse of the immediate postwar period. Adorno experienced the need to write on American race relations alongside the sense that these relations were being transformed by the larger forces of the century. He experienced the need to be a spokesperson for the survivors of the Holocaust just as an international civil and human rights movement was getting off the ground. These experiences, amplified by Adorno's sense of the insufficiency of traditional sociology and philosophy to address the issues of the twentieth century, are what informed the development of the concept of negative identity. The progressive expansion of the idea of identity to include a politics of cultural recognition, an incorporation of the mimetic basis of culture and aesthetics, and of the power of the "second sight" of the oppressed and their wounded subjectivity all continued after Adorno's death in 1969. But awareness of the fact that this transformation was based on a transatlantic conversation, itself too long obscured, may concretize the insight that negative identity does not mean an absence of knowledge but a commitment to lend social and critical depth to the identity principle. Theory remains that which identifies the non-identical within a history of expanding, plural, and contradictory identities.

2

America; or, the Stranger

In 1964, Adorno was invited to contribute to a volume of essays discussing the contributions made by the European intellectuals who had fled "Hitler's Europe" to America in the 1930s and 1940s.[1] The paper he produced, "Wissenschaftliche Erfahrungen in Amerika" (Scientific experiences in America) remains Adorno's most autobiographical essay, and it has greatly shaped the perception of Adorno's exile period, not least because for decades it was one of the most accessible pieces in Adorno's late work. The text summarizes Adorno's sociological impressions of the United States, the professional sociological work he conducted, and the intellectual challenges he and the Frankfurt group tried to address.

Since it explicitly discusses Adorno's reactions to an American scene he perceived as deeply foreign, "Scientific Experiences" can be (and has been) used to depict Adorno as hopeless in the game of immigration: a "German Mandarin" or reflexive pessimist whose philosophical training and cultural prejudices prevented him from understanding American Pragmatism or contributing to an American-style empirical social science. It has been taken as a key to interpreting the "negative" tone of Adorno's American theoretical works, including *Minima Moralia* (1945–47) and *Dialectic of Enlightenment* (1943–45). Read alongside Adorno's jazz essays and his *Philosophy of Modern Music* (1941–1948), "Scientific Experiences" has bolstered the interpretation of Adorno as a cultural elitist who failed to appreciate America's virtues and whose recondite theoretical orientation insulated him against learning anything new during long years of exile.

This chapter addresses Adorno's engagement with Kantian universalism as a theory of scientific method, ethics, and interdisciplinarity. It seeks to reframe the "cultural" reading of "Scientific Experiences" and reveal its epistemological consequences. Exploring how Adorno interpreted his experience of exile in relation to two modes of universality—Kantian autonomy and Marxian alienation—the chapter analyzes how Adorno's rejection of theories of cultural adaptation grew out of both his subjective experiences and his theories of objectivity. I argue that it was in the early 1940s that Adorno came to think social thought required a theory of alienation and negative identity in a subjective sense, and I show how this discovery was driven by a combination of social-scientific and philosophical concerns. Framed against the rise of the United States to global dominance—economic and military as well as cultural—and situated within a debate concerning the disciplinary definition of "social research" carried out by émigrés alongside Americans in the wartime world of American social science, the picture of Adorno's intellectual biography developed in this chapter is twofold. Biographically, this chapter studies what it meant to Adorno to have to reinvent his own identity as a scholar in relation to the American research industry, arguing that he came to understand the American approach to social science very well and was influenced by it even as he resisted it. Though Adorno ultimately rejected the cultural and neo-Darwinian foundations of both American empiricism and Pragmatism, his engagement with these traditions helped him develop a critical distance from the intellectual traditions of Marxism, neo-Kantianism, phenomenology, and German formal sociology out of which his later work sprang. Adorno's understanding of negative identity would become possible, intellectually, through the process by which Adorno came to have a negative—critical—relation to both the American and German sociological and philosophical conceptions of disciplinary science.

Cultural and Scientific Experiences

The first thing to observe in reading "Scientific Experiences in America" is that there is nothing naïve about the essay. It is, rather, an extended exercise in reflexivity, in narrative doubling around the meaning of return. The title's dissonant pairing of the word "science" with "experience" suggests this, but so does *The Intellectual Migration*, the collection in which Adorno's essay appeared: the title of volume and essay both play on the title and subtitle of an important 1953 volume by Franz Neumann, *The Cultural Migration: The European Scholar in America*. There, Neumann, the foremost legal thinker in the Frankfurt group, had argued that the social facts of exile during the early modern period—the fact that the law of nations provided no protection to freedom of thought—had been the driving force behind the creation of the comparative social sciences and the idea of natural law. Neumann's argument was congruent with Horkheimer's foreign policy reading of Arthur Schopenhauer and with Adorno's idea, articulated in *Minima Moralia*, that truth does not emanate from the centers of power but is the labor of those in the margin, those who suffer exile. There were good reasons for commemorating and revisiting these arguments at the height of the Cold War. The 1964 collection, put together in homage by people who had known Neumann either in the Office of Strategic Services or at Columbia before his death in 1954, was a reflection not just on how much American universities benefited from the Nazi purge of European intellectuals but also on how the experience of exile had shaped ideas of rights, historical memory, and even science.

Adorno's essay, nonetheless, has been read as a confession, an expression at once of arrogance and naïveté, and it has been read ever more naïvely by the generations of readers who have used it as an introduction to his thought. There is, certainly, a textual basis for reading it as an exercise in ingratitude—a parting shot at America. One might expect Adorno, who owed America not only his survival but also his restored livelihood in the postwar German university, to describe his experiences in America with the mixture of gratitude, nostalgia, and self-deprecation appropriate to the Festschrift-esque nature of the occasion. One might further expect that Adorno, having been bitten by the jazz controversy and other musicological disputes, might have deemphasized his involvement in music and focused on the international fame that had accrued to the empirical-theoretical synthesis of *The Authoritarian Personality*. Readers who have had this expectation have been surprised by the opening words of the essay. Translated literally, the first paragraph of the essay reads:

A suggestion from America has prompted me to say something about the intellectual experience [*geistige Erfahrung*] that I accrued in my time there. Perhaps such reflections will also cast some light, at least from one extreme, on some things that have received less exposure [*das minder Exponierte*]. From the first to the last day [of my exile], I always felt myself to be a European—this I have never denied. It was already self-evident to me that one should attempt to preserve a sense of intellectual continuity [*geistigen Kontinuität*]; but in America [the need to adapt] forced itself to the fore of my consciousness soon enough. I remember well the shock that was in store for me when I spoke to a young female immigrant—a daughter of a so-called "upstanding family"—who was, like all of us, at the beginning of her time in New York, and she explained to me: "I used to go to the philharmonica, of course; but now I go to Radio City [Music Hall], like everyone else." Under no circumstances did I want to end up like her. As a consequence of natural constitution and historical experience, I was not conceivably cut out for assimilating myself in matters of intellect or spirit. Though I would never underestimate the importance of assimilation and socialization processes for the formation of intellectual individuality in general, so, conversely, I think that both the obligation and the proof of one's individuation lies in one's ability to assure that it transcends anything that can be classified as adjustment [*Anpassung*]. This relation between adaptation and autonomy received its earliest articulation in Freud's theories, and today has become a familiar concept for American scientific awareness. But thirty years ago, as one went from here to there, things were quite different. The word adjustment was a magical one—especially for someone who, as a European refugee, was expected to prove himself professionally in the new country while not arrogantly insisting on [remaining] that which he once was.[2]

The simple reading of this passage focuses on music—on Adorno's claim that his first encounters with America were mediated by his musical judgments, his horrified discovery that immigration might require "adjustment" to local musical conditions. Radio City Music Hall looms as a fate worse than death—and the story of Adorno's time in America unfolds as story of "magical" temptation in which the new immigrant must cling to the "intellectual-historical continuity" of his superior music. Adorno has all but cast himself as an intolerant variant of Odysseus, the wandering stranger who must stop his ears to avoid being lured to his doom by the siren song of American popular entertainment—or being turned into a pig by an émigrée Circe.

If this is one's reading, the effect of the first paragraph is immediately off-putting—so much so that Adorno's translator apparently felt compelled to add three or four sentences of introductory apology at the beginning of the essay.[3] These diplomatic efforts appear, however, to have had little effect on the essay's reception. Even when buffered by preliminary civilities, the opening anecdote seems inappropriately provocative. Not only does the genre of the Festschrift not allow for provocations, but the scene as painted fits too strongly—and then not at all—into the trope of the "cultural clash." Ever since the culturalist turn in American thought, a standard introduction to academic papers has been the "failed cultural encounter," a scene that illustrates how different interpretive communities view the same phenomenon differently. Based on the democratic assumption that there is no right way to do most things—that culture is fundamentally a matter of individual habit and group perspective—the narrative arc moves from miscommunication toward a dual-sided exploration of cultural assumptions. In Adorno's case, he begins by speaking of "shedding light" from "one extreme" of experience, but seems never to describe the other extreme or to enact the self-deprecation required by the genre. Certainly, under no circumstances should the "academic encounters man-on-the-street" story end with a declamation against the woman on the street—with an "Under no circumstances did I wish to be like her." Equally, the anthropologist-observer is never supposed to suggest he is more educated, is of a higher class, or sees things more clearly than the local informant. The effect is one of utter insensitivity—rendering humorous Adorno's comment a page later that "I came to America—at least I hope so—as someone completely free of nationalism and cultural arrogance."[4] What an appalling man! With the poor émigrée standing in as a proxy for American culture, Adorno's own autobiographical words out him as an undemocratic snob.

First impressions matter: perhaps because of this, few have noticed that later in the essay, Adorno himself pokes fun at the self-isolating German academic he once was, and does so in reference to another essay in *The Cultural Migration*, that by Paul Lazarsfeld, Adorno's supervisor at the Princeton Radio Project.[5] Though written twenty-five years after the event, by men living on two sides of the Atlantic, the two essays converge to create a coherent picture, an odd-couple narrative with Adorno in the role of the self-obsessed Teutonic researcher capable of arguing about anything, and Lazarsfeld just trying to get the job done. The story that emerges from the two essays has provided a simple, almost cartoonish explanation of how cross-cultural misunderstanding governed the émigré research community. And indeed, to animate this image of Adorno does not require a will to caricature; most readers need only to hear the sound track that played, as it were, in the background. It is, perhaps, a little hard *not* to snicker at the idea of Adorno, active in the 1930s as a composer in the austere modernist school of Schönberg and Alban Berg, being brought to America to study Tin Pan Alley music, of all things. One almost has a ready-made situation comedy when one adds Lazarsfeld, a practical-minded sociologist with no musical expertise, tasked with supervising Adorno's interviews with "average Americans" about their musical tastes to produce publishable results.

Readers have rarely asked why Adorno would propagate such an image of himself; those who take Adorno's opening depiction of the young émigrée as a moment of unintentional *self*-revelation may see this as a further sign of a fundamental failure of cultural self-reflection. And yet, if we are to take this essay *as* an introduction to Adorno's thought, we must ask more critically why Adorno offered this particular contribution to a collective volume dedicated to thinking through the complexities of "intellectual migration."

As reminiscences in the social sciences go, Lazarsfeld and Adorno's memoirs in *The Intellectual Migration* are incredibly entertaining to read. Adorno set the scene for *his* first encounter with "administrative research" by remarking that "the Princeton Radio Project had its headquarters neither in Princeton nor in New York, but in Newark, New Jersey, and indeed, in a somewhat improvised manner, in a disused brewery" reminiscent of "Kafka's Nature Theater of Oklahoma."[6] Adorno's account foregrounded scenes of frustration with colleagues who believed that the categorization of a certain piece of music as "light music" was a matter of subjective opinion or was somehow derived from its effect on the listener as "a kind of stimulus," rather than understanding that "light music" was a technical term, grounded—as Adorno insisted—in the intelligible objectivity of the musical form. The frustration was compounded when Adorno was asked to confront members of public with these formal analytical skills:

In a group of radio listeners I was given the task—God knows why—of presenting a musical analysis in the sense of structural aspects of listening. In order to connect with something generally familiar and the prevailing consciousness, I chose the famous melody that forms the second main theme of the first movement of Schubert's B-minor symphony and demonstrated the chainlike, imbricated character of this theme that lends it its particular insistence. One of the participants . . . said roughly the following: what I had said was all very well and convincing. But it would have been more effective if I had donned the makeup and costume of Schubert, as if the composer himself was issuing information about his intentions and unfolding these thoughts.[7]

In his essay, Lazarsfeld complained bitterly of Adorno's pedantic and impractical personality, depicting Adorno as impossibly slow to adjust to the work of the radio project and the American standards of research. Lazarsfeld, who set Adorno to the task of these musicological interviews but who also wanted to defend the project and Adorno's role in it, painted his own role in self-ironic tones that ultimately presented methodological struggles in terms of cultural and personality differences. Characterizing himself in retrospect as a rare "curiosity," a "European 'positivist,'" and an utterly practical man, Lazarsfeld described himself as the "connecting cog" between Viennese science and the American research industry and Adorno as the "typical absent-minded German professor . . . who made me look, in comparison, as if I were a member of the Mayflower Society."[8]

Lazarsfeld, of course, was a stranger here himself, and no candidate for the Mayflower Society. Despite appearances, this was not a conflict between American Pragmatism and European theory. Both men were, after all, European émigrés, and both experienced objective alienation in their interaction with the research system. The archive that preserves Lazarsfeld's angry five-page memos warning Adorno not to condescend to those with less musical knowledge than he, alongside Adorno's notorious 120-page memorandum of protest, also reveals that the disagreement did not ultimately hinge on Adorno's snobbery but on questions of valid scientific method. Both were concerned about the absurdity of a "scientific" survey that sought to measure something that had not been defined, but their concerns led them in quite different directions. For Lazarsfeld, questionnaires must follow a market model of consumption—people would listen only to what they liked, and corporations would pay only for surveys that helped them sell their material. Working within these limitations, Lazarsfeld believed that the most important principle was that surveys should pose clear questions, not open to interpretation: "like and dislike" surveys transformed subjectivity into objectivity because they took something about which the subjects had no doubt—namely, what they liked—and objectified this information into usable results. For Adorno the musicologist, the idea of studying musical form through public opinion surveys made no more sense than shaping public health policy based on whether respondents thought that a given disease "sounded" more hereditary or environmental. The true research concern was whether radio listeners possessed or could reasonably obtain the knowledge they needed to even experience the music of the radio symphony. Thus, Adorno attacked NBC's Walter Damrosch and the *Music Appreciation Hour* for failing to provide its listeners with a true musical experience, one in which they would experience their own, autonomous subjectivity as they gained access to the objective content of the material:

[The Music Appreciation Hour] makes no mention of the historical process that led to the prevalence of the discord in modern composition nor of the expressive function of the discord. Music must be as harmonious as they want people to pretend the world is. While the *Hour*'s proponents profess a desire to educate people musically, they actually reproduce the very prejudices which responsible musical education should seek to eradicate. . . . The totality of these features of the Music Appreciation Hour is what we call the tendency to produce musical Babbitts—the promotion of a musical pseudo-culture that actually consists of some vague and largely erroneous information about music and the recognition of stiffly conventional musical values, instead of the promotion of a living relationship with music. . . . The musical Babbitt has little forthright feeling for historical distance and for the inappropriateness of judging artworks produced at a different historical level in terms of contemporary values. To him everything can be measured and expressed in quantitative terms—the notion that everything can be expressed in terms of the money he spends for it. This attitude is evoked in the Music Appreciation Hour by benevolently patronizing statements such as, "Yet, in early times, much music was produced whose artistic perfection compares favorably with that of the great works of recent years." Though there were no skyscrapers in Bach's time, his music was, after all, not so bad.[9]

Adorno writes with active disregard as to whether the research will please its sponsor; he insists that the goal of research is as stated: to ascertain the objective educational value of the radio program. With untamed outrage at the betrayal of a true educational possibility, Adorno's analysis still carries the sting of personal betrayal, a demand that people should have the right to understand the historical element embedded in music because it is part of their participation in the universal. Needless to say, neither the radio station nor Lazarsfeld approached music as objective, as an irreplaceable experience, or as something to which all humanity has a right. Their goal was chiefly to sell, to create a venue for advertising.

The humor here is that Lazarsfeld did not disagree with Adorno's commitment to music or even his avant-gardistic socialism. As project director, Lazarsfeld shared Adorno's sense of absurdity, but for him the absurdity was political, not musical. The FCC charter required broadcasters to "serve the public good": the Rockefellers and NBC thus found themselves paying émigré socialists to help the American public think about itself. Funding of this sort would not flow to science for very long, but there was no harm in finding out what people wanted. While he prided himself on the speed at which he adapted to the commercialization of intellect in the United States, Lazarsfeld saw a tragic inevitability to a situation in which *Bildung* (education) was being converted relentlessly into *Werbung* (advertising). His essay from the 1960s communicates an awareness of a trajectory of compromise: Lazarsfeld's pre-emigration project was the famous *Marienthal*, written with his then-wife Marie Jahoda, which studied the social and cultural difficulties faced by unemployed workers for the purposes of advancing the workers' cause. After the war, Lazarsfeld found himself well paid but leading such studies as "How Pittsburgh Men Choose Which Brand of Gasoline to Buy" and a study on the most effective adjectives to deploy in writing ad copy for laxatives.[10] Though satisfied with his success, Lazarsfeld, like Adorno, was bothered by the question of whether propaganda and advertising were ultimately separable—in either theory or practice. Equally, the underlying question of whether the radio would draw its central power from entertainment or education haunted all early studies of broadcast media. Implicitly, both Lazarsfeld and Adorno pose autobiographical questions about their exile that pointed to historical forces. Refugees from a civilized, technologically advanced society, they grappled with the question of why they were experiencing a migration of intellect, not just across the ocean, but into the radio, commercialization, the culture industry. The questions of exile and adaptation to economic reality were not matters of elective affinities of "personality" or "culture" but of how their experience related to defining the "objectivity" of the situation.

In the background of Lazarsfeld's reminiscence is a grinding irritation—a desire to understand how the obviously myopic and disorganized Adorno ended up being the central theorist of *The Authoritarian Personality*, a book that transformed research methods on questions of race, politics, law, and government. And this question is indeed still relevant. For if both Lazarsfeld and Adorno document Adorno's failure to negotiate cultural difference, they are also engaged in explaining Adorno's success at something else: how Adorno evaded the American demand for success, how he managed to ask—and find answers to—questions that American science considered unscientific and that American capitalism considered unprofitable. To follow them in this inquiry, one has to start not with the comedy of mismatched scientific personalities but with the difference between their initial assumptions about subject/object relations. Where Lazarsfeld saw everything as a type of market choice—one had to either take the offer or leave it—Adorno, especially in analyzing musical phenomena, immediately perceived the distance between what was offered and what was actually given and set about to theorize this gap, turning this sense of dissonance between subject and object into a mode of sociological observation. The epistemology of estrangement suggests that the essay's opening provocation was intentional. The dissonance within the title "Scientific Experiences" is amplified by the odd language in which Adorno presented his side of the encounter. Describing himself as presenting a memoir "from one extreme," he also spoke of "exposure" (*das minder Exponierte*). Both of these terms were typical elements not of Adorno's cultural expectations but of his late-life idiolect. The word *exponieren* was particularly important to Adorno in his last years: a synthesis of the double-sided impulse toward Enlightenment in his late thought, suggesting both "exposure" and "exposition," it emphasized the wounded nature of theory and its non-identical relation to its social content. Even the scientific researcher, Adorno suggested, does not fully know whether he is acting or being acted on by history.[11]

Ultimately, the discomfort of "Scientific Experiences" is not that it fails to conform to the trope of the culture clash but that it denies the trope's validity while at the same time undermining that objectivity and individuality against which immigrant pragmatism takes aim. The story Adorno tells in the essay begins with his shock at the demands of "adjustment" and "adaptation" and moves toward his abandonment of certainty about the superiority of his European individuality; the focus of the piece is on the intellectual education that led to this change. The arc of the essay thus follows that of the trope of cultural encounter, but it does not do so affirmatively. And if throughout the essay Adorno refers to the fact that foreign-born sociologists often see things completely differently than do natives, the source of this is not culture but the wound—the exile experience that requires one to change one's mind about a myriad of things, the subjective alienation that makes possible new objective insight. Deep relativism is the condition within which objective knowledge emerges. Coming as he did from immersion in two universalist discourses of theoretical reflection, Kantianism and Marxianism, he was initially greatly resistant to this idea. But when it came time to write about how America shaped him, the question of identity was clearly on Adorno's mind. One mark of this is the third sentence's reference to John Locke's definition of identity as a form of "intellectual continuity."[12] Adorno, like most, theorized the concept of identity in terms of his own experience. This story points toward the fact that Adorno grasped his time in America in terms of the problem of negative identity—and, to no small extent, vice versa: it was in American exile that he learned how to think of himself as a European, a sociologist, a scientist, a Jew, and it was in the dissonances of these subjective experiences that he transformed his way of thinking.

Read in the light of the wound, the opening anecdote reverses the logic of cultural relativism. In the place of the culturalist idea that both sides are right in their perspective, the logic of Adorno's essay suggests that both the "American" concept of "adjustment" and the "European" concept of "autonomy" are wrong, subject to a deep non-identity, at the level of the person as well as that of intellectual culture. "Adaptation"—a cultural but also a Darwinian term—leads to blindness and signifies the individual self's source in something beyond itself. The surprise is that "autonomy" and "objectivity"—the keywords for Kantian moral knowledge and universality—become possible only through a sense of alienation, the suffering of the particular: negative and non-identity before identity. The tension between these two concepts and the limits of both concepts' reliance on a sense of identity suggest that the point of the essay was to estrange his own individual reminiscences in order to interrogate the way the category of "identity" is used to mediate the relationship between subjectivity and objectivity, universality and progress, in the sociological imagination.

It is important that "Scientific Experiences in America" is a late essay: Adorno probably could not have written about his subjective alienation in America this articulately when he was in America. Yet the source for this insight into the importance of alienation to knowledge had been part of Adorno's intellectual world long before he left for the United States. In the work of Georg Simmel, Adorno already possessed a schema for interpreting the relation between subjective alienation and objective science as one of negative identity. "Scientific Experiences," I assert, unites a series of meditations on selfhood, objectivity, social Darwinism, and Freudian selfhood into a critique of the "cultural encounter," and it does so according to an idiom that, drawn from the work of Georg Simmel, was grounded in the idea of the sociologist as Stranger. In the 1964 essay, Adorno was rethinking what he learned in America through the thought-image of Simmel's Stranger and was thereby refining the kernel of his theory of negative identity. Several categories of Simmel's exposition of the Stranger are relevant: Simmel's belief that social knowledge arose originally from commerce, which disrupted the insular nature of feudal groups; that outlier individuals crystallize the meaning of group affiliation; that the Stranger articulates ideas out of his perilous "liberation from every given point in space" because "nothing at first belongs to him . . . and he brings qualities that cannot be native [to the world he joins]."[13] Of particular relevance is Simmel's analysis of the perception of difference: the Stranger, he argues, because he "is simultaneously near and far," knows that his social relations must be constituted by "general human similarities"; however, this makes consciousness so reliant on the "absolutely general that he should have in common" that he becomes intensely aware of "that which is not common." The fact that Strangers are not perceived as individuals but as a *type* of foreigner makes them cling to individuality and universality in ways that expose them to the fault lines of both.[14] Simmel's interest in the relation between foreignness and vulnerability provides a key to reading Adorno's American transformation because Adorno came to America at a time when external events made it evident—at least to the eye of the Stranger—that America had not confronted its own configurations of identity as domination, its own assertion and effacement of ethnic and racial differences.

The estranged epistemology informing Adorno's relation to Simmel helps us see the American origins of Adorno's theory of negative identity: how the concept grew out of an attempt to produce a new objectivity through a combination of scientific universalism and the analysis of individual alienation. This chapter focuses on the philosophical and disciplinary prehistory of Adorno's turn toward studying racial and ethnic prejudice. Engaging with Adorno's notion that sociology required a theory of alienation, it works through Adorno's objections to the American culturalist reception of Simmel's category of the Stranger (*Fremde*) and Adorno's resistance to the American culturalist approach to studying racism as a problem of incomplete cultural assimilation or adaptation. But it also shows how Adorno was himself changed by his empirical and theoretical alienation in America and explores the rudiments of Adorno's theory of sociological and psychological disciplinarity and its relation to the problems of woundedness, exile, and homelessness in the modern world. The latter is a question about Simmel in American consumer society; the former is about the fate of global Kantianism in a world at war. Adorno believed that when social science embraced adaptation as its central paradigm, it sacrificed the Enlightenment prerogative that drove science. His American experience taught him to believe, however, that science must ground itself on a theory of universalism that had room for thinking about individual autonomy and difference, and it must do so not (just) because it was ethically a good idea to do so but because science's objectivity and universality required this dimension of difference. Conversely, if science *failed* to defend the knowledge content of individual experience alongside universalism, it could never mount a defense of particularity. The need to understand how universal and particular were dialectically related in this way would shape Adorno's later understanding of cultural critique and bring the concept of non-identity to the center of his thought.

Sociology and Double Consciousness

To take Simmel seriously as a philosopher and sociologist, one needs to start with the category of alterity—historical and subjective. The notion that sociological observation is never contextless but always develops out of a particular history was axiomatic for Simmel's sociology, and this emphasis on the historical was paired with the equally firm belief that sociological knowledge becomes possible only when this history is understood from the perspective of alienation. A protégé of Max Weber, Simmel believed that "ideal types," as fundamental elements of sociological analysis, were conceptual-logical starting points that, though distilled from history and experience itself, preceded and organized facts. The idea of the Stranger, which served as Simmel's ideal type for sociological insight in general, contained three moments that might seem to be at odds with each other. The Stranger was defined in terms of alienation, of "otherness" in a dialectical sense; in terms of cosmopolitanism and its standards of objectivity as a balance achieved by the cultivated self; and in terms of the objectivity of an impersonal science. The idea that the sociologist's knowledge was that of the Stranger was genealogically related to the role of the landless trader, the wanderer, and the European Jew; this "type" had been transformed by the Enlightenment, by the notion of a self-made, autonomous individual, and transformed again by the Romantic movement of the nineteenth century, with its ideas of the multitalented, multifaceted self who cultivated "foreign" views for the sake of making them his own. But if it was true that without foreigners there would be no sociology, it was also true that sociology had become more than an essayistic cosmopolitanism. Simmel, who thought of himself as a scientist, an empiricist, and a positivist, argued that sociology must be cognizant of its roots in modern selfhood, in the alienation within oneself and others. Sociology had to transcend this subjectivism, but if it failed to acknowledge its debt to the experience of otherness, it would fail, and all other disciplines would fail with it. This dependence on alterity was, in Simmel's view, not a weakness but a strength. If sociological knowledge ultimately comprised formal, subjective, and objective elements, it became knowledge only by engaging the network relations of these elements with the totality of experience and the full range of disciplinarity; and just as historical modes of explanation needed to challenge formal ones, and vice versa, so there must be a constant reciprocal alienation of subjective and objective elements within thought.

Simmel's interest in alterity as the foundation of subjective knowledge had its roots in history and biography. If Simmel's life experience was that of the Stranger, his was a very modern form of cosmopolitan itineracy. A scholar of Jewish descent born in the 1850s, Simmel managed to establish himself, albeit with great difficulty and delay, within a European university. Shaped by the cultural and political power of Berlin, the city of his birth, Simmel was a polymath who sought to reconcile the positivist, historicist, and idealist strains of his thought within the expanses of his own self. Studying "folk" psychology and aesthetics and the relation between country and city, Simmel first researched law and economics before branching out into the philosophy of the natural sciences. Initially influenced by Hermann Lotze's view of scientific rationality, the young Simmel was a neo-Kantian positivist who strove to develop the social sciences and humanities into more properly scientific fields. Later in life, he pioneered the concept of material culture and the social network. Had he been allowed to become a German *Ordinarius* (a salaried full professor with the right to advise doctoral students), there would have been a "Simmel school." Unique among his generation, Simmel was both a master of the "Southwest German School of sociology and philosophy" exemplified by Max Weber and a promoter of the anti-academic tradition within German philosophy and letters exemplified by Arthur Schopenhauer and Friedrich Nietzsche within philosophy and Karl Lamprecht within history.[15] Deprived of institutional recognition, he was nonetheless influential as a lecturer and essayist, writing, in his late phase, pioneering essays on the sociology of the city, the problem of gender and sexuality in modern culture, the idea of patronage and collecting, and the tension between psychology and philosophy.

Adorno's interest in Simmel's Stranger grew out of his philosophical education. The influence of Simmel had been profound on Siegfried Kracauer and Walter Benjamin, the two men who served as Adorno's literary-philosophical mentors. Not only were many of Simmel's sociological and philosophical interests represented in their early writings, but both were strongly indebted to the monograph representing the philosophical distillation of Simmel's sociological and scientific work—his 1904 *Kant*, a historical, aesthetic, and philosophical study of subjectivity and its relation to modernity. Though Simmel was not the first thinker to read Immanuel Kant historically or to emphasize the tension between his aesthetics of nature and his philosophy of natural science, his approach served as a philosophical mediating point between the positivist and phenomenological impulses of the early twentieth century and the Frankfurt thinkers' interest in a Hegelian Marxism. Important here, too, was the fact that Ernst Bloch and Georg Lukács's early work, so formative for Adorno, was defined philosophically by Simmel's "canonical . . . accomplishment of returning philosophy to consider the concrete."[16] Yet if Simmel's work powerfully inspired and anticipated critical theory, his perceived failures were also important. Kracauer and Benjamin, both old enough to have known and admired Simmel for his materialism and aestheticism, were not only aware of the anti-Semitism that limited his career but were also disturbed by Simmel's foolish embrace of World War I in the name of the "life" in *Lebensphilosophie*. The multiple moments of Simmel's theoretical Stranger, which played so dynamically with and against each other in his extraordinarily creative and productive career, remained unreconciled in Simmel's own life: Simmel's cosmopolitanism had proven no safeguard during the wartime rush toward the vitalism promised by jingoistic nationalism.

Though Simmel had never been literally in exile, his association with exile and the inherited problems of the nineteenth century was palpable—as was the applicability of this model to Adorno's American situation. It was clear to Adorno in the 1960s that he had lived a double life in America in the 1940s and 1950s, and in a doubled sense. Adorno's Marxism, bereft of a party or a nation with which to identify, had been as disrupted as his self-understanding as a European *Bildungsbürger* (educated bourgeois) had been: what the Nazis had not literally killed off in the socialist tradition, Stalin's Show Trials and the Cold War had silenced; and whatever recognition Adorno and his fellow émigrés had won for themselves within the world of European secular culture they were required to win anew. In a land that emphasized the need for democratic expressions of equality, open-mindedness, and pragmatic "problem solving"—and did so with particular vigor during the war years—the vocation of the sociologist was often overshadowed by that of the market researcher, the role of the European *Geisteswissenschaftler* by the need to sell the idea of culture itself.

To read the 1964 article as an exercise in negative identity—in how objectivity grows out of exile and woundedness—is to see why Adorno identified with Simmel and why the process of growing beyond Simmel was crucial for his intellectual development. By invoking the ideal type of the Stranger in an autobiographical essay, Adorno signaled at once his opposition to positivism and his fidelity to the notion of science that positivism sought to represent: the divided, alienated nature of his own experience as an émigré had to unfold into a critique of the problem of identity and its legacy within science. In the first instance, Adorno chose to present this naïvely: as a musical version of Simmel's Stranger. This self-presentation invoked the lingering controversy surrounding the jazz essay, revealing the tensions not only between the Simmelian model of the Stranger and American-style positivism but also between the Stranger and the American ideal of expressive culture. But the trajectory of Adorno's thinking about Simmelian doubleness gradually developed into something quite different: a critique and defense of the categories of personality, fact, and bias in the articulation of social theory and, by extension, an analysis of excluded, irrational, broken, exilic, and wounded subjectivity for the understanding of autonomous selfhood and objective analysis of phenomena.

Autonomy, Disciplinarity, and Identity

An obscure manuscript on Simmel puts the story of critical theory in America in a new light: that of the Stranger's relation to the philosophy of science. The paper, "On the Problem of Individual Causality in Simmel's Thought," was delivered to the Sociology Department at Columbia University on April 19, 1940.[17] One of the more purely academic talks ever given by Adorno, this paper can be seen as a halfway marker of Adorno's uneasy adjustment to the American academy and as an early theoretical foray into the questions of the relations among particularity and universality, subjectivity and objectivity, positivism and idealism that constituted the theory of negative identity. Having been in America for several years, Adorno was by the spring of 1940 beginning to understand some of the challenges of cross-cultural translation. He was thus chosen to give a talk at Columbia at a moment of strategic importance for the Institute, which had been engaged in protracted negotiations with Columbia University to attach itself permanently to the Sociology Department. Adorno was aware that he had to balance between the interests of the department chair, Robert MacIver, who had an interest in the theoretical dimension of German sociology, and Robert Lynd, who admired the politically interventionist statistical survey (and was also a vocal supporter of Lazarsfeld). Contrary to the caricature of Adorno as the perpetually clueless émigré, the lecture on "Individual Causality" reveals a sophisticated understanding of the internal politics of the Columbia department at a moment of conflict.[18]

Adorno's goal was to show the Institute's ability to address disciplinary foundations while avoiding taking sides in the MacIver-Lynd rivalry. The choice of subject matter—Simmel's relation to the tradition of epistemology—was strategic, mixing things familiar and foreign. Since 1896, when Albion Small began his assiduous translation of Simmel in the second volume of the *American Journal of Sociology*, Simmel's name was familiar to almost every American sociologist of the era, though the idea of Simmel as an epistemologist was foreign.[19] Adorno's introductory claim that American sociologists must think through Simmel's origins in the German philosophical tradition of subjective Idealism to understand the foundations of their field was therefore easily plausible. Much more challenging for his audience, however, was the secondary claim: Adorno argued that Simmel's theory of science asserted that scientific validity existed as the relation between two dimensions—universality and its particularity. Science was true if it could formulate general laws of social existence while accounting for the empirical particularity and variety of individual experience. The talk thus aimed at explaining Simmel the philosopher in order to defamiliarize Simmel the (social) scientist and thereby demand the rethinking of the foundations of science more generally.

Ostensibly, the essay is purely historical, pursuing, roughly in order, five major topics: Simmel's *Lebensphilosophie* in comparison to midcentury currents within science and philosophy; the relationship between German neo-Kantianism and the development of the new social science disciplines; the relation of these new sciences to the Kantian and modern division of experience into theoretical, practical/ethical, and aesthetic dimensions; the idea of causality and evidence in the social sciences, with special regard to the question of how general lawfulness, causality, and necessity define valid science; and finally, a neo-Kantian defense of the connection between a sense of individual autonomy and objective knowledge. Only when one considers what holds these themes together—an extended meditation on Simmel's thought in relation to American Pragmatism—can one read the essay for what it was: a provocative reconsideration of the foundations of

American sociology as it approached midcentury and an initial formulation of Adorno's notion of the role of both subjective and objective nonidentity in the constitution of knowledge.

The essay's opening moves are biographical and consensus building, contextualizng what his audience already knew about Simmel within nineteenth-century philosophical and scientific debates. American sociologists remembered Simmel as an aesthete, a subjectivist, a theorist of *Lebensphilosophie*—of the higher reality of the immediacy of experience and the self. They also credited him with building the foundations of formal and scientific sociology, particularly the study of the patterns of dyadic and triadic affiliation within groups. This work extended from exploration of relations of domination and subordination within status groups to more complex models like that of the Stranger, which analyzed how transindividual structures like markets, religion, or law shaped group membership and individuality at the same time. Reminding his readers of these familiar Simmelian topoi, Adorno then challenged the contemporary fusion of empirical and philosophical approaches by asking questions about Simmel's relation to the Spencerian and Pragmatist idea of "adaptation."

Adorno's central paraphrase of Simmel's philosophical program described it as an inquiry into "how lawfulness in general was rooted in subjectivity."[20] With this compressed description, Adorno explained Simmel's *Lebensphilosophie* as an outgrowth of and reaction to the tradition of German Idealism, epistemology, and the theory of science. After Kant, Adorno argued, there emerged a push within science either to pursue the discovery of universal laws or to emphasize a pure empiricism in the collection of data. Alongside this induction-deduction quarrel, there emerged a countertradition demanding that science be more attentive to inner experience and aesthetic as well as historical particularity. Simmel's idea of a vitalistic philosophy of life sought to synthesize these fin de siècle impulses, proposing to combine a philosophy of inner experience (as pursued by Pragmatism, phenomenology, and existentialism) with the social sciences (anthropology, sociology, psychology) that had a concept of culture at their core. Simmel's goal was to combine "hard" epistemology with "soft" aesthetic and social investigations to find a *via media* that would expand the scope of scientific objectivity, make experience more open to study, and displace the tendency to make notions of dominance stand in for epistemological truth.[21] Simmel's partial success in this, argued Adorno, came from his devotion to Kant's concept of science. Where both positivism and neo-Kantianism sought to modernize *beyond* Kant, Simmel modernized through Kantian non-identity. His contribution to positivism, empiricism, and phenomenology came in resisting these movements' tendency to undermine Kant's dedication to subjective Idealism as a tension between universality and particularity. This allowed Simmel, in Adorno's estimation, to resist the Spencerian logic that turned Darwinian adaptation into a social doctrine, one that equated action with culture, conformity to the environment with the true or the ideal. Adorno here gives a first glimpse of a core idea that an accurate understanding of the nature of knowledge required science to resist coerced identities. Simmel's unique version of neo-Kantianism suggested, Adorno argued, that adaptation was an improper paradigm for the social sciences and that a true science required a very different way of thinking.[22]

Much has been made, in the last thirty years, about philosophical congruencies between American Pragmatism and critical theory.[23] The Frankfurt group aligned with Pragmatism in that both movements encouraged a demythologization of knowledge production. In the 1930s and 1940s, however, the Frankfurt School theorists were engaged in defending the scientific value of metaphysical reflection and in criticizing all theories of truth as adaptation, Pragmatism included. Demythologization of thought did not mean, for Horkheimer, equating thought with action or natural causality, or collapsing the distinctions between philosophy, science, and subjective self-fashioning. Indeed, long before Adorno, Horkheimer warned against the attempt to naturalize metaphysics, suggesting it had the terrible side effect of encouraging the indiscriminate embrace of behaviorist or functionalist models. Before and during their exile, the Institute criticized the logical positivism movement—Rudolf Carnap, Otto Neurath, Ernst Mach, Ludwig Wittgenstein of the *Tractatus*—as well the American Pragmatists—William James, John Dewey, and George Herbert Mead—for their reliance on assimilative motifs. In articles such as "Materialism and Metaphysics" (1933) and "The Latest Attack on Metaphysics" (1937), Horkheimer argued that science undermined itself if it insisted that all events and experiences could be explained naturalistically. This insistence merely placed a taboo on metaphysical and moral questions rather than answered them. He had argued, for example, that logical positivism wished to reduce all science to physics and then imagine "that the meaning of all concepts of science is determined by physical operations. [This] fails to see that the concept of the corporeal, in the sense peculiar to its use in physics, involves a very special subjective interest, involves, indeed, the whole of social practice."[24] The footnote to this passage explicitly praised Edmund Husserl for explaining how science involves subjectivity—that no science happens without the organizing interest of the researcher or the will to reduce experience to a formula under which it can be controlled. The footnote also argued against a "scientism" that suggested that lawfulness was merely the product of the objects themselves. Horkheimer was willing to strategically defend Idealism and phenomenology when they served as redoubts against domination and reductionism.

Without referring to Horkheimer's articles directly, Adorno was, in "Individual Causality," invoking Horkheimer's defense of Kantian metaphysics and epistemology against modernized action theory, arguing that apparent contradictions within Simmel's way of combining subjective Idealism and positivism were in fact refusals of reductionism, expressions of scruple in relation to the later nineteenth-century tendencies toward scientific reductionism, on the one hand, and outright subjective irrationalism, on the other. Simmel was neither irrationalist nor willfully contradictory: he sought neither to break down nor to ignore distinctions between science and the subjective. One of the ways Adorno demonstrated this duality was through a comparison between Simmel and Henri Bergson, who, argued Adorno, shared the same basic goals of understanding experience in a scientific way, of expanding the notion of science to include the temporality of the now and the particularity of subjectivity. Bergson was, of the two, the more sweepingly radical epistemologist. He pursued a special science of the mind that would meet the categorical requirements of the natural sciences—materialism, the quantum, universal, and general laws—one that would all but eliminate the role of the subject in the construct of objective materiality. At the same time he developed a pure theory of the thought-act—a realm of subjective, temporal immediacy, of time and experience as pure inwardness, internality, and individuality. Bold though it was, this dualism risked collapsing into either pure causal determinism or pure voluntarism. Simmel, though interested in the same questions of subjectivity, lawfulness, immediacy, and temporality, approached them in a way that was structured by the conflict between a Kantian sense of limits and the ambitions of nineteenth-century positivism. Simmel's Kantianism and his commitment to positivistic notions of observation, that is, held each other in check, each mitigating the scientistic tendencies of the other. Simmel's earliest work, to be sure, had attempted to understand moral experience in a scientific way, but he never argued that moral and practical reason could be viewed as a matter of physics or natural causality. Instead, his Kantian notion of limits to theoretical and practical knowledge led Simmel to think about the limited autonomy of the subject in the world, the ways in which moral action could never be theory, or vice versa. His Kantianism refused to imagine a metaphysics in which the practical and theoretical modes of reason could be reduced to one another. Instead of embracing a theory that equated individual experience with immediacy of givenness, Simmel insisted that rationality had limits within its objects and that the modes of reason could and did often conflict. He also insisted that social relations had their own proper dimensions of knowledge, each structured as much by the needs of individual autonomy as by adaptation.[25]

Bergson and other theorists had believed in developing a single, naturalistic science of experience, and they believed that by doing so, they were defending the freedom of the individual and the subjective. As mid-twentieth-century American sociologists considered what made their field a science, they accepted these assumptions. Though sympathetic to these goals of a phenomenological social science, Adorno questioned whether their pursuit of a single, naturalistic science of experience would in fact lead automatically to a defense of individual autonomy. Rather, he believed that a naïve pursuit of this goal left the *via media* vulnerable to a hostile takeover by the Spencerian-Darwinian notion of adaptation, which, since it described itself as both a theory of knowledge acquisition and a theory of social assimilation, made it impossible to defend either individual autonomy or the epistemological value of qualitative distinctions and particularity. Simmel knew that adaptation to the whole readily eclipsed the autonomy of difference, and he was too good an empiricist not to argue for the irreducibility of different spheres of experience and knowledge. Simmel linked individual autonomy to interdisciplinarity because he believed that only by confronting the dissonances of experience and knowledge could the individual hope to transcend the irrational givenness of the social world. For a Kantian, Adorno argued, the idea that *knowledge of something* is not convertible into *knowledge of something else* was foundational to the idea of individual self-governance; thus, the refusal of reductive identification of two autonomous realms is implicitly also a refusal of heteronomy, of rule by the outside. Adorno perceived in Simmel's mixture of fidelity to individual and to objective autonomy a refusal of the falsified equation of nonequals—a refusal of what he would later call identitarian thinking.

If the point of comparing Bergson and Simmel was at once to suggest a European alternative to American social science and to warn against the problematic use that Americans were making of some European traditions, Adorno knew he also needed to address his American audience on their own terms. The bridge term he chose—and chose to attack—was in the process of becoming *the* foundational concept in American social science: "culture."[26] Simmel, Adorno observed, was a lifelong advocate of the scientific study of *Kultur*, but he had remained skeptical of the pervasive use of the concept as a paradigm for individual action and subjective expression, often preferring the term *Geisteswissenschaften* for the study of, and *Lebensstil* for the practice of, self-fashioning. The reason for this scruple, Adorno later argued, could be best understood through the difference between the nineteenth-century sense of German *Kultur* and the twentieth-century definition of *culture* that dominated the American discourse.[27] The nineteenth-century concept defined *Kultur* in terms of objective spirit—*Geist*—and referred first and foremost to the production of individual works of intellectual achievement that permanently extended human universality. Though the work of subjects, *Kultur* was embedded in objects and had a double logic of possession: at one level, objective culture belonged to no nation or group in particular but all humankind; at another level, cultural objects were of course material objects, subject to near-exclusive ownership by the property-owning class and subject to the dialectic of mechanical reproduction. Artists, the makers of these objects, were the prime examples of how individuals might claim, in their need for self-expression, to be laws unto themselves; the fact that others found value in these objects demonstrated that these subjective laws were also universal. As the concept of *Geist* had come under attack as insufficiently scientific, it had fragmented into different fields: a science of phenomena had been cultivated alongside a cult of subjective immediacy, with the latter-day concept of culture loosely mediating between them. This modern concept of culture, which came to dominate in America, was Pragmatistic—grounded in the notion that the forms of meaning and action in everyday life constituted a field of "adaptation"—and also always particularistic. Because of culture's emphasis on action and adaptation to the norm, the cultural sciences readily effaced tensions between subject and object and between knowledge and action—tensions of the sort to which Simmel was particularly attuned.

In distinguishing a culture based on adaptation from a culture based on subject/object non-identity, Adorno drew on both Simmel's celebrated essay "Tragedy of Culture" (1911) and his *Philosophy of Money* (1900), which depicted the subjective enjoyment of culture rooted in material progress as the basis of a tragicomic dynamic of subjective empowerment within bourgeois civilization. The comedy was rooted in civilization's great achievements: as material progress transformed modern urban life, it was accompanied by a money and exchange economy that established the formal conditions for every individual to become a particular, to have an identity all his or her own. Money in particular allowed for the creation of cultural objects because the surplus that money represented allowed one to suspend the cycle of hand-to-mouth work in order to pursue distant ends. To be cultured in the modern sense was to enjoy the freedom to pursue one's sense of individuality and style of living, a sense of identity that one had to create for oneself. This sense of self-creating law and of identity as a kind of personal possession sponsored the potential for tragedy, however—both for individual experience and the categories of scientific judgment. For the individual, the desire to become a law unto oneself had its pathologies: one could feel that despite having all the advantages of objective culture, one had failed to live up to one's creative potential or to gain autonomy. For society, this desire could lead to a subjective relativism, injecting notions of truth and progress with a deep nihilism or even effecting a permanent disjuncture of means and ends.[28]

In the typescript for the talk, Adorno included a final note in brackets—intended to be delivered as part of the discussion—apologizing for having "so thoroughly discussed the problematic in Simmel's hypothesis." If he had demanded so much of his audience in requiring them to consider nearly fifty-year-old technical problems in German philosophy, it was because the "contradictions and difficulties that are part of Simmel's thinking are parallel to the contradictions of causality and freedom, accident and necessity . . . that are cultivated today."[29] This apology was not only a conversational nicety, a general gesture toward relevance. His goal was to encourage his listeners to consider the epistemological value of the irreducible dimensions of the subject/object conflict, the way impulses of autonomy and adaptation clashed inside the individual, and indeed clashed in every stage of the acquisition, production, and consumption of culture. Ironically, though Simmel's attunement to social non-identity had comprised his original attraction for American sociologists, his work's dialectical potential had been gradually blunted in the course of his acceptance into the American sociological canon. As the first faculty member in sociology at the University of Chicago and the first editor of the *American Journal of Sociology*, Albion Small translated Simmel into English in part because he sought to resist tendencies toward psychologistic positivism and Spencerian adaptation models. The curious American tendency to read Simmel as a Spencerian never abated.[30] Simmel's formal sociology—his interest in how life organized itself in space and time—had provided a schema of social mechanics sufficient that his work lent bona fides to the American discipline, but sufficiently individualistic to make it possible for studies of group psychology to address the alienation and internal autonomy of the individual. By the 1920s, however, Simmel had come to be read in a quite different and more reductive way: as a partisan of the American concept of culture, a concept that emphasized the ubiquity of adaptation in order to plead for an acceptance of human difference. Imported from anthropology, Franz Boas's approach to the concept of culture had become the crucial counterterm in combating the cult of scientific racism by relativizing any group's claims to superiority. If all individuals relied on their membership in a culture in order to have a sense of affiliation, meaning, and belonging, citizens of a democratic society could nonetheless learn to relativize the resulting ethnocentrism by recognizing their culture as a *par inter pares*. Pluralizing culture as the everyday form of adaptation allowed for a primitive version of multicultural citizenship. Simmel had come to be read in terms of this democratic and culturalist paradigm, which harmonized well with the near obsession in American sociology with assimilating the proverbial Polish peasant. Simmel's work was taken to be both culturalist and adaptive, while also being formal, scientific, and interested in causal laws.[31]

Seeking to attune his listeners to the knowledge value in examining contradictions, Adorno drew on Simmel's definitions of scientific epistemology to challenge the claims of the American culture concept to be scientific and progressive. Simmel's *Problems of Historical Philosophy* argued that a causal law in the strict sense intended by Kant and the natural sciences requires that when a self-identical object is introduced to a particular situation, it must "unconditionally, and therefore every time and in every situation—produce the same outcome."[32]

But neither society (as conceived by Herbert Spencer) nor the newer concept of culture was either a self-identical object or truly causal. And worse, accounts of cultural phenomena typically oscillated wildly between declaring these to be expressions of autonomy—of totally free action and expression—and declaring the opposite, the "causal determination of everything that occurs within the bounds of culture."[33] This rendered problematic the adaptation principle. Openly questioning the concept of culture at the home institution of Franz Boas, John Dewey, and Ruth Benedict, Adorno asked how a new Kantian understanding of culture as non-identity might remain true to Kant's Enlightenment intent to preserve autonomy, to define knowledge as something other than adaptation, and to expand the object domain of scientific study.

Adorno's lecture did not attack the idea of culture head-on. Rather, it gave a historical account of Simmel's neo-Kantianism that demonstrated the epistemological value in Simmel's fraught relation to "individual causality." Describing Simmel as simultaneously a defender of the idea of causal universality as the very criterion of objectivity *and* as a theorist of a special mode of individual causality, Adorno revealed Simmel's bifurcated notion of causality to be grounded in a commitment to the complex objectivity of sociocultural phenomena. This sideways critique of a singular, pan-causal idea of culture addressed the identity and non-identity inherent in the notion of cultural causality: the ambiguity of whether a culture acts through the individual, the individual acts by deploying culture as a tool, or the individual acts as an individual only to the degree to which he or she *transcends* cultural expectations. By showing that post-Kantian philosophy struggled with the problem of social causality long before it entered American intellectual life as the idea of culture, Adorno suggested that there was something to learn about scientific method from how Simmel resisted the arguments of Heinrich Rickert and Wilhelm Windelband, his neo-Kantian predecessors. In proposing the nomothetic/idiographic distinction, Windelband anchored the Kantian epistemological differentiation between theoretical and moral reason within a disciplinary argument: nomothetic categories were defined as normative for disciplinary formation in the natural sciences; idiographic categories of value rationality, as normative for the social and human sciences. Simmel accepted this conceptual distinction but found fault with its disciplinary logic. Simmel insisted that validity, perception, and practice reflected qualitatively distinct modes of living. This insistence on non-identity, made on Kantian grounds, led him to move beyond the Kantian idea that all valid disciplines must be founded in a priori conceptuality. The sociologist of values who believed in Kantian objectivity must adopt an interdisciplinary epistemology. Values needed to be studied in themselves and in terms of their ability, especially in traditional or isolated societies, to generate practices that guaranteed group cohesion. In modern societies, where individuals had the power to choose their own value orientation but were increasingly governed by large-scale social forces, values and causality needed to be approached as simultaneously moral and amoral, as personal and anonymous, as a priori and a posteriori. Simmel's notion of culture therefore acquired an interdisciplinary character. Rejecting the fetishization of values as a kind of charismatic religion of selfhood, Simmel's concept of culture required a commitment to exploring modern phenomena according to an overlapping set of anthropological, sociological, and economic logics.

In Simmel's putative dilettantism, then, Adorno perceived a pioneering interdisciplinarity and an epistemology of divided selfhood that just might rescue the concept of autonomy from totalizing models of knowledge and social action. Simmel's perspectival pluralism, in fact, defended the Kantian principle of judgment—and its value for social insight. Where categorical reason was the mode of eighteenth-century science, judgment—the subject of Kant's third *Critique*—revolved around historical and aesthetic logics that had, like modern social conflicts, no single cause or solution. Simmel's fascination with the concrete object led him to investigate how the modes of judgment could overlap or dissolve into one another. This micrological love of ambiguity inspired new inquiries—inquiries into how modern social life was driven by meaningful contradictions, embodied in nodes of concretion. Many forms of social and economic thinking could be asserted as laws but were charged with submerged values; depending on the mode of social domination, Kant's sublime example of the perception of nature was, in fact, never just about nature but shot through with values that were deeply intertwined with questions of human mastery and control. Simmel's doubts that science could uphold any absolute distinction between nomothetic and idiographic analysis ultimately led him not just to argue that values and laws viewed historically were mutually constituting but to theorize the value of confusion and contradiction. The central principle of *Lebensphilosophie*, that theory and practice—morality, science, and aesthetics—could all seem to run together in life (*Leben*) blunted the concept of reason, but it also created new objects and methods for scientific inquiry. Science could investigate the contradictions within the object, and it could map out how the conflict of the subjective faculties related to the social division of labor and domination. The imbrication of contingent and universal reason with subjective and objective non-identity could thereby be diagnosed by an epistemology that took the self's estrangement as foundational.

Kantian Subjectivity and Historical Disciplinarity

Adorno believed that neo-Kantianism, especially Simmel's version of it, was willing to specify qualitative and even categorical distinctions within lived experience in a way that allowed philosophy to combat the inherent modern tendency toward positivistic reduction. This deployment of Idealism in the name of qualitative distinctions could potentially move epistemology beyond the simple project of eradicating contradiction and toward an explanation of contradictions as historically and socially necessary correlates of an incomplete human autonomy. Simmel's great innovation, Adorno argued, was that he extended Kant's inquiry on Enlightenment into a more general effort to explain the importance of ideality to everyday, material life, and vice versa. Drawing extensively on Simmel's 1907 *Kant*, Adorno argued that Simmel's breakthrough as a social thinker came from his ability to recognize the interplay between historicality and ideality within Kant's categories of subjectivity. Kant's famous "Copernican turn" was based on the idea that the categories of pure apperception—unity, plurality, inherence, reality, negation, necessity, reciprocity, and so on—enumerated the predicates of all valid knowledge. Simmel demanded philosophy explain its late discovery of these inherent categories. And it must therefore account for how historical change affected validity. Ultimately, Simmel argued that though the Kantian categories were indeed "our timeless historical possession," they were also temporal in the triple sense that their elucidation was central to "establishing our modern world view," that they were discoverable only under certain historical conditions, and that the scope and creativity through which they were applied in everyday life was dependent on the development of individuals.[34] Adorno was interested in how Simmel could have believed in universal categories as an idealist and a scientist but thought about them in a material, social, and historical way. This combination was part of Simmel's belief in the scientific "priority of empirical research and moral-philosophical reflection of the utilitarian sort," but it also oriented his sense that the growing "autonomy of knowledge and understanding [*Erkenntnis*]" was itself an object of sociological study.[35] The Kantian category of autonomy entailed not just practical but also theoretical and sociohistorical reason.

That this historicist rereading of Kant bore implications for thinking about the relation between the autonomy of individuals and that of disciplines became clear in Simmel's reconsideration of the problematic nature of the a priori/a posteriori distinction, the question of whether lawfulness was located inside or outside the individual. Kant had pointed to "the moral law within and the starry skies above."[36] This statement suggested a relationship between inside and outside, between moral and natural science, between subjective experience and universal law; it also raised the question of their mediation. Was this dual intuition an aesthetic precondition of moral philosophy in a subjective mode? Did one, that is, need to *feel* the law *as given* in order to discover it as a ground? If so, was this sense of interconnected, given lawfulness *historically* grounded, tied to the historical experience of those living during the Enlightenment and perhaps even more specifically to the late eighteenth-century's sense of optimism in the recent "discovery" of human morality and autonomy? If the answer to these questions was affirmative, still further questions presented themselves: Did adherence to Kant's notion of rational autonomy require one to sustain this eighteenth-century belief precisely in the way Kant did, by acting and arguing as if moral and scientific reason were both cleanly separated from each other, yet mysterious and profoundly linked? What was the connection between what everyone feels and knows and a universal and passively received "is-ness" and "oughtness"? These questions were not hypothetical for Simmel. Rather, in a series of essays on sociology, Simmel had argued that the course of the nineteenth century had made this connection harder to sustain and that, practically speaking, modern identity as lived had de facto rejected Kant's sense of identity.[37] Far from seeing the natural universe as providing strict "laws" for all thinking, modern individuals sensed sources of lawfulness within their own *selves* while perceiving a considerable lawlessness amid human institutions. Since the Renaissance, argued Simmel, there had been an increasing tendency among modern individuals to feel that their sense of individuality and particularity rivaled any sense of transcendental subjectivity or necessary lawfulness. Simmel's sociology typified fin de siècle thought in that it presented most individuals as having lost a sense of awe toward transcendental universal laws of nature and morality and as feeling most intensely alive through their experience of their own individuality. Modernity saw particularity—personal identity, individuality—as the most potent source of inner strength, normativity, and lawfulness.

The rise of this emphasis on subjective identity was paired with that of autonomous scientific disciplines, each with its own foundation of validity; conversely, the growth of historical non-identity was linked to questions of disciplinary non-identity. If one could understand the changing definition of reason and its spheres from within the disciplines, one could also understand that change from without: socially as well as subjectively. The quintessential Enlightenment idea, expressed by Kant, that the capacity for individual self-governance should grow with the expansion of objective knowledge implicitly posited both a relation and a unity between theoretical and practical philosophy. Simmel's role in the late nineteenth century was to recognize modernity's imperilment of this unity in lived experience. The increased tension between the individual and the universal was threefold: a matter of lived experience, of disciplinary technique, and of how science understood itself. But historically speaking, argued Adorno, the more someone imagined rationality in terms of the technical sciences, the more one felt the increasing appeal of culture as an autonomous realm of action and a form of a priori self-certainty. Disciplinary history actually becomes a history of the self:

The technical advances of the natural sciences—take for example the strictly *a posteriori* quality of nineteenth-century chemistry—diverted the vector of aprioristic elements [of knowledge and perception] toward the social sciences, and thus toward forms of knowledge that played no role within the Kantian *Critique of Pure Reason*. The materiality inherent in aprioristic philosophy [thereafter] took refuge in the "cultural sciences" such that [cultural knowledge] appeared far more the bearer of that autonomy of subjectivity actualizable as personal freedom.[38]

The word "refuge" is not here accidentally. With it, Adorno was explaining the transformation of Kantianism during the course of the nineteenth century's explosion of disciplinary specialization through the logic of what he would later call subjective/objective non-identity. This was both a defense of disciplinary specialization and an argument about its side effects. The disciplines must, Adorno argued, be free to specify the truth of their particular objects of knowledge. This disciplinary objectivity could be said to serve the subject, acting as bearer of both an epistemological insight into the world and of a materiality that human subjects desire and need in order to live. Adorno was suggesting, however, that Simmel recognized that the rationality of science expressed in Kant was not just about the advance of the individual sciences but about their role in establishing a coherent relation between the lived application of practical and theoretical reason. For Simmel, the sense that theoretical mastery did not necessarily bring greater rationality was apparent in the relation to nature: as the sciences of nature became more technical in the control of nature, so the sense of freedom and autonomy given by nature changed, seeking refuge in other realms and other forms of practice. One could, however, see the strain between the various forms of (objective and subjective) identity and non-identity in the growth of the *Geisteswissenschaften*. As late nineteenth-century natural science rendered nature, lawfulness, and freedom increasingly "external" and "merely given" in the sense of being an object for laboratory or economic manipulation, there emerged, argued Adorno, a strong tendency for "the productivity of spirit" that Kant saw as the heart of intelligence to look elsewhere, to a prioris, to the ideal of autonomy itself, to the embrace of mere practice. The intelligent, the sensitive, and the observant sought to imagine that the "concrete substance of the human . . . could be more lawfully structured than the [very] nature that Kant imagined as prescriptive."[39] In other words, as nature seemed more objective, less open to experience, and thus less "freely given," the study of society, individuality, and spirit became the refuge for lawfulness and autonomy.

Simmel's historicization of Kant had been of crucial importance to the founding of critical theory. Adorno's mentors, Benjamin and Kracauer, had shared the dream of developing Simmel's understanding of Kant into a defense of particularity for a bourgeois world in crisis. Consider this fragment from Benjamin's incomplete *Passagenwerk*:

Simmel touches upon a very important matter with the distinction between the concept of culture and the spheres of autonomy in classical Idealism. The separation of the three autonomous domains from one another preserved classical Idealism from the concept of culture that has so favored the cause of barbarism. Simmel says of the cultural ideal: "It is essential that the independent values of aesthetic, scientific, ethical, . . . and even religious achievements be transcended, so that they can all be integrated as elements in the development of human nature beyond its natural state."[40]

Adorno's Simmel talk sought to address this "very important matter" of autonomy's relation to the value spheres. The notion that "the cultural ideal" sought to uphold the autonomy of aesthetic, scientific, ethical, and religious values by uniting them into a single sphere of action pointed for Benjamin, as for Adorno, to the contemporary crisis in science, politics, and the self. The core idea was that fascism exploits people's fear of the divisions within the self, coercing identities, while a true science would analyze and provide a refuge for the non-identities of historicity, lawfulness, subjectivity, and disciplinarity. This historicist view of the value spheres and human capacity, derived from Simmel and developed by Benjamin, stood at the head of Horkheimer's 1931 inaugural address:

> The objects of pre-Hegelian philosophy . . . are social. Kant's major works advance philosophical theories concerning the knowledge of law, of art, and of religion. But this social philosophy was rooted in the philosophy of the isolated subject [*Einzelpersonlichkeit*]; those spheres of being were understood as projections [*Entwürfe*] of the autonomous person. Kant defined the closed unity of the rational subject as the sole source of the constitutive principles of each cultural sphere; the essence and the organization of culture were to be made comprehensible only out of the dynamics of the individual, the fundamental modes of activity of the spontaneous ego.[41]

Reflecting the spirit of 1931, the idea of value spheres is articulated in the language of phenomenology: the subject "projects" itself, its autonomy, being, and forms of knowledge onto an uncertain future—a future that would make unknowable demands upon the subject and would require the non-identical to become a path to universality.

. . .

Critical theory's defense of the non-identical as a form of refuge Enlightenment had, then, a Kantian-Simmelian origin. Building outward from Simmel's commitment to understanding the problems of the philosophy of science as problems of the divided modern self, critical theory broadened Simmel's "tragedy of culture" into a model of epistemology appropriate for addressing the crisis of bourgeois society. The reason Benjamin viewed the modern culture concept as "barbaric" is that modern constellations of knowledge and identity placed an ever-heavier burden on notions of culture as action, eliminating distinctions crucial to the individual and creating whole disciplines that "administered" areas of knowledge once subject to criticism by the individual.[42] The experience of being an individual required one to differentiate and synthesize among (at least) the three core areas of Kantian rationality—the theoretical, moral, aesthetic—and the process of doing so was central to the formation of an individual's or a society's sense of experience and judgment. Conversely, Benjamin suggested that the refusal to differentiate between these spheres of rationality and objectivity led to a "barbaric" concept of culture and theory of actionism. If we follow Adorno's later paraphrase, we might say that the strength of individual, subjective identity inhered in the ability of the individual to resist demands for a logical or Pragmatic identity of these "cultural spheres."

Adorno did not delude himself into thinking his New York audience could understand the full breadth of this theory of the non-identical, the divided self, and the divided object. He believed, however, that reasserting the categories of autonomy and alienation was of utmost concern. Associating a sense of disciplinary, subjective, and objective non-identity with the resistance to a triumphant fascism, Adorno thought it important to challenge American social science's belief that assimilation—adaptation to power as a means to survive—was a good model for either democracy or science. Revisiting Simmel's divided self allowed Adorno to address both social science's concept of assimilation and the pressures that assimilation placed on the sociability of science. One mark of how strictly the concept of adaptation had come to define both categories of social adaption and the tasks of cultural assimilation is to be found in the concluding sentences of Alfred Schütz's 1944 article "The Stranger." Schütz, a social phenomenologist once capable of many fine-grained distinctions, had nonetheless come around to paraphrasing Simmel in the American style and thus to describing all knowledge as cultural knowledge, all culture as adaptation:

> Strangeness and familiarity are not limited to the social field but are general categories of our interpretation of the world. If we encounter in our experience something previously unknown and which therefore stands out of the ordinary order of our knowledge, we begin a process of inquiry. We first define the new fact; we try to catch its meaning; we then transform step by step our general scheme of interpretation of the world in such a way that the strange fact and its meaning become compatible and consistent with all the other facts of our experience and their meanings. If we succeed in this endeavor, then that which formerly was a strange fact and a puzzling problem to our mind is transformed into an additional element of our warranted knowledge. We have enlarged and adjusted our stock of experiences. What is commonly called the process of social adjustment which the newcomer has to undergo is but a special case of this general principle. The adaptation of the newcomer to the in-group which at first seemed to be strange and unfamiliar to him is a continuous process of inquiry into the cultural pattern of the approached group. If this process of inquiry succeeds, then this pattern and its elements will become to the newcomer a matter of course, an unquestionable way of life, a shelter, and a protection. But then the stranger is no stranger any more, and his specific problems have been solved.[43]

Schütz's paraphrase of Simmel's Stranger implicitly rejects the phenomenology of difference and the analysis of conflict to embrace the idioms of assimilation, adjustment, and progress. This in turn gives testimony to the degree to which exile disrupted the continuity of intellectual life. In the years between 1940 and 1944, the émigré had to make many adjustments that at best were compromises with and at worst were capitulations to the current reality. Schütz's description of Simmel's Stranger, which synthesized the language of behaviorism and immigration, psychology and knowledge, probably helped sell his work and the New School but offered no resistance to a social Darwinistic theory of action, culture, and assimilation. Everything that Schütz himself might have contributed—the ways Schütz might have *changed* American thinking—was postponed.

"Under no circumstances did I want to end up like" him: the musical judgment Adorno passed on the radio-hall fan was also one he might have addressed to Schütz. Adorno strove never to become Schütz's kind of Stranger. And he did so not only because he wanted to preserve intellectual integrity—his autonomy—but also because, faced with the looming possibility of global barbarism, he felt that sociology needed a renewed sense of that objective and subjective non-identity which could recognize what Americans loved to talk about but American social science could not explain: individualism, the possibility that individuals would use their judgment and take action in resistance to totalitarian social control. Albion Small had introduced Simmel's emphasis on alienation and foreignness to argue against the supremacy of neo-Darwinian models of adaptation. In the era of world war, an epistemology of estrangement, foreignness, and non-identity was important again. Adorno, arguing that there was no objectivity without subjectivity, used Simmel to insist that science did not understand lawfulness in the social world until it took seriously the problem of individuality with all of its exceptions, forms of domination and appropriation, conformity and nonconformity. This heterodox reading of Kant was, for Simmel and Adorno, a rescue of the original, orthodox, protodisciplinary construction of autonomous Kantian subjectivity.

The Science of Individual Causality

In the last third of the Simmel talk, Adorno developed a practical argument for the wartime utility of a sociology of the Stranger. Citing a recent Belgian newspaper report of explosions at a munitions factory just across the German border, Adorno asked how a positivist or a Kantian might assess the meaning of such an event. A strict understanding of science might ask how this event could be related to other events, such as the Nazi invasion of Norway. The everyday consciousness might ask, "Was it a mere accident, or had German workers engaged in sabotage against their own state?" If one applied a Kantian or positivist stringency of scientific explanation—the idea of a strict causality—one could hardly posit a *causal* relation between two events hundreds of miles apart, and certainly not a universal, repeatable one. One must therefore refuse to theorize this event, either on the positivist-inductive grounds that one needed to wait for more data to be collected or on the idealist-deductive grounds that this was a misapplication of the idea of causation.

Counter to this sense of scientific restraint, Adorno argued that Simmel's idea of individual causality offered a potentially useful tool for hypothesizing how connections among apparently unconnected events might be explained. The idea of the individual law offered a framework for challenging the strict distinction between natural-scientific causality and the idea of moral or value-centered reasoning. It allowed the research to ask, hypothetically, what ideas and social relations might combine to make an act of sabotage *thinkable* in a particular context. Social science should be free to construct models of the views and situations that might lead individuals to connect their inner sense of their own preservation of autonomy qua individual to a need to intervene in present affairs. One could draw on information about the labor movement, the German political opposition, and newspaper reports on the atrocities of Hitler's military expansion to the north and ask whether it was possible that some individuals would, under those circumstances, feel the need to do something in order to preserve their sense of self-continuity.[44] This kind of active construction of the object of inquiry might seem to be a leap into the Kantian "thing-in-itself," a violation of the strict, passive notion of science. Speculation on the individual law was, however, less a violation of Kant's principle than was a theory of individual adaptation, which carried the premise that the *need to adapt* to the surrounding (social, cultural, intellectual) environment was the cause of all action. At the very least, argued Adorno, Simmel demonstrated that causality and necessity were not uniformly identical. At the furthest extent of Simmel's "resistance to nominalism and positivism," he asserted that there was *no such thing* as a pure thing-in-itself or pure a priori in social science, but rather the object of social science emerged out of the need to "reconstruct the *a priori*" not as a matter of "pure facts occurring next to each other" but through active interpretation that showed the "objectively binding connections and contexts that connect facts."[45] One of the things to be reconstructed was the relation between autonomy and value: the kind of value that would impel, for instance, factory workers to rebel, to engage in risky acts of sabotage. There were, however, limits to this process of (re)construction. Values did not appear out of thin air, out of the purity of the act or the sudden appearance of the charismatic individual. They came out of individual reactions to negative experience, the sense that individuality was under threat. Simmel's Kant, as the upholder of qualitative difference, spoke to how this sense of limit and negation was a source of worldly engagement. The fact that human beings encountered limits in constructing meaning was definitive, both for the individual and the social scientist: the sense of limitation, objective necessity, and vulnerability was after all what made "[social] contexts powerful and their description comprehensible and important."[46] If the neo-Kantians had no good explanation of where values came from or how individuals could challenge the domination of social laws, Simmel had at least a partial answer: though values certainly emerged through the consensus of the community, they also emerged as individual laws, negations of the status quo (*Bestehenden*). Values could be the transcription of the *sensus communis*, or they could emerge as expressions of individuals' struggles to maintain their autonomy against a world of domination and adaptation.

Adorno posited the term *Wesensnotwendigkeit* to describe how social science might reconstruct the situational necessities under which individuals conceive of new values to assert their autonomy beyond the limits of their situation. Like the theory of adaptation, this term referred to the mutual construction of subject and object; but unlike the idea of adaptation, it posited no identity or harmony. A kind of ideal type for analyzing collective behavior, *Wesensnotwendigkeit* spoke to the constructedness of the a priori. Though the German word *Wesen* means "essence" and would be used to translate the Latin *esse*, or Aristotle's *to ti ên einai*, as that which is self-identical, it can also be used in compound words describing complex aggregates that function as a system, as in *Postwesen* (the postal system), *Vereinswesen* (voluntary associations), or *Bahnwesen* (the railway system). By pairing this concept with that of necessity, Adorno indicated a kind of necessity that emerges from communities, institutions, or nations but does not imply either that these aggregates are naturally occurring entities or that their actions and values are identical to those of the individuals who comprise them. As a form of situational necessity reconstructively posited, the *Wesensnotwendigkeit* model suggests how compound contexts (those comprising institutions, economies, states, and groups as well as fields of knowledge-based activity[47]) could be said to enforce necessity and forms of knowledge on individuals. Instead of imagining social science to be restricted to the discovery of immutable laws acting on individuals and of values animating their lives, Adorno quotes Simmel's idea that social inquiry might be built around the understanding of the kind of necessity aligned with autonomy under the conditions of partial or limited freedom. Instead of the necessity of objective action, Simmel posited a "unity of theory as a kind of necessity" under particular circumstances.[48] And in Adorno's reasoning, to speak of situations possessing a quasi-essential force was to reconstruct the concept of autonomy without assuming it was guaranteed by laws or values. Autonomy, conceptualized with great difficulty when no or limited choices were available, needed to be studied concretely. Studying the collective forms of antagonism and necessity, freedom and knowledge that people in difficult situations face could help make possible a study of what kinds of individuals resist environments that conflict with their inner sense of individual necessity. With this sense of active theoretical construction in mind, argued Adorno, one could conduct valid social research that would allow the "unity of theory [to] serve analogously [to] the role played by the universal causal law" in the natural sciences and in Kantian definitions of reason.[49] Adorno was arguing, in short, for both a strict construction of social-scientific universality and an alternative, more relaxed notion of necessity for the study of social-scientific particularity.

The conclusion presses the question of research and causality further, pointing to how ease in obtaining data can distort the theoretical formulation of research, and vice versa. The year 1940 was still early in the story of "model construction" in the social sciences: here we find Adorno—often depicted as ignorant in matters of empirical theory—addressing a cutting-edge question in the study of data modeling and the philosophy of science.[50] This was, in fact, useful speculation. As the world moved to war, the question of how to apply isolated data points to form a composite picture of intelligence was as central as how to correlate quantitative and qualitative modes of analysis. The example of how narratives and "essences" might be constructed on the basis of a single explosion involved the worldly application of philosophical questions—from existentialist notions of heroic action, to socialist notions of group solidarity, to the statistical analysis of industrial accidents. One can also see here a preliminary version of Adorno's later theories of personality type and the dynamics of group versus individual behavior. Where Max Weber's ideal types conceptually modeled practices of charismatic authority and means rationality, Adorno asked how notions of individual necessity might be formed under conditions of domination. This concurs first with Adorno's later critique of the social-scientific abuse of personalism, which he generally found to contribute to collectivist and actionistic models of identity in ways that were radically voluntarist, coercive, and violent in practice and too absolutist as matters of theory.[51] Second, it reveals Adorno's sustained engagement with the complex inheritance of the Weberian ideal type. Before the war, Adorno and Benjamin discussed using the reconstructive power of the dream image as a kind of Weberian ideal type of mass hallucination and modern myth; after the war, Adorno spoke in a technical fashion about the ideal type's mediation of objective and subjective elements as "formed by the one-sided accentuation of one or more points of view" such that "concrete individual phenomena . . . are arranged into a unified analytical construct one might call a thought-image [*Gedankenbild*]," which presents a "methodological utopia that cannot be found empirically anywhere in reality."[52] The Simmel talk shows the beginning of Adorno sorting out the scientific usage of this utopia. Threading his way between the positivist (Simmelian-inspired) sociometrics movement (which sought to map patterns of social relations without reference to qualitative analysis) and Weber's emphasis on values as fundamentally mystical and religious in nature, Adorno's exploration of autonomy and necessity in individual causality sought to navigate between positivist and Romantic-existentialist understandings of individual action. His reasoning was likely that social science must start out assuming a notion of strong agency but ultimately must construct tentative models of social understanding that assumed no one in modern society operated in natural or complete autonomy. Hypotheses framed in terms of an individual consciousness as it exists in relation to objective social factors offered a way of thinking through the dialectic between subjective and objective poles of social action. Thus, a rigorously conceived science could construct a qualitative model of views an individual might hold, apply all available theories to it, and ask whether this might be a case not of individual adaptation but autonomy according to the unity of consciousness modeled by theory. This kind of model of conflict and disciplinarity would allow one to study topics otherwise unavailable to a strict nomothetic science; additionally, it would allow science to theorize incomplete emancipation, to think through historical process in a way that assigned individuals neither too little nor too much power. The ideas of wounded or weak subjectivity and the divided self were thus part of Adorno's concept of empirical research in 1940.

Minima Moralia, written in 1944–45, includes a discussion of Simmel, phenomenology, and the problem of philosophical exposition titled "Gaps," which reflects on his Columbia presentation. *Minima Moralia* laments "the academic industry's . . . insistence" that good arguments should document "explicitly all steps that have led to their conclusions . . . so that every reader may follow it." The belief in the "liberal fiction of communicability" serves to "sabotage thought."[53] This is defiant language, transforming the moments of self-doubt evident in the Columbia talk—for instance, Adorno's concluding gesture that he "fears some might . . . think me to be engaged in the ill-reputed German theory-weaving."[54] Painfully aware of being the theoretical stranger in the room and of his task to sell the Institute to the faculty at Columbia, Adorno indeed sought to provide a series of theoretical resources to supplement empirical work. Written after only three years in America, "Simmel and the Problem of Individual Causality" hovers between a highly structured lecture seeking to overcome every gap and an almost unreadable close reading of Simmel. Adorno was still learning how to divide his activity between empirical work and theoretical speculation, with both broken off from a sense of praxis or practicability. The Simmel talk, seeking to balance these forces, bears the appropriate scars. On the one hand, the essay posits a value in resisting demands of academic clarity and assimilation to the norm. It sees autonomy as an epistemological as well as a practical principle, presenting the drive toward hyperclarity as a danger to actual social perception, and systematic closure as a threat to the analysis of social contradictions. The Adorno who would occasionally defend his later reputation as a difficult writer—who in *Minima Moralia* criticizes Simmel for having written *too* clearly—has an origin in this moment, in the need to preserve intellectual independence in the face of a demand for clarity that was also a demand for assimilation. On the other hand, the Simmel talk shows Adorno laboring to make research relevant and to apply theoretical contradictions to the needs of contemporary empirical analysis. Questions of the relation of culture and immigrant life, assimilation and social struggles, individuality and universality, bias and measurement were of direct importance. Everyone in the room was aware that there was already a proposal being floated about turning the Office of Radio Research into (what would be named) the Bureau of Applied Social Research. Adorno's two-front argument, rising to this moment, was aimed at making theory seem attractive and scientific and at discrediting the ideas of administrative research that handed out questionnaires and called the tabulation of statistics "science."

Negative Identity and Empirical Research

The fact that Adorno, five years later, was writing aphorisms on Simmel in his notebook might well be taken as a sign that the sales pitch that he was meant to give had utterly failed. The Institute for Social Research, after all, did not get a home at Columbia; rather, shortly after Adorno gave his talk, Lazarsfeld was appointed to Columbia and became the director of the relocated Office of Radio Research. The rivalry between Lazarsfeld and Adorno with which this chapter opened—expressed in essays of the 1960s—has often been taken as evidence that Adorno was simply too theoretically Germanic to participate in the kinds of projects that Columbia needed and got in the person of Lazarsfeld.

But this account gets things backward. Not only does it forget that Adorno went on to be a central figure in *The Authoritarian Personality*, a much larger-scale research project than anything Lazarsfeld directed in America; but it also misses the substantive ways in which Adorno's pitch to Columbia anticipated high-level collaboration among the very people attending the seminar. MacIver and Lynd would in fact work together on early versions of *Studies in Prejudice*, and they offered memos of support arguing that Horkheimer's group was uniquely qualified to uphold the theoretical rigor of the project. To be sure, *Studies in Prejudice* was not conflict-free—especially once it involved the codirection of the American Jewish Committee, with its more narrowly empirical researchers. But it might be better to say that the clash between Lazarsfeld and Adorno was typical of the way conflict with Americans and other émigrés helped Adorno and Horkheimer develop a model of theoretical writing and empirical analysis that transformed the presumptions of American social science: ideas about subjectivity and objectivity, about the role of speculative theory in the formation of hypotheses, about the importance of interdisciplinarity and the unified rationality of social action.

Adorno's notion of the epistemological value of the divided self—arrived at as part of his post-Radio project examination of Simmel—became the kernel of Adorno's future intellectual development, both theoretically and methodologically. Growing out of Adorno's stubborn insistence that culture must aim at autonomy, not adaptation—and growing out of his experience of estrangement in America—the notion of knowledge as internal division allowed Adorno to analyze non-identity within the subject, within objects, and within method as a way of understanding the unachieved status of the universal.

Adorno came to recognize that his encounter with American life involved a complex dialectic between assimilation and alienation. Although he continued to insist on the objective universalism of the Kantian ideal of autonomy, he came to recognize tremendous positive value in the assimilation to democratic norms. "Scientific Experiences" indeed ends with an explicit explanation of this allegiance between everyday life and political openness:

> Over there I became acquainted with a potential for real humanitarianism that is hardly to be found in old Europe. The political form of democracy is infinitely closer to the people. American everyday life, despite the oft-lamented hustle and bustle, has an inherent element of peaceableness, good-naturedness, and generosity, in sharpest contrast to the pent-up malice and envy that exploded in Germany between 1933 and 1945.[55]

This did not mean that Adorno was arguing for American cultural exceptionalism:

> I do not want to imply . . . that America is somehow immune to the danger of veering toward totalitarian forms of domination. Such a danger lies in the tendency of modern society *per se*. But probably the power of resistance to fascist currents is stronger in America than in any European country.[56]

But what it did mean was that Adorno was willing to give some credence to the notion that, in an immigrant nation in particular, the tremendous stress laid on adaptation was crucial for securing a certain quantum of civility both for the majority and the individual. This becomes much more an analysis of theories of necessary alienation:

> Yet it is an illusion sharply criticized by Goethe and Hegel that the process of humanization and cultivation necessarily and continually proceeds from the inside outward. It is accomplished also and precisely through "externalization," as Hegel called it. We become free human beings not by each of us realizing ourselves as

individuals, according to the hideous phrase, but rather in that we go out of ourselves, enter into relation with others, and in a certain sense relinquish ourselves to them. Only through this process do we determine ourselves as individuals, not by watering ourselves like plants in order to become well-rounded cultivated personalities. A person who under extreme coercion or indeed through his egoistic interest is brought to behave in a friendly manner in the end attains a certain humanity in his relation to other people, more so than someone who, merely in order to be identical with himself—as though this identity was always desirable—makes a nasty, sour face and gives one to understand from the outset that one does not exist for him and has nothing to contribute to his inwardness, which often enough does not even exist.[57]

This last passage, glossing Simmel but now in the mode of negative identity, points back to the problem of autonomy and culture but also forward to Adorno's lengthy engagement with the question of identity. Evident here is not only the basic formulation of identity as the product of coercion and self-interest but the explicit interpretation of Adorno's American experience as one of negative and positive identity. The citation of Hegel asserting that "externalization" precedes autonomy anticipated Adorno's ontological argument that negative identity is always the precursor to identity. This, paired with the argument that individual identity asserts itself as a defense mechanism against coercion, paraphrased Simmel's notion of the individual law, this time not as a matter just of self-preservation but as an objective necessity that is both illusory and a step toward enlightenment. Adorno was arguing for the irreducible importance of self-alienation and adaptation, autonomy and civility, for the preservation of humanity. These ameliorating and self-ironic comments, appearing at the end of "Scientific Experiences," suggest the same willingness to engage with the positive transformation of negative identity that we examined in Adorno's postwar essay on Heine. Just as it was possible to turn woundedness and alienated selfhood into a scientific or philosophical experience, so it was possible for Adorno, despite his opposition to the discourse of identity and ontology, to use this language to describe himself and his own woundedness and transformation.

Philosophically, one can see here the anticipation of Adorno's later critical theory. His analysis of identity and non-identity in Simmel was an exercise in a constructivist immanent critique: by showing Simmel by turns as a positivist, a strict universalist, a theorist of individual autonomy, a substantive logician interested in disciplinarity, and a theorist of the "individual law," Adorno sought to criticize and supplement the narrow picture of Simmel the vitalist philosopher of *life*. The idea of trying to understand experience lawfully moved one beyond a naïve positivism or a "feeling of life," beyond loose notions of action and adaption—whether social Darwinistic, Spencerian, culturalist, decisionistic, or statistical—and beyond assertions of existential self-immanence: *Dasein*, *Leben*, or culture as plenitude. In Adorno's later works, he would be more explicit about the dialectic of this movement: the social scientist could feel and analyze the historical movement of particularity and universality, the rise of the "ontological need," and the dangers of subjective self-assertion and positivistic celebration of domination. As an immanent critique of science, the analysis of non-identity had no fixed end point, only the inner sense of a need to articulate the opposed knowledge poles of subject and object, moving, on the one hand, toward developing a defense of the autonomy of the self and the validity of substantive knowledge, and moving on the other hand, toward a theory of necessity in first and second nature.

There were more practical applications as well. The Simmelian notion of the epistemological Stranger, the divided self, and the disciplinary concept of autonomy transformed Adorno's approach to philosophy and writing. Adorno's critique of science developed out of his critique of the idea of assimilation and adaptation. Theoretically, science needed to have a self-reflective understanding of its own alienation in order to know what kinds of subjectivity were embedded in its concept of objectivity as *techné*. Empirically, science needed to model the divisions within the self (or within culture) qualitatively before it could adequately claim to know what it was measuring. Sociologically and psychologically, the idea of the *Wesensnotwendigkeit*, paired with an analysis of the desire of each individual to be "an individual law," set an agenda for a model of empirical research that could see a place for the mixture of objectivity and subjectivity in the construction of a social physiognomy and ideal types. Disciplinarily, the idea of "unity of theory under necessity" became a model for understanding the interaction between social rationality and irrationality and the importance of the divided selfhood and multiple perspectives for the reconstruction of objectivity. As a matter of political theory, the interest in the epistemological value of alienation, estrangement, and exile pushed Adorno to apply sociological thoughts to the analysis of objective autonomy and to apply the concept of autonomy to the sociological analysis of subjective unfreedom.

Biographically, the Simmel essay changed Adorno's approach to social theory. According to "Scientific Experiences," his first breakthrough as a sociologist occurred late in his work at the Radio Project when he was assigned to work with George Simpson. Because he was not an émigré himself, and therefore was challenged rather than threatened by the process of translation, Simpson took pleasure in "encouraging me to write as radically and uncompromisingly as possible."[58] The process of estrangement, translated thus into linguistic reconciliation, encouraged Adorno to detach his theoretical speculation from the need for immediate praxis. The Simmel talk served the opposite effect: it was an exercise in applying his most radical philosophical ideas to the critique of empirical methods. Though this internal self-division, itself a product of exile, radicalized Adorno's philosophical voice, it did so in a way that made him open to negative identity, to the suffering of others, and pointed a way toward a systematic critique of unified subjective rationality.

3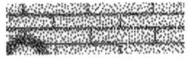

Negative Identities of the Subject in Wartime America

Radical, Multivalent Enlightenment

Some eighteen months after Theodor Adorno delivered "Simmel and the Problem of Individual Causality," he and Max Horkheimer began writing *Dialectic of Enlightenment*. The change in tone is radical. Where the April 1940 text defended the idea of scientific reason and explored the meaning of the Kantian tradition, the latter book (first circulated in 1945) bristled with sharp criticisms of Kant, the Enlightenment, and the idea of reason. Like the radical texts of the Enlightenment on which *Dialectic of Enlightenment* is modeled—one thinks of Helvétius's *De l'ésprit*, Rousseau's *Discourse on Inequality*, Diderot's *Letter on the Blind*, or Hume's *Dialogues concerning Natural Religion*—Horkheimer and Adorno's text has shocked, and remains shocking, for its frontal assault on the dignity and self-possession of rationality in the subject. The first two sentences of the work communicate a sense of urgency and betrayal—an intensified version of Rousseau's turn of Enlightenment on itself: "In the most general sense of progressive thought, Enlightenment has always aimed at liberating men and making them master. Yet the fully enlightened earth radiates disaster triumphant."[1] A few pages later appears the infamous sentence: "Enlightenment itself is totalitarian."[2] "Enlightenment" throughout is twofold: an era of human history, but also the subjective use of reason with objective consequences. Weaving between these, the book takes aim at what was then (and probably remains) the consensus view of Western progress as the linked advance of individualism, science, economic prosperity, and democracy. Behind this vision of history and behind the core concepts of the Enlightenment, there is an unconsciousness, a blindness—and not infrequently, *rage*.

Adorno's contemporaneous remark in *Minima Moralia*—that "only thoughts that do not yet understand themselves are true"—applies to the problem of interpreting *Dialectic of Enlightenment*.[3] From the beginning, readers, including friends at the Institute, were baffled by the work's fragmentary character and demanding paratactical style, which made every sentence a new thought. And what of its intent? How did a text that set out to be a comprehensive "theory of logic" turn out to be a fragmentary meditation on Homer's *Odyssey*, Hollywood and the "culture industry," the Marquis de Sade, and the nature of anti-Semitism?[4] A manifesto that hid itself, *Dialectic of Enlightenment* appeared conflicted even about who its readers were to be or what kind of intervention it was to make. Before the text was even written, Horkheimer described it as a "message in a bottle," a book for some future addressee; at the same time he declared his intention of writing a book on "dialectical logic" in the tradition of Marx, Engels, and Lenin—one he apparently envisioned as a punctual contribution to a rapidly moving debate that was in every way shaped by the political transformation of Soviet and fascist Europe.[5] In many regards, we know both too much and too little about the text. *Too much* because we know that in writing it, the authors envisioned a synthesis of modern and ancient narratives that told of human self-destruction and a return to myth; and that they contemplated, but never could finish, a positive part, to accompany the negative, that was provisionally titled "The Rescue of the Enlightenment." *Too little*, because few commentaries have been able to answer the question of praxis: Why would Horkheimer and Adorno, who had spent the previous years working to integrate themselves into the American social research industry, suddenly retreat into an exegesis of a classical text conjoined with a fragment on cultural commodification?

The hard nub of the problem rests in the fact that the book, which set out to be about the future of Marxism and the Enlightenment ideal of relieving human suffering, ended up being focused on the problem of a modern "return to myth," both in the form of fascism and a regression into commodified entertainment. A study of historical and logical regression, *Dialectic of Enlightenment* seemed almost itself to regress, and the interpretive problems this posed were slowly amplified by the receding expectation, on the part of friends and younger contemporaries, that it would eventually be finished, and then by the creeping suspicion that its authors never wanted the book to be read. Because the work circulated initially with the title *Philosophical Fragments* (a phrase later demoted to the subtitle), the book was first understood to be incomplete, and the general surmise has become that it was not finishable, that Horkheimer and Adorno never found a way to make reason reemerge from the modern mythos that had swallowed it. All that was left of reason was a heap of angry fragments.

Philology does well to enumerate its fragments before interpreting them. A glance at the table of contents reveals *Dialectic of Enlightenment* to be, indeed, an array of fragments, remnants of something apparently lost, but pointing, in their ruined quality, to something larger. Promising more than a treatise, delivering perhaps less than a completely polished selection of aphorisms, the book presents a Hegelian-style deep reading of a single concept: Enlightenment. Like the speculative histories of the Enlightenment, the initial exposition overlays ancient and modern first principles before roughly dividing into historical segments. The book's first chapter and "first excursus" comprise an extended interpretation of Homer's *Odyssey*. The book's "second excursus" explores the Marquis de Sade, Kant, and the French Enlightenment. The book's remaining sections are devoted to an analysis of "The Culture Industry," the relation of anti-Semitism to Enlightenment, and a set of aphoristic fragments off-handedly labeled "Notes and Drafts."

If the organization of the text suggests something obviously incomplete, this unnerving impression is heightened by its method of exposition, which might be described as simultaneously Dionysian and Apollonian. At the center of *Dialectic of Enlightenment* is a reading of *The Odyssey* structured around the deeply counterintuitive conceit of naming Odysseus "the first bourgeois subject," a representative of the Enlightenment. Odysseus, the book asserts, stands as the prototype of the individual who creates his individuality—his identity—by turning others into objects and servants. The narrative power of *The Odyssey*, then, derives not from Odysseus's heroism in any simple sense but from a logic of sacrifice and subordination. *Mêtis*, Odysseus's cunning, his way of taking more than he is given—and giving others more trouble than he takes—is ultimately about establishing an individual who creates laws out of suffering, his own and that of others. This makes for a strange, self-canceling form of heroism. In the first instance, Odysseus's status as a hero involves a self-identity that comes of making himself an exception: an individual who forces others to conform to the rules of sameness-identity. In the second instance, it turns out that the hero limits not only his men but himself—and all future heroes. Having himself tied to the mast while the oarsmen row on, Odysseus establishes the type of the bourgeois factory owner, enjoying the yields of nature while his servants must labor without meaningful experience of either the power of nature or that of myth. Both take more than they are given, both create a heroic image and narrative of the self, and both, having built an idol of subjective conquest out of the image of the domination of nature, ultimately become subject to the fetishized second nature that they themselves fashioned.

This is a parable of reason and subjectivity in their non-identical relation. Just as Odysseus's actions are not those of a happy, conquering subjectivity but of a suffering, conflicted individual who can be understood as the template for an internally divided notion of reason, so the modern notions of science and production delude themselves in assuming that one can have objective progress that creates spontaneous subjectivities without cost to either subjects or their objects. Odysseus has fooled himself about being enlightened: his heroism, his self-creation rely on the coerced sacrifice of others; and worse, in the process of reducing others to tools for his own fulfillment, he has objectified, instrumentalized, and otherwise forgotten many of the natural sources of the desire for freedom itself. This structural analogy between reason and subjectivity in their non-identity echoes, negatively, the city-soul analogy at the heart of classical philosophy as well as the fact/value distinction of modern thought—and in so doing foregrounds their essential instability. As is the case with Nietzsche's interpretation of the Apollonian and Dionysian dimensions of tragedy and representation, there is a parallax quality to Horkheimer and Adorno's argument that reason is *constructed* out of mythic particularity and the routinization of domination and sacrifice. On the one hand, constructions imply the Apollonian—they imply the stable and traditional, the signifier's subordination to the signified. But on the other hand, since anything constructed can be said to be arbitrary and can be unmade, constructivism implies the Dionysian—and thus not just the possibility of undoing but even gleefulness in undoing it. *Dialectic of Enlightenment*'s provocation comes from its refusal to resolve the parallax. Presenting subjective reason as a *Vexierbild* (a picture puzzle),[6] it challenges a fixed concept of subjectivity and thus a fixed concept of reason; argues that the world fragments subject and reason alike; and asks whether both can be reassembled or whether suffering has become a new law as abstract subjectivity has entered into an alliance with domination against real subjects. The epic as a genre appears, in the darkest reading, to be an enactment of the social power of collective forgetting and the growing power of domination. But like the modern bourgeois who dominates and sacrifices others, Odysseus oscillates between fantasies of complete control and the delusion that he, too, is a victim of laws (natural or economic) beyond his control. He is negative and positive identity in one.

Identity Metaphysics and Decline

In its interrogation of Odyssean subjectivity, *Dialectic of Enlightenment* placed the question of self making at the center of a speculative history of society that destabilizes the lines separating materialist from idealist, mythical from rational, narrative from logical modes of explanation. As such, its dissection of the form of subjectivity has had a profound effect on how objects of the cultural world—literature, the arts, the discourse of politics—are interpreted. Marxian theory almost exclusively focused on the questions of the objectivity of capital accumulation; works in the Kantian-liberal tradition had not dared to elaborate a theory of subjective unfreedom that radically suspended the distinction between myth and rationality. *Dialectic of Enlightenment* questioned the neutrality of everything: the concept of essence, the notion of subjectivity, the separation of writing into narrative and analytical genres. This radicality would be redoubled through reception. Republished and circulated through the 1960s in pirated editions by the student movement before Horkheimer and Adorno were compelled to reissue the book officially, the book's reception was polarized by the sense that it had been hidden from public view. For some, *Dialectic of Enlightenment*'s metaphysics provided a model for how to analyze individual consciousness and notions of civilizational progress in a material and historical manner. Other interpretations assumed the purpose of the work was to be dissociative—to diminish the categories of reason by showing reason to be nothing but fragmentary (or, conversely, falsely totalizing), to attack the idea of subjectivity by saying it is has no relation to individual freedom. Some readers, seeing this dissociative quality, concluded that the book advanced a nihilistic theory that equated civilizational progress and the development of bourgeois selfhood with sacrifice and decline.

The most prominent pessimistic metaphysical interpretation was advanced by Jürgen Habermas, the philosopher-sociologist whom Adorno had recommended to take Horkheimer's chair after the latter's retirement in 1964. Writing in the 1980s, but borrowing from interpretations stretching back to the late 1960s, Habermas positioned his "Entwinement of Myth and Enlightenment" as the pivot point of his lectures attacking materialism, Idealism, and poststructuralism, *The Philosophical Discourse of Modernity*.[7] Throughout this essay, Habermas invidiously compared what he labeled Horkheimer and Adorno's subjective and nihilistic approach to the understanding of reason to the intersubjective and constructive approach advanced in his *Theory of Communicative Action*.[8] Although Habermas elsewhere had offered more nuanced considerations of his mentors at the Institute, his analysis of *Dialectic of Enlightenment* emphasized a narrow identitarian interpretation that associated all previous critical theory with a narrative of the decline of the self, the rise of fascism, and a psychological-metaphysical language of identity:

> The idea that people develop their identity by learning to control external nature at the price of repressing their inner nature provides Horkheimer and Adorno with the model for a description in which the process of Enlightenment reveals its Janus-face: the price of renunciation, of self-seclusion, of the interrupted communication of the ego with its own nature which has become an anonymous id—all this is interpreted as the consequence of an internalization of sacrifice.[9]

Habermas thus views *Dialectic of Enlightenment* as a deterministic theory of identity producing two zero-sum equations of domination. First, there is a (logical) identity of subjective domination in which individuals suppress their relation to nature and to freedom in order to dominate others and form their (subjective) identity. Second, this postulates a (logical) identity of objective equivalence that assumes a decline of subjective reason: as external domination grows, means triumph over ends, both within the world and in the individual, and the subjective sense of truth withers entirely. The one form of identity distorts the other. The more the world is forced under the quantitative spirit—the spirit of modern science, the control of instrumental reason, and the profit motive—the more every object, each individual, appears merely as an object like any other, to be dominated or discarded at will. When the dominating self refuses to recognize the validity of anything beyond its control, selfhood starts to undermine itself. For Habermas, Horkheimer and Adorno's "Janus-faced" Enlightenment leads to a historical pessimism that is not just fatalistic but actually *demonic*:

> Domination of an objectified external nature and a repressed inner nature are the hallmarks of Enlightenment. With this thesis, Horkheimer and Adorno vary Max

Weber's well-known theory in which the old demystified Gods are seen rising from their graves in the form of impersonal powers in order to renew the irreconcilable conflict of the demons.[10]

The "dialectic" of Enlightenment becomes, then, a metaphysics of reductive identity in which the attempt to emancipate oneself mentally leads to a coercive regime of material life, and the domination of nature leads to mental enslavement: every form of civilizational progress constitutes a prelude to inevitable decline.

A theory so pessimistic may not, perhaps, be supposed to be very useful; Habermas, building on the question of what readers were supposed *to do* with such a theory, not only labeled the book nihilistic but presented its nihilism as the key to the larger story of critical theory and its failings. For Habermas, *Dialectic of Enlightenment* represented the end of the beginning of modern social theory, a summa of all the problematic developments in nineteenth-century social theory and an object lesson in what was wrong with the radicalism of post-1968 continental thought. The *Philosophical Discourse of Modernity* sees Horkheimer and Adorno drinking from two poisoned streams: first, a pessimistic theory of European culture that, originating with the French Revolution and culminating in the late nineteenth century, relied on ideas of a pathological collective subjectivity and of a salvific culture; second, the tradition of subjective rationalism that, unlike the modern communications theory Habermas was advancing, neglected the "intersubjective dimension" of reason. The twentieth century witnessed the disabling results of the confluence of these tainted traditions. Because the Enlightenment imagined progress as a process of applying the "right" instrumental vision of culture to society—as if society were the patient and culture were a medicine—modern social analyses tended to start with a theory of the subject or the group rather than with an analysis of the communicative action that should first constitute the individual-group relation. *Dialectic of Enlightenment* was one of the worst offenders because it seeks an impossible "standard for the critique of culture" that condemns "science and morality as ideological expressions of a perverted will to power" yet recognizes no outside force that could deliver society from this dead end.[11] *Dialectic of Enlightenment*, argued Habermas, culminated the Enlightenment tradition by following out a subjective logic pioneered by Sade, Schopenhauer, and Nietzsche—a logic that ends with a futile quest for a reason outside reason and a voice of resistance outside everyday life. It therefore represented a retreat from empirical research and democratic liberalism toward the illiberal speculative philosophies of the German nineteenth century. Horkheimer and Adorno thus appear as escapist and undemocratic, impractical and incurious in a way that was "insensitive to the traces and the existing forms of communicative rationality."[12]

Reading for Negative Identity

The remaining chapters of this book argue that what Habermas misses in this pessimistic reading of *Dialectic of Enlightenment* is precisely its negativity—its concept of negative identity—and that in so doing he misinterprets the history of critical theory. Though *Dialectic of Enlightenment* indeed examines the metaphysics of identity, it does not do so in the mode of historical determinism or cultural pessimism, but in terms of a social and interdisciplinary concept of subject/object relations. Though Habermas sees intersubjectivity as a kind of preexisting understanding, it is argued here that *Dialectic of Enlightenment* engages with the core problem of intersubjectivity at many levels. It does so, moreover, with a reconstructive interest in understanding the social constitution and transmission of authority in the form of knowledge, institutions, and narratives of the self. I thus argue that despite the intentional scandalousness of *Dialectic of Enlightenment*'s style and argument, it does not represent a radical break from Adorno's concerns of the previous years. Rather, it is a transformative extension of Adorno's theorization of subjectivity in the Kantian mode through an application of a concept of negative identity to Kant's scientific and subjective universalisms and to Marx's vision of a universal science of the production of autonomy and domination. Where scholarship on the Frankfurt School has often followed Habermas's lead in seeing *Dialectic of Enlightenment* as a retreat into theory and away from applied research, this book considers the way the *Dialectic of Enlightenment*'s "message in a bottle" was central to the Institute's engagement with how questions of race and nationalism were transforming the interest-based politics of Western societies.

In advancing this reinterpretation of *Dialectic of Enlightenment*, I pursue an intertextual approach that places the fragments of this pathbreaking work in dialogue with the other work of the period (completed and fragmentary, empirical and theoretical). Setting aside the notion that *Dialectic of Enlightenment* offered a unified—or even successful—argument, I emphasize the book's status as a record of Horkheimer and Adorno's need for a theoretical and speculative supplement to—and refuge from—the large-scale, empirical, and interdisciplinary projects they were engaged with during the 1940s. The central focus of these chapters is on the major projects in which Adorno was involved between the years 1941 and 1950: *Dialectic of Enlightenment, Minima Moralia,* and *Authoritarian Personality* as part of the *Studies in Prejudice* series, as well as Horkheimer's *Eclipse of Reason.* Given that Adorno and Horkheimer were proposing and developing the research that would lead to *Studies in Prejudice* alongside the writing and revision of *Dialectic of Enlightenment,* it is surprising that so little attention has been paid to the interconnections between these books and how they together address the limits that prejudice and ressentiment place on reason. I argue that this neglect springs from a central myth of the Frankfurt School scholarship that emerged in the 1980s—the belief that Adorno did not take his empirical work seriously and that it was disconnected from his theoretical work. This is ironic, because not only did Adorno critique the practice of blind empiricism that held that objects of study were a matter of indifference to theory, but he did so specifically in relation to the study of fascism. Adorno believed that a true empiricism emerged from using theory to relate details to the whole, but that this whole was not totality as such but the reflection of a divided social totality in its subject/object. The guiding hypothesis is, thus, that if one reconnects the speculative and practical, philosophical and empirical, hermetic and public dimensions of Adorno and Horkheimer's work in the 1940s, a new picture emerges of both the empirical and the theoretical. Arguing that the writing of the *Dialectic of Enlightenment* served as a catalyst to the research activities of Adorno and the entire Institute circle, I show how sparring with the "extreme" theses of *Dialectic of Enlightenment* allowed them to engage with the American world of social-scientific research that had not been able to comprehend Adorno's Simmel talk. *Dialectic of Enlightenment* and *Minima Moralia* were, during the American years, private fragments that served as a rich source of testable (and untestable) hypotheses challenging the conceptions of science and concrete research methods relied on by the Institute's members and their American collaborators.

The foregoing discussions of woundedness and estrangement, of Heine and Simmel, provide the framework for a reconstruction of Adorno's concept of identity, non-identity, and negative identity. The Odyssean model of a woundable self—a self simultaneously empowered by and diminished by the myth of his own self-sufficiency—was part of Adorno's revised concept of subjective universalism. Out of this consideration of the divided self, he would develop both a new theory of valid interdisciplinary empirical research and a diagnosis of the sources and dynamics of political extremism. This book relates the story of how a concept such as identity—which had largely meant logical unity in a systematic or mathematical sense—came to be used (and then rejected) by the Frankfurt School theorists as a linguistic marker of unalienated subjectivity. This story of the rise and fall of a critical theory of identity in the 1940s is deeply related to Adorno and Horkheimer's critique of the unity of rationality and disciplinarity, on the one hand, and to their analysis of racism, authoritarianism, and anti-Semitism, on the other hand. Identity as we use it today still carries within it these meanings. But out of a historical understanding of the origins of identity, one can build a compelling case for a broader dialectical use of it, positively as well as negatively.

Lived Negative Identity and the Genesis of Interdisciplinary Theory

One of the most durable ways in which a book's reputation can eclipse its actual argument occurs when a politically motivated attack presents a negative image of the author that becomes fused with reception of the book. In the case of *Dialectic of Enlightenment*, Georg Lukács's characterization of the psychology of Horkheimer and Adorno undoubtedly preinterpreted the work in a way that few analyses have shaken off. The sketch of Adorno and Horkheimer that appeared in the 1962 preface to Lukács's *Theory of the Novel* presented them as spoiled radicals who, living the good life at others' expense, developed an upper-class pessimism that displaced the guilt for their inactivity:

> The leading German intelligentsia, including Adorno, have taken up residence in the *Grand Hotel Abyss* . . . a beautiful hotel, equipped with every comfort, on the edge of an abyss, of nothingness, of absurdity. And the daily contemplation of the abyss between excellent meals or artistic entertainments, can only heighten the enjoyment of the subtle comforts offered.[13]

This passage tells us more about Lukács's relation to his earlier *Theory of the Novel* than about Horkheimer and Adorno. Written to underscore the divide separating his authentic Marxism of the Eastern Bloc from the spoiled life of the West, Lukács's preface was written to disavow his own 1914 book, which had been the single most important inspiration for the cultural wing of the Frankfurt School. As Lukács tells the story, *The Theory of the Novel* pointed to disaster because it combined the analysis of genre and society with an unacceptable metaphysics of subjectivity. On the eve of World War I, he, a student of Max Weber's, developed an analysis of inauthenticity and alienation in an age of "absolute sinfulness" and greed.[14] Longing for the heroic action of the older epic tradition, the bourgeois novel conveyed a metaphysics of dehumanization. And so, as Lukács would have it, when the Great War came, he realized his error and found the proper antidote to cultural pessimism: Marxism and objective social analysis. Adorno, presented as the pampered epigone of Lukács's younger, foolish self, lived in the past: he was a nihilist longing for salvation from a nonexistent God, a theorist whose notions of negativity were merely a cloak to hide inner decadence and faux radicalism.

So few commentators on *Dialectic of Enlightenment* have been able to resist Lukács's brilliant ad hominem attack that the image of intellectuals living at the "Grand Hotel Abyss" has come to be identified not with West Germany but with coastal Los Angeles. A simple sense of cultural geography indeed must find some humor in two would-be radicals seeking to write an esoteric book on socialist dialectics in 1940s Los Angeles, of all places. And once one sees the irony of being pessimistic while living in sunny California in its heyday, it is hard to resist using decadent terms in describing Horkheimer and Adorno's move from the decision-making centers of Washington and New York to Tinseltown. Before one reads a single line, and as one reads any available preface (such as Habermas's), Lukács's presumption that inner decadence led the way to an outer one has prefigured the interpretation of *Dialectic of Enlightenment*. It takes little creativity to fold into this narrative the "evidence" of Adorno's preface to *Minima Moralia*, which defends the utility of decadence for the formulation of theory.[15]

Theoretical works such as *Dialectic of Enlightenment* are, however, shaped more by the interaction of ideas with worldly problems than by questions of decadence and enjoyment. And indeed, however optional it was to come to Los Angeles in particular, the flight of the Institute from New York was largely dictated by necessity. In the course of 1941–43, the Institute for Social Research, having failed to establish a permanent arrangement with Columbia, found its financial resources severely strained. A year after changing its journal's name to *Studies in the Philosophy and Social Science*, and thus embracing the American world and the English language, the Institute was forced to cease publication entirely. This was a defeat but also a new beginning. As America moved to a war footing, the Institute at Morningside Heights faced diminished prospects for domestic or foreign engagement. With students and dollars moving toward the war effort, the Institute could not uphold its original role as a center for research and teaching.[16] The Institute during these years followed two contrary dynamics: it was in the first instance diasporic, with members instructed to seek work and projects elsewhere; but all the while, Horkheimer was seeking to find a long-term project that would, in the language of his 1937 "Traditional and Critical Theory," assemble "an interdisciplinary group of researchers trained to collaborate for the evaluation of complex social material."[17] Even as the Institute fragmented into separate islands of research, it was finding new ways to connect those groups and make ties to others.

The genesis of *Dialectic of Enlightenment* (written between 1941 and 1944, first distributed as a mimeograph in 1945, published in Amsterdam in 1947) and the production of the five-volume empirical work *Studies in Prejudice* (developed between 1942 and 1949, published in 1950) must be told as a bicoastal tale, one in which research and theory interacted, reinterpreted, and invigorated each other. On the East Coast, members of the Institute, including Herbert Marcuse and Franz Neumann, ended up finding work in the State Department and later academia. On the West Coast, Horkheimer and Friedrich Pollock moved to Los Angeles, where the relatively low costs permitted them to live without an office and avoid seeking full-time employment in the American research system. While a series of grant and project proposals continued apace, Horkheimer began work on the "dialectical logic book," soon to be joined by Adorno in November 1941.[18]

Horkheimer and Adorno shared a research interest in the power of modern media, and Los Angeles, home of the movie industry, offered an intriguing vantage for extending the Institute's work on radio, film, and mass culture. The first, 1941 proposal for the Institute's study of antiSemitism set forth the idea of surveying different audiences' prejudiced reactions by watching two different short films of the same script—one group with "typically Jewish" actors and one with non-Jewish actors.[19] No other city was better for investigating what Adorno and Horkheimer taught succeeding generations to call "the culture industry." But even leaving this motivation aside, it is clear that in moving to Los Angeles,

Adorno and Horkheimer were not isolating themselves from intellectual community, but joining one of the few centers of free, creative thought open to German and Jewish thinkers during wartime. Adorno the artist was less isolated than he had been on the East Coast. In Santa Monica he found a lively community of émigrés with diverse political views, many involved in the film industry—including, for example, the once-conservative, later-reluctant liberal Thomas Mann; the avant-garde liberal Fritz Lang; and hard-line "Cultural Bolsheviks" such as Bertolt Brecht and Hans Eisler. In his daily work with Horkheimer, moreover, Adorno finally shed his status as the Institute's enfant terrible. The partnership resulted in Horkheimer's most important books and established the working basis for the division of labor that would emerge in the postwar years, in which Horkheimer would return to administrative positions, trusting Adorno to serve as the chief theorist for what would come to be known as the Frankfurt School.

Dialectic of Enlightenment was written in a commuter fashion. Horkheimer had a home in Pacific Palisades within walking distance of the Pacific Ocean; Pollack, his closest ally and the Institute's economic theorist, lived in the adjoining house. Meanwhile, Adorno's residence was in Santa Monica, some three miles away, just west of the Hollywood Hills.[20] After Horkheimer spent the morning in correspondence, Gretel Adorno would drive her husband down Sunset Boulevard to the Horkheimers', where the three would either edit the previous day's transcript or begin a new philosophical conversation. The scene seems idyllic until one recalls that there was a horrific war going on. Some months after starting their "retreat," Adorno and Horkheimer found themselves engaged in a huge, ever-expanding project that they understood as wartime research. Wartime could allow isolation and even idyll to overlap with a sense of exhaustive, total commitment. The dual identity as researchers and philosophers, Marxists and cultural theorists was, moreover, redoubled by the realities of public identity in myriad ways. When President Roosevelt issued Executive Order 9066 on February 19, 1942, Horkheimer and Adorno became legally identified with their persecutors. On account of their German nationality, they were restricted from traveling more than five miles from home and had a strict 8:00 p.m. curfew. Their correspondence had to be written in English; their daily comings and goings were registered and monitored.[21] Negative identity, the wound of split and divided subjecthood, was part of their daily lives in more ways than one.

The exposure to lived negative identity was pivotal for the transformation of a book devoted to universal subjectivity and logic into a book that addressed questions of anti-Semitism, racism, and right-wing agitation. Once the war began, the need was to understand the historical function of anti-Semitism and racism as the sign of a changing capital structure, an essential ingredient in the making of a new global and mental order. As the war moved forward, the study of anti-Semitism became about the Holocaust but was no longer just about the Jews. A study that emerged from minority concerns, intended to track the activities of the irrational fringe, became an attempt to understand the failures of rational subjectivity, democracy, and science, addressing the question of how liberal society might foster irrationalism and totalitarianism within itself.

In 1941, the Institute first proposed a systematic study of anti-Semitism to the American Jewish Committee, one that was, in its first draft, articulated largely along historical, economic, and social lines and was implicitly European in focus. The revised proposal of 1942, however, explicitly expressed an ambition to study the growth of a totalitarian anti-Semitism that could be understood as a new logic of political and mental organization, one that was not just the province of conspiracy theorists and fringe political agitators but could be embedded in everyday life, in the structures of personality, judgment, and subjectivity. This was a tectonic shift: Horkheimer wrote to Harold Laski in March 1941 that global citizens needed not merely to understand sociology to explain anti-Semitism, but that "society itself can now only be understood through Antisemitism."[22] This application of an epistemology of estrangement would allow the American situation to be understood in terms of the European experience. As capitalism and anti-Semitism were theorized together, so alterity and subjectivity grew more dialectically entwined.

The Institute's view that anti-Semitism was not simple or timeless hatred but a complex modern phenomenon that required psychological and philosophical, political and economic, sociological and historical study, did not develop spontaneously or in isolation. Rather, it emerged from the conflict between the Institute's ambition to have a total theory of subject/object relations and its need to draw upon the social-theoretical resources of America and make America its object of study. As Horkheimer developed an understanding of science and epistemology's relation to universalism, he charged Pollock with making regular flights to New York to meet with the anti-Semitism project's sponsors, the American Jewish Committee.

The story of how identity moved to the center of Adorno's theoretical concerns is bound up with that of how Adorno became the person with whom Horkheimer would cowrite the "Dialectical Logic" book, and both of these stories are writ large in the final issue of *Studies in Philosophy and Social Science*. The shuttering of the Institute's journal has largely been interpreted as a matter of financial necessity and lack of interest in empirical research. Though the financial problems were real, the deeper problem was global. On the eve of the US entry into the war, Institute members were divided over the philosophical foundations of their paradigm and whether it had an audience, a focus, and a future orientation. Throughout the 1930s, the Institute had sought a psycho-social mediation that would achieve the materialist goal of a Marxist-Hegelian synthesis while challenging the increasingly calcified definitions of "totality" emanating from the Soviet and German state realities. The last issue of *Studies* attests that, while many members of the Institute remained engaged with the question of psycho-social mediation—of combining the insights of psychology, sociology, and economics to theorize the subject's relation to totality—they were increasingly torn between positive and negative conceptions of this mediation. None of them would have said at the time that the term "identity" was at the crux of their disagreements. However, it was in the context of debating how totality mediated individual consciousness that Institute members first used the term "identity" in its fully modern sense, and the differences between how members understood the pairing of social totality and individual identity would prove decisive for their future careers.

4

Critical Theory Goes to War
The Critique of Positive Identity and Positive Science

Final Issue: Identity and Particularity in Theory

Published in March 1942, the final issue of the *Zeitschrift*, renamed *Studies in Philosophy and Social Science*, consisted of five main articles: Horkheimer's "The End of Reason," Adorno's "Veblen's Attack on Culture," Marcuse's "Some Social Implications of Modern Technology," Friedrich Pollock's "Is National Socialism a New Order?," and Otto Kirchheimer's "The Legal Order of National Socialism." The review section included long reviews of Marcuse's *Reason and Revolution: Hegel and the Rise of Social Theory* (written by Paul Tillich) and Erich Fromm's *Escape from Freedom* (written by Fromm's friend Ernst Schachtel). Horkheimer's preface informed readers that Pollock, Kirchheimer, and Marcuse's articles were delivered at Columbia as part of the Institute's lecture series, while his article and Adorno's were part of an emerging "joint effort."[1] It thus suggested a future direction as well as standing commitments. Kirchheimer, Pollock, and Marcuse's articles pursued an objective, materialist theory of basic state and legal forms, examining how technology, institutions, and economy change the public world. Horkheimer and Adorno's contributions, by contrast, spoke to each other and to *Dialectic of Enlightenment* and in so doing pointed toward a revised understanding of cultural criticism.

Adorno's engagement with Thorstein Veblen is indicative of the sophistication and fertility of his encounter with American thought. Admired by the Columbia sociologists whom Adorno had sought to cultivate, Veblen had nonetheless been a lifelong outsider, a sociological Stranger to the American university system. The reason for this, Adorno realized, was that Veblen both typified the connection between Pragmatism's equation of reason with action and the pluralistic concept of culture *and* was one of the few insiders to have examined this equation critically.[2] In "Veblen's Attack on Culture," Adorno explored how the notion of "conspicuous consumption" implied a new, modern "barbarism of culture," in which people consume wastefully to display their status and work in order to consume conspicuously. For Veblen, this system was both characterized by a deep, internal rationality—the logic of workmanship as domination—and devoid of any true rationality, and this double fact pointed to an equivalence between the modern and the barbaric: the animal spirits of the marketplace and the competitions of status guide the putatively rational, modern individual as blindly as they guided any savage. Adorno was deeply impressed by this insight, which grounded reason in culture, in society as a totality. Yet he rejected Veblen's nihilistic conclusion that all cultures are equivalently rational (or irrational). Veblen had not quite understood the implications of his own insights—the fact that his contemptuous gaze pushed the misery of consumer shallowness to such an extreme that its counterimage became visible. It was not that there is no rationality but that rationality exists only within a history of its Other. If the "totality" of culture must be interpreted in terms of a rationalized system of identities—a totality of production-consumption-distribution—it was also possible to imagine that rationalization could move toward a system that valued labor and planned equality. Moreover, Veblen's attention to the incongruous object offered Adorno a model for understanding how particular cultural objects both embodied and resisted the totality of the culture that produced them. Here, too, Veblen had not quite understood the objective meaning of his derision. When Veblen looked at a train station designed to look like a medieval castle, he saw "nothing but a reversion" of culture to barbarism; but for Adorno such retro-commodification was kitsch—an objective field of contradictions reflecting the divided self. Ostentatious anachronism is a sign of a specific modernity—an awareness of abject aesthetic failure and capitulation to the system of mass production that attests to "a desperate compulsion to escape from the abstract sameness of things by a kind of self-made and futile *promesse de bonheur*."[3] Arguing that kitsch is subjectively irrational and objectively rational, Adorno read the train station for its incongruity and for the way power manifests itself as a coerced identity and bad totality:

> Veblen has noticed the temporal disparity between the castle and the railway station [made to look like a castle] but not the law behind this disparity. The railway

station assumes the aspect of the castle but this aspect is its truth. Only when the technological world is a direct servant of domination is it capable of shedding the disguise. Only in fascism does it equal itself.[4]

The castle/station is what Benjamin called a "dialectical image."[5] It must be viewed in two ways at once: as representative of the social trend and as a gap within the field of cultural knowledge. Read dialectically, it is an expression of the universal's power and of its limitations. "Memories" of the primitive are also specifically modern—revealing a desire to regress, they also represent a moment of resistance against the law of universal sameness and a momentary insight into the fragmented whole. Unstable in its meaning, kitsch reveals that domination is ongoing, demonstrates how co-option works, yet shows that pleasure is not dead.

Readings such as this represented an objective breakthrough. Throughout his intellectual development, Adorno struggled with squaring his Kantian and Marxian commitments to the universal with his Romantic and modernist concern for the analysis of the particular. Reading Veblen allowed him to extend an approach he had initiated in the Simmel talk, seeing the incongruous particular as a challenge to the universal. Horkheimer summed it up in philosophical terms: "In the most decisive fashion, you deliver Veblen out of rationalism, deliver him from theses such as the identity of thinking and being, the category of totality, or that of freedom. I've been wasting my time with exactly these [dead ends] in my work."[6] The essay pioneers several approaches that would be hallmarks of Adorno's later theory: his emphasis on immanent criticism and totality; his concern for what he would later call the "non-identical" status of subject/object relations; and his interest in the tensions between the different modes of rationality represented by different intellectual and scientific disciplines. In the case of the castle/station, its unsuccessful architecture reveals, like all kitsch, the poor and falsified state of non-identicality in an age of mandatory universality and thus opens a window on the conflict between the underlying value spheres: economic, political, aesthetic, and social reasoning fuse into a confused expression. "In a society in which productive powers develop and are fettered at the same time and as a result of the same principle, each progress in technics always means an archaic reversion somewhere else."[7] Veblen's laughter at modern archaisms is, for Adorno, the beginning of social critique—a transformation of the non-identical into an epistemology of division in the entire system of representation. In this late 1941 essay, Adorno discovered that claims to universality were forgeries in economic as well as aesthetic discourse and that social theory (like modern art) would do well to discover and defend the universal in the mutilated particular.

Horkheimer's "End of Reason" is, like Adorno's "Veblen," about the relation between mental and material totalities. Its focus is on reason rather than culture, however, and the concern is much more narrowly focused on how changing concepts of reason affect the idea of the self and what selves can imagine. Surveying the conflict between rationalism and universalism across the Christian Era, Horkheimer speculated on how those at the pinnacle of the "social pyramid" cultivated a view of "rational civilization" to justify their cultivation of "political and spiritual powers" while setting narrowly rationalistic goals for society. The maintenance of these goals in the individual as well as in social planning was supposed to (and partially did) create a "harmony between universal and particular interest." Even as rationalistic ideology defined the lower classes as irrational, instinctual, and requiring coercion, it placed real limits on the dominant class. In modern society, by contrast, those on the bottom increasingly attacked the falsified element of "universal concepts and pointed to existing reality instead." This new empiricism promoted a logic of social leveling. Yet it also bifurcated the concept of truth along lines suggested by economic logic. It saw truth as collective insofar as society was organized around a calculus of scarcity, and it saw truth as individual insofar as subjective self-preservation was the proof of correct understanding. This contradictory definition of truth discounted the substantive needs of human beings and promoted the formation of new group antagonisms. Modern philosophy, from Locke to Kant, had promoted individualism and attempted to build a world of law and order around the self, yet eviscerated the substantive legal claims of the self. Seventeenth-century rationalism contained far more social substance: it "upholds the potential solidarity of men as an ideal against the actual state of affairs in which solidarity is asserted with violence and catastrophe." The later world in which "all men have become empiricists" is also one in which individuality is reduced to self-preservation, creating the basis of possibility for a monopoly capitalism in which there is no true individuality but only the self-assertion of the power of the elites.[8]

On the basis of this dialectic of universalism and selfhood, nominalism and idealism, economic and political systems of collectivism, Horkheimer analyzed two trends of contemporary modernity. The first involved a definition of "cultural authority" as a weak replacement for both religion and reason, between which it splits the difference. Culture, which he characterized as the "attempt to tame the element of brute force immanent in bodily strength," ceased to be a matter of intellectual cultivation and now involved conditioning human beings through their physical pleasures.[9] Intellectual life had succumbed to cultural practices that worship strength, and physical culture had turned into an ideology of intellectualized bullying symbolized by the way the monster stadium echoed the Wagnerian *Gesamtkunstwerk*. This cultural totality favored action over contemplation, facts over concepts, markets over solutions, immediacy over reflection. This led to the decline of the ego, reflective reason, cultivated human relationships. Even the natural impulses of sexuality were unrecoverable by psychoanalysis, which, Horkheimer argued, had fallen behind the times in its understanding of gender roles and the commercialization of sexuality. Culture, emptied of all serious thought, had become the mental hygiene program of a unidimensional self.

Horkheimer's second argument turned this critique of the decline of reason and the rise of a national culture toward a new concept: "identity." Using this term in a fully modern, if also directly negative way, Horkheimer spoke of the modern situation of identity as a form of loss and coercion, a system of time-labor indebtedness. Where the Renaissance began to think of death as the end of life and thereby valued life all the more, the modern era saw meaninglessness as a universal condition that one must simply labor through. Individuals become divided against themselves and must sacrifice their egos to heteronomy and external domination:

> Everyone feels that his work perpetuates an infernal machine from which he manages to wheedle enough time to live, time that he proceeds to lose back by attending to the machine. Thus he keeps going, expert in handling every situation and in understanding none, scorning death and yet fleeing it. To men in the bourgeois era individual life was of infinite importance because death meant absolute catastrophe. Hamlet's line, "the rest is silence," in which death is followed by oblivion, indicates the origin of the ego. Fascism shatters this fundamental principle. It strikes down that which is tottering, the individual, by teaching him to fear something worse than death. Fear reaches farther than the identity of his consciousness. The individual must abandon the ego and carry on somehow without it. Under Fascism the objects of organization are being disorganized as subjects. They lose their identical character, and are simultaneously Nazi and anti-Nazi, convinced and skeptical, brave and cowardly, clever and stupid. They have renounced all consistency. This inconsistency into which the ego has been dissolved is the only attitude adequate to a reality . . . defined . . . by concentration camps.[10]

The passage resonates with Albert Camus's *Myth of Sisyphus*, the pioneering work of the existentialist movement, published in Paris a few months after Horkheimer's essay.[11] The contemporaneity of the two essays is striking, yet a crucial difference of commitment and trajectory is also already visible: Horkheimer here approached existentialism in mood and analysis but negated all its affirmations. His Sisyphus is not happy. Like his French counterparts, Horkheimer focused on the absurdity of modern work, of modern death—the concentration camp as the epitome of modernity—and the passage corresponds with a host of existentialist tropes, from Kierkegaard's angst (which unfolds once human beings lose the simplicity of instinct) to Heidegger's *Geschlossenheit* (the determination to do things in the face of death and meaninglessness) to Jean-Paul Sartre's *bad faith*. Yet Horkheimer refused positive identity as the recovery of faith or meaning in the face of these realities. Horkheimer diagnosed the current state of affairs as one in which the individual experiences a negation of the "identity of consciousness" that requires her to both "abandon the ego" yet "carry on somehow without it." The vocabulary of existentialism was thus countered with an invocation of Freud (through the English word "ego") wrapped around the language of Marx and German Idealism. The idea of a "bad infinity" invoked Hegel's *Logic* as well as his attack on Johann Gottlieb Fichte's identity concept in the *Differenzschrift*—the claim that everyday understanding misconceives the concept of infinity if it imagines quotidian sameness without end. A monotonous identity of consciousness effaces the identity of a self that lacks a concept of meaning to rescue it.[12] And for Horkheimer, this crisis of meaning was rooted in the increasing meaninglessness not just of labor in the modern factory but of consumption under the conditions of modern culture.

Horkheimer's bitterness regarding the "disorganized self" of modernity came from seeing how fascism diabolically exploits the weak self. Fascism turns the strength of the individual—the ontological aura of individuality itself—against itself to create tolerance for authoritarian domination. To live in a contradictory state but suffer no crisis of conscience and to feel none of the spontaneities of rebellion is to enable horror. This consciousness can embrace heteronomy and non-identity and be "Nazi and anti-Nazi, convinced and skeptical, brave and cowardly, clever and stupid." From 1942 on, the problem with existentialism for Horkheimer, as for Adorno, would come from its obsession with overcoming the problem of internal division—creating identity—by pretending that the immediacy of being, death, or nothingness will come to the rescue of a world rendered lawless by a bad infinity. As this passage suggests, Horkheimer had embraced the historical argument of Adorno's Simmel talk: the idea that phenomenology, existentialism, and *Lebensphilosophie* all shared the false hope that a new immediacy could heal the rift between universal and particular. "The End of Reason" extends this critique into the core expressive totalities of bourgeois existence. The myths of personality, culture, and subjective identity now need to be criticized *as* myths, uncritical assertions that a substantive and objective identity of reason can be grounded in the self. Rather, argued Horkheimer, the opposite was true: those seeking to defend reason needed to conceive of and study the negativities of identity.

Horkheimer's use of the subjective identity concept—the "identity of consciousness"—is startling here not only because it was one of the earliest uses of the modern social-psychological concept of identity in any language, but also because it appeared in the form of a sharp critique—an argument that to understand a multifarious subjective identity, one must study it negatively, study it in crisis. The crisis of identity represented a new concern for Horkheimer and the Institute. Horkheimer had previously used the concept of identity once, in 1935, to refer to the subjective sense of selfhood that comes from the certainty of religious conversion.[13] Here that existential motif is negated, in that it contemplates an unraveling and dissolution of the subjective reason and autonomy of the Enlightenment and Romantic sort to which Horkheimer was most committed. The existentialists were not the first to find value in a vision of an individual whose wholeness might counter a divided world. Existentialism's theories about the self must be located in a longer history of concern about how the divided self exemplifies—or fails to exemplify—the ideally free self in a world of objective potential.[14] In previous essays, Horkheimer had meditated on the long tradition of worrying about the unities of social reason through consideration of the unified self. Aristotle's concept of *phronêsis*, the reflective judgment of a knowledgeable and active intellect, found a point of refuge in Romantic reflection on nature and objects of aesthetic beauty. Friedrich Schiller's *Letters on the Aesthetic Education of Man* depicted Kant's "free play of the intellect" as that mental practice of judgment that brought the semblance of unity and harmony to a world that reason tore asunder; Wilhelm von Humboldt's notion of a cosmopolitan universalism embedded in the diversity of the individual personality sketched out a model for the modern university that cultivated a balance of talents transcending the narrowness of mere *techné*.[15] More recently, thinkers such as Wilhelm Dilthey, Simmel, and Husserl (who directed Horkheimer's *Habilitation*), had defended the idea of cultivating a harmony of diverse interests within the individual, within reason, and within culture. While "The End of Reason" finds Horkheimer developing a critique of existentialism, the gaps in the essay's history of philosophy suggest uncertainty about how far to push this critique and how much it would undermine his long-standing defense of subjective metaphysics.

The uncertainty around the edges of Horkheimer's analysis attests to what he would ask of his younger collaborator in writing *Dialectic of Enlightenment*. The second half of 1941, during which "The End of Reason" and the Veblen essay were written, was a crucial moment in Adorno and Horkheimer's working relationship. Emotionally framed by the struggle to recover Benjamin's manuscripts after his suicide, and by Gretel Adorno's insistence that Benjamin's project of a new objectivity be continued, these months saw Horkheimer increasingly turning to Adorno to help articulate the core theory of subject/object non-identity.[16] Adorno's novel combination of Marx, Kant, and the analysis of narrative content equipped him for the role of unpacking existential identity's relation to its Enlightenment and Romantic precursors. And although there remained many problems to work out, the affinities between Adorno's and Horkheimer's contributions to the final issue of *Studies* speak to convergence on the question of subjective reason. In considering the relation between individual identity and the totality of culture, both essays asked whether looking at culture as a totality of subjective meaning represented a new way of conceiving of reason's validity. Both writers answered "no" to this question: for both, a static, synthetic concept of subjective identity was emerging not as the answer but *the problem*. Horkheimer's programmatic essay was more ambitious, more conceptually focused on the linked definitions of "rationality" and "subjectivity," and it took as its purview almost the entire history of rationalism; Adorno's much more narrow focus on immanent objectivity promised to move past attack into a determinate (rather than absolute) negation and discover a truth content in the non-identity of subject and object. Arguing that the object told the truth of subjective non-identity, Adorno had begun to transform critical theory's notion of reason and of science into a theory of negativity and subject/object mediation.[17]

Positive Identity in *Escape from Freedom*

The final issue of *Studies in Philosophy and Social Science* looked forward to the analysis of dialectical subjectivity, but it also looked back, consolidating some of the Institute's gains and cutting some losses. As Horkheimer moved closer to Adorno, he was moving away from some of the Institute's original personnel. The two headline reviews of books by Institute insiders—Fromm and Marcuse—may be taken as summaries of the theoretical achievements and dead ends of the Institute's decade of publishing. Both reviews were friendly but pointed in opposite directions across the divide of Horkheimer's guiding philosophical question: Whither positivity in theory? As such, they registered the new situation.

The review of Marcuse's *Reason and Revolution* was written by Paul Tillich, the existential theologian who shepherded Adorno's 1932 *Habilitation* on Kierkegaard through university review. Praising Marcuse's analysis of the development of German Idealism in relation to the politics of the French Revolution, Tillich affirmed that the book was an "extremely valuable interpretation of Hegel's philosophy" because it combines "historical analysis" with a conceptual focus on the problem of negativity. Seeing Marcuse as reflecting the Institute's synthesis of historical and conceptual method, Tillich emphasized the significance of Marcuse's main thesis:

> Hegel's philosophy is indeed what the subsequent reaction termed it, a negative philosophy. It was originally motivated by the conviction that the given facts that appear to common sense as the positive index of truth are in reality the negation of truth, so that truth can only be established by their destruction. The driving force of the dialectical method lies in this critical conviction.[18]

At stake for Tillich, as for Marcuse, was the status of the Hegelian dialectic at a moment when the Soviet Union was claiming a monopoly on both Hegel and Marx. For Tillich, Marcuse's historical reading of Hegel debunked the totalitarian view of Hegel as a defender of the rights of the state and church above those of the individual. The key to rescuing Hegel from positivity was to embrace his immanent method. Hegel's rationalism was not apologetic but a view that "everything is something other than it immediately is, and uniting itself with 'its other' tends to fulfil the law of life and progress which is at the same time the law of thinking and being." Tillich saw Marcuse's critique of immediacy and his championing of negativity as a triumph that pointed to greater things for an Institute whose central mission had always included rescuing what it asserted was "orthodox" socialist theory from revolutionary dogmatism.[19]

In looking at the second half of Marcuse's book, which explores positivism and positivity, Tillich offered some criticisms, lamenting Marcuse's failure to specify how right-Hegelianism unified state-based models of social science with legal and scientific positivism to create new formulas for domination of external and internal life that devalued the individual. Tillich then asked whether Marcuse's lack of analysis of spiritual and eschatological matters might not feed the decline of subjective rationalism needed for revolutionary thought. Without questions of "the ultimate," argued Tillich, "criticism becomes positivistic and contingent." Moreover, he added, "no successful revolution can be made without a group of people who . . . believe that the 'freedom of the personality' is the meaning of existence and are ready to live and die for this belief."[20] With this move, Tillich reconnected existentialism to religion and existentialized revolution: value rationality required conversion. This defense of transformative subjective value rationality stands in direct opposition to Horkheimer's antiexistentialist arguments in "The End of Reason." The contrast between their two positions—with Humboldt figuring hilariously in Tillich's account as a revolutionary—points to how controversial the question of affirmative subjectivity had become for the Institute. Marcuse's emphasis on Hegelian negation in *Reason and Revolution* stood in marked contrast to Tillich's claim that a subjective or revolutionary rationalism should be grounded in theology or an existentially conceived positive self. Tillich and Marcuse's debate was ready-made for Horkheimer and Adorno to develop into a negative analysis of identity.

The review of Fromm's *Escape from Freedom* is, however, a purely positive review in every sense of the word. Though Adorno had suggested to Horkheimer that they coauthor a review, Horkheimer decided to make no official commentary, instead allowing the task to fall to Fromm's longtime protégé and collaborator Ernst Schachtel.[21] This was a strategic decision. Fromm's book was already a best seller, and his name's association with the Institute was invaluable for grant applications: *Escape from Freedom* is probably *still* the most widely read book written by a member of the Institute. The problem was that Fromm had been forced out of the Institute in 1939 and was no longer on speaking terms with most of its members. *Escape from Freedom* was thus at once, awkwardly, the Institute's calling card and a prime example of what it no longer was.

The story of how this break happened is negatively legible in Schachtel's positive review. Fromm had, throughout the 1930s, been the Institute's most prominent member, and for good reason. If the Institute sought to mediate between Marx and Freud at a theoretical level and to apply methods drawn from psychology and sociology to social domination at a practical level, Fromm's task was to fill in the psychological parts of the equation. Fromm was both shaped by and shaped the Institute. Trained by Alfred Weber in sociology and by Frieda Reichmann (also his first wife) and Hans Sachs in psychoanalysis, Fromm long seemed perfectly suited to address what Horkheimer called in "Traditional and Critical Theory" the core problem of social research: that of how the "role played by a group in the economic process" related to the "psychic structures of its members."[22] But relations between Horkheimer and Fromm began to chill in the mid-1930s. Adorno's sniping letters and Fromm's polite, business-like ones to Horkheimer comprise the backbone of many histories of the Frankfurt School, with the consensus view that antagonism arose out of what was a personality conflict, at best, or jealous or malicious scheming on the part of Adorno, at worst. The divergence between *Escape from Freedom* and the directions pursued by the Institute's final issue suggest, however, a different story: one centering on intellectual disagreement over positivity and identity. If Horkheimer, Adorno, and Marcuse all began to emphasize the language of negativity and identity in their writings at this moment, it appears to have been in direct reaction to Fromm's *Escape from Freedom*, the first English book to employ the word "identity" as a technical, psychosociological term.[23]

To pick up *Escape from Freedom* is to be struck by an immediate difference between Fromm and his former colleagues: his writing style is far more intelligible. This difference is not trivial. Fromm's career in America followed a different tack, personally and intellectually, from that of the Adorno of "Scientific Experiences." The gregarious Fromm adapted easily to American life and prided himself on his many American contacts and English fluency. Writing without a translator, he adopted plain language and naturalized many a philosophical and disciplinary idiom. When he used the term "identity" and posited the crucial importance of preserving "the identity of our personality," he was advancing a psycho-social concept that drew on such existentialist sources as Heidegger, Kierkegaard, and Nietzsche. But he did so in a language that appealed to 1940s Americans' love of the common man, their dual emphasis on individualism and cultural adaptation, and their aversion to complex syntax. The book is a testament to Fromm's creative ability to bridge the differences among intellectual traditions: *Escape from Freedom* cites from the *Zeitschrift*, but the intellectual weight of citation and argument is toward American Pragmatism and the Columbia school of culturalist relativism. In conceptual terms, this meant that where Marcuse, Adorno, and Horkheimer would emphasize negativity, Fromm naturalized the positive qualities of the individual and identity.

Fromm's thesis in *Escape from Freedom* is that fascism should be understood as "a psychological problem."[24] Fromm emphasized the historical origins of this psychology. The modern self, he argued, began in the Renaissance and Reformation, when theological arguments for the limitation or strength of the individual will aligned with the needs of the emerging economic system, which required a dissolution of the feudal bonds that both gave the individual a sense of belonging and fettered him in a static social order. This articulation of negative freedom—freedom *from*—destabilized the normative meaning of everyday life and effectively isolated the individual. Because Fromm considered it axiomatic that human beings seek "relatedness"—a sense of connection to others—he believed they find abstract negative freedom insufferable. But positive liberty was also increasingly fraught. The individual needed increasing amounts of courage to be free in the modern sense—so much so that the necessity of finding one's own identity in the world of free labor and personalized religion became a burden. As the economic and spiritual economy increasingly demanded that individuals answer the questions of "who am I?" and "what is meaningful for me?" in the terms of positive liberty, selfhood could seem at once the most valuable thing and utterly empty of meaning. The social contradictions of demand for personality caused a concomitant growth in the psychology of "escape mechanisms" and the politics of authoritarianism and "automaton conformity."[25]

This historical analysis prepared for global war against fascism through a liberal-optimistic rewriting of Freud's *Civilization and Its Discontents*. Rejecting the idea of any inherent tendency toward violence, and arguing for the creation of a culture that would build humanistic values through a more expansive notion of love and a nonconformist notion of the self, Fromm saw a chance to address psycho-social conflict by using the Renaissance as a heuristic model for examining contemporary problems of individuality. A kind of golden age, the Renaissance's integral culture had made possible a new, autotelic subjectivity. Leon Battista Alberti had rightly called the "Renaissance Man" the "Universal Man" because he could now "do all things if he will." The self thereby acquired a new goal—to be the subject of history and enlightenment, of science and art, in such a way that reconciled these conflicting logics within the wholeness of the self.[26] Interpreting the positive/negative liberty distinction in a sunnier fashion than Isaiah Berlin would when he borrowed it from Fromm a decade later, Fromm argued that a liberated culture can emerge if it learns to cultivate positive identities that fulfill the human need for relatedness and meaning embedded in the notion of positive liberty.[27] As Schachtel's review pointed out, Fromm's book tied human psychology to the environment, exploring the social psychology of positive freedom as that which a free society would make possible:

> Positive freedom can be achieved only in a society which, on the basis of a planned economy, permits the individual to participate actively in the social process, to find a spontaneous relation, in love and work, to the world and to realize his individual self. The concept of spontaneity is thus established as focal for the psychological meaning of positive freedom.[28]

This vision of happy identity clearly met the formal criteria of the synthesis of the social and the psychological that Horkheimer had originally imagined. Yet Adorno and Horkheimer did not believe that the cultural adaptability that sponsored subjectivity was as free as Fromm asserted. Though Fromm saw his pluralistic concept of culture and emphasis on individualism as a product of his conversations with American interlocutors, his German colleagues discerned—underneath the influence of Freud and Marx—the cultural models and historical narratives of Alfred Weber, Ernst Troeltsch, and Jacob Burckhardt. Fromm's almost folksy American English appeared, disturbingly, to have allowed him to slide toward a Romanticism that would have sounded archconservative *auf Deutsch*. Horkheimer and Adorno distrusted such visions of unalienated golden ages, finding calls for more love and community recklessly Panglossian amid the murderous conformities that were engulfing societies globally. Adorno was certainly horrified by Schachtel's startling assessment that "man's striving for freedom is part of his historical evolution and has become an inherent part of human nature which cannot be crushed and eliminated"—and would have been more horrified if Fromm authorized this paraphrase.[29] The idea that freedom, once achieved, was *irreversible* was not a critical concept, nor would he have agreed that the language of identity sanitized the social Darwinistic language of "evolution." Indeed, the whole project of critical theory was endangered if these ideas allowed a book about Nazism to be read as a defense of the untrammeled nature of human spontaneity. For if freedom was now part of human nature, how was Nazism possible? And equally, why could the argument for identity not be brought to Hitler's defense—presenting sadomasochist nationalist mass murder as an expression of *his* freedom? One could hardly be less dialectical than Fromm's acolyte Schachtel.

The modern language of identity was not something that Horkheimer intended to sponsor when his inaugural address had launched the Institute on a decade-long project of uniting questions of individuality and reason, materialism and culture. That the concept of "identity" emerged from the *Zeitschrift*'s debates—and was met with a reinvigorated concept of *negation*—says a great deal, both about the concept of identity and the position of the Frankfurt School in twentieth-century thought. Both the turn toward Hegelian negativity and the subjective turn in the concept of identity were fissive by-products of a search for a postmetaphysical psycho-social synthesis. Fromm's notion of identity provided an easy version of this synthesis, one palpably inadequate to a world shaped by the nexus of fascism and consumer capitalism. Marcuse's reevaluation of Hegel as a primarily negative thinker challenging common sense offered an electrifying answer to Fromm's positive concept of identity as *immer aufgehoben*—always preserved, always progressive, always liberating. Just as Hegel had sought to overcome a static conception of objective and subjective knowledge and to discover how subjects made themselves by making their objects, so critical theory's relation to the concept of identity aimed at synthesis. But Fromm at this moment appeared to follow the model of the Right Hegelians who sought permanent, implicitly conservative synthesis. For Horkheimer and the reduced circle of the Institute, the paramount goal became avoiding false syntheses.[30]

If we regard the final issue of *Studies* as a seminar on the faults of Fromm's *Escape from Freedom*, we can also understand it as preparation for writing *Dialectic of Enlightenment*.[31] Where Fromm offered the first English-language use of the concept of subjective, expressive identity as a way of imagining the integration of the self with the world of culture and society, Horkheimer delivered a scathing analysis of how the language of selfhood served as an ideological cover for manipulating the self's internal divisions in an age of dehumanization. Where Fromm argued for a culture that incorporated a more powerful sense of rootedness, connection, and meaning, Adorno argued that these desires for wholeness imperiled the individual and theory under modern conditions, becoming indistinguishable from a desire for the archaic *Gemeinschaft*. The dissection of this ontological desire moved to the center of social analysis. While Horkheimer emphasized the importance of understanding the historical nature of a universalistic, subjective reason and criticized misguided forms of group solidarity, Adorno sought to break open the monolith of culture as a form of conditioning and locate a societal rationalism in particular forms of expression. This was the issue of the final issue: Marcuse's negative reading of Hegel already informed both Adorno and Horkheimer's essays. Rejecting positive identity for its inherent alignment of subjectivity and science with the status quo, critical theory made a negative turn toward the object that was understood as defense of subjective autonomy. Indeed, Horkheimer and Adorno began to argue that science as a whole had not faced the problem of how society mediated consciousness through positivity: it had preferred to emphasize the positive result, the optimistic theory, the good totality. Even their own search for a psycho-social empiricism had been structured by science's demand for a univocal concept of reason and methodology. But as the early 1940s dialogue made clear, the emphasis on negation redefined the meaning of Hegelian synthesis and the theory of conceptual mediation, rejecting Hegel's notion of progress, of history moving in irreversible stages, with each stage marking a higher level of self-conscious understanding. The march of progress could run in reverse. Subjectivity could in fact exist in a negative relation to itself. And a science of social interpretation could comprehend these inverted states of affairs by recognizing not only that such false syntheses took place, but that their positivity might be socially necessary. Thus, identifying a falsified identity became an important step in seeking to "negate" it: a false synthesis could be transformed into a diagnostic tool for recognizing bad forms of social reasoning and causation or for articulating the rudiments of immanent critique.

Total War, the Object of Research, and the Theory of Extremes

When one reviews the Institute's proposals for research in 1940–43, their debt to Fromm's psycho-social model of empiricism is inescapable.[32] In proposing the project that became *Studies in Prejudice* to the American Jewish Committee's (AJC) research group, the Institute continued to promise, as it had in the 1930s, to find a way to mediate between Marx and Freud. This project required modifying the classical modes of both theories: Freud, for instance, had quite emphatically rejected most notions of a "group psychology" and emphasized that psychoanalysis was centered on defining and treating the individual.[33] Until Fromm left the Institute in 1939, his role had been to innovate on the psychological side, designing psychologically oriented questionnaires and personality profiles, correlating these with sociological and demographic data, and interpreting them according to Fromm's own sociologically modified version of Freudian theory.[34] Fromm was originally recruited to the Institute by Horkheimer in 1929 to work on a survey of attitudes among German white- and blue-collar workers first proposed by Carl Grünberg; later he was assigned the pivotal research position in the 1936 *Studien über Autorität und Familie*. This project, which pursued the idea that the crisis in family life was being shaped by the crisis in capitalism, and vice versa, drew on the core of the Institute. Marcuse, for example, offered an "intellectual history" survey, and Horkheimer produced an introduction with a general theoretical overview, while Fromm's role was to explore whether the psychic development of individuals was being affected by social change and, by extension, whether Freudian theory was contingent on historical or class conditions.[35] In these studies and accompanying articles in the *Zeitschrift*, Fromm intermingled classical Freudian theory with interpersonal psychology drawn from a variety of theorists (Karl Abraham, Alfred Adler, Anna Freud) to posit a portrait of class "personality structures" and "character traits," seeking to connect these types to relevant political attitudes. When the Institute began, in 1940, to propose research on "the anti-Semitic character" or, eventually, "the authoritarian personality," it was acknowledging the influence of Fromm's central theoretical innovation over Freud, the socially analyzed character type.

Fascism, of course, taught everyone that reactionary group behavior was real and could be amplified by modern institutions. The challenge for critical theory involved finding ways to translate psychoanalytic methods designed to study individual psychopathology into a sound method of analyzing group behavior. And this inevitably led to questions of interdisciplinary method, of how to bring different kinds of science to bear on a single subject. The Hegelian doctrine of negation provided the template for systematically relating distinct but opposed forms of knowledge.

Psycho-socially, this meant one had to have a theory about how the individual psyche mediated and transformed social conflicts into mental representations and how the forms of social conflict were recognizable to the individual. Because Horkheimer considered Marxism a method of (materialist, dynamic) universalism, he saw this question of individual mediation in psychoanalysis as parallel to the Marxian questions of how the factory system or regimes of capital accumulation mediated class consciousness. Though some members of the Institute complained about the mushiness with which Fromm applied Freudian typologies to Marxian class categories (Adorno insisted Fromm needed be less sympathetic, "read some Lenin," and think about how authority *really* works[36]), for the first eight years or so, Horkheimer was largely satisfied with Fromm's work. As long as the logic of collaboration predominated—and Horkheimer had the privilege of choreographing the production and writing the introductions—he also tolerated work that did not quite conform to the standards set by his own programmatic essays on disciplinary method.

Horkheimer was, nonetheless, listening to Adorno's complaints that Fromm's schematic typologies represented not just a lazy methodology, but also a failure to recognize the underlying philosophical and disciplinary problems posed by the research and its object (the authoritarian state). And these complaints were in fact borne out as flaws became evident in the design, collection, and analysis of the survey. By the end of the 1930s, Fromm had left behind a trail of unfinished and apparently unfinishable research projects—projects which Horkheimer had hoped to leverage into future collective research. The study *Arbeiter und Angestellte (Blue- and White-Collar Workers)*, Fromm's first major survey for the Institute, had been an exercise in naïve empiricism, constructed without concern for respondent self-selection to its 248-point questionnaire nor for how its pointed questions might cue the respondents. Assuming a direct correlation between workers' libidinal economy and their political preferences, the survey engaged in a fishing expedition for correlations among pleasures, repressions, consumer habits, and political orientations—all without filtering for Type I (false positive) statistical error. Worse, the central concern—the relation between the mode of employment and class consciousness—drowned in demographic detail: respondents were asked how often they did laundry; how many hours they worked per week; and whether they ate jam, honey, or margarine on their bread.[37] Operating on a "pleasure principle" model, Fromm sought to assemble a set of personality profiles that categorized the workers' responses according to enjoyment and labor in three major areas: attitudes toward politics, authority, and general social benevolence (hostility or solidarity).[38] The unprocessable data soup sloshed around foreordained conclusions. As Rolf Wiggershaus has observed, workers who responded according to the official Communist Party line were coded as "revolutionary" with a strong social-historical consciousness, while those who failed, say, to blame the hyperinflation on capitalist machinations were considered irrational and reactionary.[39] *Quod erat demonstrandum*: Fromm concluded that the lower middle class—largely deskilled white-collar workers—were sadomasochistic, jealous of other people's pleasures, and projective in their sense of violence. They thereby were prone to identify with sadists and authoritarians who sought to exploit the organizational weakness of the proletariat. Despite repeatedly advertising the study's contributions, Horkheimer never published it. And though many factors contributed to this failure—including Fromm's health issues and the logistics of international collaboration—its unmanageable design was the real problem. The next major empirical survey project in which Fromm was assigned a central role, the 1936 *Studies on Authority and the Family*, studied unemployment in Newark, New Jersey, but despite the assistance of Paul Lazarsfeld, this too concluded without a publishable data set. Though the experience—from Fromm's perspective—was a useful one, as he used it to argue for an evidentiary-based revision of orthodox Freudian concepts of paternal authority, only the section on theoretical psychology was actually published.[40]

These misadventures in interdisciplinary empiricism played a significant role in triggering Fromm's ouster, and they framed the question of how the Institute would reinvent itself when pivoting toward research on fascism. Once America entered the war, the Institute became a group of affiliated scholars seeking either grants or professional positions on an ad hoc basis. They still sought to present themselves as an interdisciplinary team with significant knowledge of the political and economic situation in Europe and America, but they had to make themselves salable in wartime. In pitching themselves to the AJC, the earlier Institute strengths in economic analysis were downplayed, reduced to things such as Pollock's speculative "fascism scenario for America," based on the thesis that the economy after wartime stimulus might bring a reactionary political wave.[41] Concomitantly, the Institute had to downplay its theoretical and philosophical work and earlier internationalist focus. While some employment was available through the State Department (Marcuse, Neumann, and Kirchheimer did research on postwar political and legal scenarios), government groups aimed at US civilian life and private groups like the AJC asked questions of a psychological or cultural nature. The continuities between the Institute's style of psycho-social research of the 1930s and the initial proposals to the AJC pointed to the importance of maintaining the appearance of continuity after Fromm's departure—as well as to the urgent necessity of developing methods that would actually produce publishable data.

Both methods and subject matter would evolve rapidly as the Institute adapted to working for the AJC and to the strictures of a sponsored and collaborative project. If the Rockefeller Foundation promoted a vision of American progress and technology, the AJC had an ethical and scientific mandate to reflect on universality in terms of minority questions.[42] The AJC sought a pragmatic and empirical study measuring the extent of contemporary anti-Semitism with an analysis of how it could spread in a democratic society. Between 1941 and 1945, the Institute engaged in a series of proposals, meetings, and memoranda on the "Project on Antisemitism," followed by an extended process of reaching out to collaborators; establishing institutional networks; designing a survey and research methodology; conducting surveys, interviews, and document requests; holding a conference and a series of lectures; creating a preliminary report; and then, in 1944–45, creating an expanded request for additional funding, which required a further iteration of research and reporting, an even broader inclusion of other American academics, and further meetings and hypothesis building.[43]

The concrete result, conducted by two teams of researchers on the East and West Coasts, was the five-volume *Studies in Prejudice*. *The Authoritarian Personality* was the capstone volume, focused on understanding the psycho-social elements of authoritarian politics, while other volumes studied the changing nature of public emotional response, mass media manipulation, the logic and history of hate politics, and the psychopathology of anti-Semitic individuals. *Dynamics of Prejudice*, by Bruno Bettelheim and Morris Janowitz, studied how perceptions of individual inequality interacted with practices of ethnic intolerance (including anti–African American sentiment) among war veterans. *Prophets of Deceit*, by Leo Lowenthal and Norbert Guterman, investigated American and European agitators, focusing on the speeches of leaders and radio personalities advocating reactionary economic, political, and moral change while delivering little more than ressentiment, false moralism, religious nationalism, and conspiracy theories. *Rehearsal for Destruction*, by Paul Massing, analyzed the history of anti-Semitic and illiberal politics in Germany in the decades before World War I, with a particular focus on the role of the Social Democrats in trying to defeat political anti-Semitism. *Anti-Semitism and Emotional Disorder*, by Nathan W. Ackerman and Marie Jahoda, engaged in a content analysis of psychoanalytic casework on questions of group hatred or intolerance, speculating on how the social perception of otherness distorted individual emotional self-perception and could lead to neurosis. *The Authoritarian Personality* was, by design, a synthesis of the findings of these investigations. It made an extensive social survey of American life, examining the relation of individual/group dynamics to a set of empirically and theoretically developed sociopsychological political profiles. Adorno and Horkheimer's combined role throughout was to develop the scientific and theoretical method, integrating a dizzying array of researchers in disparate fields of psychology and psychotherapy, pedagogy, sociology, law, economics, religious studies, area studies, and classical studies.

Such a massive undertaking presented its directors with profound intellectual challenges. Horkheimer could not control this group as he had the Institute, and he could scarcely pretend that all collaborators represented a unified position. As Adorno had found in working with Lazarsfeld at the Princeton Radio Project, the émigré scientists struggled with questions of translation even among themselves. The social survey methods of the Institute group—Weberian-Simmelian—did not always register as "empirical research" to their American patrons and collaborators: when the Institute generated a set of "ideal types" of "the anti-Semite," their collaborators were uncertain whether this was considered the beginning or the result of research. Or was it more a confession of presuppositions—a sign of needing to be more inductive and open-minded?[44] The project, involving collaborative work with scores of coinvestigators and a university's worth of disciplines, constantly threatened to devolve into incoherence.

The Institute understood, however, that the fate of critical theory rested in the outcome of the research. That each of the challenges also represented an opportunity is suggested in the revised, 1942 research proposal:

Anti-Semitism is the synthesis of all reactionary features of present day social life; it cuts across every scientific discipline and touches on every problem of our social, political and economic existence. Hence it can only be studied by a synthesis of all the sciences covering the various aspects of the problem. Our project aims at such a synthesis. The problem cannot be adequately attacked by juxtaposition of scholars from various fields. A mere symposium of scholars without experience in team-work would be incapable of producing an integrated study.[45]

Two points are crucial to this new conception of the totalitarian character of anti-Semitism. First, the collaborative project is presented as an opportunity to pursue the kinds of syntheses once understood to be the main work of the Institute: social totality in theory. Second, even at this early stage of the project, they were recognizing that if anti-Semitism must be viewed as a kind of totality, it was a negative one—a "synthesis of all reactionary features." To study universality through the minority required understanding the negativity of the contemporary social system.

From the very beginning, the key intuition was that this reactionary totality of anti-Semitism required a new methodological sophistication that did not assume a uniform totality, either in psychology or society. This required moving beyond the mechanical collection of opinion data and the account of the "origins" of political hatred. Finally, it required moving beyond the hyperpsychologization of ideal-typical analysis and beyond a notion of cultural causality toward one of institutional effects and fractional ideologies. Even as the Institute launched into a project with the Frommian keyword "personality" in the title, the specter of Fromm's empirical and theoretical shortcomings was before them, and the fear of failure to turn theoretical synthesis into a workable methodology was legible in the proposal with the words "mere symposium of scholars."

Adorno's ascendency in the Institute came from Horkheimer's belief that philosophy defined interdisciplinary mediation and that he needed a partner in theorizing disciplinarity's role in a constructivist empiricism. As the editor of the book review section of the *Zeitschrift*, Adorno had earned the nickname "Archibald, King of the Hippopotami" because of his formidable powers of intellectual digestion, which went beyond consuming hundreds of pages of disparate materials to distilling the theoretical and disciplinary kernel of the argument at hand—frequently elucidating implicit theses beyond the author's understanding.[46] This synthetic capacity, startling and sometimes irritating on the part of a junior colleague, proved useful for large-scale collaborative work that aimed to be more than a "juxtaposition" of studies. Horkheimer could count on Adorno to push premises to the point where they became arguments or broke on the rocks of disciplinary limits. Though *The Authoritarian Personality* has often been considered a kind of alienated labor—work for hire that dragged Horkheimer and Adorno unwillingly from the grand hotel of abstract speculation—there is significant evidence that the collaborative work gave Adorno the opportunity to play a central role in the Institute, that he enjoyed the work, and that he flourished on the challenge of mediating across the gaps between different disciplinary approaches. A November 1944 letter to Horkheimer, for example, finds Adorno recalling that he "had a lot of fun" meeting with the Berkeley Public Opinion group to develop preliminary questions on the "F-scale," intended to measure respondents' authoritarian, reactionary, and fascist tendencies. His role, he reported, was to "distill a number of questions out of 'Elements of Antisemitism' by means of a kind of translation"—presumably from dialectics to the language of academic psychology.[47] Contrary to legend, not Hektor Rottweiler but Archibald, the King of the Hippopotami, loped through the Sather Gate and presided over the material challenges of *The Authoritarian Personality* and the need to develop subject/object mediation out of the necessary plurality of disciplinary approaches.

In 1945, when much of the survey work for *The Authoritarian Personality* was complete but the analysis was still ongoing, Adorno offered an assessment of the importance of extreme theses for the progression of thought. It took the form of a joke on German culture and Hegelianism, but it also expressed Adorno's attitude toward the notion of extremity and interdisciplinarity in philosophical thinking:

The Echternach dancing procession [three steps forward, two backward] is not the march of the world spirit; limitation and caution are no way to represent the dialectic, which advances by way of extremes rather than qualification, driving thoughts with the utmost consistency to the point where they turn back on themselves. The prudence that restrains us from venturing too far ahead in a thesis is usually just an agent of social control, and so of stupefaction.[48]

The claim that philosophy should make thoughts "turn back on themselves" might seem like an overstatement, but for Adorno it was a lived practice of research as much as philosophy. Horkheimer and Adorno believed a "speculative philosophy" that went to extremes was central to preventing research from reproducing hidden normative assumptions that were morally pleasing but epistemologically and ideologically undigested. Dialectical thought compelled the reversal of subject and object positions. A concrete example of the applied dialectic of negative identity can be found in a letter from October 11, 1945, in which Horkheimer reflects on Adorno's draft typology of different "anti-Semitic personalities," and he asks Adorno specifically to consider the meaning of anti-Semitism in childhood or early adolescence:

> I think, we discussed this point of view in Los Angeles. If in a family with two boys where the respected father or beloved mother complains repeatedly about having been cheated or outsmarted by Jews, one boy sticks to the general doctrines of good behavior and neighborly love advocated in school and home, and the other boy goes out and hits a Jew, who, do you think, acts more neurotically? I admit, the problem is not easy, particularly so because the latter boy does usually not confront the Jew alone.... Our whole educational system functions in a way that any child or adolescent grasps the undertones in the moralistic and religious teachings and clearly experiences their ideological aspect. He understands that the universal values which form a regular part of the instruction in school and church must be professed and exhibited at innumerable occasions and yet be practiced with definite limitations. He is fully aware of the relativity of such values in our society and probably practices the esprit du corps of its members in this respect long before he is able to use the word "society" properly.[49]

This extraordinary document shows what it means to push a theory to its dialectical limit. To common sense, the violent son is the more neurotic one. But the examined theory challenges the underlying notions of authority and ego health. What if, as Horkheimer argues, the parental discussion cultivates social paranoia? Or what if the violent son believes he is acting in a calculated, political way that challenges the preaching of tolerance as ideological? Or what if the nonviolent son refuses to engage in violence not out of a conscious commitment to universality but out of an anxious desire to act in conformance to the norm—and thus in a way that will change whenever norms change? Horkheimer is not advocating violence as a form of mental hygiene but rather pushing a thesis to an extreme to show the breaking point of a hidden premise about healthy ego identity. Though Horkheimer did not see "neuroticism" in every failure of conformity, nor did he think conformity was a panacea, he insisted that the empirical theoretician must be willing to ask such extreme, reciprocal questions. A philosophy that acknowledges a damaged universality learns this reciprocality, learns that a theory never tested through collapse of moralizing assumptions is no theory at all—it merely abuses the technical language of psychoanalysis to defend the investigator's presuppositions, assuming that human essence is always untrammeled. Given the strong tendency for social psychology to devolve into theories of normative adjustment—for second nature to be naturalized—psychoanalytic terminology must truly add something diagnostically powerful rather than serve as camouflage for unexamined sociological premises. If the tension between the modes of inquiry collapses, all epistemological value is lost.

If one considers that Adorno fit Horkheimer's need for a philosophically and methodologically sophisticated interlocutor who understood the importance of the dialectical extreme for achieving methodological clarity, it becomes possible to see the overlapping work on *Dialectic of Enlightenment*, *Minima Moralia*, *Eclipse of Reason*, and *The Authoritarian Personality* in a new light. *Dialectic of Enlightenment* was not the "real" project, from which collaborative empirical research was an annoying if remunerative distraction. Rather, written in the background and alongside a series of applied empirical research projects, *Dialectic of Enlightenment* and *Minima Moralia* were at once refuge, laboratory, and playground: intellectual spaces in which one could freely make mistakes, invert subjectivities, radicalize empirical investigations, and move through the extremes of disciplinary fusion such that the premises and logics of research could be better understood. The motive for this was not intellectual perversity, or even love of abstract speculation, but the belief that urgently needed and practically applicable research required rigorous theorization of subject/object relations that need to challenge the way in which knowledge fused with power. One gets a sense of how closely intertwined practical—even martial—considerations were with speculative questions for the joint working group when one sees memoranda such as the following, which Pollock circulated on May 7, 1943, quoting Horkheimer:

Principles:

Teamwork. (basic assumptions, etc.)

Use short-cuts, avoid duplications whenever possible. . . .

Concentrate on new approaches. Partly experimenting with methods used in other fields, partly doing pioneering work with new ideas.

This is total war. If you want to succeed, you must throw in everything you have got. Will therefore try every approach which seems to hold any promise.

". . . While the ideas of great creative minds in natural sciences are methodically checked, differentiated and given the highest degree of precision in a cognitive process chiefly determined by the logics of the subject matter itself, research into obscure social reactions such as Antisemitism, has not yet been emancipated from the tutelage of practical fears and has been hampered by the postulate of immediate applicability. Many an important path has not yet been pursued because it seemed like a detour. Yet, history of science will teach us, that, what appeared to be a side track more than once proved decisive for the final discovery." (M.H.)[50]

In this bizarre motivational memo, the Kantian language of "tutelage" and the idea of "truth in theory, falsity in practice" suggests the degree to which, for Horkheimer, "immediate applicability" was at once the goal and enemy of enlightenment. Horkheimer and Adorno agreed that to make *Studies in Prejudice* a practical success, they needed to push every prefabricated disciplinary solution until it broke against the totalizing phenomenon of anti-Semitism. This meant that one had to think of the problem as a totality and develop a provisional assemblage of tools to attack the real problem from multiple angles. One also had to take these theoretical tools and ask whether they were universally true, particularly true, or shadows of a weak or neurotic normativity. Doing so required a willingness to follow detours, be impractical, and seek multiple perspectives. It meant cultivating skepticism over and against the positivistic belief that the facts speak for themselves, but also in relation to unexamined idealist and humanist assumptions that people will choose the moral course as soon as "normal" conditions reassert themselves. Having undertaken large-scale data collection with little scientific yield, they could not ignore the basic question of what constituted legitimate science. They also found themselves without a consensus theory of "psychology" but in possession of a plurality of techniques. And between these two questions ran what was, for both Adorno and Horkheimer, an increasingly pressing question: that of the status of subjective reason.

Science, Totality, and Alterity; or, Orthodox Marxism as Interdisciplinary Method

Dialectic of Enlightenment represented a pivotal moment for Adorno's career in multiple ways. It was through this project's thought experiments that he learned to manage the relationship between empirical research and philosophical speculation; and it was in reaction against the book's speculative scenarios that his work became focused on countering languages of logical and subjective identity with theories of negative identity and alterity. So far, we have represented Fromm as a kind of antagonist in this story. If, however, Fromm and *Escape from Freedom* loomed large on Adorno's intellectual horizon at this moment, the dispute over personality was not merely a personality dispute: it was about the role of subjective rationality in socialist and scientific theory. Fromm's success rendered evident the limits of his fundamentally culturalist-assimilationist approach to personality and social change. Fromm's brilliant and readable synthesis of European and American thought, his attempt to unite the logics of psychology and sociology, empirical research and historical-philosophical speculation, realized much of what the Institute had set out to do and had clarified both the assumptions behind and the implications of his generation's project. In particular, his focus on identity exposed the problems with which many of his colleagues were struggling. The idea of the individual as the bearer of rationality was fundamental to the work of social scientists, philosophers, and Marxist political partisans. Each field depended on the idea that the self is an autotelic bearer of rationality, guiding society by unfolding the possibilities of self creator and world creator. And each discipline was, at this moment, facing a crisis over the validity of this subjective rationality—a crisis whose name was not Fromm but fascism. If Fromm became a target at this moment, it was because his near successes and real failures pointed back to the mistakes of the Institute and critical theory and clarified the challenge of designing a rigorous social survey that neither juxtaposed nor collapsed interdisciplinary approaches.

Dialectic of Enlightenment engages profoundly with the theory of science at the place where subjectivity is identified with data and where scientific validity is defined purely through the category of utility. Effectively crystallizing the fear of these two émigré scientists engaged in wartime research is the assertion in the second excursus that "the perception that is supposed to prove the theory is typically reduced to an electrical signal registered as data on the experimental apparatus. Its nonappearance is generally of no practical consequence, for it destroys no more than a theory—or at most, the career of the responsible research assistant."[51] Science becomes meaningless when researchers ask only simple questions, producing preschematized data. But because careers and grants, institutional and personal survival are at stake, the forced equation of data collection with scientific objectivity drastically narrowed the scope of every question. In the natural sciences, where the utility of the project is technical in nature, this is less of a problem: if "the bridge collapses, the crop fails, the medicine causes illness," social utility will intervene to save scientism from itself. However, if the question is of broad human consequence—having to do with combating domination, exploitation, or suffering—there is a powerful systemic bias toward "useful" and "measurable" research uncomplicated by concepts or analyses. Data-driven research is indeed driven by the economic, psychological, and social needs of the research *system*. This systematicity fosters aversion to any subject/object model that does not serve the data-capital nexus, anything that requires thought to be produced or consumed.[52]

The idea that scientific systematicity degrades the ability of even intelligent subjects to understand the world in which they live is advanced in the book's opening passages, which quote Francis Bacon's *New Organon*, the most important Renaissance treatise on the scientific method. According to Bacon, modern knowledge naturally falls into two categories: virile, strong, and productive knowledge—the stuff that "makes man lord"; and the "useless" knowledge of speculation, which is the "coquette of the mind" and which, in Bacon's terms, delivers a kind of whorish pleasure that is fleeting, ephemeral, enslaving, and lustful.[53] Bacon's choice of words was not incidental. To render substantive reason hysterical, to describe speculation on the human condition as whorish, was, as Horkheimer pointed out in the "End of Reason," an attempt by the spokesman for the new subjective rationalism of the Renaissance and the bourgeoisie to counteract the aristocratic (ideological but real) investment in substantive rationalism. There was a reason that Lord Bacon was the lead prosecutor against Thomas More, the utopian. Classicism does not discover a natural harmony; rather, it channels emotion away from substantive social concerns. By castigating speculation as feminine and trivial, Bacon imposed a division of labor upon research that defined a bourgeois, rational identity in terms of its ability to bracket awareness of totality. To think socially is to be a whore and to violate the classical manly ideal of reasoned virtue.

Horkheimer and Adorno needed to critique the ideological character and estrange the truisms of bourgeois science as they engaged in it. Feeling themselves both subjects in the American research system and subject *to* it, they considered the anti-Semitism project equivalent to a "total war" that must be won. Adorno wrote to his parents in 1943 that he hoped his research might "contribute to . . . something more than idle talk . . . [and be] a serious counteraction."[54] The reflections on Bacon were thus written by thinkers neither sneering aloofly at research nor puffing themselves up with thoughts of Baconian "virility" but trying to contemplate the whole of the system in which they were enmeshed. What if, they asked, advances in research on social science and fine-tuning of the wartime economy could absolutely transform the world, as Bacon contemplated, by erecting utility as a new God? But what if these advances did so in a way Bacon never contemplated? What if science, by becoming social science and taking humans as its object, actually succeeded in stripping people of the spontaneity and freedom they had gained in overturning the "old idols"? One could put this question in Weberian-Simmelian terms: What happens if the spirit of science, aimed at perfecting the means of transforming nature, undermines all sense of human ends to the point where the chain of extended ends snaps and the thinking subject can no longer uphold the Enlightenment ideal of attaching the most useful means to humane ends? Or one could put it in Hegelian terms: What happens if objective spirit—the subject of history—succeeds first in liberating itself, uniting itself with a system of domination, and then proceeds to turn itself into an object, effectively reversing the subject/object dialectic? The idea of unintentional reversal of Enlightenment and of the master/slave dialectic is at the center of the book: it considers the way systems of knowledge in wartime could lead to self-destruction insofar as systems produce and coerce identities. All weapons of warfare—psychological tools as surely as weapons of steel—could be turned on their developers. Equally, the "weaponization," masculinization, deemotionalization of knowledge already implied a reification of the difference between means and ends, between qualitative and quantitative reasoning, between the subject controlling the object and a new totality of subjectless subject/objects.

There are both historical and theoretical reasons why Horkheimer and Adorno developed these arguments in the mid-1940s as an extension of their critique of Fromm. At its core, *Dialectic of Enlightenment* called attention to the contradictory claim of modern science to stand on both sides of the subjectivity concept. A science that claimed to be objective (and therefore free from subjective bias) and to be expressive of the subject (insofar as it fulfilled Renaissance or Enlightenment potentialities of subjective knowledge) was ideological in its claims to always serve humanity and advance the cause of the subject. Because Adorno and Horkheimer came to believe that socialist as well as liberal claims to progress created blind spots, they believed that all such moralisms in service of power needed to be challenged by an *Echternach* hermeneutic of non-identity, by a reversal of the subject/object terms of analysis.

Nothing could have provoked this critique more forcefully than Fromm's identity concept and its underlying theory of interdisciplinary science. Its mode was disciplinary fusion: drawing on Pragmatism and existentialism, the choice of the word "identity" reflected a decade of Frommian assertions that personality structure determined social structures, and it did so in a way that cast new light on the philosophical meaning of a word that had long been naïvely shared between positivist and Hegelian-Marxian concepts of science. Prior to Fromm, "identity" was, for the social sciences, a purely objective term, but one that had been used in different ways by positivists, systematic social scientists, and Hegelian-Marxists.

First, identity within the positivist tradition stood for a notion of closure and certainty, of unambiguous facts, objective data, and singular frames of reference. One had positive *idem*-identity whenever one eliminated ambiguity. According to Bertrand Russell's famous example, the phrase "morning star" could not logically mean the same thing as "evening star" because meaningful reference required identity; philosophy triumphed when it disentangled the sense of the words from their reference until one was speaking about a singular identical thing—the planet Venus.[55] Logical positivism saw identity as an ideal to be achieved through the removal of the subjective element of expression and language's potential for irrationality.

Second, identity in the social science traditions of economics and sociology stood for a different kind of epistemic closure, the exhaustive analysis of systems. In the analysis of capitalism, "identity" was a system and accounting identity, encapsulating the proposition that, in relation to totality, production needed to equal consumption and that the sum of money in circulation needed to equal the sum total of surplus labor value.

Third, Marx inherited the social-systemic notion of identity but added to it a Hegelian notion of perspective-shifting or historicist non-identity. Two sides of an equation meant two perspectives and a reciprocal analysis of domination. Drawing on an objective sense of the historically non-identical, the Hegelian-Marxist could cite *Capital*'s critique of the fetishism of commodities or its critique of bourgeois economic theory, which took as foundational the "identity of labor in general with wage labor." Such false identities required historical analysis. The Hegelian-Marxist critique of identity attacked the ahistorical slippage in conceptual usages, unearthing an objective dialectic of appearance and reality. Doing so moved theory toward recognizing that what one grasped first as a simple, natural identity was a complex, historical one. A fetishization of value was required, Marx argued, to make the "produced means of production" appear equivalent to money capital, when in fact historical changes in the mode of labor created the category of wage labor that now stood in for the whole and was denominated in money form.[56] Labor appeared identical to money but was non-identical.

Fromm's subjective use of the otherwise objective concept of identity attempted to create interdisciplinarity through a redefinition of social subjectivity. This was in keeping with Fromm's program to remake social psychology into a foundational element of Marxist social science alongside political economy. Identity was the key concept to invoke because it had long been used, in the social-scientific and Marxist-Hegelian senses, as a tool for broadening the scope of a narrow economism. The pursuit of a Marxist-Kantian universalism, invoked by Horkheimer in his inaugural address, was itself rooted in a program of scientific inquiry into the meaning of universalism and logical identity. This program, which we discussed in relation to Simmel, had its origin not just in Lukács's epochal 1923 *History and Class Consciousness* but in the intra-Marxist debates that led up to and informed it. Indeed, the struggle over identity within the Frankfurt circle was a struggle over the meaning of "orthodox Marxism"—a struggle initiated by Lukács's startling assertion that Marxism as a positive, economic science had mutilated Marx's concept of knowledge, science, and human subjectivity and that the title of "orthodoxy" would belong to the theory that could restore Marx's original vision.[57] Fromm, seeing himself contributing to a debate that had long been under way, sought to fold the debates about objective identity into his concept of positive identity.

The pursuit of this revisionist "orthodoxy" as an argument about the historical nature of logic must itself be understood historically. It emerged from debates about the rationality, systems identity, and scientific nature of Marxism that had animated Western Marxism around World War I. These discussions, articulated at a moment when social democracy and militant Communism were advancing through the nation-states of Europe, explored how much concepts of subjectivity and humanism mattered to Marxian theory. A crucial contribution to this debate, published in 1907, was Otto Bauer's *The Nationalities Question in Social Democracy*, which offered a theory of national identity and its relation to systems identity. Bauer, the most talented student of Carl Grünberg, the Institute's first director, argued for the notion of emergent, lawful national communities that embodied a balance between Kantian and Marxist universalism. Though he believed in the rising power of an international vanguard workers' party, Bauer questioned the economistic assumption that the tendential decline in the rate of profit would force the end of capitalism, and he thought it politically necessary for socialists to theorize the future of the nation-state. In an anticipation of Keynesian economics, he suggested that the state was not *necessarily* the enemy of the worker but could, through taxation, potentially save itself and the market economy by redistributionist and public works policies. This functionalist, scientific concern with the national economy had a psychological side, in that workers who identified with the nation should not be expected to think they had "nothing to lose but their chains." Everyone feared loss, and socialists needed to theorize it. Bauer thus made the Kantian-phenomenological argument, echoed in Benedict Anderson's *Imagined Communities*, that workers did not see themselves first as "workers of the world": they imagined political self-understanding, emotional belonging, and worldly community first by belonging to a family, followed by a cultural group, and by extrapolation, a nation.[58] Ethno-national particularity first defined one's reflective sense of self and modes of valuation, essence, ownness, and belonging. In a multiethnic empire such as that of the Habsburgs, the dominant national culture—Germanness—served as the first tutor of who one universally was and of what one considered valuable. A socialism that could be taken seriously, Bauer argued, had to recognize that universalism was always an abstraction and a negation away from this first perceived sense of essence:

The curious phenomenon of national valuation [*Wertung*]—the fact that we regard anything German as good, regardless of what it is, and call anything that is good "German" in order to praise it—arises from the causal linkage of the individual member of a people with his nation. Because the individual is the child of his nation, its product, all the specific characteristics of his mother nation appear to him as good; they are, after all, his own. For this reason, he is capable of adopting anything that conflicts with this particularity only by overcoming a powerful feeling of reluctance; he must reinvent himself, transform himself, if he wishes to move beyond the boundaries of his own national particularity.

However, man is not only a knowing being [*erkennendes Wesen*], one who becomes conscious of the causal link between himself and the nation, but above all a being of will and of action who sets himself goals and selects the means of achieving these goals. This fact gives rise to another form of valuation, which comes into conflict with national valuation . . . [the fact that] our reason attributes value to a means according to its utility. . . . This is the form of valuation—arising from rational choice of a means of realizing a particular end and the rational choice of a goal as the means of realizing the supreme end, the moral idea [*des Sittlichen Ideales*]—that constitutes the form of evaluation employed by *rationalism*.[59]

Culturally relativist and hermeneutically immanentist, Bauer nonetheless viewed the rootedness that Fromm called "an identity" as the opposite of true autonomy and knowledge. Universalism as the gradual negation of particularity spoke to how the universalisms of the nineteenth century were confounded by the demands of particularity. Such passages also attested to the ways in which a Kantian-Marxian thought sought to reassert universality in the cultural sphere, imagining how, at a practical and everyday level, utility might lead outward and upward from a more primary, national-cultural model of affiliation. Universality was not a given but something achieved, which thus had to be approached in negative terms and with awareness of the objective constitution of the collective.

The Frankfurt theorists' notion of Marxian universalism inherited not only Bauer's exploration of national non-identity but also Rosa Luxemburg's analysis of the non-identity of the state with the common good. Like Bauer, Luxemburg addressed the relation between nation and state in socialism, but she emphasized questions of authority and rationality. An attentive student of Weber, she applied his concept of a "bureaucratic rationality" (as opposed to "charismatic," "value," or "scientific" rationality) to a logic of perpetuation. Arguing that a revolution tied to nationalism tended toward absolutism, she speculated that Bolshevism's identification with state bureaucracy had corrupted the revolutionary project in a fashion parallel to German nationalism. Her insistence that socialism, nationalism, and the state were not to be equated with one another was recognized as prophetic after her murder in 1919. As the Institute analyzed the Soviet Union as a variant of state monopoly capitalism, the lesson to socialist theory became that of refusing to allow emancipation to be equated with national, state, or bureaucratic systems that claimed to represent the totality and that instead blotted out the individual workers' access to the universal and turned reason to unreason.[60]

Lukács's *History and Class Consciousness*, drawing on and criticizing *both* Bauer and Luxemburg, advanced a vocabulary of subjective and objective consciousness aimed at revising Marxism to consolidate its theory of subjectivity, its notion of autonomy, and its concept of systems identity and disciplinarity. A student of Weber and Simmel, Lukács viewed "economy" broadly, as the overall historical relation between notions of spirit, community, and selfhood. He argued that neither science nor economics was a natural way of seeing the world; these disciplines were outgrowths of bourgeois domination. Lukács thereby redefined heterodoxy as the tendency—

which he detected in Luxemburg and Bauer, Karl Kautsky and the Russian Machians—to have a narrow concept of reason and of subjectivity, one rooted in self-enclosed logics of the state and the positivistic fetishization of science. While trying to uphold Lenin's concept of vanguardism, Lukács embraced an expansive notion of a Hegelian-Marxian divided selfhood that still today informs the reading of Marx. Approaching questions of identity and consciousness as part of the social production of totality, Lukács argued that "orthodox Marxism" should approach the praxis of the sciences as Marx had material production, theorizing how ideas emerged as part of the lived practice of labor, how the highest levels of production related to everyday praxis. Consciousness needed to be interpreted in terms of its distortion by the productive system, and socialism needed a theory of true and false consciousness. In slogan form, this meant socialism should seek to understand the "identical subject/object of history" and to theorize the "identity of theory and praxis" out of the current false state of affairs. The vocabulary that Lukács discovered through his reading of the "young" Marx—terms such as "alienation," "reification," "second nature," "divided" or "false consciousness," "fetishization," "totality"—furnished a catalog of transformative keywords that brought out the dual subjective and objective nature of economic vocabulary. Effectively, the non-identity that Lukács made visible required the economics of Marxism to address all the other disciplines in their non-identity to each other and to human autonomy. If one properly understood Marx, argued Lukács, then coerced identity equations—such as the definition of "labor as wage labor"—could be shown to be not only ahistorical but *unscientific* in nature. Positivist economics revealed the ideological character of narrow disciplinary thinking and thereby showed how much science had adopted a form of false consciousness that it had imposed on the rest of the world.

Fromm's redefinition of subjective "identity" invoked this entire tradition in a most peculiar way. Seeking to make social psychology as important to Marxism as political economy had long been, and redefining identity not just in the terms of systematic Marxism but those of nationalism and disciplinarity, Fromm saw himself as drawing on Lukács's subjective and interdisciplinary turn. Identity was a kind of Renaissance totality in selfhood. By the early 1940s, however, historical events had opened a split already present within Lukács's original concept of an "orthodox Marxism." Lukács, out of both personal and theoretical necessity, had renounced *History and Class Consciousness*, aligning himself with the Stalinist conception of the Party. In doing so, he had embraced the notion that the true form of consciousness was strictly objective, with no basis in the consciousness of actual workers who suffered from necessarily false consciousness. But since workers were the identical subject/object of history—the ones in direct relation to the concrete material of production—theory needed to break away from the bourgeois sciences and articulate a class consciousness objectively and scientifically from the position of labor. *History and Class Consciousness*'s theory of science—its argument that the bourgeois sciences individually and as a whole needed to be subjected to a critique that would include the categories of autonomy and subjectivity from a universalist position—was effectively dropped, submerged under Lukács's new insistence that Marx's *Capital* contained a complete theory for determining objective class consciousness. *History and Class Consciousness*'s theories of consciousness remained, nonetheless, of crucial importance for younger Hegelian-Marxists. The question was whether to emphasize the political totality suggested by Lukács's idea of the "subject/object of history" or whether to pursue the epistemological insight inherent in the non-identities of both self and science.

Dialectic of Enlightenment, aware that Lukács's innovative criticisms were no longer acceptable under Stalinism, sought to salvage the connected notions of disciplinarity, divided selfhood, and logical non-identity. Part of the quarrel between Fromm and Adorno in the 1930s came from Adorno's insistence that the critique of fascism required one to reject positivity and totality and to embrace immanent critique. Fromm was not interested in the idea of immanent critique; his decision to place personality structures at the center of social causality, though interdisciplinarily informed, was an attempt to understand false consciousness without a concept of subject/object non-identity. Instead, Fromm had embraced a notion of disciplinary fusion in which psychology (wedded to a Pragmatist notion of culture) had created the pan-causal totality of subjective identity. Where Lukács came to denounce psychological and sociological ideas as irrational distractions from the pursuit of social objectivity, Fromm redefined identity and disciplinarity as a kind of totality that gave no purchase for the analysis of social objectivity other than as the materialist input to social psychology. *Dialectic of Enlightenment*'s concept of science insists, to the contrary, that if one cannot develop an immanent critique of false consciousness and its negative relation to universality, one no longer has a critical theory. Wanting to preserve Lukács's insistence that social consciousness within an antagonistic society is necessarily false, Adorno and Horkheimer also refused both the claim that the consciousness of the oppressed was meaningless and the claim that the consciousness of the liberated epitomized social harmony. Beginning with the Veblen essay, Adorno argued that by diving into the contradictions within the object, critical theory could develop an interdisciplinary notion of critique and an analysis of subjective alienation capable of transforming the contradictions of the most wretched kitsch into an insight into the alienated state of humanity. This movement out of the immanence of false consciousness promised to reground life lived among the contradictory value spheres of modernity. Adorno and Horkheimer saw Fromm's concept of identity as a sleight of hand, an attempt to give the appearance of critical theory fulfilling its purpose, that of analyzing fascism as an intensification of bourgeois false consciousness.

Fromm's theoretical concept exposed problems not just in Lukács's approach but in Horkheimer and Adorno's own. Fromm's method of disciplinary fusion and his elision of the contradictions of objective identity into a subjective identity pointed to the need for a better concept of a universal science and its subconcepts: disciplinarity, subjectivity, psycho-social mediation, and logic. A central passage in *History of Class Consciousness* suggests why the language of subjective identity was the overdetermined intersection of logical, systems, and subjective identity. In a passage describing how the non-identical spheres of economic activity determine and mediate the fetishization and reification of thought, Lukács argued how the divided objectivity of social domination draws a veil over historical consciousness:

> The category of totality does not reduce its various elements to an undifferentiated uniformity, an identity. The apparent independence and autonomy which they possess in the capitalist system of production is an illusion only insofar as they are involved in a dynamic dialectical relationship with one another and can be thought of as the dynamic dialectical aspects of an equally dynamic and dialectical whole. "The result we arrive at," says Marx, "is not that production, distribution, exchange and consumption are identical, but that they are all members of one totality, different aspects of a unit. . . . Thus a definite form of production determines definite forms of consumption, distribution and exchange as well as *definite relations between these different elements*. . . . A mutual interaction takes place between these various elements. This is the case with every organic body." But even the category of interaction requires inspection. If by interaction we mean just the reciprocal causal impact of two otherwise unchangeable objects on each other, we shall not have come an inch nearer to an understanding of society. . . . [Theory] must go further in its relation to the whole: for this relation determines

the objective form of every object of cognition. Every substantial change that is of concern to knowledge manifests itself as a change in relation to the whole and through this as a change in the form of objectivity itself. Marx has formulated this idea in countless places. I shall cite only one of the best-known passages: "A Negro is a Negro. He only becomes a slave in certain circumstances. A cotton-spinning jenny is a machine for spinning cotton. Only in certain circumstances does it become capital. Torn from those circumstances it is no more capital than gold is money or sugar the price of sugar." Thus the objective forms of all social phenomena change constantly in the course of their ceaseless dialectical interactions with each other. The intelligibility of objects develops in proportion as we grasp their function in the totality to which they belong. This is why only the dialectical conception of totality can enable us to understand reality as a social process. For only this conception dissolves the fetishistic forms necessarily produced by the capitalist mode of production and enables us to see them as mere illusions which are not less illusory for being seen to be necessary. These unmediated concepts, these "laws" sprout just as inevitably from the soil of capitalism and veil the real relations between objects.[61]

This passage, one of many in which Lukács approaches and then retreats from immanent critique, revolves around Marx's concept of non-identity, applied first to sectors of the economy; then to the distorted perception of "intelligible objects" as isolated, self-identical entities; and finally to the "laws" of the social sciences. Insisting that each sphere of capital production—indeed each "intelligible object"—must be analyzed as mediated through the totality, Lukács suggests that the unity of capitalism embeds itself within the disunity of the subject and that the divisions of the subject create a fragmentary field of knowledge. Because each subject mediates the overall social metabolism in its own particularity by incorporating the formalism of reason dictated by the fetishization of commodities into its own consciousness, the bourgeois structure of mental and material life reproduces itself in everyday consciousness as well as in the abstraction process of labor. Consciousness is stripped of its social and historical ground. Individuals are trained instead to see things as possessing a transcendent, timeless value, while viewing the living labor of those dominated as a mere resource for the accumulation of capital. The fetishization of commodities and the division of labor thereby create necessary false consciousness.

Lukács's brilliant Hegelian Marxism works very well as long as one does not try to put its totality concept to work as a tool for moving from false consciousness to true. If one attempts, as the Frankfurt School theorists of the 1930s and 1940s did, to engage in epistemological reciprocality and to theorize false consciousness from the position of weakness, one runs into difficulty. The mention of slavery here is a wound, a marker of negative identity. Immanent critique becomes a refuge for a subject hemmed in by domination and false consciousness who cannot otherwise analyze the untruth in his or her situation. Where Marx worked immanently out of the political economy of David Ricardo and Adam Smith, Lukács's theories were an exercise in abstract negation: one had to theorize consciousness from the position of the strong and universal subject who could explain away irrationality as an illusion. Fromm's belief that the Renaissance Man had declined—fallen out of the plenitude of identity—pointed toward a concept of alienated selfhood, but it did so at the price of romanticizing one historical period of early capitalism and defining negativity in terms of this plenitude. Fromm, needing to theorize totality as something to which everyone had access, drew on the positivist and social-scientific concept of identity without addressing the Hegelian notion of non-identity. This exposed Lukács's sacrifice of the Simmelian-Kantian notion of autonomy. By using identity as a second version of the totality concept and rendering it subjective, Fromm plausibly forged a method to interpret the pathologies of daily consciousness as an extension of the decline from the universally capable subject; however, it had all the problems inherited from the Pragmatist theory of assimilation. If one rereads the Lukács passage in terms of "identity" in Fromm's sense of the word, it becomes a nonsense theory of the self as well as the disciplines. The self, completely assimilated to the world, has a consciousness that reflects the world perfectly yet irrationally. This concept of the self offers no basis for criticism because it sees no position outside the self and its totality, and *this* violates the principle of disciplinary non-identity that had been so important to Lukács's concept of a universal science. Adorno and Horkheimer, reacting to the substitution of psychology for economics as a master science of interpreting totality, decided to salvage the concept of a science of negative universality by subjecting the notion of identity to a critique in all its forms: disciplinary, social-systematic, logical, epistemological, subjective, and objective. They developed Lukács's submerged concept of subjectivity in order to save his notion of science. Critical theory's goal, then, became that of developing a theory of non-identity—an immanent critique of subject and object that could work backward as well as forward, moving from distorted consciousness (here, that of the slave) and the "intelligible objects" of production, through the division of labor and the social totality of value spheres, to the systems of domination. Here is where the logic of non-identity militates against implied ontologies.

The problem that Horkheimer and Adorno discovered was that Fromm's concept of Renaissance science exposed flaws in their own understanding of Kant and Idealism. The concept of Enlightenment and the Kantian conception of subjective reason itself was one-sided and blind in the way Adorno had stumbled over in "On Jazz" and confronted in his exposition of Simmel. Though addressed to a world of changing knowledge, the theory of enlightened subjectivity presumed that any subject who had the knowledge to liberate herself and know the world would naturally do so. Such a theory required an account of how the reification of consciousness under capitalism that occurred in bourgeois society more generally related to the attempt in bourgeois science to see "intelligible" objects or subjects against the backdrop of their lived totality. The Simmelian concept of estranged epistemology, balanced against the Kantian notion of autonomy, offered the first frame of reference for critical theory. But what if Horkheimer and Adorno's own concept of science had deluded itself into thinking that it alone had the tools to see truly? Fromm's embrace of identitarian self-knowing exposed Lukács's own strange historicization of the classical age of Idealism and its relation to the distortions of consciousness. For Lukács, when Hegel had used the phrase *das zerissene Bewußtsein* (torn consciousness) or had spoken of the *absolute Zerissenheit* (absolute torn-asunderness) of the modern age, he was speaking about the divided subject of capitalism, the ways in which capitalism, in order to produce commodities, requires the opposition of subject and object. Lukács saw bourgeois consciousness not only as reified but as divided against itself: theory was divorced from practice, the individual alienated from the whole. Crucially symptomatic of this state was the division of science into disciplines:

The specialization of skills leads to the destruction of every image of the whole. And as, despite this, the need to grasp the whole—at least cognitively—cannot die out, we find that science ... based on specialization and thus caught up in the same immediacy is criticized for having *torn the real world into shreds* and having lost its vision of the whole. ... The more intricate a modern system of science becomes, and the better it understands itself methodologically, the more resolutely it will turn its back on the ontological problems of its own sphere of influence and eliminate them from the realm where it has achieved some insight.[62]

Taking as his example the degeneration of political economy into a system of positive and conflicted economic laws aloof from all human suffering, Lukács argued that disciplines emerged out of an interest rooted in human ontology and degenerated into reified and abstracted laws that served only to fragment the image of the whole subject. His answer in 1923 was to turn the dialectical analysis of totality, reification, fetishization, and positivity toward reassembling not just reason but the dividedness of subjectivity and consciousness. If reason was to restore the ability to reason, the partial truths of bourgeois science must be reunited through a dialectical method of interdisciplinarity that restored the unity of theory and praxis. Horkheimer and Adorno subscribed to this vision of interdisciplinary totality and insisted on asking why Lukács had abandoned it and whether he was correct in arguing that Kant, Hegel, and Marx lived in a golden age where the "tornness" of the world was somehow still visible. Or was it possible that even Kant and Marx, in their divisions of science and the self, were contributing to the division of the self, the division of labor, and the positivistic erosion of social reflection?

While *Dialectic of Enlightenment* shows its debt to Lukács as a scientist and theorist of identity and non-identity, it attempts to solve the Frommian-Lukácsian problem of the golden age by pursuing the problem of system identity into the concept of subjective and objective reason. Lukács's relation to Kant and German Idealism more generally—though it never brought him into conflict with the Soviet authorities—was at least as complex as his struggle with more politicized orthodoxies. Idealism represented, for Lukács, a moment when ideas came together and when they fell apart. Kant was a hero for Lukács in that he articulated a notion of critical reason without which there could have been no Marxian dialectic; but Kant was, in his contradictions, the thinker who systematized and imported into science a real social rift within the subject—a subject divided between value and form, theory and praxis, subjective understanding and objective reason. Lukács's sensitivity to these divisions and their philosophical articulation in the bourgeois era made him one of the greatest expositors not just of Idealism but of the genre and subjectivities of the bourgeois novel. Yet, in no small sense, his thought remained trapped in the world of philosophical Idealism and its identities. In Lukács's vision of history, Kant and his era marked the moment at which the subject had become irrevocably split; yet the period of bourgeois realism in the novel, the first half of the nineteenth century, was depicted (as was his earlier vision of the unalienated world of the classical epic) in the same light as Fromm's Renaissance: as a period in which true subjectivity was still legible. Adorno, a committed modernist, disagreed with Lukács's increasingly classicist (and Stalinist) aesthetic choices and considered Lukács's historical myth making to be as problematic as Fromm's. However, Lukács's approach to critiquing and yet preserving Kant was crucial. Lukács saw Marx as being made possible only by a Kantian analysis of individual autonomy. An Idealist analysis of subjective rationality is a prerequisite for understanding how systematic unities of capitalist production relied on the creative powers of constitutive subjectivity; it was also crucial for developing a science of the social constitution of reality.

Where Lukács believed that objective rationality was still obtainable once theory pierced the veil of commodity fetishism, and where Fromm saw Renaissance scientific community as a model, *Dialectic of Enlightenment* argued that even theoretically informed subjects have great difficulty in picking up the tools of reason to see beyond pragmatic reason. This is not just because reason has been transformed by notions of survival and domination borrowed from the marketplace but also because the fear of being dominated has always driven scientific activity. The true totality theorizes knowledge as a relation of non-identity and considers that for a subject to know itself and its world, it must consider knowledge in terms of the possibility that the subject can become object at any time, that individual groups of people can become "problems" that need to be solved quickly or disposed of immediately:

> The [system of science-world identity] that most accords with the concept of Enlightenment is that which most efficiently dispenses with problems such that the mastery of nature can continue uninterrupted. Its principles are those of self-preservation; and if one is not emancipated [*unmündig*], survival is in doubt. The subject of Enlightenment has always been the bourgeois subject, unfolding from slave owner, entrepreneur, administrator. The concept of reason itself is vexed by the real contradictions created by these layered forms of subjectivity; reason stands for both self-possession and difficulty within the very concept of reason—difficulties and contradictions that can only be papered over by the seemingly clear-eyed judgment of the [Enlightenment's civilizational power] in the West.[63]

A "layered subjectivity" carries the history of domination within itself as a set of potential subjective identities with the economic-material system. The metaphor suggests accumulated and conflicting identities without suggesting originary wholeness. The fear of becoming a victim, just like the belief that history is on one's side, can sponsor a variety of actions against others that define social roles. This analysis of intersubjectivity, more psychological than Lukács's and more materialist than Nietzsche's, draws on both thinkers to create a model of the imposition of role identity through systematic domination and fear. Bourgeois subjectivity is figured here as a kind of class identity that forms a second nature and therefore a consciousness that serves the needs of the economic system. The bourgeois character type prides itself on favoring means over ends, views survival and domination as definitive, and is indifferent to suffering outside the particular sphere it defines as universal.

To speak of the layered self was to speak of non-identity, a model of subjective rationality and disciplinarity that did not assume a moment of wholeness, purity, or foundational unity. Non-identity is the rule incorporated into the measure of all things. The model of measuring science against the concept of negative autonomy and wounded or weak subjectivity that had been developed in relation to Lukács's teacher, Simmel, came into focus as a way to retheorize the relation between the Kantian principle of a science of autonomy and the non-identities of disciplinarity. Instead of reaching toward an abstract idealism untainted by negative identity, Adorno and Horkheimer sought to purge the concept of science of its myths of subjectlessness and the idea of the unified or singular object. Radicalizing Kantian subjectivity, they sought to think through the notion of the layered subject as a model of both autonomy and heteronomy. In so doing, they were able to recover a Marxian dialectic that had previously been effaced.

Claiming Orthodoxy

Lukács's *History and Class Consciousness* finished what Kantian Marxism had started. Declaring "orthodox Marxism" Hegelian, interdisciplinary, scientific, and aimed at restoring the actuality of universal autonomy, it pushed aside narrow notions of methodology, specialization, static identities, and reified concepts and asserted that a universal Marxism was epistemological, concerned with knowledge as something both independent from and inside the division of labor. Lukács's Kantian Enlightenment anticipated Fromm's concept of identity—its invocation of a Renaissance golden age in which individual creativity and autonomy seemed to drive the division of labor rather than the other way around. But both visions were humanist to the point of being borderline restorationist, drawing on the notion that subjectivity and knowledge were once whole, before being lacerated, torn asunder, divided into positive and negative freedoms. *Dialectic of Enlightenment* wished to reclaim Lukács's "orthodox Marxism" from Stalinism. But to do so, it had to attack not just the golden age but the sleight of hand through which it was born: the notion that subjectivity was positive before it was negative; the idea that subjective identity preceded the division of labor; the idea that something, in order to be wounded, must have originally been whole, and that this inference of wholeness could serve as the basis for a science of autonomy. A true Marxian orthodoxy would not reify reason but see it as emerging from the division of labor, the development of human productive powers, and the exchange of human powers with those of nature; and it would critique the notion of a golden age as a fetish of an inadequately theorized concept of subjectivity and disciplinarity, idealism and materialism.

Dialectic of Enlightenment's opening chapter deals with questions of narrative and sacrifice in order to address how individuality is an inscription of class privilege and the domination of the global over the local, of second nature over first. By extending Fromm's search for wholeness to and beyond one of the earliest-known texts, the Odysseus chapter pushes aside the Renaissance community of understanding as surely as it does Lukács's vision of an unalienated epic subjectivity. If the Homeric poems are driven by the subordination of ends to means and create as their by-product an epic narrative that can be instrumentalized for the defense of the self or for its liquidation into the collective, notions of a narrative return to a past origin are ideological in nature and must be negated. If, however, Odysseus appears as the "first bourgeois subject" and thus the first divided subject, then the mythical quality of all narratives that begin with plenitude is exposed, and theory can begin to analyze the exchange between knowledge and domination rather than assert their eternal opposition. The reading of Odysseus shows that there is no moment prior to the separation of subject and object, of subjectivity from domination, or domination from the division of labor. This in turn challenges the notion that *any* form of knowing—even epic subjectivity—can be exempted from the charge of false consciousness. Fromm's golden age was rolled back to the beginning of the distinction of myth from history.

To lay claim to orthodox Marxism, however, Adorno and Horkheimer had to effect a second reversal. They had to turn the myth of reconciled, holistic, positive subjectivity into a critical analysis of a divided subject and object. This they did by pushing the origin of Enlightenment back to the origin of identity and pushing the Enlightenment concept of subjective Idealism and disciplinarity forward to Hollywood. False consciousness can be made self-critical by negating disciplinary autonomy, exaggerating existing social tendencies, and imagining functional fusions of separate ontic realms. *Dialectic of Enlightenment*'s exploration of the "hidden affinity" between the philosophies of Immanuel Kant and the Marquis de Sade thus delves into the reification problem posed by the Veblen essay, not in terms of culture but in terms of the Simmelian-Lukácsian notion of alienation. It asks whether, if one defines Enlightenment as the right to individual reason, it is still possible to find a "natural" limit to the use of reason, or whether the principles of domination, control, and the covert appeal of barbarism will overwhelm any individual mandate to autonomy. "The Culture Industry" chapter ties together the Odysseus and Kant/Sade considerations of Enlightenment's non-identity by asking whether the pleasure principle can drive systems of objective reason and domination. The answer is that the reciprocal relation between the entertainment industry and a consumerist economy can fuel economic demand forward into almost endless psychological frontiers of created needs and distractions from the burdens of self-governance or self-reflection. The final chapter, "Theses on Antisemitism: Limits of Enlightenment," addresses the "functional" role of racism and alterity in the psychic economy of the surplus, the way in which images of hatred and desire can create a primacy of politics and subjective identity that can suspend economic concerns and notions of objective rationality. The question that hangs over the book is whether these aspects of subjective identity—narrativity, rationality, psychology, distraction, alterity—constitute the foundation for a permanent subordination of reason to the objective needs of the capital system.

Dialectic of Enlightenment continues in the tradition set by Lukács's *zerissenes Bewußtsein* but does not, as Lukács did, assume that objective reason is untouched by the subjective turn.[64] Rather, the legacies of Kant and Marx are equally at stake. Lukács, like Tillich and Fromm, hoped that a residual existential, ontological, teleological, or social awareness might preserve critical social reason. Horkheimer and Adorno believed that a Marxism dependent on an Enlightenment Idealism it could not justify must find another way. F. H. Bradley's aphorism that "where everything is bad, it must be good to know the worst" was placed at the head of part 2 of *Minima Moralia* (1945) for a good reason. Like the Idealist Bradley,

Horkheimer and Adorno sought to use subjective Idealism to "know the worst," pushing every speculative thesis to its ultimate point and then stepping back, creating a fusion of logical, systemic, and class identity that presented a negative version of a Kantian regulative ideal. *Dialectic of Enlightenment* wished to put an end to the historical referentiality of all classicist harmonies or scientific laws of equilibrium, speculating freely about utopia and disaster without Romantic illusions of past wholeness. Such blank checks written against reality would ultimately come due when reason or science called substantive morality into question. In an age of fascism, theory could not afford to hope that *is* could be transformed into *ought*, that spontaneity would resist conformity, or that one could access some classical harmony that would restore reason.

The interpretation of Kant in terms of Sade is illuminating for understanding the self-inoculation of reason that Horkheimer and Adorno wished to perform. Though Kantians may have good reason to complain of the unfairness of reading Kant in terms of Sade, the warrant for this bit of dialectical criticism follows the same Hegelian logic by which alterity emerges as a consequence of epistemological negation: the theory of individual rights (and thus of human rights) must be capable of thinking its logical other, an absolute individual right to domination. Because Sade and Kant had a common starting point—in the theory of rights, freedoms, and the limits of action—their core positions, as opposite, extreme approaches toward the notion of rational duty, are required to make sense of one another. If Kant imagined individual emancipation to transcend all social and class boundaries, Sade imagined a world in which individuals began unbounded by any intragroup shame or moral feelings. There thus exists an affinity between Sade's idea of "knowledge without the guidance of another person" and the impersonality of the Kantian moral imperative of duty performed "purely for its own sake."[65] When "reason fails to scrutinize its relation to power and domination,"[66] it can easily side with the dominant class, with any party promising an expedient route to survival. Sade, by extending these Kantian ideas of pleasure and utility into the bedroom, made the utilitarian redoubt of morality—pleasure—itself into a kind of grim, repetitive work. Both Sade and Kant are interested in alterity not as such but in terms of what the fact that there are other people must imply about the power of self-legislation. This kind of aloof formalism invites the mind to create an ontology of otherness that would bring the self into a fuller engagement with the qualitative dimensions of self or otherness, but the impulse toward the ontological is thwarted by Kant and Sade's emphasis on constitutive subjectivity. Where the Middle Ages looked to religion to define the ideological and moral meaning of social domination, after Enlightenment this role fell to subjective and class identity. One may do whatever pleases oneself, and one can do unto others whatever one can get away with.

This critique of Kant's moral philosophy redounds on subjective universalism and its legacy in social thought. Kant's strict division of reason into practical and theoretical categories, his attack on substantive and teleological reason, his emphasis on formal types and natural laws: all of these undercut the ability to use reason for its Enlightenment intent, to address social problems. The bourgeois character and subjective reason are constituted by an emotional coldness that enforces categories not just on others but also on the self. To a powerful degree, argue Horkheimer and Adorno, Kant's concept of cognition bears the deep traces of Sade. Cognition is chained to both reason and to consciousness, and this threatens a two-sided conformism, eventuating in a consciousness that seems vital insofar as it conforms to social reality or that seems inert insofar as it pursues the ideal. The ideals of pure reason, like the concept of a rational god, seem to be nothing more than impediments to the progress of knowledge and an irrational restraint on the will. The result is that substantive reasons—the reasoned articulation of particular goods based on experience—get pushed aside, and human, moral, or social categories must be squeezed into the universally conceived categories of survival, profit, or necessary conformity.

Adorno and Horkheimer, then, remain orthodox Kantians in the same way they, through a modified reading of Lukács, saw themselves as orthodox Marxists; though they wish to defend philosophy's universalism and objective rationalism, they find they must argue with and against its identities and non-identities. This explains their remarkable reevaluation of the truth content of the *Critique of Pure Reason*. Extending the argument of Adorno's Simmel essay, *Dialectic of Enlightenment* attacks the idea of a lawful consciousness—the schematism of the understanding—as a sleight of hand, a scientistic subordination of philosophical experience to science. The truth of Kantianism comes in its moments of logical non-identity: in those moments of methodological scruple where the actual is not the real, where the Other is not reduced to its instrumentality, where particularity bears the marks of not being fully subsumed under the universal. There is a moment of utopianism, and thus the kernel of a future immanent critique, where *Dialectic of Enlightenment* describes Kant's "unclear relation" between the empirical self and the lawful, enlightened self:

> As the transcendental, supraindividual self, reason comprises the idea of a free, human social life in which men organize themselves as the universal subject and overcome the conflict between pure and empirical reason in the conscious solidarity of the whole. This represents the idea of true universality: utopia.[67]

This brightly optimistic statement can only be registered negatively. But it is the truth of *Dialectic of Enlightenment*. The universal subjectivity of Kant is paraphrased in Marxian terms, and the Marxian freedom of a self-organized, laboring humanity is likened to the supraindividual self of the intelligible world, the Thomistic-Platonic *mundus intelligibilis* of rational objects invoked by Lukács. Material and ideal freedom conflict with each other until achieved in reality. Kant allows only momentarily for the transcendental self to appear as emphatic lawfulness before quickly moving on to the business of everyday cognition and the submission to necessity. But Adorno and Horkheimer undoubtedly believed that the momentary awareness of such non-identities was the beginning of real thought and true individuality. This rearguard defense of Kant's Idealism is also a defense of the reciprocality of a true universal law as well as a defense of the ideal that every subject can obtain not just Enlightenment and self-knowledge, but also ideal universality in the emphatic sense—the possibility of entering the Kingdom of Ends, of autonomous subjecthood. This includes everything that Fromm meant by the goal of "having an identity" but quite a lot more, both qualitatively and socially. For Horkheimer and Adorno, freedom is not subjective desire but an objectively achieved state of conscious non-identity.

Before philosophy can have a better understanding of freedom's rationality, subjective and objective, one must ruthlessly criticize the definition of reason that equates it with mere consciousness in accord with the world. Failure to do so promotes the bad identity of the self as a kind of lawless reproduction of the same—a layered subjectivity of heteronomous second nature where the individual consciousness is just a policeman enforcing cognitive and social conformity. Thus, the sentences directly following the utopian vision cited previously point to the possibility of negative identity under the culture industry:

> The true nature of [Kant's] schematism of the general and the particular, of concept and individual reconciled from without, becomes legible in contemporary

science as well as in industrial society. Being is apprehended under the aspect of manufacture and administration, and everything—even the human individual, not to speak of the animal—is converted into the repeatable, replaceable process, into a mere example of the conceptual models of the system. . . . The conceptual apparatus determines the senses, even before perception occurs; a priori, the citizen sees the world as something made from raw material that he manufactures. Intuitively, Kant foretold what Hollywood consciously put into practice: in the very process of production, images are pre-censored according to the norm of the understanding which will later govern their apprehension. Even before its occurrence, the perception which serves to confirm public opinion is adjusted by that judgment. . . . Reason is deployed as a mere systematic science, a means-calculation to level everyone down to the same identical interest. No one is other than what he has come to be: a useful, successful, or frustrated member of a vocational or national group.[68]

This passage delves into one of the famous sore spots of *The Critique of Pure Reason*. In describing how intuitions are converted rationally into concepts, Kant proposes a mediating function of "the schematism of the understanding." Schematism is what makes it possible for sense data to become conceptual and to be applied to a priori logical rules. These rules, the "categories of the pure understanding," provide the outline for perceiving particulars as universals and for performing logical or conceptual operations on bare facts or imagined objects. In terms of intellectual history, the fact that Kant limited the schemata to the twelve concepts that he believed could be applied to any object—unity, plurality, totality; inherence, causality, reciprocity; reality, negation, limitation; possibility, existence, necessity—was highly significant, as this aligned the underlying categories that "made perception possible" with the twelve categories of logical operation identified by Aristotle. Kant probably feared that allowing a single further category of prereasoned reasoning would have opened the door to a relativism that would make pure reason indistinguishable from everyday consciousness or cultural perception.[69]

Horkheimer and Adorno both had their philosophical training in phenomenology and knew how to mount a defense of the categories by means of the Husserlian *epochê*, a route quite different from schematism.[70] But in retaining the category of schematism as a synonym for prejudice, stereotypes, or formulaic cultural productions, they required themselves to interpret Kant not just as a defender of subjective metaphysics but—as Sade or the culture industry would—also as a technician who applied rationalistic systems of categorization to human questions. The distinction between epistemological, aesthetic, and moral reason quickly dissolves under the pressure of a technique that makes no distinction between subjective and objective meaning. Instead, the attempt to overlay moral philosophy onto a naturalized metaphysics corrodes all moral objectifications. Objects (Beings or Concepts) that once seemed morally charged now have the gravitas of so many fake castles: they appear as kitschy as the theory of moral sentiments itself, no different than saccharine films made by committee. Moralism becomes a market-tested, cookie-cutter genre, populated by pseudo-choices in the form of differently packaged clichés aimed at particular communities. "Public interest stories" are just the gloss of morality in commercialized news. And even science makes the headlines only if it can reinforce people's prejudices, moral or amoral. Sade, applied to Kantian divisions of reason, points to the end product of capitalist identities: a fusion of culture, capitalism, and statistical science that lacerates the rationality that Kant imagined would be produced when his schematism fused reality and consciousness. The culture industry takes this to its logical conclusion: the forces of the personality are harnessed for more production, against the interests of actual persons, to play to and reinforce their prejudices and to make them essentially identical if superficially different. Instead of perceiving the non-identical relation between the real and the ideal, one senses only the ontological discomfort of being a "useful, successful or frustrated member of a vocational or national group." A new type of subjectivity is created that cannot fundamentally relate to universal subjectivity except through the negation of group identifications. Because reason has become, essentially, a cultural procedure, identity becomes subjective, an owner's pride in one's group memberships and settled prejudices.

This extreme image paints, like the *Echternach* hermeneutic, a radical picture of what happens to the theory of the divided subject as the World Spirit travels westward to Hollywood. But it was also a dire private warning that Kant and Marx's notions of an objective science of subjectivity stand or fall together, and that their deathbed would be made up of culturalism, relativism, stereotypical thinking, and the love of cheap immediacy. Horkheimer and Adorno were terrified of a fusion of bourgeois amoralism with the power of data-driven propaganda. Wanting to preserve a memory of Idealism and universalism to negate a future bad possibility without lending positive value to the notion of a cultural or communal golden age, they imagined a social world governed only by psychological assimilation to the images of mass culture. Doing so meant that they "knew the worst" and negatively anticipated the need to analyze racial and ethnic stereotypes. Trembling at the possibility of perfecting a stimulus-response science of prejudice, they were aware that every technique developed for the study of public emotion had likely been created for commercial purposes and would be available for fascism. Theory lacked the tools of criticism for grappling with the social consequences of such advanced techniques, but an awareness of the sadistic inversion of Kantian reason preserved a sense of the non-identical and the consequences of negative identity. Caricatures and stereotypes, backed by highly sophisticated statistical techniques for shaping the audiences, had their uses as surely as did schematisms of the pure understanding. And so the essay "Schema of Mass Culture," which remained for Adorno's lifetime "the unpublished portion of the Culture Industry Chapter," was drafted in October 1942, just as Adorno was at work on his study of anti-Semitic radio preacher and personality Martin Luther Thomas. Both the Thomas study and "Schema" offer the same understanding of "technique": once the "advertisement" aspect of culture comes to the fore, culture loses all concept for describing its quarrel with or non-identity to practical life (*Differenz vom praktischen Leben*).[71] Both books grapple with the meaning of psycho-social "identification," using stereotypes as a kind of screen idea and role model.

The reconsideration of Kant's schematism on the subjective ground of the culture industry transformed the interpretation of Marx and Marxism's concept of subjective identity. If *Dialectic of Enlightenment* expressed the concern that the natural and social sciences had tied themselves to compliance with external nature, this was doubly true of contemporary Marxism. Socialism as dialectical materialism, whether one considered it scientific or speculative, had put itself in the business of prognostication. But in the 1940s, blind faith in science, progress, or the inexhaustible good of nature and production required demythologization. These lessons, learned from socialism, were important for liberalism. After the collapse of the Second International in the vote of European countries to join World War I, followed by the Russian Revolution, socialist theory had largely contracted into Stalinist-Leninist theories of an absolutist state with single-party rule. For political and theoretical reasons, Horkheimer's agenda at the Institute had addressed this situation through questions of interdisciplinary method, investigating the question of the state in the making of the economy and probing the question of collective subjectivity. When the Institute for Social Research was conceived in the 1920s, there was still a functioning socialist public sphere that could address economic-political issues in a humanist mode. By the time the Institute immigrated to America, not only had Lukács been forced to renounce the parts of his theory that analyzed the non-identity between subjective and objective class consciousness, but the power of mass media for harnessing feelings of national and group belonging had eroded large parts of the socialist network of communication and theorization. Whereas *The Communist Manifesto* dedicated a whole section to the development of national and world literature, even Otto Bauer lacked an equivalent socialist understanding of how social theory would be articulated in a world of radio, film, and television organized by national and international conglomerates.

The structure of the public sphere had changed. And this amplified the problem of the broken systematicity of science and the disciplines. The double transformation highlighted a daunting historical fact: revolution had come not from below, or the Left, but from the nationalist, ontological Right. The elements of systematicity that should have paved the route toward the universalization of the worker had empowered reaction. This pointed toward the need to engage psychological and cultural explanations—matters of personal and group identity—rather than retreat behind the old universalisms. In the mid-1940s, Adorno and Horkheimer sought to understand how changes in the public sphere had blocked the advance of progressive politics and how structural change had made the fragmentation of individual consciousness as powerful a tool for domination as was the monopolization of labor power. Where others were using the language of culture to describe the universal non-identical, the Frankfurt group had followed Lukács's lead in using the language of (systematic) identity and non-identity both to understand the deficiencies in a systematic theory of mediation between mental-material totality and to explain why the experience of capitalism in everyday life did not lead to critical class consciousness. In describing the decline from the "salutary individual distinctions that bolster the common interest" to the requirement that one become a "useful, successful, or frustrated member of a vocational or national group," they were describing a decline in the public self, and thus in bourgeois subjectivity, but they were also describing problems with the structure of theory, its failure to engage with the increasingly consumeristic, cultural, and national nature of economy and the erosion of class relations and class consciousness.

Disciplinary Psychologies: Techniques and Narratives

Lazarsfeld's recollections in the 1960s set the pattern by which the American parerga of Adorno and Horkheimer were interpreted as a retreat into theory and away from the empirical. Though Adorno has been the focus of this hermeneutic, a famous 1943 letter by Horkheimer has lent support to the view that even the Institute's master administrator found himself lost in the administrative and theoretical farrago of American psychological academe. Writing to Marcuse, Horkheimer complained:

> The problem of Antisemitism is much more complicated than I thought in the beginning. . . . Since we have decided that here in Los Angeles the psychological part should be treated, I have studied the literature under this respect. I don't have to tell you that I don't believe in psychology as a means to solve a problem of such seriousness. I did not change a bit my skepticism toward that discipline. Also, the term "psychology" as I use it in the project stands for anthropology and anthropology for the theory of man as he developed under the conditions of antagonistic society. It is my intention to study the presence of the scheme of domination in the so-called psychological life, the instincts as well as the thoughts of men. The tendencies in people which make them susceptible to propaganda for terror are themselves the result of terror, physical and spiritual, actual and potential oppression. If we could succeed in describing the patterns, according to which domination operates even in the remotest domains of the mind, we would have done a worthwhile job. But to achieve this one must study a great deal of the silly psychological literature and if you could see my notes . . . you would probably think I have gone crazy myself.[72]

Horkheimer's words have seemed, if not quite despairing, at least dismissive: psychology, if it means anything at all, must be read as anthropology, and anthropology as materialism. If one understands "anthropology" as code for "Marxism," then American psychology is entertained only as a Trojan horse through which to smuggle class politics into the American disciplines. The letter, however, can better be read as invoking the project of theoretical reconstruction of the disciplines outlined by Lukács as "orthodox Marxism." The challenge was to relate the study of the "so-called psychological life" to a mediated sense of the disciplines and autonomy to yield a theory of objective social mediation. Far from dismissing all empirical psychology, Horkheimer is expressing a kind of dual attitude: a determination not to neglect any form of technical mastery that would reach into "the remotest domains of the mind," while also trying to integrate psychological research into his sense of dialectical materialism—even if the attempt takes him to the edge of insanity.

An understanding of how "technical mastery" relates to identity in the interdisciplinary as well as psychological sense explains why Adorno's version of "crazy" appealed at this moment and why this led Horkheimer to place Adorno at the center of the dialectics project and then the anti-Semitism project. Surprisingly, it was in reading Adorno's forbiddingly technical musicological text *The Philosophy of Modern Music* that Horkheimer saw the possibility of a theory that allowed multiple disciplines to be combined beyond the mere "juxtaposition of scholars." Horkheimer was not a musician, and modernist music could hardly lie further removed from empirical psychology. But Horkheimer recognized the implications of Adorno's argument about dissonance as an argument about non-identity. Music, like metaphysics, encountered the death of God in the rejection of harmony. But in approaching metaphysics via music, Adorno also added something new, something that pure philosophy had much more difficulty seeing: the conceptual power of *Philosophy of Modern Music* comes from its attention to technique. Adorno's introduction argues that immersion in technical disciplinary concerns can transform that which makes a discipline closed, opening up its insights to a broader inquiry. By pushing the internal logic of musical tonality to its breaking point—to the point where the underlying metaphysics of harmony are laid bare—*Philosophy of Modern Music* argued for an analogy between the end game of tonality and that of metaphysics.[73] This idea of inverting technique to study subjectivity's limits was the one that Horkheimer sought. On reading the manuscript, the usually reserved Horkheimer wrote to Adorno: "If I ever felt enthusiasm for anything in my life, it was while reading this. . . . This study will in the broadest sense form the basis for our common efforts."[74]

Adorno argued that music was always about channeling the flow of emotion through technique, but the untapped possibilities of musical technique could, if understood properly, do more than merely manipulate the formal needs of the tonal system: they could, in fact, address the logic whereby mute suffering had disfigured emotional response. Horkheimer immediately recognized that the book's historical schematism—its interest in finding unarticulated suffering within details, such as the expressive power still dormant within individual chords—as well as its skill in thinking through the epistemological value of representation, were useful for rethinking technique in psychology in relation to the models of normalcy that haunted psychological studies. Music did not assume a normal, unalienated state of freedom, nor had it been plagued by a positivist laboratory model. Adorno's historical and wide-ranging analysis of the relation between universality and particularity, emotion and technique in the decomposition of classicism was needed for rethinking the psycho-social synthesis. Thus, though Horkheimer lacked Adorno's mastery of musical technique and could not, he confessed, follow Adorno in the details of the musical analysis, his invocation of the word "enthusiasm" (a word he clearly meant in the fully philosophical and religious sense, as a synonym for madness, an overflowing of affect) explains why he felt he did not need to. Adorno's strength as a reader involved his ability to identify the site at which the technical rules of music intersected with their impossible antithesis: music as pure emotion, the outflowing of transcendent expressivity.

Written within weeks of each other, Horkheimer's letters to Marcuse and Adorno show that the goal in the early 1940s—of both *Studies in Prejudice* and *Dialectic of Enlightenment*—was not just to transpose the technical insights of one discipline into another but into the study of disciplinarity itself and, beyond that, into a reinvigorated notion of the divided subject and object of theory. This philosophical understanding of technique aimed at a Marxian anthropology was not a matter of formalist analogy but of turning the subjectivity implied in the disciplinary concept inside out. In each of the disciplines in which he worked—music, philosophy, psychology, sociology—Adorno argued that technique at once represented a connection, and a block, between particularity and universality. Drawing on the epistemology of estrangement, Adorno sought to show how each technique disfigured subject and object and could also be transformed into a historical-social understanding.

It is not coincidental that as part of their articulation of this notion of disciplinary technique, Horkheimer and Adorno used the language of identity in a way that upheld a dual prerogative. On the one hand, identity meant a pursuit of the universal concept of autonomy, as expressed in a September 1941 letter in which Horkheimer reflected on "the identity of reason and speech" creating an ever-renewed situation in which "language chafes against the tension between the dominant form of praxis and the true universal . . . aiming, completely independent from the intent of the speaker, at that universality one ascribes to reason."[75] Three weeks earlier, Horkheimer reflected on the problem of identity in terms of the value spheres, telling Adorno, in relation to the *Philosophy of Modern Music*,

To be sure, your treatment of the different spheres as identical does not always appear justified. The danger of the philosophy of identity, and thus of idealism—of which you were naturally as cognizant during the formulation of the text as I was while reading—does not yet appear to me to have been entirely overcome.[76]

While arguing that one could not create an identity between the "problematics of music" and "those of capitalist society," Horkheimer tied Adorno's successful analysis of technique back to the Veblen essay's concept of immanent critique. Convinced that Adorno's failure to fully synthesize the relation between inner and outer experience in a model of identity constituted a stunning success, Horkheimer argued for the need to rethink disciplinarity not as a search for a permanent synthesis but as an exploration of the non-identical, nonreducible qualities of systematic knowledge. Adorno's idea that "it is not artists, but rather works of art that know the world (*erkennen*)" reoriented Horkheimer toward reading the state of society from the contradictions inscribed in the object, and toward the concept of the non-identical as the key to understanding the search for identity.[77]

For the rest of the 1940s, the goal of critical theory became that of transforming its existing empirical model of psycho-social synthesis by finding technical resources within the "madness" of American empirical psychology that would lead outward toward a dialectical social theory. Adorno saw this as a procedure of applying the *Echternach* model of the dialectic to Fromm's concept of identity and turning it into a theory of non-identity, and thus of transforming Fromm's implicit psychological and subjective takeover of social thought back into a theory of subject/object relations. Rather than look to create a transdisciplinary master synthesis, Adorno emphasized the importance of not reducing any form of knowledge to another but of bringing many disciplines to bear on how the externally structured inner lives of imperiled individuals had become building blocks for modern forms of domination. Psychology, for this same reason, needed to be broken up. Because psychology was threatening to absorb all other forms of social inquiry, Adorno directed his interest toward psychology's clinical ability to generate techniques of subjective manipulation rather than its claim to provide a totalizing explanation. It is a fact little commented on that *Dialectic of Enlightenment*, though it is widely credited with synthesizing Marx and Freud, largely sidelines Freudian psychology. Though *Totem and Taboo* is referenced in passing, the structural model, for example—id, ego, superego—is seemingly neglected. Far more prominent in *Dialectic of Enlightenment* are the aspects of psychological research that could be described as "psycho-technics"—methods of psychic manipulation that were provably "true," in empirical research, insofar as they could predictably shape the behavior of those subjected to them. *Dialectic of Enlightenment* reads like a tragic playground of psychologisms, a contradictory tour of how subjective irrationality can be manipulated to the undoing of individuals and societies. Just as Adorno the musicologist looked for expression in the most technical dimensions of music, so in *Dialectic of Enlightenment* he looked for the subjectivity that emerges at the grinding margin where the role of science is to strip away autonomy and turn subjects into objects. In the course of Adorno's experiences in America he had plentiful opportunities to see the range of psycho-technics being developed by American researchers: as Lazarsfeld well knew, there was a catalog of techniques to induce people to buy a particular brand of gasoline and consider it a form of self-expression. Because *Dialectic of Enlightenment* ran riot with the separability of technique from social context, it is hardly possible to canvass the variety of psycho-technics it deploys. But a summary of the three dominant forms of applied sociopsychology helps define how the non-identical element emerged from a logic of exaggeration.

The most prominent psychologism of *Dialectic of Enlightenment* is what might be called media or narrative psychology. Just as Odysseus reordered his world through storytelling, so the culture industry develops "tricks" to make narratives superficially substantial and emotionally compelling. The difference between ancient and modern forms of organization is that the modern is governed by a commodity fetishism that forges narratives whose appeal is detached from any sense of labor, social solidarity, or responsibility. Where *The Odyssey* tells a story of self making and even individual education that leaves traces of sacrifice and the pain of domination, the culture industry, like its model in advertising, is based on a commodified amnesia of social bonds. At worst, this psychology is one of education in reverse: consumers who know the social function of work but who wish to forget their reliance on society can be mechanically distracted by images of the cash value of celebrity, the wanton waste of resources, the moral luck of the lottery or the gambler, or the sheer rush of violence. These pathological invocations of unreal wealth and gratuitous violence can make films or political speeches seem engaged in a high moral deliberation at the precise moment when they are cynically eroding the possibility for culture or meaningful action. Culminating years of study in the *Zeitschrift* into how consumer capitalism had created new narrative techniques that interpellated the viewer into an emotional network of pseudo-social relations, *Dialectic of Enlightenment* explored how new mass media such as soap operas and situational comedies create networks of cathexis that incite fear while reinscribing bourgeois normalcy into the emotional projectivity of its listeners.

The second psychologism developed in *Dialectic of Enlightenment* involves the exploitation of a divided, fragile, and heteronomous self. Asserting that modern individuals are exploited both through their fear of division and dissolution and their longing for wholeness, *Dialectic of Enlightenment* explores the question of whether modernity's increasingly complex institutions and forms of knowledge operate by fostering this inner division. The power of commodification, the division of labor, the pseudo-concrete quality of money and quantitative reasoning provide a logic of free-floating consumer choice that appears, at first blush, to provide a calculative unity to the self. Simmel envisioned money as a means that allows autonomous individuals to pursue ever more complex ends, but autonomy breaks down if individual psychic life is hollowed out by powerful forms of conformity and by social complexity beyond individual control. Wholeness becomes the commodity that can be sold to the divided self again and again, and thus wholeness and autonomy become a central ideology of self-imposed tutelage:

> The bourgeois whose existence is split into a business and a private life, whose private life is split into keeping up his public image and intimacy, whose intimacy is split into the surly partnership of marriage and the bitter comfort of being quite alone, at odds with himself and everybody else, is already virtually a Nazi, replete with both enthusiasm and abuse; or a modern city-dweller who can now only imagine friendship as a "social contact": that is as being in social contact with others with whom he has no inward contact. The only reason why the culture industry can dispense with individuality so readily is that individuality has always reproduced the fragility of society. On the faces of private individuals and movie heroes assembled according to the patterns on magazine covers vanishes a pretense in which no one now believes; the popularity of the heroic models comes partly from a secret satisfaction that the effort to achieve individuation has at last been replaced by the (more breathless) effort to imitate. It is idle to hope that this self-contradictory, disintegrating "person" will not last for generations, that the system must collapse because of such a psychological split, or that the deceitful substitution of the stereotype for the individual will of itself become unbearable for mankind.[78]

This attack on the identity of the divided self echoes the discussion in "End of Reason," though with important modifications. It is strikingly more concerned with the identities of gender relations and consumption than was the 1941 discussion. Media culture works as a solvent of traditional ideals and subjectivity such that "personality" under this situation "scarcely signifies anything more than shining white teeth and freedom from body odor and emotions."[79] An important shift in emphasis appears here in the critique of spontaneous individuality: instead of merely criticizing the ideological character of positive identity, one sees an empathy with the *fragility* of the divided self. As in many passages of *Dialectic of Enlightenment*, the question is left open of whether a wounded or vulnerable subjectivity will be pushed to total dissolution, endlessly exploited, or eventually find the autonomy that has been marketed to it but that it has never enjoyed.

Finally, the "Theses on Antisemitism" added a third psychologism: the functional, dialogic enemy. This theory draws on Nietzsche's idea that values are created negatively through ressentiment and merges Nietzsche with the Nazi jurist Carl Schmitt's twin arguments that politics had assumed a "new primacy" over (economic) interest—a primacy capable of trumping class conflict—by making the identification of an enemy the "essence" of politics.[80] Critical theory argued that there was no social substance to this essentialized enemy other than negative identification. The "need for an enemy" was no "psychological *existentiale* of man."[81] In the age of fascism, having an enemy was a first move in a functional game of modern mass politics, the goal of which was to possess a wounded enemy so weak as to pose no threat, who, contemptible on account of weakness, authorized a new authoritarian politics that allowed the aggressor to mask his own inner weakness. This drama of subordination produced a pseudo-activity of perpetual self-assertion charged with a falsified religious zeal. "Now the Jews are in fact the chosen race," the text comments ironically: chosen out of the cold political logic of instrumental negative identity.[82] Nazi ideologues do not believe that Jews are objectively responsible for German weakness; they know, however, that identifying Jews as their chosen enemies defines Germans as ontological warriors and simplifies politics to this identity. This mirror game is even a form of "loving one's neighbor" in the form of negative identity: Nazis can cultivate their own desire for world domination by projecting it onto the Jews.

In *Dialectic of Enlightenment*, these three forms of analysis are not psychoanalytic but psycho-social and psychotechnical—they explore the possibility of social formation through a mimetic model of psychic adaptation. To the point of parody, they follow the central doctrine of psycho-social dynamism advanced by Erich Fromm in his 1942 methodological appendix to *Escape from Freedom*, "Character and Social Process": the idea that critical theory should study social character as "the essential nucleus of the character structure of most members of a group . . . developed as the result of the basic experiences and mode of life common to that group."[83] As the media provide images of unfulfillable desire, as the division of labor requires a divided and compartmentalized self, as the world of political economy becomes more social Darwinistic, so the social-psychological character has a more attenuated relation to the common good, a weakened sense of its own self, and finds meaning only in the crudest form of competition, the sense of having an enemy.

Dialectic of Enlightenment indeed imitates, and then pushes to the extreme, these theories of cultural adaptation and identity born out of disciplinary fusion. Visions of autotelic liberalism, of society moving the individual or the collective naturally toward health and freedom, are not just self-deluded but dangerous. But the same could be said for visions of inevitable decline. Theory must construct the worst-case scenario—the one in which the divided self, exposed to the negative identities of the division of labor and a desubstantialized politics, becomes the basis for a new, sadistic, and inverted form of rule following, one constructed of empty pleasures and functionalist concepts of a convenient enemy. The assertion that ontological conflict was a metaphysical inevitability served as false interdisciplinarity, as non-identity without self-conscious reflexivity. Psychology needed to invert and test its normative assumptions, working to understand that even the form of subjectivity could become a means for the perpetuation of domination. The desire to *be* a self had nothing inherently positive about it and was indeed infinitely exploitable by those wishing to turn subjectivity into an object.

Dialectic of Enlightenment's interest in narrative explores the relation between negative identity and disciplinarity by examining three interlocked theses: that technical mastery begins with narrative, that the self is always already divided, and that narratives of woundedness mediate between myth and Enlightenment, defining the heroic story of the disciplines and their limits. Long before modern natural science, stories were "useful" because they divided up and controlled the world. And they were useful because they did openly what Baconian science did covertly: fashion the self by dividing the self. This allowed for a self-identity to be fashioned out of thing-identities, the material—words, experiences, forms—of the non-self. Mastery is not just primarily heroic action but the orchestration of emotion, knowledge, technique into identities that forge reason and myth at the same time:

> Though trembling and shipwrecked, the hero anticipates the work of the compass. Though he is powerless, no part of the sea remains unknown to him, and so his powerlessness also points toward the mighty powers that will be conquered. But the evident untruth in myths, the fact that the waters and the earth are not actually inhabited by demons . . . is, when seen through the eyes of Enlightened autonomy, transformed into something merely fanciful in comparison to Odysseus's goal of self-preservation and return to homeland and settled property relations. . . . The knowledge that comprises his identity and enables him to survive has its substance in the experience of the multitudinous. . . . And by the same token, "the knowing survivor" is he who throws himself most audaciously into the greatest dangers. Consequently, epic is not the antithesis to myth, nor is the self the antithesis to peril, but [both genre and self] are shaped through opposition. [Epic identity] is a form of Being that emerges from the assertion and denial of all unity in its multitudinousness. . . . Like the heroes of the bourgeois novel, Odysseus loses himself to find himself, and the estrangement from nature that he effectuates is realized through the processes of nature with which he contends. . . . In Homer's moment, the identity of the self is so much a function of the unidentical, of disassociated, unarticulated myths that it must derive itself from those myths.[84]

This passage, which notably places the Heideggerian concept of Being in apposition to the concept of identity, insists on the importance of non-identity for the construction of identity and for the inescapability of the subjective and objective poles of knowledge. Its message of originary negation is central for understanding how Adorno and Horkheimer thought of the relation between identity and difference—connection and separation—in both the self and in knowledge. The word "identity," used here in a fully subjective sense in that it describes who Odysseus is and how he feels and thinks, also describes a falsified unity. Odysseus, and subjectivity more generally, is understood as something made, not given, and therefore as something that must always be understood in terms of the relation that technical mastery creates between subject and object, between internal and external nature. The idea that reason is not just opposed to myth and narrative but that narrative is itself a form of reason points to the possibility of recovering a broader context of subjective/objective nonidentity. The subject, whose internal life begins by negating the undifferentiated nature that would destroy him, learns to establish islands of narrowed object relations, which, through the magic of narrative, are internalized to form a layered and divided self capable of external domination but incapable of mastering his own internal world. This leads to the conclusion that narratives of knowledge or selfhood before specialization are themselves a form of myth that undermine the individual, for there never was an unalienated knowledge or an undivided subjectivity. And it leaves open the possibility of forestalling the regression to myth through the creation of an identity capable of preserving the memory of its objective, dialectical relation to the non-identical.

Far from being a metaphysics of inevitable decline, or a capitulation to a new mythology that creates victimhood in response to vulnerability, this analysis of myth and identity poured cold-water tonic on naïve empiricisms and created new possibilities for empirical research. The writers, both Kantian-Marxist universalists, knew they were embarking on a scientific study of race and racism. They did not believe in the reality of the underlying object (race), nor did they believe that there was liberation to be found in embracing value relativism or validating the reality of symbolic struggle or ideologies of hatred. Their goal was to enlighten themselves—to understand how their own concepts of universalism could foster the very techniques that social power used to exploit the divided self. In studying identity as effective truth, one needed to develop a kind of negative ideal type: identity as a reactionary, outward-directed cult of self-assertion that seeks to find a new essence in ontologized racial hierarchy and permanent, static identities. As an attempt to force theories of identity and wholeness back onto themselves, requiring their heroic narratives to be looked at as technique and instrumentality, *Dialectic of Enlightenment* argued that models of subjectivity and otherness and models of disciplinary objectification are something other than neutral or passive. It advocates that all narratives develop a practice of self-reflexivity that cultivates a recollective memory of what is sacrificed and obscured to create narrative unity.

Every aspect of critical theory's research program was shaped by this speculative work of negating identity. Written as a prelude to studying the empirical dynamics of instrumentalized particularity, *Dialectic of Enlightenment* engaged in a critique of how capitalism necessarily divided consciousness against itself in an ideal, system-theoretical form. Whereas Lukács had sought to differentiate permanently between subjective and objective class consciousness, Adorno and Horkheimer sought to show how even subjective universalism, when divided against itself, could be exploited into a form of domination. This critique of the divided consciousness of theory was not a destination but a step toward a social science free from the presumption that the united self was the obvious answer to the divided self. Ceasing to equate truth with unity freed them to study the ways in which the logics of subjective universalism—without which Marx and Kant made no sense—had already been alloyed to the techniques of an exploitative negative identity. A few examples of hypotheses of inverted universalism advanced by *Dialectic of Enlightenment* help show how this speculative work structured Adorno and Horkheimer's concurrent empirical work.

Narratives and Techniques of Victim Formation

Dialectic of Enlightenment's study of the culture industry narratives and their psychologisms should be read in conjunction with a significant empirical spin-off, Adorno's unpublished *Psychological Technique of Martin Luther Thomas's Radio Addresses*. In the summer of 1943, while writing *Dialectic of Enlightenment*, Adorno researched how a Los Angeles "radio minister" encoded anti-Semitism and reactionary politics for American audiences. The intent was to produce a "field handbook" for countering fascist rhetoric in the media. Adorno argued that Thomas was a master technician of narratives that harnessed democratic themes for reactionary purposes, analyzing how Thomas told redemptive stories about himself and his movement, about a future America "freed" from Jewish control, about the America of good heart, and about the conspiracies and misinformation aimed at hiding the truth. Adorno's tropological interpretation of transcripts yielded a catalog of thirty-four techniques of emotional-political appeal to an American national identity that could reorganize any understanding of economics, social power, familial function, or social violence into a question of belief in Americanness. Among Adorno's list of techniques were the cultivation of emotionalism and irrationalism in defense of the people; the call for a rebellion against bureaucrats and civic institutions; the posturing of the agitator as a "truth teller" willing to speak uncomfortable truths about national enemies within; the deployment of victim blaming both for enemy baiting and as rehearsal for violence; the claims of the leader having superhuman "stamina" and powers of empathy; the appeal to the "good old times" and falsified "human-interest stories" to smuggle in hate rhetoric amid avowals of decency; the castigation of one's opponents as "weak" while implying that they should be eliminated by force; the tendency to dignify small-grade tactical struggles or even investigations into one's wrongdoing as epochal historical struggles of a liberation "movement"; mock participation in civic debates where the performance of self-righteousness authorizes juvenile name-calling and disparagement of "enemies"; pseudo-rebellion against authority coupled with the active cultivation of fantasies involving much more extreme authority; deployment of economic rhetoric to suggest that one must hurry to join the movement before some (less fully American) person takes one's spot. Arguing that these techniques were borrowed from advertising methods for creating a brand identity, Adorno underscored their antithetical construction—the way in which Thomas exploited the new medium of radio to form a negative image of Jews prior to establishing any positive message his own.[85] In considering this study of technique and narrative an empirical investigation, Adorno was redefining empiricism and theory as *Wesensnotwendigkeiten*.

Liberalism, Emotion, and Actionism

Dialectic of Enlightenment addressed how the forms of liberalism—economic, philosophical, political—had a tendency to foster an emotional regime of indifference or disdain while lending a kind of erotic appeal to illiberal elements. The operative myths of the bourgeois nineteenth century were that "irrational anger no longer exists" and that a genuine "unity among men had been established in principle" because the economic system now managed scarcity and conflict through quantitative rationality.[86] These were universalist ideas, but they imbued liberalism with a sense of abstraction and restraint that made its opposites—the cult of authoritarian action, notions of a gender or racial essentialism—seem robust, vital, and invigorating. Authoritarianism was not just a psychological phenomenon, but a system of techniques and cultivated knowledge aimed at activating these short-circuits in the body politic as if they were a form of love: anti-Semitic and segregationist "personalities" often shaped themselves by developing an obsessive interest in the superior emotional expressivity of a despised group. This knowledge of the Other could then be turned many ways, transforming into a transparent imitation of the racial or ethnic characteristics of the minority, a taste for conspiracy theories involving the minority, or a general tendency to delegitimize minority rights and the "bureaucratic" role of the state in protecting the minority. Speculating that this passion for national, racial, or gender essentialism in the Other appealed most to those afraid of losing economic status and those ill-suited for the division of labor, Adorno and Horkheimer showed how the ascription of subjective identities displaced social analysis. Fascists lust after the undisciplined mimicry of dominated peoples—the mimicry that has made a school of "influencing purchasers by flattery, debtors by threats, creditors by entreaty" or by telling jokes objectifying their powerlessness.[87] The passion for Otherness could readily turn to contempt and hatred. The intoxication of immersing oneself in the gestures, tastes, sights, and even smells of the imagined enemy could serve as prelude to soberly "track[ing] them down and destroy[ing] them" while indulging in "unconditional" but subconscious "identification" with both the pleasures of particularity and the liberal "authority which has prohibited" such expressivity.[88] Adorno and Horkheimer wished to research whether the logic of tying identity to survival had given rise to a grotesque modern desire to extirpate all difference: "Everything which stands for difference in society is threatened. Everyone is either a friend or an enemy; there are no half measures. . . . Ethnic groups are forced across the border, while those branded Jews are sent to the gas chamber."[89]

Anti-Semitism and Incomplete Emancipation

Dialectic of Enlightenment imagines that the psycho-social interaction between class struggle and the struggle for national emancipation could potentially lead to intertwined, mutually disrupting forms of emancipation. The Jews and the bourgeoisie, for example, defined themselves subjectively and objectively through negative reciprocality. Jews constructed their self-image around the ideal of the rights of man, becoming, alternately, apologists for its incompleteness, defenders of its ideality, and architects of rearguard attempts at amelioration, such as the minority treaties of World War I. The liberal bourgeois order cultivated a special vision of the Jews as simultaneously weak (nationally) and powerful (economically) to justify economic aggressiveness and congratulate themselves as protectors of the weak.[90] But when the economic vision of the capitalist order began to fall into crisis and the bourgeois as a class started to fear the inability to reproduce itself, the bourgeois liberal self-understanding started to lust after the internal cultural coherence of the Jewish community and to find the anti-Semitic argument of a "natural order" deeply compelling. The bourgeois, wanting to join the *Volksgemeinschaft* (national community), castigated the Jews by turns as mere and then special nature, as attenuated and then essential Being. Out of a series of pseudo-concrete identity struggles, anti-Semitism and bourgeois liberalism fused into a new conceptual identity—race—and a new spiritual and collective identity, a national economic version of the "in itself, for itself."[91] Scientific studies of prejudice needed to examine how threatened groups might assign such essentialism to themselves or be compelled to internalize its imposition.

The Ticket Mentality

Dialectic of Enlightenment introduced the question of whether the practice of market choice, civil elections, and strong forms of party or brand affiliation fosters not just intolerance of difference but hatred of any minority position. *The Authoritarian Personality* extends the speculative work's analysis of the "ticket mentality" as the all-or-nothing idea of personality: the notion that if one agrees to one policy idea of a political party, one must agree with all.[92] Such reasoning—whether by democrats, liberals, socialists, or conservatives—becomes a form of mechanical reduction of the self and a taboo on thinking. When this reasoning invents new ways of identifying individuals as enemies, it short-circuits the social reflection that once defined the social constitution of law and society. The ticket mentality wants the rule of the majority of the majority. Fascism exploits the Sadian (and sadistic) view that a group identity can be imposed on others negatively and far more efficiently than education can create informed citizens. The ticket mentality thus bespeaks the triumph of subjective psychology over objective social governance, inclining toward identity positions that are symbolically majoritarian, rather than seeking to be representative of the social whole. Fascists believe in declaring everyone other than themselves (the self-appointed representatives of the national majority) equal in weakness. Fascism then exploits the proceduralism of democracy to impose the ticket mentality at a higher level of abstraction: the progressive idea that the African and the Jew alike are bearers of values is inverted into a ticket logic to reimpose the "natural" rule of the strong.[93]

Identity Thinking, Musterung, and Scientific Ethics

In titling his *Minima Moralia* aphorism on Carl Schmitt *Musterung (classification/call to arms)*, Adorno pointed to the fatal spiral of an identity thinking that collapses social and psychological struggle and grafts it onto the notion of science. Schmitt had called for a scientific ethics of social classification; *Dialectic of Enlightenment* expressed an awareness that an agonistic theory of the enemy possesses a lurid, pseudo-concrete appeal—one capable of so overstimulating the ingrained impulse toward survival and dominance that, even in the researcher who aims at objectivity, identity thinking can overwhelm any residual impulses toward Kantian universality or the preservation of autonomy.[94] The purely psychological, abstractly negative quality of nationalist identity was unfortunately wholly compatible with an aggressive form of sociological definition of the Other. The ambiguity of the word *Müsterung*—which can mean "labeling" but also "preparing to fight"—speaks to the neo-essentialism and pseudo-concretion of the Schmittian concept of the political. The process of labeling and defining groups—and contemplating their distance from the true essence of the *Volk*—had been imbued with the political zeal of religious conversion. Schmitt's horrific recasting of the Gospels' "You are either for me or against me" was indeed part of the end game of liberal nationalist thinking in the age of alienated selfhood. As part of its definition of the problem of typology, *The Authoritarian Personality* devotes considerable attention to counteracting the notions that identity thinking represents a kind of collective *Wesensnotwendigkeit*.

Erikson, American Identity, and Interdisciplinarity

In 1950, Erik Erikson published *Childhood and Society*, the book conventionally credited with introducing the concept of "identity" to social-scientific discourse and the first to attempt to make psychology a kind of master science by placing a positive notion of ego identity at the center. Because his theoretical approach to the concept of identity derived from a combination of Freud, Fromm, and empirical studies of culture and society, a brief look at his approach helps contextualize the Frankfurt debate over positive and negative identity.

Erikson's novel claim was that identity was a fundamental need: all individuals needed to experience themselves "as something that has continuity and sameness, and to act accordingly."[95] As was the case with the earlier usages by Fromm and Horkheimer, Erikson's "identity" had a sense of crisis attached to it: identity was what one needed in a world of change. Identity was thus for Erikson an achievement shot through with dualities. It was universal but also historically changing. It involved the individual's claim to be something unique in the world, but it required participating in and finding a place in a culture or group. Despite or perhaps even because of the not fully articulated antinomies within Erikson's vision of identity, this was a concept that would, slowly in the next two decades, and with accelerating velocity in the subsequent three, take root in almost every conceivable vernacular and specialization, becoming one of a handful of once-technical concepts in psychology and sociology used so frequently that many assume its timeless, descriptive value. To have an identity means to take seriously the duty and responsibility of self-ownership and self-definition. No matter who one is, or when one lives, one must have a sense of self that locates oneself as one among many.

Though Erikson's concept of identity was always dual in nature, he was actively contemptuous of the Hegelian or dialectical critique of identity as it had emerged among the critical theorists. Erikson did have a concept of "negative identity," but it referred to the *attraction* of a negative role model—that desire adolescents often experience toward those who violate the norms they are struggling to integrate.[96] Identity was otherwise for Erikson a purely subjective and positive concept, a reflective understanding of one's sense of self as it had emerged over time as part of maturation and as part of history—although this latter question was unclear. The search for individual identity, both an anthropological constant and a product of Renaissance culture, was basic to psychic life. *Childhood and Society* articulated a general theory of the psycho-social stages of childhood development, arguing that humankind has eight crucial stages of identity formation, beginning with the need to achieve trust, autonomy, initiative, and industry, and culminating in having an identity and learning to share one's inner meaning with others. The second segment of the book consists of group studies Erikson conducted before and after his immigration to the United States: studies of Hitler youth, shellshocked American soldiers, Native tribes of the Sioux and Yurok Nations, and children with developmental delays. The third part involves historical and cultural studies, including an attempt to sketch an American identity, and psychobiographical studies of Maxim Gorky's and Hitler's identities. Erikson's identity concept was articulated explicitly in terms of the concept of culture as the medium of meaning that allowed adaption to social change. Thus, he surveyed his different studies through the lens of "the problems that face the youth of the world today":

Industrial revolution, world-wide communication, standardization, centralization, and mechanization threaten the identities which man has inherited from primitive, agrarian, feudal, and patrician cultures. What inner equilibrium these cultures had to offer is now endangered on a gigantic scale. As the fear of loss of identity dominates much of our irrational motivation, it calls upon the whole arsenal of anxiety which is left in each individual from the mere fact of his childhood. In this emergency, masses of people become ready to seek salvation in pseudo-identities.[97]

This passage typifies how Erikson extended Fromm's basic formulation of an anthropologized Freud, treating identity as an extension of culture. In traditional cultures, identity is the equivalent of maintaining a traditional role; in modern societies, identity is weighted toward self-invention; in mass societies, Erikson argued, identity enters into a state of "emergency" that inspires the widespread adoption of falsified "pseudo-identities." Literalizing Fromm's Renaissance origin story of the individual, Erikson tightly linked the notion of identity to a conception of cultures and tied both to reason and health. The "fear of loss of identity" replaced the fear of freedom, and Freud's notion of castration anxiety or fear of superego destruction is turned into role/ego anxiety. If one's social role is dissolving, one will be gripped by existential fear; if the desire for social integration meets with favorable social conditions, then one will be able to develop a healthy sense of "ego-identity."[98]

In formulating his blockbuster idea of positive identity, Erikson was exposed to both Fromm's positive concept and Adorno's negative one. Though Erikson's biographer, Lawrence Friedman, sees no evidence that Erikson engaged deeply with *The Authoritarian Personality*, there are good reasons to think that Adorno and Erikson were familiar with each other's work and that Erikson made a conscious choice to align with Fromm's positive interpretation of the nature of personal identity, while Adorno made a conscious choice to emphasize negativity.[99] This is not just because Erikson's work on the Hitler Youth is cited in *The Authoritarian Personality*, while the latter is cited in *Childhood and Society*, but because the writers were connected through a network of personal and institutional affiliations. Starting in 1939, Erikson had an appointment at the Berkeley Institute for Child Welfare; in 1944 he would be joined there by Else Frenkel-Brunswik, one of the chief investigators on *The Authoritarian Personality*. Erikson had regular lunches with Henry Murray, whose work on the Thematic Apperception Test (TAT) was central to *The Authoritarian Personality*. Additionally, Adorno and Erikson were both members of the San Francisco Psychoanalytic Society, presenting papers at its annual conferences in the mid- to late 1940s. It therefore seems likely that the "architect of identity" thought about his own career and identity as a therapist in a way that was negatively formed in relation to the Institute's work. Consider, for example, the way *Childhood and Society*'s final essay seems to refer to the Institute and the "emergency" research both Erikson and the Institute members had engaged in during wartime:

> Emergencies prevail upon us to offer our judgement regarding societal and international events. Some of us respond by analyzing the problems of social organization as clinical situations. Others put their faith in what is called interdisciplinary teamwork, a kind of halt-and-blind cooperation, in which a social scientist with little psychological vision carries in piggy-back fashion a psychologist who has not learned to move with ease in the public events of this world, so that together they may grope their way through contemporary history. But I think that our work must contribute more significantly to a new manner of man, one whose vision keeps up with his power of locomotion, and his action with his boundless thinking. Only in so far as our clinical way of work becomes part of a judicious way of life can we help to counteract and reintegrate the destructive forces which are being let loose by the split in modern man's archaic conscience.[100]

The phrase "interdisciplinary teamwork" makes invidious reference to the Institute for Social Research. Psycho-social work, Erikson had argued on the previous page, is akin to atomic research, where the splitting of the atom perfects "work of the highest theoretical and most far-reaching practical significance" but forces the scientist to decide whether to be a healer or a warrior. There is "a point where scientific ethos and armament races do not live well together in one identity, and on being forced to merge endanger the very spirit of inquiry."[101] Returning to this critique of instrumental technique, Erikson associates clinical work—what he and Fromm were engaged in—with the healing power of atomic medicine, while associating "interdisciplinary social research" with the Manhattan Project and the "unleashing of destructive forces." Thus, Erikson depicts himself as a loving and engaged clinician, working to heal the world by cultivating relatedness, while suggesting that the members of large interdisciplinary groups suffer from an unethical division of labor that translates into epistemological confusion and internal identity problems. This depiction of critical theory as having retreated from the clarity of identity suggests that Erikson knew quite a bit about the Institute and its notion of system identity and interdisciplinary research. Erikson believed by 1950 that the engagements of wartime research now had to be offset by the pastoral work of clinical therapy.

Erikson had good reason to want to take a swipe at *The Authoritarian Personality*, for this much-anticipated book would for years overshadow Erikson in shaping how American science looked at questions of prejudice and how Americans thought about what Erikson called identity. The book did much to redefine the public meaning of psychoanalysis and sociology, while calling attention to how prejudice endangered democracy and how perceptions of American racial injustice undercut America's moral authority in the Cold War. Well before Erikson's language of identity filtered into book and article titles, ideas from *The Authoritarian Personality* about overt and latent prejudice, victim blaming, and the functional value of racism in politics were shaping American political and social thought. Given that it was more than a thousand pages long and filled with statistical data and raw interview material, *The Authoritarian Personality* was probably seldom read cover to cover, but parts of it nonetheless made for riveting reading, revealing the widespread nature of prejudice and antidemocratic thinking. The immediate comparisons to Gunnar Myrdal's *An American Dilemma* suggest the breadth of *The Authoritarian Personality*'s social survey and the depth with which it addressed topics far beyond its original conception.

In the five years it took to produce, *The Authoritarian Personality* evolved from a narrow wartime study of anti-Semitism to a general study of racial prejudice and personality. Its assertion that authoritarianism and racism were linked transformed social science. Adorno expected, in fact, comparison to Myrdal's work, citing, in the unpublished afterword to *The Authoritarian Personality*, Herbert Aptheker's criticism that Myrdal had viewed the problem of the American Negro as a psychological problem "in the heart of the American" and that "social trends have their main significance for the Negro's status because of what is in white people's minds."[102] Adorno extended this to say, "The gist of Aptheker's argument is that the Negro problem is [in Myrdal] abstracted from its socio-economic conditions, and as soon as it is treated as being essentially of a psychological nature, its edge is taken away."[103] The approach of *The Authoritarian Personality* was to move beyond mere psychology—or weak psycho-social "syntheses"—and to study anti-Semitism simultaneously as something objective and as forming a peculiar new type of individuality.[104] Adorno sought to embed this dialectical approach into the study's interdisciplinary analyses by emphasizing the need to take an "integrative" approach to the study of problems, while also upholding a theoretical understanding of the non-identity of disciplinary analyses. Economic concerns, for example, cannot be absolutely separated from psychological questions because

> the concept that there is economy on the one hand, and individuals upon whom it works on the other, has to be overcome by the insight into the ultimate identity of the operative forces in both spheres. Per contra, however, the division expresses

the truth that in our society neither the total nor the individual can be identified forthwith; they have to be understood as being opposed to each other while still being aspects of the same whole.[105]

The Authoritarian Personality sought to go beyond the question of whether prejudice is fundamentally a matter of "the moral conflict in the hearts of the Americans."[106] Instead it asks how individuals' necessarily nonidentical relation to themselves leads them to classify others according to a logic that looks like mere psychology but in fact is shot through with concerns of economic and social domination. Here the subjective and objective, universal and particular, descriptive and ascriptive dimensions of positive and negative identity touch. The Frankfurt School, through Fromm's *Escape from Freedom*, had already contemplated the question of seeing positive identity as the solution to the problem of fascism, and Horkheimer, Adorno, and Marcuse had broken off to reject this solution on the grounds that it took developmental and ego psychology as a self-enclosed totality that one could treat in separation. As we continue to explore the grounds for this rejection, it is important to recognize that they were not alone in this assessment or in thinking that "the Negro problem" spoke to "the Jewish problem" in this regard. In 1941, Ralph Ellison, in reviewing *An American Dilemma*, complained:

In our culture the problem of the irrational, that blind spot in our knowledge of society where Marx cries out for Freud and Freud for Marx, but where approaching, both grow wary and shout insults lest they actually meet, has taken the form of the Negro problem.[107]

This was a decade and a half before Ellison would write *Invisible Man*, which presented a devastating critique of the dangers of a normative theory of positive identity and the attempt to turn problems of racial prejudice into a psychological problem to be solved by offering positive role models. But we know that before Ellison wrote his review of *An American Dilemma*, he had been reading Erich Fromm's *Escape from Freedom*, and his conversations with the Trotskyist circles of Greenwich Village and Harlem undoubtedly shaped his desire for a social survey that moved beyond economic analysis.[108] The Frankfurt and Harlem theory of negative identity brushed against each other at this moment.

To consider Erikson and Adorno's work in the course of the 1940s is to see how the need to develop an interdisciplinary synthesis of psychology and sociology torqued its way around the American race problem. Though the basic outlines of this development take the form of a schism—Fromm's split with the Frankfurt group, Adorno and Horkheimer's rejection of languages of identity, and Erikson's reclamation of the term—the career of the concept of identity does not map out as a set of divergent lines but something more like a helix: at key moments in this story their disagreements led them, warily (as Ellison would put it) shouting insults, back toward each other. Erikson, we have seen, was more influenced by the *Studies in Prejudice* group than he let on. Adorno, for his part, would nudge the collective project toward finding points of compromise with psychologists who had a culturalist understanding of prejudice more akin to Erikson's than his own.

Like Fromm and like Erikson, a number of American psychologists of the late 1930s, dissatisfied with the applicability of Freud to modern social problems, looked for new inspiration to the relativistic conceptions of culture associated with the Columbia Anthropology Department, most prominently Ruth Benedict and Margaret Mead. The culture and personality movement, true to its name, sought to develop a psycho-social synthesis through the study of the mutual determination of culture and personality. Deemphasizing Freud's schema of the divided psyche (in which the ego is always dogged by the id or schooled by the superego), they emphasized the way the mature ego emerges through adaptation to culture.[109] Erikson, along with his contemporaries Fromm, Karen Horney, Abram Kardiner, and Nathan Ackerman, believed that a kind of recuperative pacifism could be achieved through a psychological science that aimed at helping children, adolescents, and adults readjust to societies to which their internal identity was misaligned. This might mean reforming the culture or tutoring the individual toward success and adjustment; or it might mean taking a stance of nonconformist individuality. In their vision, psychoanalysis contributed to healthy adaptation to culture while advancing the development of better cultures through ethical nonconformity.

Adorno and Horkheimer's war against Nazism was paralleled by a war against the idea of adjustment. However, making the *Studies in Prejudice* project work at all meant finding ways to collaborate with these theorists of personality. Though *Dialectic of Enlightenment*'s high-theoretical concern with the negative construction of identity seems removed from the empirical task of typologizing individuals according to their susceptibility to prejudice, a closer look at the choice of collaborators on the project suggests a more complex story. For though Daniel Levinson, Nevitt Sanford, and Else Frenkel-Brunswik were all oriented toward a combination of ego psychology and the personality and culture movement, what made it possible for Adorno to work with them was that these psychologists also shared a common interest in a topic of great importance to *Dialectic of Enlightenment*: the psychological function of narrative. Frenkel-Brunswik, for example, a student of the great Gestalt theorist, philosopher, and laboratory psychologist Karl Bühler, was an expert on narrative theory and psychological defense mechanisms whom Horkheimer had known since she was employed as an assistant, along with Paul Lazarsfeld and Marie Jahoda, at Bühler's Viennese Psychological Institute. Her 1939 book, *Mechanisms of Self-Deception*, explained Freud to American audiences in terms of the narrative habits of personality that caused one to evade unwelcome truths. Employed at the same Institute of Child Welfare at Berkeley as Erikson, Frenkel-Brunswik was useful for fulfilling the AJC's desire for a survey covering anti-Semitism among women and children, but she was important for her theoretical expertise as well. Combining narrative forms was not only her specialization, but she and her husband, Egon Brunswik, were expert at relating experimental data and psychoanalytic observation and had published on the ethics of psychoanalytic work. It was through Frenkel-Brunswik that Horkheimer contacted her colleague Nevitt Sanford, who had received a grant from a Jewish theater owner to publish in 1944, with the assistance of Berkeley graduate student Daniel Levinson, an initial articulation of a sociometric scale for anti-Semitic opinions.[110] When Adorno proposed collaboration with the Berkeley group, he was meeting with people who had already developed a psycho-social synthesis that drew on concepts borrowed from Fromm and Bühler. Both the theory of the life cycle and the lab techniques of Henry Murray—Sanford's Harvard thesis adviser—were integral to the collaborative project.

Though the collaborators on *Studies in Prejudice* perhaps could not have agreed on a single definition of "psychology," their empirical work was thus united by a common interest in relating narratives and ideas about the self to the formation of public opinion. Horkheimer and Adorno learned much from this conversation. They were already familiar with psychometrics—the *Zeitschrift* had run several articles on the statistical measurement of qualitative data. But undoubtedly, their collaboration in *Studies in Prejudice* brought them a substantial education on the use of projective tests in creating a psychological profile that let the interviewee define the question. The Rorschach Test was the first and remains the most famous projective test, but central to *The Authoritarian Personality* was the TAT, developed by Murray with assistance from Sanford at Harvard, which involved showing the interviewee a set of photographs of social situations and asking him or her to narrate a story onto the scene. Photographs, as Walter Benjamin had argued, were never just pictures of a person but of social types, enmeshed in the narrative of the city as surely as the typology of faces in paintings were entwined with the family histories of the aristocrats who commissioned them.[111] Murray and Sanford understood that one could show a picture of a person and ask for a narrative, and the interviewer would gain a general image not of a person but a social type as projected through the dominant schema of intersubjective understanding. Murray's biography confirms that the disclosive power of narrative originally came from epic literature: he was so obsessed by the famous "doubloon scene" from *Moby-Dick*—in which each crew member of the *Pequod* projects on the coin's image his own view of human purposiveness—that in 1925, as a young psychologist, he gave a copy of the book to Sigmund Freud.[112] Years later, after being denied tenure at Harvard, Murray began writing a book that used the doubloon scene to conceptualize psychology in terms of the logic of cultural projection of the self onto objects. The idea that psychology could do meaningful survey work by requesting a narrative projection onto images proved a perfect way to interview subjects freely about social topics that they would not otherwise discuss and to apply psychoanalytic ideas both to their perceptions of others and to their unconscious wishes for reshaping public life.

Collaboration developed around the concept of narrative and content analysis ushered the American ego psychologists beyond psycho-social identity. This is demonstrated in a term borrowed from Henry Murray and introduced to the project by Sanford. Part of Murray's approach to profiling personality was to rate an individual's overall ratio of "intraception" versus "extraception." The first term was defined by Murray as "the dominance of feelings, fantasies, speculations, aspirations" as a way of explaining events, while the second term indicated "the disposition to adhere to the obviously substantial facts. A practical, 'down-to-earth' skeptical attitude."[113] *The Authoritarian Personality* redefined "intraception" as "the tendency toward introspection, as well as a readiness toward gaining insights into psychological and social mechanisms" and replaced "extraception" with "anti-intraception." This rendered a purely psychological category into a social-psychological one, allowing for the measurement of an individual will to false consciousness through a reversal of Murray's original assessment of which group was more oriented toward objective reality. Where some people actively think about how domination (legitimate or not) structures their world, others actively evade such reflection.[114] Though Adorno allowed that it might be difficult to measure why some people are resistant to objectivity while others engage with it reflexively, his broadly Freudian hypothesis was that this resistance was correlated with the successful or unsuccessful resolution of the Oedipal complex. In Adorno's social understanding of the Oedipal complex, the child inevitably encounters the conflict not just between desire and the law but also between the arbitrary law of the father and that of society. In the modern world, the child cannot merely imitate her parents but must acquire a socially determined set of skills as part of the process of entering the world of labor. The Oedipal conflict is the first entry into the social hierarchy, where the personality is compelled to accept "the hierarchical social orders that permeate the individual's thinking, attitudes and behavior."[115] Individuals must adapt to the standardized rules yet desire as solace to have unique selves, with their own narratives, interpretations, and insights into the objective order that both made and opposed them. But this kind of selfhood is also hard to achieve, because it requires mastery of a whole realm of interpretive ideas that are not inherited through imitative praxis. Here we have Odysseus again: individuality is at some level an injury that comes out of trying to heal an injury. But the conflicting perspectives that one must introject into oneself in order to become unique can seem, as they did even to Nietzsche, to be potential poisons, luring one away from simple, authentic selfhood unless one can ground them in some sort of intraception. If one has a sense of how one is object as well as subject, it can actually help one retain a sense of individual subjectivity. But if one acquires an aversion to intraception, one can become neurotically obsessed with the process of individuation, seeing individuality as decadent and diseased and seeing ambiguity as an enemy. In the development of this theory, which became one of the building blocks of the analysis in *Authoritarian Personality*, both the German and American participants were required to make substantial compromises. Working with Sanford's term required Adorno to start from what must have seemed a crude and abstract typology of "personalities"; Sanford had to accept not only Adorno's more social interpretation but also his reference to the Oedipal complex, which probably seemed to him a quaint European throwback to Freud's dated system.

Part of what made such a multidisciplinary project work, in practice, was the balance Adorno and Horkheimer struck between criticism and cooperation as they worked with people they did not necessarily agree with. In order to reach a public, they had to set aside concerns about the weak, sloppy, and even dangerous theoretical cultural conceptions of Fromm, Erikson, and Horney. Yet they did not simply suppress these concerns, but developed a multilayered critique of the culture and personality movement and its implicit concept of interdisciplinary mediation through the concepts of identity to culture. Much of this criticism had to be expressed in other venues: marginal writings clarifying theoretical ideas while also processing what they learned from their American colleagues. Some of this theoretical reflection was published in separate papers by Adorno; some was put into private notebooks and manuscripts, published later in the form of *Dialectic of Enlightenment* and *Minima Moralia*. Before returning to Germany, Adorno and Horkheimer had developed a critique of the Erikson-Fromm identity concept in three important dimensions: a systematic critique of social psychology as a "fused" discipline; an immanent critique of psychology as subjective rationality; and an interdisciplinary defense of Freudian psychoanalysis as the only approach suitable for theorizing the social crises of the twentieth century. Importantly, however, the partition between private theory and collaborative practice was not impermeable: Adorno tirelessly confronted the research with questions about fundamental assumptions and provoked confrontations leading to methodological refinement. In terms of both the ethics of research and the project's attempt to achieve objectivity, *The Authoritarian Personality* project went to great lengths to avoid the problems that had distorted the Institute's previous work. The theorists who had been concerned about the relationship between the individual as bearer of rationality and the kinds of totality constructed or presumed by research as a system developed a technique of upholding an empirical and theoretical concept of non-identity that made the linkage between authoritarianism and racism applicable to the analysis of every modern society.

5

Negative Modeling
Objectivity, Normativity, and the Refusal of the Universal

Methodological and Hermeneutic Circles

The Authoritarian Personality attempts to study the real power of something unreal: identity and its shadows, race and anti-Semitism. The technical challenge was to create a method for studying these real problems without creating a "methodological circle" that would reproduce in thought the injuries of incomplete emancipation and the woundedness of the universal that the authors sought to study. This chapter examines the conceptual construction of *The Authoritarian Personality*, considering its method of analyzing data, thinking through narratives, and repurposing definitions. The standard account of Adorno's career suggests that the time spent on empirical psychological research was time lost for the true work of philosophical speculation; it emphasizes Adorno's disdain for his American colleagues, as well as his American research subjects, and implies that designing surveys was perhaps not the one-time musical composer's forte. This chapter seeks to show that the opposite was true: that Horkheimer had made an astute choice when he saw Adorno's musical analysis of technique and expressivity as the key to understanding how subjectivity is produced and expressed in modern societies, and that the speculative work on the problems of both subjective and objective identity pursued by the pair during the mid-1940s laid the ground for constructing a large-scale multidisciplinary research project that produced valid data because it did not presume what it sought to prove.

The central focus of the work that went into *The Authoritarian Personality* involved the problem of identity, and a central part of this work involved the researchers' reevaluation of their willingness to dignify the ideas of identity, race, and projective alterity as worthy of scientific inquiry. This was not a war they had ever wanted to fight. As Kantians and Marxian universalists, they resisted contaminating fundamental definitions of social thought and subjective rationality with a vocabulary tinged by racism or social Darwinism. They had, however, to be pragmatic in the acceptance of Pragmatism. In the previous chapters we have seen Adorno and Horkheimer build alliances with Americans associated with a number of disciplines, a collaboration requiring them to compromise on the objects they were willing to study and on the languages and methods of scientific research they would deploy. To read *The Authoritarian Personality* is to see how far they went in adopting the American language of race and culture; it is also, however, to witness how successful they were, through a negative deployment of these languages, at adapting the existing tools of American social science toward a critique of the identity concept. This work, performed by émigrés in a quest to understand the forces that had made them émigrés, was applied not just to American society, but to the entire layered, non-identical selves and value spheres implied by sociological, psychological, economic, and political analysis.

If *The Authoritarian Personality* is a monument to the kind of work Adorno could accomplish by persisting in his refusal to adapt to American standards, the project ultimately demonstrates how much Adorno had been changed and had learned by being forced to consider the relation between the American logic of identity—its racial and ethnic construction of reality—and the ways in which identitarian logics structured the disciplines. This chapter argues that the work of *Studies in Prejudice*—the study of racism and systematic oppression—could be accomplished only after *Dialectic of Enlightenment* had commenced the critique of science, subjectivity, and identity, and only after Adorno developed a working theory of the necessity of interdisciplinary work for understanding the divided self. It argues, moreover, that the insights won through the confrontation with the American research industry would inform their speculative work and their understanding of the basic concepts of philosophy. Five years prior, neither Horkheimer nor Adorno could have written the critique of definitions one finds in the 1947 *Eclipse of Reason*:

Theories embodying critical insight into historical processes . . . have often turned into repressive doctrines. . . . Definitions acquire their full meanings in the course of a historical process. Each concept must be seen as a fragment of an inclusive truth in which it finds its meaning. It is precisely the building of truth out of such fragments that is philosophy's prime concern. There is no royal road to definition. The view that philosophical concepts must be pinned down, identified, and used only when they exactly follow the dictates of the logic of identity is a symptom of the quest for certainty, the all-too-human impulse to trim intellectual needs down to pocket size. It would make it impossible to convert one concept into another without impairing its identity, as we do when we speak of a man or a nation or a social class as remaining identical, although its qualities and all the aspects of its material existence are undergoing change.[1]

This passage ties personal and group identity to the question of conceptual identity and non-identity, and thus to the idea of constructing truth out of fragments and converting one concept into another without impairing it. The art of conceptual mediation, of injecting a sliver of dialectical and disciplinary thought in order to get to the truth of negative identity, became central to critical theory during the years 1943–44. It became a way not just of negatively preserving the memory of a universal but also of unraveling the evasions that allowed individuals to falsify their own identity according to the dictates of an antagonistic society. The goal of *Studies in Prejudice* and midcentury critical theory became that of studying the wound of identity without further wounding universality. Identity had to be analyzed without hypostatizing it, approaching its sedimentation in divided subjectivity through a multidisciplinary inquiry and, dialectically, through a redefinition of terms and methods whose essential truth they denied.

Interdisciplinary Definitions and Negative Ideal Types

The question that governs the entire *Studies in Prejudice* is a political-psychological one: the series asks whether democratic, subjective universalism is undercut by the logic of group identity and, if so, what can be done to address such ruptures in the polity and the individual subject. Anti-Semitism and other forms of racialized and stereotyped thinking are approached in *Studies in Prejudice* as social pathologies attendant to the dominant psychological and political roles in modern society. Negative subjective identification of the Other is *psychologically* useful to the pathological individual because it bolsters his or her otherwise ungrounded self with the energy of negative cathexis. Negative subjective identification of the Other is *politically* useful because it injects a sense of movement-like religious zeal into an otherwise alienated and atomistic political world, charging everyday life with a sense of zealous purposefulness and creating a plenitude of emotion-laden objects that blunt social solidarity and distract a media-rich public sphere from focusing on questions of objective inequality. Social identification, both subjective and objective, is described across an array of overlapping, non-identical fields of experience. The project's negative framing, a reflection of the epistemology of estrangement, stands in a general analogy to the problem of historical experience. The working premise appears to be that when individuals encounter the social power of economics, politics, culture, or status, it is as negation—a kind of law that thwarts autonomy as if a quasi-natural force, a form of social gravity.

In keeping with American expectations, however, the book presents authoritarianism first and foremost as a psychological problem. As *The Authoritarian Personality*'s opening definition of "personality" explains, personalities constitute coherent wholes and therefore represent legitimate objects of scientific investigation:

> The political, economic and social convictions of an individual often form a broad and coherent pattern, as if bound together by a "mentality" or "spirit," and this pattern is an expression of deep-lying trends in the personality. The major concern was with the *potentially* fascistic individual, one whose structure is such to render him particularly susceptible to anti-democratic propaganda.[2]

This cautious reference to personality as a totality is signaled in the title of the book itself: there is a sense of compromise in the definition of psychology between Adorno's notion of the individual law and the ideas of the culture and personality movement. As we have shown, mainstream American psychology made the idea of the personality the fundamental datum of social-scientific observation—the most concrete thing to study in looking at cultures. And indeed, this first definitional sentence can seem like a transcription of the notion of "personology," the main idea of Henry Murray, the doctoral advisor of Nevitt Sanford, one of Adorno's coauthors. Murray believed that the distinctive shape of a personality defines the hyphen in the psycho-social synthesis. *The Authoritarian Personality*, in suggesting "political, economic, and social convictions" as the first principles of "a broad and coherent pattern," accepted Murray's basic idea while bumping it out disciplinarily, suggesting that the personality structure is not purely psychological, but founded on a network of convictions derived from objective and subjective relations: social facts, observations, rumors, or mass-mediated experiences of others. One can already see a sociological shadow hanging over the concept of the self-generating "personality."

Sociologically, the chief term of *The Authoritarian Personality* is the "ingroup/outgroup" distinction. As the simple idea that every group defines itself against others, this concept is a dialogical one, speaking to the play of *alter* and *ego*. But the ingroup/outgroup concept was also an American one, with an ugly past. Drawn from the American social Darwinist William Graham Sumner, the idea of the ingroup was originally defined as the mental structure produced by barbaric tribalisms in conflict over scarce resources. The "me-group" or "ingroup" struggled against the "they group" or "outgroup" as a way of regulating domination over space and establishing hierarchy among the groups.[3] Sumner's term, incorporated into German national historical sociology and Chicago School notions of spatialized conflict, emphasized the priority of conflict over contemplation in the formation of the habits of mind. Because membership in one group implied struggle against the others, groups were who they were because other groups defined them as outgroups.

Given the vigor with which Adorno attacked the mere whiff of social Darwinistic reasoning in Fromm (and even Freud), one might well ask how *The Authoritarian Personality* could casually adopt as its core sociological concept an idea burdened with this social Darwinistic heritage. A likely answer is that Sumner was, at least, not Carl Schmitt. Better to embrace—and prophylactically rework—American social Darwinism than to subscribe to a Nazi distillation of *Müsterung*. Such an accommodation to practice could perhaps be made with the comforting thought that unlike Schmitt's famous identification of "the enemy" as the "essence of politics," at least Sumner's concept had its moment of historical objectivity. Deeds were not one-way events for Sumner, nor was violence the poesis of peoples.

A second answer comes when one recognizes the interdisciplinary moment. Just as the concept of personality is defined sociologically, so *The Authoritarian Personality* redefines its central sociological concept of outgroups in terms of individual psychology. This meant, in practice, that the study went out of its way to avoid naturalizing identitarian logics. In conducting interviews, the interviewers were instructed to make no assumptions about outgroups—neither their membership, nor mutual antagonism, nor even their actual existence. Outgroups were analyzed as they existed in the mind of the interviewees. Though Adorno contemplated the idea that most people and cultures construct some notion of outgroups along with their own ingroup concept, he allowed and even expected that within American society, most individuals related to group collectivities first through the law and property relations, and then through a sense of shared vulnerability. Groups therefore formed not organically but as a network among similarly situated individuals. Therefore, though interviewers probed whether self- or ingroup concepts were formed antithetically, they were careful neither to suggest identitarian thinking is necessarily neurotic, pathological, or aggressive, nor to cast notions of group antagonism as inevitable or natural. To do so would tribalize individuality and define conflict as normative. As *Dialectic of Enlightenment* already suggested, *The Authoritarian Personality* identifies "the neurotic" as a social type who cultivates an excess of knowledge about his or her "chosen" outgroup, injecting this "knowledge" with an anxiety, projectivity, and paranoia that spill over to obsession and a loss of reason. Approaching group definition in this psychological and dialogical way allows questions to be open-ended rather than ampliative, and it presumes no essential conflict. We should recall that before and after conducting a study of anti-Semitism that understood Jew hatred as a generative form of socially distorted consciousness, Adorno, glossing Simmel, had asked, "Why must the Stranger be hated?" This was intended to counter the sociological premise that the Stranger was *naturally* the enemy. One of Adorno's fundamental successes in shaping the *Studies in Prejudice* project involved preventing his colleagues from making this kind of assumption. Although the book places anti-Semitism at its center, researching the degree to which Jews define "the" American outgroup, it is scrupulous not to impose the idea that Jews are naturally an outgroup, the outgroup, or some foreign entity—or even the idea that national ingroups should naturally have outgroups. Ideal types are treated negatively across the psychosocial gradient.[4]

This paired use of interdisciplinarity and open-ended definition of the social relation defined by negative identity constitutes an innovative way of negatively exploring identity in its subjective and objective, negative and positive, real and imaginary dimensions. Adorno's preferred title for the book, *The Potential Fascist*, suggests caution against assuming, projecting, or perpetuating notions about selves and their Others and points toward the theoretical value that might come from analyzing the nonidentity of negative identity. Instead of presupposing natural groups in conflict, the book examines the general patterns of "political, economic, and social convictions" that define everyday public life and asks how these patterns prompt engagement in hate politics, political passivity, or resistance. Thus, though the book is constructed methodologically around the study of racism and anti-Semitism, these forms of ascriptive projection are not assumed to be rooted in actual "race relations." Equally, the subject of the book is not the psychology of racism but the question of how forms of racism can be incorporated into modern-day reactionary politics; the book prepares no typology of human relatedness nor presupposes how or where reactionary political groups form.

The Princeton Radio Project had conceived of questionnaires as menu items. The researcher effectively took orders by listing clearly defined objects of general taste or consumption and asking whether the interviewee liked or disliked the thing on offer. *The Authoritarian Personality* rejected such preference polling as both ethically and scientifically unacceptable. It was just as foolish to take individuals' declaration of stringent egalitarianism at face value as it was to assume that they were naturally locked in a Hobbesian war against their neighbors. To address this, *The Authoritarian Personality* framed questions about the subjective construction of self obliquely, in relation to the otherness that emerges out of objective relations. Such objective relations can include the expressive dynamics and social knowledge of the interviewee and, necessarily, of the interviewer as well. In accord with its concept of objectivity, the book begins with the claim that it will study not just surfaces but also depths, not just direct expressions of emotion but also oblique reactions of fear or weakness, and not just beliefs about experiences but whether those experiences are substantive or charged with delusion. This standard of objectivity requires a model of how overt expression differs from private thoughts and how private thoughts connect to deeper trends:

Opinions, attitudes and values . . . are expressed more or less openly in words. . . . Psychologically they are "on the surface" . . . but when it comes to such affect-laden questions as those concerning minority groups and current political issues, the degree to which a person speaks will depend upon the situation in which he finds himself. There may be a discrepancy between what he says on a particular occasion and what he "really thinks." Let us say that what he really thinks he can express in confidential discussion with his intimates. This much, which is still relatively superficial psychologically, may still be observed directly by the psychologist if he uses appropriate techniques, and this we have attempted to do. It is to be recognized, however, that the individual may have "secret" thoughts which he will under no circumstances reveal to anyone else if he can help it; he may have thoughts which he cannot admit to himself, and he may have thoughts which he does not express because they are so vague and ill-formed that he cannot put them into words. To gain access to these deeper trends is particularly important, for precisely here may lie the individual's potential for democratic or antidemocratic thought and action in crucial situations. What people say, and to a lesser degree, what they really think depends very largely on the climate of opinion in which they are living; but when that climate changes, some individuals adapt themselves much more quickly than others.[5]

The notion of technique is here borrowed directly from *Dialectic of Enlightenment*, as is the idea of the layered and divided self; the two concepts are in fact theorized in relation to each other. Techniques must approach a divided self that is fundamentally a guarded self—an object closed to research, accessible only to those who ask the right questions by invoking particular objects in an indirect fashion. This is a self whose layers correspond to layered spheres of economic, legal, political, social, and cultural value. Individuals possess multiple schemas for organizing information, and they live in a world flooded with information and stimuli; information is encountered in the experience of objective trends, in science, in the general "climate of opinion" structured by media, and in the intimate sphere. If one wishes to do more than study general public opinion and understand how subpublics relate to the classification and treatment of minority groups, one must approach the divided selves and divided publics of modern life obliquely, through an interdisciplinary survey that uses psychological analysis to negate and draw limits to sociological analysis, and vice versa. Menu-item questionnaires do not suffice. The decision was made to combine quantitative and qualitative methods: to create a multifactorial personality profile via statistical surveys and then to conduct "depth interviews" whose narrative flow was analyzed for its assemblage of particulars and its use of evasion techniques. Using narrative techniques to analyze the transition between identity logics helps assess the negative identity within the self and its relation to the negative identities of others.

Since prejudice and reactionary thought can have many sources, their study required a broad social survey with broad qualitative metrics. *The Authoritarian Personality*'s overall methodology aimed to avoid creating a preconceived ideal type of fascist; rather, it sought to have the ideal type emerge dynamically from the respondents themselves. The study's chief assumptions (drawn from a historical analysis of ideology) were (1) that authoritarian politics relied on mobilizing a caricatured image of a minority group to enforce the kind of polarization and conformity necessary to invoke a hard-line version of the "ticket mentality"; and (2) that the study of authoritarian politics must concern itself with three types: agitators, followers, and resisters. The genesis of these political "roles" was then modeled and refined according to an iterative process. First, hypotheses were framed concerning the social nature of anti-Semitic and racist beliefs based on publicly available sources of ideology and propaganda. Next, a preliminary survey of reactions to these ideas was conducted, and those most responsive to anti-Semitic ideas or patterns of opinion were interviewed. Transcripts of these discussions were subjected to social and psychoanalytic analysis for elements of wish fulfillment, projection, displacement, neurosis, ethnocentricity, and prejudice. These qualitative data were then compared with the qualitative construction of the quantitative component of the data, and the questionnaires were revised to seek to differentiate between the two types of "potential fascists": those subjects who are ideologically and psychologically committed to a racialized form of social perception, and those who are predisposed to quickly adapt themselves should those in power begin to tolerate or promote anti-Semitic and racist expression. From these data the first positive ideal types of anti-Semitic and racist personalities were created, leading to a refinement of the original questionnaires and the categories for their analysis. A psychometric model for questioning and measuring the particular types of reactionary thought was now developed with an eye toward creating a composite scale. The subscales measured (1) political, economic, and moral conservatism; (2) ethnocentrism; and (3) projectivity and resistance to analysis (what they called anti-intraception). A composite scale—the "F-" (fascist) scale—was thus constructed by examining the qualitative correlation of questions on these scales, themselves already developed through an iterative process of survey refinement and subscale design. These scales were weighted by correlation to analysis of how statements of explicit anti-Semitism developed a pattern for identifying Others, articulating revenge fantasies, and conceiving of political action. As part of the whole process, researchers looked into the response distributions of particular scales and the composite scales to select subjects for further interviews and qualitative analysis. Neither deductive nor inductive, this methodology featured a high degree of recursivity and back-construction: just as the surveys were constructed by content analysis, theoretical hypotheses, and preliminary survey results from previous work, so the final analysis of and presentation of material from the depth interviews were structured by a series of intermediate reviews of the survey results that allowed for the late addition of categories, subpopulations, and ideal types.

Love, Hate, and Method

The Authoritarian Personality set a new standard for combining theoretical and empirical, qualitative and quantitative data analysis. Those working on the study agreed that the most important quantitative-qualitative innovation was the dynamic psychological profile of the F-scale. Having observed a high degree of correlation between two metrics—those who scored high on P-E-C (Political-Economic-Conservatism) and A-S (Anti-Semitic)—the researchers discerned a pattern in which a heightened concern about the conventionality of values and social norms could feed a sense of distrust of the outgroup, or vice versa. The researchers identified nine variables that seemed highly correlated with fascistic potential: conventionalism, authoritarian submission, authoritarian aggression, anti-intraception, superstition and stereotypy, concern with power and "toughness," destructiveness and cynicism, projectivity, and sexual paranoia.[6] When statistical covariance among these variables was detected, the correlation was examined in semantic terms that recognized the mutual construction of the category by the subject and the investigator. Sometimes a category that seemed diagnostic proved a mere projection. An excellent example is "conventionalism," which was first included in the conservative ideology profiles to assess the "well known hypothesis" that susceptibility to fascism was simply "in the culture" of the middle class.[7] When the first round of questions yielded a negative correlation between conventionalism and fascism, the researchers recalibrated, crafting questions that distinguished between the traditionally conservative dislike of imputed "morally loose" behavior of minorities or the lower classes and the kind of conventionalism that outsources moral authority to an external agency outside the ego. The example given in this case was of "the perpetual convert," a type who serially "finds" himself through Catholicism, then Communism, then conservatism, and so on through the alphabet.[8] With the revised concept, the researchers reversed their initial hypothesis, arguing that the "conservativism" of the fully integrated ego might "resist the violence and delinquency that characterizes the advanced stages of fascism," whereas the perpetual convert who orients himself toward an externally referred social authority is more likely to assimilate rapidly "to the standards of the collective powers to which he is, for the time being, identified."[9]

Two immediate discoveries required the researchers to revise methods as well as hypotheses. First, they were startled to find that apparently everyone has the ability to resist certain stereotypes; and second, they came to understand that, contrary to common belief, ignorance was neither the first nor the strongest incubator of prejudice. Citizens learned how to resist social prejudice both internally and as part of his or her public self, but this training had varying outcomes. The research discovered one group of respondents who, though volubly opposed to stereotyping, engaged in it anyway; while finding others who actively avoided all expressions and even thoughts of bias. Some low scorers with little education seemed to be gifted at criticizing prejudicial perceptions, and some well-educated high scorers actively resisted self-reflective analysis of their own prejudices. Applying a multidisciplinary approach, the researchers worked to discern when people were actively deflecting analysis. Observing this active relation to cultural and public stimuli—the fact that consumption of images of the Other was an active process even when it might appear passive— allowed the team to refine the F-scale in a very important respect. Fascist ideology was not a matter of blind id-driven identification with the totality but of learned and active behavior. The opening chapter indeed argues that though research must, by necessity, build a general profile of public opinion, its main goal is twofold: to create one profile of the truly small number of likely authoritarian activists and another for a much larger group of passive compliers. The book is careful to note that some conservatives and conformists do not end up being authoritarian, and it argues that this group also merits a dedicated study. *The Authoritarian Personality* thus constructs its object with the aim of studying both the pathological extreme and those who will align with it in a divided, non-identical social world. In all these ways this is not a study of culture or any other given totality but a study of what Adorno considered the "phenomenology of prejudice," analyzed as a totality that entwines with the divisions within modern society.[10]

These extensive interview protocols and their often lengthier analyses produced a detailed and still-provocative archive of American identity, circa 1944, in its cultural and psychological dimensions. But the recognition that neither conservatism nor ignorance alone is the source of prejudice also led the researchers to important methodological reflections on the two-way relationship between researcher and subject. Adorno addressed the ethical concern explicitly:

> In all probability, the presentation of extreme anti-Semitic statements as if they were no longer disreputable but rather something which can be sensibly discussed, works as a kind of antidote for the superego and may stimulate imitation even in cases where the individual's "own" reactions would be less violent.[11]

Research should not normalize racism. Crucially, the research model sought to record responses to questions of social stereotypy without actively eliciting them, reifying racial concepts, or legitimizing the expression of negative attitudes toward any group. Follow-up questions sought to elicit further specification of an interviewee's specific complaints against a group or a subgroup without encouraging the individual to perfect or imitate a racialized schema of social interpretation. Open-ended questions encouraged spontaneous answers. Thus, interviewers were instructed to ask, "Can you tell a Jew from other people? How?" If the person indicated that Jews were identifiable because they were to be blamed for something, interviewers were to tag their spontaneous explanations against a long list of "bad Jewish traits" that was not shown to the subjects:

> Aggressive; bad mannered; controlling the banks; black marketeers; cheating; Christ-killers; clannish; Communists; corrupting; dirty; draft dodgers; exploiters; hiding their identity; too intellectual; Internationalists; overcrowding many jobs; lazy; controlling movies; money-minded; noisy; overassimilative; overbearing; oversexed; looking for privileges; quarrelsome; running the country; too smart; spoiling nice neighborhoods; owning too many stores; undisciplined; unethical against Gentiles; upstarts; shunning hard manual labor; forming a world conspiracy?[12]

These characteristics, contradictory and strangely arbitrary, defined a pattern when chosen from the subconscious menu—a pattern that might correlate with specific variables of the F-scale. What the researchers found, however, was that, in practice, those who volunteered one of these menu items were usually willing to follow up with the "inclusive" list—as long as they felt secure that they were perceived by the researcher as simply confirming something "pre-established, as if commonly accepted."[13] While the expectation was that the social, political, or religious fragmentation of American society might encourage different groups of respondents to foreground, say, economic over moral or religious over international concerns in the deployment of negative alterities, it turned out that one of the hypotheses of *Dialectic of Enlightenment*—the ticket mentality—was decisive, at least for anti-Semitism. If an individual was willing to "vote" for one part of the anti-Semitic platform, he tended to be willing to accept any and all "reasonable"— generally available—stereotypical frameworks of perception. The ability to populate a schema defines identity thinking and therefore reason.

There is a perceptible determination throughout the pages of *The Authoritarian Personality* to let these words emanate from the interlocutors while also not letting them stand as descriptions of reality: the point is to allow the conceptual dissonances within the statements speak to the larger question of socially distorted consciousness. Inevitably, the conceptual non-identities that emerge from the "dialectics of the interview" expose complex contradictions that cannot be accounted for in statistical surveys. Sometimes, the analysis addresses these moments only in passing, such as in the case of the culturally fascinating subject 5052, whose concerns are encapsulated in the phrase "I am not a Negro, I am an entertainer." This man, who is strongly anti-Semitic and defensive about his homosexuality, receives only the brief comment that "the element of social identification [as an] outcast is clearly responsible for his prejudice."[14] *The Authoritarian Personality* cultivates an interest in the individual suffering behind this kind of intersectional negative identification but recognizes that it is beyond the scope of the book to address such cases *in detail* because the "whole complex of anti-Semitism among minority groups, and among Jews themselves, offers serious problems and deserves a study of its own. Even the casual observations provided by our sample suffice to corroborate the suspicion that those who suffer from social pressure may frequently tend to transfer this pressure onto others rather than to join hands with their fellow victims."[15]

The care the researchers took not to cue their subjects came from an equal mix of concern with producing objective psychological science and with the ethical implications of the research situation. The survey form required typologies; yet any typology might cut two ways. The following passage, though it addresses the projections of its subjects, speaks to a self-reflective awareness of the dialectic of enlightenment: "Sometimes the projective aspect of the fantasies of Jewish domination comes into the open. Those whose half-conscious wishes culminate in the idea of the abolition of democracy and the rule of the strong, call those antidemocratic whose only hope lies in the maintenance of democratic rights."[16] To be concerned about the weakness of rights theory under demagogic pressure dovetails with a legal-political caution against helping perfect ethnocentric typologies into a psycho-social *technique*. Once someone becomes used to "spotting the Jew" or identifying the Other as weak and in need of protection, such a person has become aware of the wounded nature of universal subjectivity. Though such a schema could amplify the liberal impulse to impose a sense of right and could use the power of equal protection to protect such vulnerable identities until they can become regular, universal subjects, the ideal-type modeling of an ethnographic imagination can easily be manipulated into a tool for conspiracy theorists to claim that they are defending democracy by attacking the vulnerable who need state protection. Sociology in an age of identity must work to articulate social types without encouraging such conspiratorial counternarratives of inverse emancipation, for every typology could be misused by the media, culture, and the state. This tragic awareness of an arms race in the *techné* of social typologies was underscored by the fact that the Europeans on the anti-Semitism project—Adorno, Horkheimer, Marie Jahoda, Frenkel-Brunswik—were highly aware that the National Socialists had already used ideal types and narrative profiling to imagine a more perfectly illiberal society. In German sociology there was a Nazi version of the culture and personality movement, the most technically sophisticated proponent of which was Erich Rudolph Jaensch, who published in 1938 the book *Der Gegentypus: Psychologisch-anthropologische Grundlagen deutscher Kulturphilosophie, ausgehend von dem was wir überwinden wollen* (The type of the antagonist: Psychological-anthropological foundations of a German cultural philosophy, based on that which we must overcome). Already the title reveals abject *Gleichschaltung*—assimilation to the Nazi norm. A member of Alfred Rosenberg's Militant League for German Culture, Jaensch combined Jungian analysis of heroic types with statistical profiling methods to come up with images of the ideal Nazi type who exercised unwavering leadership and of the "opposite type," or Semitic Type, who represented "that which we must overcome." Jaensch had a statistical model for rooting out those inclined toward ambiguity, aestheticism, synesthesia, and complexity of perspectives.[17]

Aware that systems like Jaensch's were negative identification machines, used for "labeling live human beings, independent of their specific qualities" in ways that "resulted in decisions about their life and death," Adorno insisted that *The Authoritarian Personality* include an ethics of applying social typologies. Any study produced by researchers in America might potentially be used by some local "militant culture league" to supply its state or agitators with the technology for identifying its enemies. For this reason, "enquiries regarding the study of prejudice must be particularly cautious when the issue of typology comes up." Typologies are dangerous distillates of applied subjective and objective categorization. Interviewers should not prompt subjects into expressing violent prejudice they otherwise would not, and the typologist should also remain aware of the potential use of their findings and their categories, working neither to advance the science of negative identification nor to unintentionally render the categories of research "undynamic, 'anti-sociological' or quasi-biological." The problem with Jaensch was not merely ill intent but bad science: to be actual science, Jaensch's inquiry would have to be self-reflexive, capable of explaining what social forces would first compel science to group people into types such that they would be commanded by rigid stimulus-response models. One must negate negative identity to make it knowledge.[18]

Partly because the study was restrained in the framing of its questions, it was judgmental in its analysis. This duality has been the source of many critiques of the project. The researchers' willingness to state that some interviewees *knew* what was objectively true, but were resistant to saying it or thinking about it, has indeed offended the sensibilities of many public opinion survey-makers. Violating the tacitly relativist and culturalist assumptions of American research, the study was accused of presuming the existence of an objective reality, and of presuming that individuals had the ability to question biases. As early as 1956, Edward Shils would call the study on this ground "biased," suggesting that the researchers thought they "knew better" than their subjects. Adorno certainly believed that the truly condescending researcher was the one who believed that subjects could neither transcend their cultural assumptions nor hide their true opinions. Research should remain Kantian in interpreting the objective meaning of subjective categories of understanding up until the point that Freud was required; the book's most forceful analyses look beyond the realm of immanent consciousness and intragroup perceptions and speak to the conscious and unconscious sources of the social impulse to impose identity on others. We might summarize this by saying that Adorno's standards of rationality are Bauerian for the interviewees and Lukácsian for the researcher. Though not everyone has the training to reflect on the role and meaning of social science and the ethics of stereotyping, everyone is, nonetheless, capable of some perspectival reflection that can carry her beyond her own worldview to see things from someone else's point of view—as an outsider to one's own ingroup, as an object for some other subject's observation. The negative construction of selfhood among those who score high on the quantitative F-scale made clear that their inner mental life was typically driven by (stereotypical) reflections about others that served as source material to define, negatively, their own sense of identity. Although Adorno shared Otto Bauer's Kantian view that comparative reflection on ingroup/outgroup constitutions should naturally progress from a sense of inner ontology or essence toward a comparative view of cultural immanence and, finally, to an interest in objective universality in its epistemological and legal forms, Adorno also found that his subjects possessed a wealth of evasion tactics to forestall exactly this circuit of thinking through non-identity, allowing them to settle for positive identity, even in a negative or aggressive form.

Applying a model of phenomenological-psychoanalytic reduction to the interview transcripts, the researchers looked first for contradictions, then classified underlying evasion tactics, and finally, when appropriate, analyzed the "functional" character of the individual's negative projection. Following this procedure, the study found anti-Semitism "useful" to the individual for providing a ready-made structure of reality that is "not so much dependent upon the nature of the object as upon the subject's own psychological wants and needs."[19] A typical example is subject 5051, a Boy Scout leader with "strong unconscious fascist leanings" who denies the common saying that the "average Jew is smarter in business than the average white" but insists that Jews need to learn to be "more cooperative and agreeable"—and who then adds, "Armenians are much more underhanded . . . but not nearly as conspicuous and noisy."[20] To this man's uncanny distrust of the Stranger in general—foreigners per se—is appended a "semirational" qualification: a sense that he indeed knows some Jews he likes assures him that he is making objective sociological observations. This is, for Adorno, psychologically a matter of neurotically keeping some group always available to stand in for the bogeyman, the unknown; but it is functional in the way that he maintains a militant outgroup nationalism: implausibly he "tempers his Antisemitism and anti-Negroism by referring to a third group . . . the Armenians." This "mobile" prejudice is, as Adorno puts it, "relatively independent of its object" and, for that, oddly self-reflexive: even as it acknowledges that the Jews can be quite smart, this positive identification of the Other is used merely to glorify his own ingroup.

Once a subject finds the promulgation of stereotypes functional for his or her self-construction, things can go in two directions: semirational, half-objective ideas can become conscious, rationalistic theories of the "problem" with the Other, and/or they can become erotically and emotionally charged matters of active subjective obsession.

The first, "rationalistic" category becomes a kind of perceptual schema, according to which the individual begins to "see Jews everywhere" and to equate their new "awakened" perception with a heightened insight into reality, especially the reality of social struggles. Sometimes a clear motive precedes the distorted perception: "One does not need to conjure up deeper motivations in order to understand the attitude of the farmer who wants to get hold of the property of his Japanese neighbor."[21] At other times the Stranger becomes the personified form of the subject's own inability to explain the complex operation of "supra-individual laws" or failures of bureaucratic rationality: "Political stereotype and personalization can be understood as devices for overcoming [the] uncomfortable state of affairs" created by the alienation of the individual from society and by the inscrutable "objectification of social processes." If one can create a logic according to which the "real" society can still be loved even as one hates the bad groups that have somehow corrupted it, then one can create a vision of a "pure" society that can be restored once the bad group is eliminated. This definition of Jews, Negroes, or others as "a problem" simultaneously serves to give a pseudo-rationalistic label to social problems, and it allows the rationalistic anti-Semite to feel enlightened for having seen through to the essence of things.[22] The whole language of "the problem" "take[s] over from the sphere of science and is used to give the impression of a searching, responsible deliberation" and thus makes it sound like the prejudiced person is somehow engaged in a "detached, higher objectivity."[23]

The second form of hardened racist identity is antirationalistic and deeply emotional. Just as Plato had maintained that knowledge was always motivated by love, so stereotypy also has an erotic component for those who have come to perceive the form of the negative Other in all that they see. "The whole complex of the Jew," says Adorno, "is a kind of recognized red-light district of legitimized psychotic distortion,"[24] in which the racist thinker cultivates a deep, eroticized love of the object of his or her deepest fantasies. "Falling negatively in love,"[25] the anti-Semite actively cultivates knowledge of the Jew so that he or she can externalize pent-up social aggression through personalization and thereby authorize the release of emotions that otherwise would be taboo. Once this epistemology of eroticized hate takes root, both subject and object are damaged, and experiencing the other person starts to become impossible.

Worse, the eroticized knowledge starts to connect itself to the rationalistic forms of racialized seeing that become hardened against reflection. This forms the perfect subject/object identity of the anti-Semite—one immune to perceiving actual difference or actual people. "One cannot 'correct' stereotypy by experience," especially one that has come to be bonded by an eroticized attachment that systematically distorts all forms of knowledge.[26] Adorno gives the example of subject 6070, a forty-year-old woman who ties this all together in a number of startling ways:

I don't like the Jews. The Jew is always crying. They are taking our country over from us. They are aggressive. They suffer from every lust. Last summer I met the famous musician X, and before I really knew him he wanted me to sign an affidavit to help bring his family into this country. Finally, I had to flatly refuse and told him I want no more Jews here. Roosevelt started bringing the Jews into government, and that is the chief cause of our difficulties today. The Jews arranged it so they were discriminated for in the draft. I favor a legislative discrimination against the Jews along American, not Hitler lines. Everybody knows that the Jews are back of the Communists. This X person almost drove me nuts. I had made the mistake of inviting him to be my guest at my beach club. He arrived with ten other Jews who were uninvited. They always cause trouble. If one gets in a place, he brings two more and those bring two more.[27]

As Adorno points out, though the opening passage expresses dislike of the Jews, the whole passage is charged with erotic language and wish fulfillments of unrequited attraction-repulsion. This woman, "doubtless attracted by the [musician's] fame," invited him to her club but quickly free-associates her way from this eroticized attraction to a bizarre construction of the threat Jews in general pose now that they have been invited to America. The rationalization that "the refugee, forced to leave his country . . . *wants* to intrude and expand over the whole earth," to control governments near and far, draws on "imagery . . . derived from the fact of persecution itself."[28] By projecting global persecution onto her antithetical ideal type, subject 6070 makes herself more important and powerful, and yet indulges in the fantasy that the Jew-entertainer is himself both persecuted and a member of an all-powerful conspiracy (backed up by the strange pseudo-rationalization of an imminent Malthusian population explosion). Here one sees the limits of almost every model—rational or irrational—of combating projective negative identity. The anti-Semite who is truly "negatively in love" can transform everything according to her special racialized vision. Like the romantic lover who sees her love everywhere, the identity-obsessed lover believes that the current object of her attraction holds the "key to everything" and perceives everything and every group according to this schema. Once the scientist encounters someone like this—someone who has assembled stereotypy, rationalization, and inverted love into a negative identity such that the person can narrate major humanitarian disasters in personalized terms—the reformer has to recognize that there are limits to what can be achieved merely by "advocat[ing] improv[ed] intercultural relations . . . between the different groups." Rather, one must "reconstitute the capacity for *having* experience in order to prevent the growth of ideas which are malignant in the most literal, clinical sense."[29] Adorno will later describe this state of affairs as wounded subjectivity. When the subject loses the ability to experience the world or to encounter the Other, then life—subjectivity—in the emphatic sense, is damaged, and false identities are reproduced.

Separate Spheres and Broken Universality

It was terrifying to behold the anti-Semite who created a new totality—a masterable world of inverted knowledge, love, and identification of the Other. This was a new barbarism that defined the ingroup by the power of the outgroup. But *The Authoritarian Personality* further showed that there is a horror beyond wounded subjectivity: the possibility of a damaged objectivity. Psychological projections, fantasies of domination and submission, can alloy with high principles, idealisms, outgroup identifications, and historical tropes to create virulent strains of socially distorted perception that shade off into a kind of conceptual violence. The late nineteenth-century age of empire had, as Hannah Arendt would put it in 1954, made possible the notion of extending popular sovereignty of one people over another without civil or legal representation.[30] This was a way of damaging the object through a transformation of the subject concept, such that a populist or emancipatory ideal needed only the smallest twist to break with the universality that held subject to object. Thus, concepts that would seem the very bulwark of democratic thinking could become schemas for the misperception of others, for the mapping of psychological fears onto real social antagonisms. Americans were not likely,

Adorno believed the research had found, to espouse fascist ideas outright. Most Americans embraced the American ideal of democracy and its associated doctrine of equality and were therefore resistant to explicitly fascist ideologies. But resistance could be worn down by the kinds of revenge or domination narratives that transformed ideals into their opposite. An example of this conflict can be seen in subject 5054, a middle-aged woman who insists that she always tries to "see the other side" of social conflicts and to "fight prejudice on every side." In other words, the interviewee understands and subscribes to the ideal of enlightened subjectivity and understands how prejudice threatens it:

> She would not subscribe to a "racist theory," but does not think that the Jews will change much, but rather that they will tend to be become "more aggressive." She also believes that "they will eventually run the country, whether we like it or not."[31]

This subject speaks directly about theories of racial domination, only to reject such views as horrid and to prescribe a general perspectivalism. It is almost as if the interviewed subject had read William Graham Sumner's account of the ingroup mentality and decided in favor of the *Genealogy of Morals*. The problem, however, is that she protests too much, and despite her explicit antiracism she adheres to a historical narrative that sees intergroup struggle as inevitable and escalating. Her moral belief in the equality of humans has run afoul of her perception of empirical inequality, and she is unable to recompose these perceptions into an understanding of social objectivity. One who holds such views would not need to believe in conspiracy theories to endorse some vision of "heroic action" or pre-emotive purge to stave off a fate of domination: one would need only to damage the object—to create a psychologically distorted image of the outgroup and a feeling of historical necessity. While the high-scoring "total" fascists were more frightening, such relatively mild forms of potential fascist inclination raised particularly involved questions. What is one to do with the large number of people who understand—and present themselves as embracing—some variant of Kantian universalism? What is one to do with the people who are fairly well adjusted and proud of their explicit antiracism, yet have exposed vulnerabilities or incomplete theoretical impulses which could be readily exploited by a skilled agitator or a corrupt transformation of traditional authority? Here we must recall the question that Horkheimer asks in his 1945 response to Adorno's typology memo: Who is the less neurotic individual, the son who is well behaved out of a nervous embrace of conventional morality, or the young man who, out of a desire to define who he is, goes out and beats up a Jew to prove he has an identity? In cases like these, it does not appear that the problem is one of psychological weakness or maladjustment. The theorist must instead consider how psychologically stable people, with largely integrated egos and superegos, may nonetheless lose their purchase on social objectivity. Psychological or cultural theories alone could not account for such cases; Horkheimer and Adorno concluded that such cases called out for a better theoretical account of the public function of reason.

One of the key areas of the survey in which questions of psychology in everyday life intersected with the problem of reason, and cast light on how the category of objectivity itself could become distorted, involved its examination of gender relations. Partly because of the wartime circumstances, the project surveyed an unusually high percentage of women. This accident proved opportune, not only because it spoke to the interests of the large number of distinguished women researchers on the project (the personnel for *Studies in Prejudice* reads like a *Who's Who* of feminist researchers in midcentury psychology) but also because Adorno and Horkheimer had a deep interest in the way the divisions within the modern subject were rooted in social divisions, the conventional separate spheres that cut through the bare universality of an exchange society. The "typology letter" of October 11, 1945, in which Horkheimer responded to Adorno's critique of types, offers an example of the way he saw divisions of reason as rooted in spatial divisions that were also markers of pure irrationality, traditional domination:

My first remark is a very fundamental one and I know well that nobody agrees more with it than you do. However, I think this point of view should possibly be brought out much more strongly. If, in this current period, one is born into an average Gentile family one does not have to be a "type" in order to be an antisemite. One simply learns to speak disrespectfully of Jews as one would learn to curse, tell dirty jokes, drink heavily, or to rage about taxes and strikes. In a democratic society one does not exhibit antisemitism at somewhat formal occasions, as, at a good puritan party, the men do not have their whiskies in the presence of ladies, or, as in the semi-dry provinces of Canada, the place in the hotel where beer is served (but no meals!) is often found in the basement and not too far from the W.C. (whose walls are anyway the predestined blank pages for antisemitic slogans and caricatures). True, as long as certain decisive forces of society have not given the *mot d'ordre* for open fascism, it is not respectable to become involved with violently antisemitic organizations, but in the meantime the swankiest clubroom offers its members not a few compensations for the pleasures of the unknown artist in the W.C. The affinity of the two spheres, by the way, becomes quite obvious in the exclusion of women from the clubs. A thorough historical and social analysis of phenomena such as this exclusion would certainly yield interesting revelations. We would probably find that the anti-civilizatory tendencies which were tolerated throughout the bourgeois ages in a pseudo-domesticated form, presumably as a safety-valve, had from the beginning the teleological meaning to become the arsenal of counter-revolution and reaction.[32]

This memo, written four years before the publication of *The Authoritarian Personality* but in the midst of preparing its surveys, signals the entire postwar trajectory of critical theory. The overall theoretical interest here is in how subjective identity is produced and how internal divisions and negative identities are important for the formation of illiberal ideologies. The spatial divisions that separate the abject from the public and the body from the mind intersect with a different set of divisions demarcating the subordination of the feminine as a sphere of putative gentility and civilization set aside from the roughness of the men's world. Both are reinscribed with a binary conception of the division between reason and emotion that at once assigns reason to the "public" space and routes it through the backrooms where men go to escape feminine flapdoodle and talk straight about hard facts. These divisions, at once absolute and flexible in their contradictions, became, Horkheimer suggested, the channels through which prejudice circulates through the body politic, in part because the spatial exception to universality legitimates and creates special license for the expression of anti-universal thought but also because these divisions within the built world are reproduced in the divisions within the subject itself. All men—and all women—carried within them, insofar as they were socialized into the normal divisions of modern life, mental public spaces and mental backrooms into which irreconcilable thoughts were channeled: the public space for generally acceptable—democratic, egalitarian—truths; a basement space "not too far from the W.C." where dirty jokes express conflicted perceptions about empirical domination and identity projection. Women are not exempted; the system of bias expresses identity through difference. This explains subject 5054: The inner contradiction between her expressed hatred of prejudice and her actual belief in antagonistic human difference is rooted in her locating them in different mental categories. The first is a moral truth, the other a pragmatic one, and each is assigned its special sphere: but there is no doubt as to which—when push comes to shove—would be sacrificed for the other.

The prefix "pseudo-" appeared frequently in *The Authoritarian Personality*, affixed to words such as "pseudo-domestication," "pseudo-conservativism," "pseudo-masculinity." This pattern of language that seeks to distinguish between objective and subjective meanings has proven controversial. For the same reason that readers have been taken aback by the study's willingness to pass judgment on its subjects, the term "pseudo-" seems—with its affinities for that other favorite word of the 1940s, "phony"—to reveal something "pseudo-scientific" about the study. American-style empirical research is supposed to neutrally record opinions, map out the contours of a whole culture, not declare its subjects to be evading their duty to universality. Yet the terms "pseudo-feminine" and "pseudo-masculine," which play particularly prominent roles in the study's discussion of gender, speak to the ways that objectivity and subjectivity could be wounded at the same time. Horkheimer and Adorno believed that people are "educated" to the non-identities of anti-Semitism alongside their education in the norms of polite society and the high ideals of civilization: both kinds of knowledge are acquired in the process of learning the proper places and occasions for expressing particular kinds of emotions. The idea that the divisions of social space formed and corresponded to subjective intellectual and affective categories points to the damage to autonomy involved in the making of subjectivity itself. But the idea that these divisions within the self are then instrumentalizable—that individuals can partition emotion from reason according to conventional notions of masculinity or femininity and then deploy the differential when authority demands it—speaks to how practices of gender exclusion created routes for racial exclusion and how practices of pseudo-domestication could, far from reinforcing the rule of public rationality, function as placeholders for authoritarian tendencies, ready to be pushed aside the moment that the order for open fascism is given from above. Not surprisingly, *The Authoritarian Personality* documented how the core fascist types were obsessed with *non plus ultra* forms of masculinity defined in terms of violence. The "tough-guy persona" that defined a form of "pseudo-masculinity" played a crucial role in redefining the social acceptability of violence. But women, the study showed, also cultivated anti-civilizatory tendencies. Whether through their inner conviction that men's realities were the true ones or the overt demand that men perform the dirty work necessary to create a civilization fit for women's purity, "pseudo-feminine" women could play a constitutive role in forming the "arsenal of counter-revolution and reaction." Eliminating social discrimination against outsiders might be necessary for overcoming prejudice, but the gendered division of reason suggested it might be far from sufficient. As long as gendered divisions dictated who could feel what about whom, and as long as they distorted the perceptions of identity and selfhood in ways that could be exploited by agitators—as long as the divergence between subjective and universal identity was a definitive part of people's lives—there was always the possibility of a total distortion of the space of public reason and solidarity. To use the prefix "pseudo-" is, then, to think about how notions of the normative can create seemingly scientific sociological observations that do not just smuggle spurious normativity into everyday notions of the reasonable but can also give birth to pathological distortions that go beyond confusions of fact and norm. Acting according to pseudo-masculine principles can mean imposing an identity on oneself as a necessity and actually choosing a "ticket slate" of enemies or victims who violate that norm.

The Projectivity of Negative Identity

Gender is not the only pseudo-norm or pseudo-science that can be weaponized. Pseudo-democracy, pseudo-liberalism, pseudo-individualism, and pseudo-progressivism are all forms of asserting negative identity or ideals that create new possibilities for reactionary identity formations. Here again, the concern is not about public opinion as a statistical average but about how sociological group identifications can ground a system of violence on falsified knowledge and referred responsibility. Such an identity relation can be a very powerful way of activating latent prejudice even within broadly tolerant people. The most terrifying objective misconstruction of identity and ideals in *The Authoritarian Personality* has to be the following testimony from subject 5061a, a woman who scored low on the F- and P-E-C scales and only middling on the Ethnocentric scale:

"My relations with the Jews have been anything but pleasant." When asked to be more specific it was impossible for her to name individual incidents. She described them, however, as "pushing everybody about, aggressive, clannish, money minded. . . . The Jews are practically taking over the country. They are getting into everything. It is not that they are smarter, but they work so hard to get control. They are all alike." When asked if she did not feel if there were variations in the Jewish temperament as in any other, she said, "No, I don't think so. I think there is something that makes them all stick together and try to hold on to everything. I have Jewish friends and I have tried to not treat them antagonistically, but sooner or later they have also turned out to be aggressive and obnoxious. . . . I think the percentage of very bad Jews is much greater than the percentage of bad Gentiles. . . . My husband feels exactly the same way on this whole problem. As a matter of fact, I don't go as far as he does. He didn't like many things about Hitler, but he did feel that Hitler did a good job on the Jews. He feels that we will come in this country to a place where we have to do something about it."[33]

These words come not of ignorance, nor active theorization of racism, nor social isolation and the failure to encounter difference. Rather, the issue here is one of distorted or pseudo-knowledge that is disturbingly proximal to the Kantian ideal. Knowledge, according to the Kantian formula, has two sources, experience and rationality. Unlike the high-scoring subjects, this woman does not actively embrace any theories of racialized global conflict or ideologically sponsored conspiracy theories. Nor is she ignorant of global affairs, economic and political theory. She indeed recognizes that racism is wrong and is quick to suggest that she has Jewish friends. She does, however, "know" they have, as a group, done her wrong—even though, when the interviewer followed up and asked how she had been injured by Jews, she could not name a single incident. This nonexperienced experience and her quickness to refer her ideas to her husband point toward the conclusion that her sense of a need to "do something" vaguely genocidal arises from deference to two sources of external authority: explicitly, her husband and the man's role in determining the correct boundaries of violence; and, tacitly, mass media and culture, from which she has absorbed a great deal of distorted information about events and ideas.

The problem posed by subject 5061a is that racism is not a rejection of human universality but a pathologically distorted version of it. If this is a kind of ignorance, it is au courant. Bolstered by a variety of pseudoscientific observations and cultivated feelings of national urgency and self-defense, this distorted social perception creates an "imaginary foe" that helps otherwise disoriented individuals define their own identity and values by projecting their fears onto an outgroup.[34] Drawing support from "statements which are either plainly self-contradictory or incompatible with facts or of a manifestly imaginary character," such damaged modern knowledge creates distorted fantasies that make everyday life meaningful while allowing inherited stereotypes to be "emancipated" from all probative evidence.[35] The essence of reaction, this statement also represents a distorted form of Enlightenment, one that pays lip service to democracy while expressing pointedly antidemocratic values and rationalizes the exceptions it makes to universality by citing others who would do even worse things in the defense of normality and decency.

Adorno and Horkheimer's goal was to turn the social Darwinistic language of ingroup/outgroup conflict into a critical language of social theory, but they could not do this by presupposing conflict or harmony, identity or atomization as the norm. One had to remove the Darwinism from Max Weber's concept of reason. Adorno therefore pushed for a negative ideal-type model that sought to avoid either reifying conflict or essentializing group identity. By placing extensive interview protocols alongside a minimal framework of critique, the analytical apparatus of research can point to internal contradictions in the interviewees rather than judge them by an outside standard or assume that conflict is inherent to subjectivity. Proceeding in this way was designed to avoid the "pseudo-democratic choice" model of polling that could push both researchers and survey respondents toward anticipated answers and thereby obscure their paradoxical alliance with extremism. The goal of *The Authoritarian Personality* was not to measure an average public opinion but to understand, qualitatively and quantitatively, the circuits by which opinion could move from center to extreme and to understand how the rules of normal politics could be played against themselves to create a damaged public or a politics of antipolitics.

Pseudo-choices can also work in the other direction, effectively rendering opaque the difference between choices that are worlds apart. *The Authoritarian Personality* explores how American rhetoric represented the Soviet Union as a "vast experiment" of a sort not all that different from the United States. The pattern of falsified personalization, whether xenophobic or xenophilic, breaks with actual social analysis based on questions of class interest, institutional integrity, or concern for the integrity of traditional institutions and the deliberative process. Adorno argues, for example, that the excess identification in pro-Russian sentiments means that ardent convictions are founded on intellectual laziness. Discussions of the "experiment"

> implicitly translat[e] Russian phenomena into ideas more familiar to Americans, often by presenting the Russian system as more harmless and "democratic" than it is, as a kind of pioneering venture somehow reminiscent of our own tradition. Yet indices of a certain inner aloofness are rarely missing. The low scorers' pro-Russian sympathies seem to be of a somewhat indirect nature, either by rigid acceptance of an extraneous "ticket" or by identification based on theoretical thinking and moral reflections rather than on an immediate feeling that this is "my" cause.[36]

This is just the mirror image of high scorers who express the conflict with Russia in terms that are little more than a dressed-up version of ethnocentrism. They fear the "bogy" of Communism, stripped of all policy reflection, imagining it through a kind of "economic superindividualism"—as if Stalin will personally seize their property. Communist and anticommunist rhetoric have in common, in fact, forms of identity thinking that can turn into an antidemocratic populism and the pseudo-politics of identification of enemies:

> During the last several years all the propaganda machinery of the country has been devoted to promoting anticommunist feeling in the sense of an irrational "scare" and there are probably not many people, except followers of the "party line," who have been able to resist the incessant ideological pressure. At the same time, during the past two or three years it may have become more "conventional" to be overtly opposed to anti-Semitism, if the large number of magazine articles, books, and films with wide circulation can be regarded as symptomatic of a trend. The underlying character structure has little bearing on such fluctuations. If they could be ascertained, they would demonstrate the extreme importance of propaganda in political matters. Propaganda, when directed to the antidemocratic potential in the people, determines to a large extent the choice of the social objects of psychological aggressiveness.[37]

This passage underlines a central concern with trying to combat prejudice: one never knows how deep knowledge goes in a constantly changing world of media messaging. The powerful antidemocratic potential of propaganda operations stems from the mass media's power to bring that which is near far and that which is far near. But in so doing, the media-identity nexus seems to unmoor traditional forms of social knowledge—religion, community relations, and so on—and create a higher degree of suggestibility to the public use of emotions. Thus, one never knows how grounded any sense of tolerance is. "Local" concerns of ingroup/outgroup formation could become the manipulable objects of mass attention and could be used to define new pseudo-problems that made politics a narcissistic medium of self-definition and distraction. Horkheimer's belief that "Anti-semitism was now the general pattern of modern culture" was not just a statement about how widespread Jew hatred had become but an assertion that anti-Semitism had created a new template for politics, transforming it into something more subjective, more irrational, and more concerned with creating non-problems than solving real ones.[38] *The Authoritarian Personality* equivocates as to whether in America the Ku Klux Klan preceded the importation of anti-Semitism in articulating a modern politics of ethnocentrically defined negative identity, but the result is the same: this new fringe-group politics redefined the mainstream. A new logic to the politics of ethnic "questions"—for example, the Jewish question, the Negro question—established a hate politics mobilizing authoritarian power while pretending to put an end to power. Fascists identify victims, label the target group a "problem" to solve, and then run an antipolitical campaign to delegitimize government while actually working to forge a powerful, lawless state that enshrines action without responsibility. Modern media techniques combined with the increasing power of military technology such that the survival of minority groups might well now depend on the ways in which the media could "direct . . . antidemocratic potential" through propaganda, through advertising, or through news supported by some more or less objective version of these images of the Other. This new form of political targeting thereby "determined . . . the social objects of psychological aggressiveness."[39]

Though the language of "pseudo" positions would sound problematic to later readers, it represented, in its moment, an innovative way to measure the shortest social distance between norm and extreme and a creative way to understand the problems of liberal governance as those of identity in nonidentity. One example of the productivity of this idea can be found in the work of Richard Hofstadter, who, citing *The Authoritarian Personality*, defined "the paranoid style" in American politics as a form of liberalism or progressivism that is, in the end, actually a form of destructive antipolitics that puts antipolitical energy back into subjective identities.[40] Adorno's idea of "the pseudo-conservative" was the model: "a man who, in the name of upholding traditional American values and institutions and defending them against more or less fictional dangers, consciously or unconsciously aims at their abolition." This type of antipolitics "[rages] about taxes and strikes" as if they were conspiracies, or about bureaucrats and politicians as if they were usurpers, or about the need for "payback" to teach a group a lesson, or about gleefully having "no pity for the poor."[41] All of these look like forms of action or the democratic expression of opinion, but they are pseudo-activity in that they do not try to solve any problems but instead make Others into "problems." Pseudo-politics undermines the democratic form while appearing to participate in it and thereby serves authoritarianism: its antipolitics typically leads to a personalization of power, where the leader is hated or loved politically for symbolic stances that have little to do with policy.

The memoranda traded among the Institute members engaged in *Studies in Prejudice* reflect their fears for science, the public, and the language of criticism. They believed a new ethics of social science was necessary to avoid reifying the logic of group politics. But they were extremely reticent to confront the identity logic of the culture industry publicly, lest they help perfect fascist techniques of identity production. One can sense a great restraint in *The Studies in Prejudice* as a whole, especially when compared to the private writings: an aversion against stating explicitly how easily the culture industry's push to gain consent through entertainment could be combined with the nationalist search for identifying foreign enemies and agents. The critical theorists apparently decided that it was better to appeal to democratic values—to appeal to Americans' knowledge of the truth and their faith in equal protection—than to directly confront the potential fascist within liberalism. It must thus have been for both strategic and ethical reasons that *The Authoritarian Personality* provides such extensive raw materials from the interviews and marks the transcripts with such lightweight cues for interpreting their inner contradictions. The interviews from this era still speak today, and it is possible to read with a critical compassion the blundering, unintentionally racist expressions of people who believe in democracy. They inspire the hope that with the mildest of pressure—mild external scrutiny or skepticism encouraging reflection about the performative contradictions of ethnocentric projection—contradictory thoughts might yield to a critical perspectivalism that would convert potential racism into productive democratic knowledge of the Other.

The dialectic of social knowledge can, however, injure rather than make whole. Every attempt to think defensively and show how the subject might himself become object might be turned into a weapon for identifying victims. Unfortunately, this danger existed not only in the subject and in the research process—the danger of teaching subjects to become anti-Semites—but also in the research industry itself. The ticket mentality could prevail among sociologists, especially when the Cold War redefined science's enemy; the fragile alliances that made *Studies in Prejudice* possible could crack open and transform scientific disagreement into political binaries.

If *The Authoritarian Personality* proved influential to centrist liberal thinkers such as Hofstadter, it also became one of the objects against which the energies of an emerging neoconservative movement were invested. Thus it was that, in the midst of the Army-McCarthy hearings, the Chicago sociologist Edward Shils penned the political critique of *The*

Authoritarian Personality that has shaped most later interpretations of the book. Shils's main argument is that the book is conceived on a strict Left-Right dichotomy such that it never even conceives of the possibility of a left-wing authoritarianism. This is in fact patently false, as the previous discussion shows. *The Authoritarian Personality* emphasizes the pseudo-conservative nature of authoritarianism, but pseudo-progressive ideas could also feed into reaction, and Adorno saw the Nazi appropriation of the word "socialism" as a case in point. Adorno believed that the pseudo-politics of the ingroup versus the outgroup, just like the social Darwinism from which it sprang, has an inherent right-wing bias capable of appropriating and distorting liberal and scientific ideas. Thus, while the project's wartime context oriented it against fascism, the larger point of *The Authoritarian Personality* was that the new politics of typology and identification destroys the whole system of objective interest politics by grafting radical, antidemocratic positions onto methods tested in the realm of ethnocentric politics such that the entire democratic form is delegitimized from within.

Shils should have understood the history of his own discipline and recognized the pains that *The Authoritarian Personality* took both to establish the ethical role of scientific research and to describe the ways in which the new authoritarian politics evaded the defenses of the Left-Right framework. As a student of Louis Wirth of the Chicago School—a reader of Park and Sumner as well as of Weber and Simmel—Shils certainly knew the American origins and use of the ingroup/outgroup distinction. Having, moreover, served as an assistant to Bruno Betelheim (and, therefore, indirectly, under Horkheimer) in the writing of *The Dynamics of Prejudice*, Shils had every opportunity to grasp the critique of Left-Right schema in *The Authoritarian Personality*. But in 1956, well on his way to becoming one of the original neoconservatives, Shils decided to attack *The Authoritarian Personality*'s use of the ingroup/outgroup distinction as a mere cover for a "bolshevist" politics.[42] The ingroup/outgroup distinction was "immediately recognize[able] . . . for anyone well acquainted with the works of Lenin and Stalin," argued Shils: the idea that the Right harbors extreme hostility toward "outgroups" was Bolshevik code for "the demand for complete and unqualified loyalty to the Party." Equally, the "extreme submissiveness toward 'ingroups'" was obviously equivalent to the Bolshevik insistence on the necessity of class conflict.[43] Somewhat apologetically characterizing *The Authoritarian Personality* as "a product of war time collaboration, Communist tactics and a well-intentioned lack of political and economic sophistication," Shils condemned its corruption of "the intellectual currency of American humanitarian liberalism" through the influence of a "Marxist outlook" or a "Bolshevik *Weltanschauung.*"[44]

That Shils's review was an exercise in political manipulation is confirmed by the fact that, sure enough, a few pages later he performed the ritual naming of names, effectively outing many of his former colleagues and supervisors on the project as Communist fellow travelers. Whether or not the list was used by the House Un-American Activities Committee is unknown; Adorno undoubtedly recognized the review as a political attack. When warned by Marie Jahoda about Shils's article, he expressed his dismay; asked her, as editor of the volume, to demand revisions; and, barring that, asked Jahoda to include introductory remarks noting that the discussion of the Soviet Union in *The Authoritarian Personality* was sharply critical and that the Russian-themed questions were in the context of the US alliance against Hitler, not the Cold War conflict.

By the time Shils's essay was published, Adorno and Horkheimer had, in any case, left the country, and it is perhaps true that this bout of Red baiting claimed fewer victims than it might have. But Shils's attack nonetheless left its mark. His critical article, probably the most cited in the voluminous literature on *The Authoritarian Personality*, created a confection of misunderstandings that has fed bad interpretations for decades—and had a surprisingly influential effect on American sociology. Although Shils would later oppose McCarthyism as a political movement, his critique of *The Authoritarian Personality* helped feed it. By imposing a Left-Right dichotomy on the book, by failing to understand the book's critique of Weber, and by insinuating that Sumner's (nineteenth-century, Pragmatist) ingroup/outgroup distinction was somehow a biomarker for the Bolshevist infection of social science, Shils set the course for the Cold War transformation of Weber into a positivist. He influentially cast suspicion on any future concern with right-wing agitators or politics in the United States and insinuated grave danger to the left-wing bias among sociologists. His basis for this claim, again, shows failure to understand *The Authoritarian Personality*'s interpretation of liberalism. At the end of his article, he says that American sociology can ignore right-wing agitators because they lack—and will permanently lack because they are rooted in the Midwest and West Coast—"any framework of action" that would allow them to succeed and that their "personality structure" was such that they would always, in trying to start their movement, fall into leadership struggles that would cause their own collapse.[45] Implied in Shils's critique, in other words, was the idea that East Coast universities and the structures of capital were plausibly in danger of being infiltrated by Bolsheviks, while it was impossible to imagine a working alliance between the world of small-town America and the strange logics of California media personalities. (Shils had not, apparently, noted the rising political career of Ronald Reagan.)

On the American side of the Cold War, the political damage was done. Adorno would, however, continue to work through the intellectual problems implied by Shils's misunderstanding, and it was in the context of addressing what was wrong with American sociological positivism of the 1950s that he fully articulated a theory of the necessity of interdisciplinary mediation and opposition. Six years later he prepared an extensive critique of what he saw as the pseudo-scientific, uncritical, positivistic distortion of Weber in American sociology. Aimed at Shils's collaborator Talcott Parsons, and framed by the latter's sparring with Marcuse, Adorno's "On the Relation between Sociology and Psychology" addressed the reductionism caused by theories of action in sociology. It was erroneous to assume, as American researchers such as Shils and Parsons did, that both the object of social science and the "context of action" were essentially timeless, structural features of the scientific observer. This was sociology's version of a bad psycho-social reduction: where the psychologists were proposing "personality" as the mediating point between self and society, sociologists imagined that the magic word "action" explained away the antagonism between social structure and subjective drives and desires.[46] In each case—the "personality" and "action" frames—the discipline asserted a keyword that was supposedly transdisciplinary and foundational but which in fact begged essential questions of the relation between truth and power, domination and legitimate authority. For Adorno, social action was too shaped by domination to be the basis for an "objective" science: just as politics was subject to a complex, ever-changing dynamic with authority, so too was science. It was a mistake to hypostatize the interview situation and pretend that it was akin to studying inert matter in the lab; one must have a theory of the historical nature of technique, of subject/object relations, and of the domination potential inherent within the typological models. Sociology needed to be placed in tension with a robust psychology to develop such a theory. This was, in fact, the method that *The Authoritarian Personality* sought to promote; and it was, in a very different way, what the often maddeningly unclassifiable, antidisciplinary work of *Dialectic of Enlightenment* sought to understand. It is with this need for a robust psychological counter to sociological reduction in mind that, turning back from *The Authoritarian Personality* to its paralipomena, we can understand why Adorno and Horkheimer, having engaged with almost every variety of "crazy" American psychology, ultimately moved toward the position that an orthodox (Lukácsian) Marxism required a return to an orthodox Freud.[47]

6

Subject/Object and Disciplinarity

What Is Orthodox Freudianism?

In "Remarks on *The Authoritarian Personality*," the unpublished 1949 afterword to *The Authoritarian Personality*, Theodor Adorno wrote a few sentences about Sigmund Freud that almost certainly surprised his collaborators:

> The fundamental problem of whether and to what extent prejudice can be approached with psychological methods in general, and depth-psychology in particular, will be discussed more systematically later. However, mention should be made here of the relation of our research to other psychoanalytic investigations in this field ([Otto] Fenichel, [Ernst] Simmel, and many others), that have exercised considerable influence on our method. Our whole study, though its subject-matter falls into the area of social psychology, is in full harmony with psychoanalysis in its more orthodox, Freudian version. On theoretical grounds, our group opposed the attempts to "sociologize" psychoanalysis through the softening of basic concepts, e.g., the unconscious, infantile sexuality, the psychological dynamism of the monad, by looking for environmental influences which would have to be registered in terms of the ego rather than the unconscious.[1]

If one looks at this passage in terms of the politics of coauthorship, the invocation of "Freudian orthodoxy" might be put down as another erratic move by Adorno the academic enfant terrible. As a whole, Adorno's collaborators—Daniel Levinson, Nevitt Sanford, Else Frenkel-Brunswik—as well as those directors of *Studies in Prejudice* not from the Institute—Hadley Cantril, Robert MacIver, Gordon Allport, and Samuel Flowerman—were interested in producing social surveys informed by psychological research. Even for Frenkel-Brunswik, the most Freudian of this group, the question of maintaining Freudian orthodoxy was subordinated to the disciplinary need to be scientific, sociologically as well as psychologically, and this meant being pragmatic in applying qualitative judgments and theories to quantifiable psychological and sociological data. Adorno's insistence on orthodoxy appeared to put theory ahead of practice, disciplinarity ahead of empiricism.

Yet Adorno, as we have seen, was rarely disruptive for no good reason. And when we ask why he would, at this moment in his career, suddenly espouse an orthodoxy in which he had shown little previous interest, a serious answer emerges. The passage brings together two well-established aspects of Adorno's theory of interdisciplinary epistemology. First, it continues Adorno's practice of attacking the psycho-social synthesis, rejecting the organism/environment analogy. Second, the passage reveals an ongoing, clear preference for heightening rather than "softening" the tensions between disciplinary approaches and concepts. "Orthodox Freudianism," with its clearly demarcated divisions of the psychic apparatus—id, ego, superego—appealed to both impulses, even if Adorno's next (highly unorthodox) move was to assert the social nature of this psychology. The programmatic statement that he intended to connect while accentuating the difference between the sociological imagination and psychoanalysis's most inwardly closed, monadic qualities indicates that for Adorno, the key thing was not to reduce theory to the ego or psychology to the id. Rediscovering Freud's vision of the divided self became crucial as Adorno began to emphasize the epistemological value of negation and mixed objectivity and moved toward a theory of the non-identical character of truth.

In signaling a return to Freud, the passage registers Adorno's willingness to rethink basic theoretical assumptions. For all its apparent lack of diplomacy, moreover, the passage offers insights into Adorno's evolving approach to interdisciplinary method during the 1940s, dropping important clues about the relation between his largely private, speculative writings and his public-facing interdisciplinary work. As we have seen, Adorno's thought in the 1940s was divided between two quite different modes, which we might roughly designate as speculative and analytical-objective. The speculative mode, which predominates in *Dialectic of Enlightenment* and *Minima Moralia*, is fusional and freely associative, applying the *Echternach* epistemology of radicalized acceleration of psycho-social logics to try to think arguments, or historical tendencies, through to their logical, practical—often absurd—extremes. This speculation aims to diagnose the crisis in bourgeois life without concern for solutions until the last moment, when it takes a step back. The analytical-objective mode, which is deployed in *The Authoritarian Personality* and other public writings, is probative, reconstructive and empirical, speaking in language Adorno's American collaborators could understand—even if it often resignified their terms—and it is aimed at producing valid data. Applying itself not to a crisis but to a world of laws that might potentially fall back into crisis, the analysis also addresses questions of objectivity with much more concern for the boundaries among disciplines. Where the speculative mode largely disregards differences between distinct dimensions of a "layered" personality or of different "value spheres" to generate speculative hypotheses concerning the mediation of the totality, the analytical-objective mode is attentive to the processes of mediation within both the subject *and* the object.

If this dual approach was crucial for Adorno's exploration of the epistemological dimensions of non-identity in the 1940s, the recovery of the necessity of Freud's structural model is indicative of what he learned in the process. In the effort to rescue psychoanalysis from panpsychologism and define its interdisciplinary value, Adorno honed his theory of objective and interdisciplinary negation, his understanding of the importance of the *not-I* in the analysis of identity. Seldom, we might say, has the pursuit of "orthodoxy" been so heterodox; seldom has a theory been so interdisciplinary in its pursuit of disciplinarity purity. One might even call it negative orthodoxy—a counterintuitive usage aimed at the underlying construction of rationality at stake in the construction of subject/object relations. As we saw in Adorno's analysis of Kant and Simmel relative to sociological alienation, or of the Lukácsian understanding of the fetishization of value relations, so here with Adorno's examination of Freud, the question of the non-identical nature of positivity plays a central role in defining Adorno's understanding of how to apply theoretical speculation to the analysis of empirical models and data.

This chapter seeks to understand Adorno's defense of Freudian orthodoxy as a model for critical theory's approach to the divided self, a divided society, a divided notion of truth. In so doing, it seeks to achieve an initial understanding of the idea of subject/object reciprocality and wounded subjectivity in relation to the Freudian and Marxian concepts of universal objectivity. Following Adorno's evolving understanding of Freud's interdisciplinary uses, the chapter explores how the critique of Fromm's concept of the psycho-social synthesis led toward the analysis of both social science and liberalism's forms of abstract subjectivity, authority and reason. Picking up on the previous chapter's analysis of how the genres of emotional constraint and expressivity of bourgeois life incubated within themselves patterns of incomplete emancipation, negative identity, and reactionary potential, this chapter explores how subjective negative identity formed the foundation for authoritarian politics. The second half of the chapter examines the epistemologies of practice and political theory, examining how Max Horkheimer's 1947 *Eclipse of Reason* applied these logics of non-identity to a critique of American Pragmatism and liberalism's formalist evasion of objective social relations. Freud's structural model connects these two endeavors.

Orthodox Freudians: The Inversion of Identity in Fascism and the Reconstruction of Legitimate Authority

To access what "orthodox Freudian" meant for Adorno in the late 1940s and to understand why he connected it to a specifically disciplinary argument, we must consider the process whereby Adorno concretized his criticism of the positivity of Fromm's concept of psychological identity. By 1945, Fromm and Karen Horney were the leading figures in the neo-Freudian revisionist movement. Adorno, writing in the notebook of aphorisms that would become *Minima Moralia*, attacked "business-like revisionists" for declaring Freud bourgeois and repressed and for advocating a simplistic vision of increasing sexual emancipation through decreased hierarchy in social, personal, and familial relations. There can be no doubt whom Adorno is attacking, nor can there be doubt about the trajectory of this attack. Preserved in *Minima Moralia*'s entries from 1944, one can find a kind of "Freud suite" of aphorisms that address the question of the Freudian system and its relation to questions of social integration and epistemology.[2] Preferring the analyst who preserves "analytical coldness" over those who pretend that the world is in a happy state or can be brought into one by modeling positive interpersonal relations, Adorno puts Freud and Marx in the column of the power of negative thinking and underscores the danger of the liberal model of sympathetic universalism:

The repressive traits in Freud have nothing to do with the want of human warmth that business-like revisionists point to in the strict theory of sexuality. Professional warmth for the sake of profit fabricates closeness and immediacy where people are worlds apart. It deceives its victim by affirming in his weakness the way of the world which made him so, and it wrongs him in the degree that it deviates from the truth. If Freud was deficient in human sympathy, he would in this at least be in the company of the critics of political economy, which is better than that of Tagore or Werfel.[3]

Adorno is here defending the importance of moving between a speculative-theoretical and an analytical-objective mode of theory and research, while refusing to jump into the trap of liberal sympathy. Only with the category of negative identity—and the reciprocality of the subject/object relation—does it make sense to compare Fromm's "business-like demeanor" to the spiritualized stance of Rabindranath Tagore and Franz Werfel's literary attempts to cultivate sympathy with the sufferings of the non-Western. Adorno is thinking about how notions of identity, self, and culture structure the broadest form of objective knowledge about others and otherness. Forging a complex analogy between Freudian revisionist attempts to reform the clinical situation in order to improve the world and the attempt on the part of novelists and poets to address violence by reshaping the patterns of global transcultural understanding, Adorno attacks the idea that emotional empathy and a vision of the good can ground analysis. Freud's clinical detachment is compared to Marx's critique of political economy: both theorists are seen as having more sympathy with the whole by denying false warmth and false identities because they understand the economic and psychological order for what it is, a complex system of humanity and inhumanity structured by power. Adorno is challenging whether, in the age of the culture industry, aesthetic or scientific universality can argue for increasing the public flow of emotion and identification in a nonreactionary way.

The problem with Tagore, Werfel, and Fromm in Adorno's eyes—and the reason that their mystic subjectivism compared badly to the hard-headed objectivity of Marx and Freud—came from their attempt to create a subjective counteridentity to the modern world: to make a negative identity into a positive one. Werfel was best known for his 1933 *Forty Days at Musa Dagh*, which depicted the Armenian Christians bearing the stigmata of human suffering; Tagore, the great Bengali poet, had won the 1913 Nobel Prize for his transreligious poems preaching universal harmony. Though it is not surprising that Adorno, an austere and circumspect modernist, was suspicious of Werfel and Tagore's aestheticized notions of cultural-religious reconciliation, the linkage to Fromm can be illuminated by probing the aphorism's later critical remarks on Freud as a global theorist of individualism who "vacillated between negating the renunciation of instinct as repression contrary to reality, and applauding it as sublimation beneficial to culture." Freud at his objective best "grasps the Janus-character of culture objectively," knowing that "no amount of praise for healthy sensuality can wish it away."[4] Adorno saw Marx and Freud as materialist thinkers who understood how consciousness repressed the facts of domination. Echoing Freud's criticism of Romain Rolland's "oceanic feeling," Adorno here doubted whether a general sense of love and common feeling can guide critical thoughts of universalism. Whereas Freud rejected the notion of a universal longing for reconciliation, oneness, and wholeness emanating from the infant's connection with the mother, he concluded that there was indeed a universal sense of guilt, brought about by the vulnerability of the child in the Oedipal situation. One could, in other words, explain the longing for wholeness as one of many possible psychological screen ideas that shield one from examining the relation between selfishness, weakness, and the imposition of the law. When arguing for the redemptive possibilities of a subaltern identity, one should, argued Adorno, be wary of reification; the attempt to point out the redemptive qualities of other religions, nationalities, or selves fosters suspicion that one is being manipulated into caring for a bad cause. Sympathy with identities (positive or negative) unguided by materialist critique breeds contempt and fosters ideology.

Using the word "materialism" to describe how Freud and Marx incorporate the non-identical in their theory of objectivity, *Minima Moralia* explores how every identification embeds within itself questions of social power. Freud spoke of "identification" in terms of the Oedipal drama and paternal authority. Individuals forced to renounce the pleasure principle rather than violate the incest taboo ultimately identify with the father or the mother. Equally, the "primal horde," after rebelling against the father and killing him, comes to deify the father and to identify with his image as a way of assuaging their guilt. Seeing psychic identification as a mode of symbolic-material exchange, Adorno ties the idea of role identification to the question of economic exchange, arguing that under capitalism people who receive something of non-identical value for their labor also start to see "all of culture as a lie" in that nonequivalent exchange seems to infiltrate all forms of social authority, from the highest levels to the lowest. In this idea of identification, the symbolic becomes the real at the same moment that pleasure is renounced. Dialectically, Adorno then proceeds to examine the non-identity of this identity. To believe in identification as the real is delusional, because to do so not only makes culture equivalent to the oldest forms of fate, but "such identification undercuts every possible oppositional thought."[5] By failing to make a distinction between speculation and analysis, Freud's theory of identification describes a bare functionalist schema of adaptation and assimilation to domination and fails to articulate how much authority, legitimate and illegitimate, is created in acts of such identification. Such non-identities plague the application of psychoanalysis to social theory. Adorno, wanting to rescue the Freudian ego from being a mere vehicle for social adjustment and adaptation, attempted to show that the theory of identification with scientific authority (and transference) does more than endorse the now-dominant culture. Worrying aloud that Freud himself had no theory of scientific objectivity other than a loose and general appeal to Darwinian adaptation, and that Freud evinced no theory of logicality and objectivity that could separate itself from "psychologism," this aphorism reflects on the question of whether, in an age in which truth has come to be defined as the mode of one's identification with power, it remains compelling to see the ego as a refuge of rationalism.

Minima Moralia shows Adorno drawing on an interdisciplinary idea of identification in search of a Kantian, even a Hegelian Freud—in search of a body of theory that would transform the subjectivistic approach to identity into something lawlike, materially grounded in emancipation, and insulated from extremity. Echoing his earlier interpretation of Simmel, Adorno wished to update Freud and fit him into a general social epistemology. The problem was that both Freud's concept of the libido and the materialist concept of knowledge kept misaligning, sometimes appearing as mere techniques of total domination, sometimes as a misplaced sympathy with the irrational. In judging psychoanalysis as a stand-alone therapeutic doctrine, Adorno often deemed it so incomplete as to be harmful; whereas when he looked at identification as a global phenomenon for the transfer of symbolic and material authority, he found it a helpful diagnostic tool for the inner contradictions of the pleasure principle. On the one hand, *Minima Moralia* struggles with what one might consider the "culture industry" interpretation of Freud's focus on the weak ego. This view holds that Freud's defense of emancipation and happiness can be deployed as mere superficial palliatives to individuals displaced by domination and that Freud's hand-wringing defense of repression as the price of civilization may indeed leave little room for the subject to express a rational sense of love for himself or others. On the other hand, *Minima Moralia* weighs the problem of the *strong* ego—the notion of a self who takes pleasure in aggression and domination and sheds all inhibition other than the need to identify libidinally with the most powerful force. Gesturing to an orthodox Freud in a parallel fashion to his "orthodox" Marxism, Adorno here was working through the subject/object distinction from the standpoint of epistemology, exposing the fact that Freud himself had trouble defining the proper scope and role of repression in holding together civilization. Adorno's engagement with the problem of global racism did not just lend urgency to the need to reconstruct Freud's materialism; it suggested a negative means of grounding. Adorno's Freud aphorisms—among them, "This side of the pleasure principle," "Ego is id," "Outside and Inside" and "Free Association"—suggest that even the analyst's ego provided no safe "Inside" insulated from the external irrationality. For Adorno in 1944, even Freud's highly qualified defense of ego rationality was too weakly theorized to provide the tools to counter the ego relativism of fascism. Though Freud suggested the ego had a law of its own, Adorno saw this as the modern version of the "cogito ergo sum" of identity that fell victim "to agoraphobia . . . or in the existential exposition of Being-in-the world, to the racial community."[6]

Accusing psychoanalysis of cultivating *techné* without responsibility other than to whoever is paying the bills, Adorno doubted whether introspection was still possible. He worried whether labor and consumption have been so intermingled in the concept of identity as to obscure the line between reason and unreason, waste and fulfillment, in both theory and practice. Thus, meditating on Freud and Fromm, Adorno asked whether psychoanalysis had not just become a particularly corrosive part of the division of labor:

If all psychology since that of Protagoras has elevated man by conceiving him as the measure of all things, it has thereby also treated him from the first as an object, as material for analysis, and transferred to him, once he was included among them, the nullity of things. The denial of objective truth by recourse to the subject implies the negation of the latter: no measure remains for the measure of all things; lapsing into contingency, he becomes untruth. But this points back to the real life-process of society. The principle of human domination, in becoming absolute, has turned its point against man as the absolute object, and psychology has collaborated in sharpening that point. The self, its guiding idea and its *a priori* has always, under its scrutiny, been rendered at the same time non-existent. In appealing to the fact that in an exchange society the subject was not a subject at all, but in fact a social object, psychology provided society with weapons for ensuring that this was and remained the case. The dissection of man into his faculties is a projection of the division of labor onto its pretended subjects, inseparable from the interest in deploying and manipulating them to greater advantage. Psycho-technics is not merely a sign of psychology's decay, but is inherent in its principle.[7]

Psychology is here viewed as a weapon in the class struggle: a way of dissecting the self and the narratives of the world through the psychological measurement and categorization demanded by technical specialization. It is out of this dynamic of hollowing out the self—of making the self an object for the purposes of consumption—that Adorno saw the notion of identity emerging. Less an attack on Fromm or Freud than on objectification in general, Adorno's charge was that psychological objectification undermined individuals and their spontaneities by developing techniques for the transformation of inner life into the measured predictability of human capital. If the self is reduced to a single point, if the "I" appears "a mere prejudice," there is no "residue" of non-identity and domination is unstoppable.

Adorno's relation to psychoanalysis evolved through his work on *The Authoritarian Personality*. Though he never stopped seeing it as involved in the "psycho-technics of domination," he came to see its epistemological one-sidedness as useful for understanding the woundedness of divided subjectivity. This transformation occurred when he applied his theory of subjective negativity to situations beyond those of the transference of clinical or cultural authority to theorize about questions of lawfulness and autonomy, transgression and heteronomy. A clear indicator is found in *The Authoritarian Personality*'s approving citation of Erikson's 1942 article "Imagery of the Hitler Youth." Erikson had argued that Hitler and other fascist leaders did not, as both Fromm and Horkheimer had hypothesized, put themselves forward as leaders by exploiting the traditional roles of father figures in the authority vacuum created by the economic crisis of the Great Depression.[8] Rather, the fascist circuit of appeal, argued Erikson and Adorno, was deeply *fraternal*: it did not attack the category of legitimate authority but trashed its core concept of lawfulness through abusive practice. The authoritarian and fascist leader gives lip service to "law and order" but creates an exception in the fashion of an emotional, protective, sexually incontinent, and violence-prone "big brother," who, out of the red-blooded impulse to protect his compatriots from a world out of control, occasionally lashes out. The symbolism of fascism is one of *abrogating the law* to restore its emotional power as immediate rather than mediated justice. This allows the fascist to engage in a vendetta-style politics to define his identity negatively in terms of his victim yet uphold the idea that his motives are apostle pure: the fascist leader comes Jesus-like, here to break the law and thus to fulfill it. The rise of such identity thinking displaces all understanding of actual social relations.

By the time Adorno wrote his 1951 "Freudian Theory and the Pattern of Fascist Propaganda," he saw his interpretation of the logic of heteronomy, victim blaming, and the assertion of a negative identity in accord with an orthodox Freudianism. In the later article, Adorno cited Freud's 1921 *Group Psychology and the Analysis of the Ego* to show that Freud himself refuted notions of the collective violence of crowds as a matter of mass hypnosis invoked by the image of paternal authority. Rather, argued Adorno, Freud saw fascist violence as arising from a kind of regression to an early stage of psycho-social development, one in which intragroup fears and the hope of a stabilizing erotic bond between brothers in the primal horde served to nurture the delusion that they were capable of living without paternal authority, purely according to the sympathetic bonds of brotherly mutual protection. The deployment of negative identity could reshape the content of lawfulness to the point where it resembled its opposite.[9]

Two ideas go together in this (culturalist) understanding of fascist lawlessness, neither of which *requires* psychoanalysis: the fascist makes himself by choosing his victim, and aggression comes out of weakness. Both involve the idea that the subject could become object. The bit of (Hegelianized) "Freudian orthodoxy" that *The Authoritarian Personality* added to this mixture was the insight that it was not primarily the ego or the id that forged the bonds of social aggression *but the superego*. For Adorno this came from realizing that authoritarian behavior developed not from the ego or the id's economy of pleasure and reality but from the superego's woundedness, its vulnerability and ability to wound. Its agency was the one capable of transmuting the ordering narrative principles of worldly authority and content analysis, and it was the superego, ironically, that served to authorize violence in an age when negative identity could organize politics. *The Authoritarian Personality* in fact uses this scenario to understand how the punitive superego could be deployed instrumentally by the modern state and economic power—in concert with the politics of hate—to turn the classical concept of personality against civilization and to inspire a new, identity-based notion of ideology, action, and violence.

The philosophical framework for arguing this point was Adorno's reconstructed Hegelianism, which interpreted Freud in terms of the theory of primary and determinate negation. Adorno's interpretation of Hegelian negation involved, as we have seen, the idea that philosophy as speculation grew out of the limitation rather than the experience of immediacy. Reflection occurred not in the pursuit of a primal essence but in the aftershock of one's encounter with negativity—the realization that one was not identical with one's environment or with Others but that one's subjectivity could be rendered into an object. This idea of the primacy of negation and woundedness sought to debunk the ideological function of all mythic notions of primary wholeness. In seeking to reconcile Marx to Freud through these ideas of negation and the internally divided self, Adorno's concept of the priority of negative identity was more than a mere swipe at the ideological notion of plenitude. It drew on a Hegelian interpretation of Freud's notion of introjection and Freud's concept of the divided self, or "structural model."

In Adorno's view, Freud's structural model made sense based only on the premise that there is no ego, id, or superego without wounded negation. The ego, which develops first out of the id, separates itself from the id through the negating voice of the superego, an "introjection" of paternal selfhood and social authority forbidding the ego-id from being one with either itself or the world. This linkage of introjection to negation served as the avenue through which Adorno embraced not just Freudian orthodoxy but also the Freudian controversy surrounding the source of aggression and self-destruction in the infamous "death drive." Historically, Freud's definition of the superego was conjoined with his articulation of a death drive or drives. Both were articulated in relation to Freud's attempts to understand the destruction of World War I. The death drive was first described in Freud's 1921 *Beyond the Pleasure Principle*, while the superego first appeared in the 1923 *The Ego and the Id*. These texts, read alongside the 1921 *Group Psychology and the Analysis of the Id* and Freud's 1929 *Civilization and Its Discontents*, are considered to constitute the core of the "late Freudian" approach to both technical matters such as the structural model of the personality and political-cultural matters such as the regressive character of mass politics and war. It is beyond dispute that Freud, in positing an innate impulse toward (self-)destructive behavior, broke with his earlier understanding that all libidinal forces were inherently pleasure seeking. After Freud's death, however, it was highly contentious whether there was such a thing as a destructive instinct or a primary masochism comparable to the fundamental drive of libido. Otto Fenichel, a central figure of the orthodox Freudian Left, doubted in his 1945 commentary whether the concept was useful or necessary. As ego psychology became a movement focused on the structuring role the ego played in shaping consciousness, it increasingly disfavored the idea of a libidinal drive, preferring, as did Anna Freud, to consider egoic impulses toward destructiveness a consequence of trauma, or as Heinz Hartmann, to reject as counterproductive any speculation on an unconscious drive toward masochism when masochism was better understood as a kind of maladaptation to a hostile environment.[10] Adorno's Hegelianized Freud fused negation to the structural model in a way that took trauma as a given but rejected the displacement of the super-ego by the ego.

The Authoritarian Personality fully incorporates Adorno's determinate negation of the Freudian structural model, which held that the ego itself was a product of negation that emerged from the unavoidable circumstance in that subject is an object to others. Differentiation within the personality structure thus came not merely from an internalization of a "hostile" environment, or oppressively narrow social roles, or the repression of inner drives, but from the fact that the personality was, like knowledge itself, built on internal negations. In many instances in the collaborative work, this notion of a deep, imbricated negativity helped Adorno evade theoretical dogmas that might have sidetracked the entire project. An excellent example of this might be seen in his careful use of the word "integration," a largely Jungian term favored by Murray, in describing the personality structure of an "authoritarian" individual:

> The most essential feature of [the authoritarian] structure is a lack of integration between the moral agencies by which the subject lives and the rest of his personality. One might say that the conscience or superego is incompletely integrated with the self or ego, the ego here being conceived of as embracing the various self-controlling and self-expressing functions of the individual. It is the ego that governs the relations between self and outer world, and between self and deeper layers of the personality; the ego undertakes to regulate impulses in a way that will permit gratification without inviting too much punishment by the superego, and it seeks in general to carry out the activities of the individual in accordance with the demands of reality.[11]

If one acknowledges that work on *The Authoritarian Personality* could have easily been derailed by controversies involving superego and the death drive, one sees how adroit it was to draw on the "layered" model of the personality to sidestep questions of fundamentalism or innateness. Here the crucial assertion is not whether aggression is innate, or whether the environment can be transformed, but whether the ego, as it governs or fails to govern the personality's relation between inner and outer world, must necessarily engage consciously with the impulses of the id and the superego and try to avoid a rupture such that any one agency of the personality dominates the other. This is a kind of structuralist interpretation of the structural model, one that has no predefined notion of health, and defines pathology on a case-by-case basis. Thus it notably avoids the usage suggested by Jung's concept of integration, which names the moment when the ego joins with the collective unconscious and bonds to the world of meaning as an individual. It is in its eclecticism fairly close to Abraham Maslow—also cited in *The Authoritarian Personality*—who viewed integration as a totality concept for how "the wholeness of the organism" achieved an internal balance relative to external pressures.[12] Adorno's invocations of Freud's structural model in *The Authoritarian Personality* conform to the basic contours of ego psychology's emphasis on the defense mechanisms of the ego. Equally, the book adheres to empirical psychology's notions of a "structured moral agency" and resistance to intraceptive narratives. Nevertheless, it insists that for the purposes of studying fascism, a punitive superego (rather than the id or even the ego) should be viewed as the key agency in generating aggression.

As part of a systematic notion of social theory, Freudianism was complete and coherent only if it renounced the idea that the personality emerges as a thing with its own unique essence, seeing the self instead as a product of internal division and negation that unfolded as a material-historical process. Adorno advocated this divided epistemology in his afterword but had already integrated it subtly throughout *The Authoritarian Personality*, and it would become the consensus view for critical theory in the postwar period. Herbert Marcuse, whether or not he read "Remarks," clearly understood Adorno's position. A decade later, his 1956 *Eros and Civilization* articulated the definitive Frankfurt School statement on Freudianism by arguing that Freud was clearer than widely suggested on the superego genesis of aggression, and that the superego was for Freud himself an inversion of a fundamental, preconscious biological tendency of all nature to return, through death, to inanimate matter. Quoting Freud's argument that "in the construction of the personality, the destruction instinct manifests itself most clearly in the formation of the superego," Marcuse clarified that the superego emerged from the determinate negation of the most archaic part of the self, the death drive. Life, to become life, must first negate death. A by-product of the original energy that negated the impulse toward death and turned into libido, the superego—as the reserve of the individual's highest ideals—is, paradoxically, a creation of the most primal instincts.[13] This definition of the superego sees a duality of ideality and destructiveness. The voice of the paternal, social authority telling one to become one's ego ideal is coeval with the impulse to destroy the self, ideals, and all of civilization. Freud, if interpreted negatively as a theorist of objectivity and negation, thus defined both the id and superego as elements of the not-I, of objectivity embedded in the subject and its field of object relations.

Marcuse's goal in defending the connection between superego and the death drive had its roots in two dimensions of Adorno's response to fascism: its concern about the reactionary potential of the liberal subject, and its deeper subject/object model of how to study social conflict. The question of liberalism's relation to fascism and the utility of a theory of rational subjectivity became deeply entwined in the research. The search for the social and psychological preconditions of fascism was of course central to a book with the working title *The Potential Fascist*. Though Adorno and Horkheimer had speculated on questions of a general desubstantialization of reason and the rise of an identity logic of vilification, the statistical inference and interview material from *The Authoritarian Personality* had placed the question of the liberal convert to fascism front and center. The alchemy of fascism forged a common cause between active ideologues and passive authoritarians, between people who had allowed id to dominate superego and to express their need for self-definition as aggression against others and those who ratified this aggression by redefining revenge as lawfulness, authorizing the superego not just to ignore revenge but to see it as an expression of the need for more punishment, more legality. Both types of authoritarian, the active ideologue and passive fellow traveler, depended on social structures that invested heavily in an externally referred superego, conjoined with a willingness to deflect introspection by orienting negatively toward others.

If one focuses on the destructive social power of this negative orientation, it becomes clear that a publicly asserted negative identity has two moments: when it makes the activist and when it acquires political assent from the mainstream. Critical theory, concerned with both the agitator and the followers, thereby realized that it needed a better understanding of how social divisions were exploited inside the liberal democratic state. It was important to understand the substantive conceptual pathways whereby a subject such as 5061a, a low scorer who referred her judgments to her fascist husband, could be converted from being a tolerant liberal with an ordinary sense of propriety to someone who could be mobilized to invoke good democratic principles of fairness to finally "do something about" a "problem" group. The possibility of agitators converting liberals to tolerate fascism provoked the question of what kind of theory could diagnose and counteract this kind of conversion. Adorno had already developed the hypothesis that notions of a conformist totality—whether cultural or institutional—conjoined with a stimulus-response model were useless in protecting divided selves in a divided society from the kind of rapid slippage experienced in a subject such as 5061a. To deal with a woman capable of converting, almost instantly, from theoretically informed expressions of the love of universal man to abject stereopathic visions of group eradication, theory needed to explain how the superego's investment in lawfulness could, when faced with a strong vision of negative identity, be converted into a horror of the continued existence of the Other.

To analyze the potential for fascism within liberalism, one had to think about how scientific or legal ideas could become objects for different layers of the personality, generating regressive configurations of the id, ego, and superego unforeseen by the advance of civilization and culture. To analyze how objects of the externalized superego could appeal to the ego and id was to ask how agitators could convert liberals to reactionary thought. Adorno, drawing on his musical technique of interpreting the smallest transitions of thought as symbolic slippages, pushed *The Authoritarian Personality* to consider the question of "falling in love in reverse" with a given minority. Content analysis showed how ideas about the law and the Other could "fill in the gaps" between a liberal frame of mind and extremist views. Tracing out how a damaged ego and an excessively harsh externalized superego infused the objects of conventionalism with a fascination for a particular type of negative identity, Adorno sought to understand the layered psychological, social, and cultural logic of these projection fantasies and how they cut across religious, ethnic, political, and cultural lines of affiliation. The result is a stunning definition of the economic and normative origins of projective negative identity:

> The individual who has been forced to give up basic pleasures and to live under a system of rigid restraints, and who therefore feels put upon, is likely not only to seek an object upon which he can "take it out" but also to be particularly annoyed

at the idea that another person is "getting away with something." Thus, it may be said that the [measurement of authoritarian aggression] represents the sadistic component of authoritarianism just as [the measurement of authoritarian submission] represents its masochistic component. It is to be expected, therefore, that the conventionalist who cannot bring himself to utter any real criticism of accepted authority will have a desire to condemn, reject, and punish those who violate these values. As the emotional life which this person regards as proper and a part of himself is likely to be very limited, so the impulses, especially sexual and aggressive ones, which remain unconscious and ego-alien are likely to be strong and turbulent. Since in this circumstance a wide variety of stimuli can tempt the individual and so arouse his anxiety (fear of punishment), the list of traits, behavior patterns, individuals, and groups that he must condemn grows very long indeed. It has been suggested before that this mechanism might lie behind the ethnocentric rejection of such groups as zootsuiters, foreigners, other nations; it is here hypothesized that this feature of ethnocentrism is but a part of a more general tendency to punish violators of conventional values: homosexuals, sex offenders, people with bad manners, etc. Once the individual has convinced himself that there are people who ought to be punished, he is provided with a channel through which his deepest aggressive impulses may be expressed, even while he thinks of himself as thoroughly moral. If his external authorities, or the crowd, lend their approval to this form of aggression, then it may take the most violent forms, and it may persist after the conventional values, in the name of which it was undertaken, have been lost from sight.[14]

This interpretation integrates Freud and Marx in a dialectical theory of identification and negative identity. Economic oppression and individual isolation serve to create individual alienation and repression. People who are reticent to express fears about survival or impulses of rebellion against state or economic authority will readily apply the ticket mentality to a perceived group. This cathects the libidinal energy and conscious suffering of individual negative identity into an outgroup image without violating the core ideas of liberal society. There seems to be no natural limit to the logic of negative identity; although anti-Semitism and Jim Crow established the pattern, every group from homosexuals to zoot suiters and every emotional channel from patriotism to economic theory can be used to deflect liberal fears about one's wounded subjectivity onto those more vulnerable. Psychoanalytically speaking, though Freud frequently theorized prejudice and shame, he did not theorize an economic source for the formation of such negative "love-objects," but he did of course give plenty of thought to the mechanism of the screen idea and its attendant notions of projection and deflection.[15] Sociologically speaking, the passage analyzes the functional power of such aggression and makes it clear that it is all but unrelated to the reality of group relations. Hatred of others comes not from an inherent ressentiment or competitive antagonism but from the universal imperilment of modern capitalism and the transfiguration of authority inspired by the frustration of libidinal drives. The motivation for aggression is in fact extraneous to the objects of desire and/or sadism, resting in the original damaged subjectivity that has been asked to sacrifice its imagined wholeness—not for minorities, in fact, but for the reproduction of capital and the maintenance of traditional authority.

Regression, Fraternal Love, and Scars

Ever since the publication of the final issue of the *Zeitschrift*, Adorno and his colleagues had sought an expanded theory of objectivity addressing the ways fascism and the modern culture industry had distorted social theory in general and the theory of subjectivity in particular. By asking how the superego interacted with the ego and id to structure the personality, they developed a theory of how the subject could become object. This was not the dream of a new, general theory of objectivity, but it allowed culturalist theory and ego psychology to counter their subjective tendencies and speak to objective conditions. Erikson's vision of fascists as a "band of brothers" who had cast off the superego as father figure spoke not just to the changing structure of the personality (and thus the desire to eradicate legitimate authority) but also to psychoanalysis's need to investigate how falsified notions of a leveling impulse could feed radicalized hierarchies or allow for the reversal of allegiances. The idea that a radicalized "band of brothers"—the modern primal horde—could transform a normal bourgeois person into a pogrom participant not through mass psychological appeal but by transformation of the object—a transformation of the terms of legitimacy—became a reason to engage with the substance of cultural perceptions. No vision of scientific objectivity alone could restore social perspective: one had to delve deeper into the divided self's claims to be an identity, to analyze its impulse toward self-destruction.

"Remarks on *The Authoritarian Personality*" shows how much Adorno sought to anchor the divided subject in the question of divided objectivity. Arguing that liberal theory consistently misunderstands the nature of fascist activism because it imagines activism to be a totality—a kind of subjective unity of meaning—that creates a totalitarian state, Adorno insists that fascism was driven by its internal divisions and their congruence with those of liberalism. Franz Neumann's *Behemoth*, published in 1941, taught the Institute that it was a fascist fantasy to see the state as a functional totality modeled on a revivalist concept of cultural totality. Any social analysis that accepted *Gleichschaltung* at face value fell into the fascist trap of exploiting liberalism's blind spots: the cult of efficiency, the belief in the invisible state, the functionalization of human beings, the romance of a "total" culture. Fascism fostered the desire for a unity it not only never produced, but against which it constantly labored. Neumann's central point in *Behemoth* was that the Nazi state was no Hobbesian Leviathan but an erratic nonstate loosely held together by internal social antagonisms, the zealotry of a few, and the passivity of the many.[16] Nazi ideology was totalitarian, cultivating true believers filled with passionate hatred, but that was not the terrifying thing about the fascist state: far more horrifying was its ability to mobilize elements within liberal nationalism that rendered fascism reasonable at a psychological, political, or social level. Violence against others produced a sense of fleeting unity that needed to be ever renewed. In "Remarks," Adorno adapted the Neumann analysis of the state to the psychological and sociological findings of *The Authoritarian Personality*:

There was no immediate relationship between spontaneous anti-semitic outbreaks and the extermination policy of the Nazis. Spontaneous anti-Jewish demonstrations in the Third Reich were, without exception, manipulated, switched on and off. Districts which had a strong traditional link with anti-semitism, as e.g. Oberhessen, never made any particular show under Hitler; Frankonia, on the other hand, with no such tradition, became notorious because of a few exceptionally violent leaders. Gregor Strasser, the most efficient organizer of the Nazi party, stated shortly before the seizure of power, that the time of *Radau-Anti-semitismus* (hoodlum-anti-semitism) was over—an utterance which gave spurious comfort to many Jews. Under totalitarian rule, anti-semitism is no longer a matter of primary hostilities on the part of the people and of truly spontaneous actions. It is an administrative measure which uses existing prejudices and, to an even higher degree, psychological dispositions. Naturally, hoodlums who molest Jews on a beach are ideal Stormtroop[er] material, but the triumph of anti-semitism does not depend on them. The problems of alienation as stressed in our discussion of the political and economic interview material, and also envisaged in Nathan Glazer's article on the alienation of modern man, affects the very structure of anti-semitic attitudes. What matters today is not so much that people might hate the Jews sufficiently to start a pogrom, but that they might endorse a movement which includes anti-semitism in its platform. It is much more important to ascertain the type of people who might be willing to join movements or back governments that plan to exterminate the Jews, than to probe for the specific cause of anti-semitic troubles in a given area.[17]

Fascism need not aspire to be a cultural movement: success did not require converting a whole nation into "Stormtrooper material." All it needed was to functionalize and normalize hatred until people feared for their survival and made the movement itself seem like the only force capable of doing the rough business necessary for the state to survive. That required already weakened and alienated subjects who no longer equated the rule of law with mutual interests and common survival. Nazi street violence played a powerful role in delegitimizing the state, eroding confidence in the fairness of judges and the effectiveness of government, and these Nazi acts of making the state ungovernable tacitly honored agitators (violent brothers) as the redeemers of the impotent law (of the father). Just as one can blame the victim, so one can reward the perpetrator.

Fascists are politicians who purport to solve problems either that they themselves caused or that are caused by the very structures of the liberal state and therefore can become unsolvable amid illiberal agitation. For Neumann, this dissolution of authority came from the erosion of a public sense of equality. Capitalistic hierarchy, worker displacement, and nationalist rhetoric watered seeds planted elsewhere. This was reflected in the economic disarray of the inflation caused by the failures of the international system, which undermined individuals' sense of continuity. This humiliation of laissez-faire allowed the democratic state to look weak and incapable of action. The legitimation crisis was also intensified by the failures of the law to counter moments of direct action, whether these were "direct action" marches on Fiume or Rome or attacks by Brownshirts on foreigners and strangers to demonstrate that they could take the protection of the nation into their own hands. The doctrine of equality and universalism is deeply interwoven in practice with Weber's functionalist definition of the liberal state as that entity that has the monopoly on the legitimate use of violence. Civil and legal equity is destroyed next. By failing to uphold doctrines of equal protection and equal punishment, or by actively exploiting notions of emergency powers, the nationalist courts skewed law to embrace its replacement: actionism and new hierarchies of identity, nation, and race.[18]

Adorno understood this mode of analysis to be objective and publicly oriented. Adorno's goal in *The Authoritarian Personality* was to push psychology toward rediscovering the importance of Freud's structural model disciplinarily in such a way that it could recover an understanding of the importance of negation and objectivity for social theory and public reason more generally. Combining the Veblen essay's understanding of reified consciousness with new ideas about disciplinarity initiated a new model for the immanent critique of sociocultural institutions. If cultural or symbolic authority could be analyzed in terms of the categories of psychosocial authority, one could reexamine how everything that Hegel called "objective spirit" constitutes material for the "externalization of the superego." Though Frenkel-Brunswik authored the section discussing the crucial questions of the relative strength of the ego, the punitive nature of the superego, and libidinal identification with parental authority throughout the life stages, she did so in close coordination with Adorno, referencing Adorno's previously cited passage on the importance of "not-too-drastic repression of instinctual tendencies" for low scorers' "greater ability for integrating and expressing aggression, for a successful fusion of sex and affection, for 'love' in general, and for creative work."[19] By contrast, high scorers tended not to identify with the limits that their parents placed on the pleasure principle. The former was compatible with "a more responsible and judicious sense of citizenship," while in cases of failed integration, the "externalized superego" was typically invested with quasi-superstitious or metaphysical properties that developed into a sense of punitive and harsh moralism, a distortion of reality, or a strenuous "counter-cathexis of unacceptable impulses."[20]

Adorno brought the question of the Kantian and Weberian implications of Freud to the fore in "Social Science and Sociological Tendencies in Psychoanalysis," delivered in April 1946 at the first meeting of the San Francisco Psychoanalytic Society. This was Adorno's first talk publicly airing his complaints against psychological revisionists and ego psychologists. Karen Horney's 1939 *New Ways in Psychoanalysis* was specifically singled out for criticism; Erich Fromm was implicitly a target, as the two were lovers when *New Ways* was published. Colleagues and rivals such as Frenkel-Brunswik and Erikson were likely in the audience. The first part of the talk equivocates on the question of culture, arguing that Freud himself occasionally attempted to psychologize a milieu or a civilization, looking at its laws as a transcription of the collective superego. However, mature disciplines sought to eject milieu-type explanations for the sake of developing their disciplinary laws. Sociology and psychology should, Adorno reasoned, refuse to combine their modes of analysis into one super-perspective of mental and cultural totality. Instead, conflicting perspectives should be constructed in opposition to one another, lest theory turn into a version of conformity, reinforcing the idea that the goal of sociology is to compel integration and compliance and the goal of psychology is to create a self who experiences no friction in the world. This attack on Freudian revisionism called upon the social sciences to resist two kinds of disciplinary inertia. First, the disciplines needed to stop imagining themselves as furnishing evidence for a general functionalism, a kind of stimulus-response model of what is "effective." Second, the social sciences needed to resist creating false totalities that blurred the line between the *subject* of knowledge production and the *object* of it. Failure to manage positivistic and totalizing tendencies created pseudo-facts that were just by-products of the theoretical system, reifying subjectivity in ways that not only were unethical but would inevitably become part of a "psycho-technics" of mass manipulation. Social science could no longer imagine a way out: its only model became to collect facts and observe the mysterious operation of power on a totality that stubbornly did not conform to the scientist's good reforming wishes.

At the heart of the talk was the question of ego psychology's emerging assimilation to the logic of positivity and functionalism, its tendency to sideline the notion of id and superego and the theory of the divided self. The problem that immediately arose, Adorno pointed out, was that of explaining how the ego, all by itself, could mediate the relation between knowledge as rationality and desire as irrationality. In explicating this problem, Adorno returned to his long-standing interest in the relation between Kant and Freud, specifically between Kant's notion of *bindingness* and Freud's structural model. The core question of moral bindingness in Kant came from his postulate of reason as the true basis and ultimate governor of conscience; Kant argued that intellectual maturity—becoming a subject—meant developing to the point where moral reason replaced dogma and unreasoned moral taboos. In Adorno's way of understanding Freud's object theory, Kant's idea of (explicit) reason absorbing (dogmatic) conscience had its parallel in the Freudian idea of the ego absorbing the id. But this parallel raised questions that complicated both Freud and Kant and shook the foundations of Freudian revisionism. Sandor Ferenczi's idea in *Building Blocks of Psychoanalysis* "that a real character-analysis must remove, at least provisionally, every kind of superego, and thus even that of the analyst" was for Adorno a deeply problematic idea, because it seemed to represent an uncritical desire on the part of psychoanalysis to negate its foundational clinical impulse. It seemed to suggest that the superego could be set aside in discussing aggression and that the ego was, after all, *naturally* the master in its own house, that desire moved inherently toward self-regulation, that assimilation to the whole anchored reason.[21] The problem here was not the wish itself—there was nothing *wrong* with wishing for a society in which the conscience was replaced by reason or in which desire wrote the laws. But this wish did not address the non-identity at hand: that there was an objective content to law and that the superego was central to the objectification of aggression. These problems were compounded by Kantian questions of whether the object (be it a person or a thing) had needs and particularities of its own that gave it meaning beyond the bounds of a primary narcissism: at some point the object needed to be looked at also as a thing-in-itself, not merely a projection of desire or a means of fulfilling the ego's needs. Adorno believed that the failure to treat the object as something other than a projection of subjective desire led to a pure functionalism.

Autonomy could not be achieved through notions of strong subjectivity but only through a recognition of the woundedness and vulnerability of the subject. In addressing Horney and Fromm in 1946, Adorno expressed these considerations in terms of a fear of a lazy fusion of psychoanalysis with functionalist sociology. In particular, Adorno feared that Horney's notion of the ego as a mechanism for sociocultural adaptation would be directly instrumentalized for purposes of psychotechnical manipulation by the culture industry. This corresponded to the fused disciplinary frameworks in *Dialectic of Enlightenment*, where theory worked to exaggerate the contradictions within socially manipulated objects in order to raise the underlying *techné* to a concept. Pointing out the superiority of Freud's reality principle over milieu-assimilation models, Adorno focused on how the substitution model of pleasures and identifications allowed for more precise objectivity. The association of the ego with the stream of consciousness, Adorno argued, needed to be squared with the idea of trauma theory. A narrative theory exploring woundedness could help psychoanalytical theory recognize that its model of therapeutic learning was closer to the notion of recovering from trauma as theorized by Ferenczi than to the kind of stimulus-response model advocated by Horney:

> Those who, like most Freudian revisionists, criticize contemporary society should not close their mind to the possibility that society is experienced in shocks, in

sudden, abrupt injuries that are determined indeed through the alienation of the individual from society—the exact same kind of shocks that are correctly foregrounded by some Freudian revisionists when they are speaking sociologically. [The problem is that they] hypostasize the "character" that is far more itself the effect of such shocks than it is of continuous experience [in the emphatic sense]. Its totality is fictional: one could almost call it a system of scars that only under great suffering—and even then, not fully—can be integrated. These afflictions are in actuality the form in which society reproduces itself in the individual, not that illusory continuity that the revisionists detach from the shock-bound structure of individual experience because presenting it as continuous would seem to help their argument.[22]

Knowledge is a system of scars: the ability to perceive the non-identical comes from woundedness. It emerges from an impulse of self-preservation to try to insert a sense of objectivity into the encounter between character and a world that wounds it. The distinction between "continuous" and "broken" experience is placed in parallel to the distinction between the psychological and sociological mode of analysis, and the observation that the two are not the same signals two things: the "shock" is now over and learning can begin, and the subject who was once powerless might begin to recover itself as part of coming to terms with the past suffering. Loosely paraphrasing the Oedipal encounter and the substitution of the father's law in terms of the possibility of "experiencing society," Adorno was setting the foundation for how to rethink sociology in terms of psychoanalysis, and vice versa. In positing that scientific reformers' model of the self and their science might both be considered a "system of scars," Adorno was holding out an olive branch to ego psychology in the form of the suggestion that the shock of the lab equipment, the stimulus of culture, or the experience of violence might be thought of as wounds that could heal into a form of subject/object non-identity.

If this talk represents a moment in which Adorno's reflections on Kant and broken universality helped him explain the weaknesses of ego psychology, the idea of the self as a "system of scars" points to the productivity of his speculative writing. In *Dialectic of Enlightenment*, Adorno had represented Odysseus not just as the first bourgeois subject and inventor of scientific objectivity but also as the hero who grows through his wounds and who wounds others through his *mētis*, the cunning that allows him to act as subject through the domination of nature. The wound and wounding are what open up the subject to the world and allow the subject to *experience* the object as something real but also to stand over and against the object.

Odysseus has one visible wound, of course—which was inflicted before his journey to Troy in his attempt to fight, as Hercules had, the wild boar. Odysseus learned from this event that the man who identifies action with truth, facing nature head-on, will suffer the mythic hero's fate. He thereafter, in good bourgeois fashion, becomes an antihero, seeking to have others do the fighting for him or to use the forces of nature to defeat nature and still experience nature. The scar partly disfigures Odysseus, and it is indeed possible that he inflicts damage on the world as a consequence of the scar; but Homer, by building his entire narrative around the scar, makes historical sense of what would otherwise be blind objectification. Narrative turns blind stimulus into meaning possessing a subject and an object, transforming the scar into a record and structure of experience that simultaneously amplifies the power of the self. This creates a structure of heroic action that becomes a new form of blindness—and preserves a sense of individual suffering and memory that could potentially turn into a vehicle for understanding not just how to control self and world, but also for understanding the Other and that which wounded the self in the first place. Where Freud said, "Let ego be where id was," the revisionists essentially say "Let id become ego" and make the ego the center of desire; but the point of orthodox Freudianism is to interpret myth as a narrative structure that allows the woundedness whereby id was forced to become ego to reflect on itself as being, as Odysseus was, the author of its own story.[23] Doing this, and taking account of the drowned and the saved, might make Odysseus's self-knowledge a paradigm not for the power of revenge fantasies or the force of id turned into ego, but for the possibility that with great difficulty, a system of scars can be largely, "but not fully . . . integrated" with civilization. Under the conditions of being able to redeem the individual shocks of everyday life into a scientific narrative capable of reflecting on its objectifications, Adorno is suggesting that he, too, might be willing to join the Freudian revisionists.

The translation of the language of scars from Adorno's exploration of narrative into a formal presentation delivered to an audience of ego psychologists speaks to Adorno's developing work methods. During the next decade, Adorno would develop a more precise language for the kind of interdisciplinarity he hoped to promote, arguing that preserving the differences between disciplinary perspectives was the key to discovering the non-identity within the object and bridging between speculative and analytical modes of thought. At this moment, however, the more poetic language of the philosophical fragment allowed him to articulate ideas that were foreign to all the disciplines in which he worked, to amplify the friction between disciplinary perspectives, and to force the disciplines to confront their relation to the disasters unfolding in the world around them. We see this again in the way he used the metaphor of scars as experience to relate Freud's concept of science to the problem of historical and mythic narrative in *Minima Moralia*'s stunning aphorism "Far from the Line of Fire" a few months earlier. There Adorno observes that every news report of air bombardment is "sure to mention the name of the military contractor who designed the plane" because such heroic narratives of corporate identity have replaced mythic narrative for how people make sense of the inhuman scale of the war alongside its intimate relation to every aspect of life, reproduction, production, and consumption. As the names "Fokker-Wolf, Heinkel, and Lancaster appear where one once talked about cuirassiers, lancers and hussars," so the idea of a battlefield experience is broken by "the sheer incommensurability of the body relative to a war of attrition . . . that makes authentic experience impossible." Participants in the war can have no "sense of continuity, history, of the 'epic' element" because each "shock," each "trauma" is punctuated by a further stimulus that breaks every mental attempt at closure that would build narrative out of the "pause between healing forgetting and healing memory."[24]

That modern war had only wounding—no scarring, no narrative—implies the possibility of learning absolutely nothing from the war. Shock without experience would mean the disfiguration of reason. It would mean that modern destructive technology provokes reversion into myth. The possibility of shock without memory was for Adorno presaged in the prewar cult of action-as-meaning—itself analogous to the stimulus-response models of the culture industry—that decried in fascist style the apparent inactivity of "the phony war" (*Sitzkrieg*) or that projected human significance onto Hitler's senseless V-1 rocket launches. In "Hitler's Robot-bombs" Adorno saw a confirmation and brutal inversion "of Hegel's notion of the world spirit on horseback," but this "subject is absolutely subjectless . . . like fascism itself, exemplifying high technical perfection with total blindness." These thoughts about heroism, experience, healing narrative, and the inability to analyze events in an objective fashion culminate in a final reflection about horror. Adorno, a social scientist living "far from the line of fire," experiencing everything at a distance and through the media, has lost the ability to judge concretely. He says that he can neither pronounce a "punishment" that would be commensurate with the crime nor imagine himself using "the apparatus of the law" to stay the hand of those wishing revenge: both are bad options, speaking to the decay of the ability of the subject to form an object of judgment in the face of such events. The loss of objectivity unravels the worldly role of the integrated superego, that of judgment: in this dark moment, Adorno says he can do little else but let history judge.[25]

Pragmatism, Neoliberalism, and the Objective Minority

In 1946, in the middle of his work on *The Authoritarian Personality* and toward the completion of the writing of *Minima Moralia*, Adorno found himself working intensively with Leo Lowenthal to edit, rewrite, and structure the lecture series that Horkheimer presented as *The Eclipse of Reason*. At first blush, these lectures appear a summation of Horkheimer's work from the *Zeitschrift* years, filled with questions of scientific method but with little on the question of psychoanalysis, anti-Semitism, or racism. This has led many scholars to treat Horkheimer's essays, delivered to a general audience at Columbia, as a kind of halfhearted contractual obligation—a weak attempt to produce a "popular" version of the fragmentary and putatively pessimistic *Dialectic of Enlightenment*. If one understands, however, the logic that connected Adorno and Horkheimer's attempt to recover an orthodox dialectics of subject and object from the thought of Weber and Nietzsche, Marx and Freud, Kant and Hegel, one sees *Eclipse*'s interest in scientific method and subjectivity as directly relevant to public debates about the postwar order. The introduction states: "These lectures were designed to present in epitome some aspects of a comprehensive philosophical theory developed by the writer during the last few years in association with Theodore W. Adorno. It would be difficult to say which of these ideas originated in his mind and which in my own; our philosophy is one."[26]

Eclipse is a history of the concept of divided objectivity, cast not from the standpoint of theory's inner logic but from the point of view of the need for a workable concept of public reason. Unlike the "End of Reason," which considered objective reason in terms of a sense of a *shared goal* for humanity and the attempt to recover it through a Marxian theory of objective rationalism and causation, *Eclipse* focused on social legitimation structures and their relation to thinking about minorities. It did so by first asking about everyday reason, in a distinctly American manner: "When the ordinary man is asked to explain what is meant by the term [reason] his reaction is almost always one of hesitation and embarrassment. It would be a mistake to interpret this as indicating wisdom too deep or thought too abstruse to be put into words."[27] This non-identical twist on the classic American "man on the streets" beginning quickly accelerates into an investigation into the relation between common sense and scientific reasoning. Questions of survival and minority views are, interestingly, related to validity questions in the Weberian sense, with Horkheimer sketching out, still in relation to his imaginary "ordinary man," the deep connection between contemporary notions of reason and the individual's ability to do things. Reason inherently has, *Eclipse* argues, a subjective and an objective "aspect." The history of reason, however, has seen the displacement of the objective dimension in favor of the subjective, as the growth of human means for doing things has overwhelmed human ability to understand ultimate ends.

Though this argument appears to reproduce Weber's understanding of the nature of reason, Horkheimer announces in an early footnote his critique of Weber, rejecting his "pessimism with regard to the possibility of rational insight and science," and arguing that "Max Weber . . . adhered so definitely to the subjectivistic trend that he did not conceive of any rationality, not even a 'substantial' one, by which man can discriminate one end from another." And then comes the telling sentence, which bears the marks of Horkheimer and Adorno's collaboration on *Studies in Prejudice*: "If our drives, intentions, and finally our ultimate decisions must *a priori* be irrational, substantial reason becomes an agency merely of correlation and is therefore itself essentially 'functional.'"[28] By Habermas's assessment in *Philosophical Discourse of Modernity*, this sentence is laughable: how could the author(s) of the "demonic" *Dialectic of Enlightenment* argue that *Weber* was too irrational and pessimistic after they themselves had equated Kant with Sade? This is not a simple puzzle. Horkheimer appears to be fundamentally agreeing with Weber's schema yet asserting that Weber could have philosophically addressed reason in its objectivity—that is, "reason as a force not only in the individual mind but also in the objective world—in relations among human beings and between social classes, in social institutions and in nature and its manifestations."[29] Horkheimer quotes Socrates in defining the concept of objectivity:

The term objective reason thus on the one hand denotes as its essence a structure inherent in reality that by itself calls for a specific mode of behavior in each specific case, be it a practical or a theoretical attitude. This structure is accessible to him who takes upon himself the effort of dialectical thinking or, identically, who is capable of *eros*. On the other hand, the term objective reason may designate this very effort and ability to reflect such an objective order.[30]

The equation of dialectical thinking here with *eros* seems bizarre until one considers it objectively, rather than subjectively. Drawing on a reading of Plato's *Phaedrus* and the doctrine of intellectual development outlined in *The Republic*, Horkheimer argues that knowledge in general begins with and is motivated by an experience of particular things—a kind of engagement with the object and its qualities and a desire to preserve the objects of one's *eros* because they are good in themselves and demand a particular kind of comportment from us.[31] The first speculative step comes in saying love (as opposed to instrumentality) is connected to the qualities of the object. (This is a completely understandable definition of *eros*, as the lover actually does not love loving but loves loving the object.) The surprise comes in defining the engagement with the *particularity* of objects as one of the foundational poles of reason. Horkheimer sees this objective pole of reason and its attendant mode of behavior and engagement in a dialectical and historical fashion, asserting that out of the objective side of reason there emerge the defining impulses of both disciplinarity (breaking knowledge into parts) and governance (dealing with particular issues in society according to their special character). An acknowledgment of Fromm's ideas of relatedness and loving that rejects Fromm's existential and communitarian foundations of these ideas, Horkheimer's notion that *eros* stands behind objectivity, disciplinarity, and control seeks to define rationality not just as a means for a subject to follow its *daimon* but also as a form of engagement that seeks to understand what qualities in the object will legitimately respond to the knower. This theory of non-identity brushes against objective ontology, but in the name of the (incomplete) subject.

Eclipse traces out a speculative history of the relation of subjective reason (the cultivation of particular means) to objective reason (the interest in the qualities of the object). This history moves forward from Socrates and Aristotle through Thomas (the pinnacle of objective rationality), up and through the French and American Revolutions, Darwinism, and American Pragmatism. The increase in subjectivistic thought and instrumental rationality is unrelenting. Pragmatism is merely the most mild-mannered of the pure subjectivisms: reason is conceived as a matter of subjective belief, action, decision, survival value. The first major discussion of crisis and conflict in the book takes aim at the central Pragmatist concept that characterizes democracy as an "experiment" in the threefold sense that it operates in public, draws on the spirit of collective problem solving, and will be decided according to majority rule. Arguing that William James and John Dewey's ideas of "pragmatic truth" first emerged from and remained broadly tied to Darwinistic ideas that equated truth with survival, Horkheimer points to the subjectivistic and even irrationalist dimension of pragmatic reason—its tendency to equate the "cash value" of truth with the power of domination. As James Schmidt has shown, Horkheimer came to New York bracing for this battle, having drafted a response to a series of articles in *Partisan Review* in which Sidney Hook had attacked the call of Reinhold Niebuhr and Jacques Maritain to return in wartime to a neo-Thomistic sense of the value of man. Hook characterized this move as an expression of philosophical timidity, a recoil from the kinds of fights that defined and protected America's sense of self. The survival of democracy was at stake.

For Hook, a Trotskyist on his way to neoconservatism, the wartime defense of religious values signaled a retreat from liberalism, which he defined as "an intellectual temper, as faith in intelligence, as a tradition of the free market in the world of ideas."[32] This kind of pursuit of value mysticism constituted a "failure of nerve" of the sort that had led to the decline of Greece. Horkheimer did not of course object to a war against Hitler, but he took umbrage at Hook's instrumentalization of Enlightenment and philosophy as a vehicle for name-calling and national self-definition. And as an adherent of Nietzsche and Schopenhauer, Horkheimer objected to the cheapness of Hook's attack on Niebuhr's doctrine of "moral man, immoral society." Though it was wrong for the Trotskyists to denounce the war as "fundamentally imperialist," it was also foolish to be so aggrieved at those underscoring the sinfulness of the war as to embrace war as a good in its own sake. Wryly commenting that "this age needs no added stimulus to action,"[33] Horkheimer questioned Hook's association of American democracy—"the American experiment"—with manly "nerve" and scientific method: it was not fair to either democracy or to science to equate them or to judge them by the outcome of the war. In invoking John Dewey and William James for nationalist ends, Hook was reactivating a residual social Darwinism within Pragmatism and reemphasizing its link to late nineteenth- and early twentieth-century decisionism: the belief that truth was in fact a form of common sense whose value came from its victory. This notion of effective truth, argued Horkheimer, essentially equated truth with power and therefore had little critical to say about domination. Just because science reached consensus by a method that allowed dissent, or just because democracy arrived at its decisions according to a procedure, did not mean that science was democracy. Nor did good means and good technique guarantee proper ends: doctrines of pure proceduralism in fact virtually assured that the interests of the minority were not going to be taken into account, that the ends guiding science were not going to be socially reflective, and that nature would be subject to blind domination and amnesia. In many respects, argued Horkheimer, the humanist and lover of humanity should prefer Darwin himself to warmed-over social Darwinism. For Horkheimer, as for Adorno, the only way for subjective reason to recover a sense of the objective was to have a memory of objectivity, of suffering, and to interpret it as a historical text:

> Instrumentalized subjective reason either eulogizes nature as pure vitality or disparages it as brute force, instead of treating it as a text to be interpreted by philosophy that, if rightly read, will unfold a tale of infinite suffering. Without committing the fallacy of equating nature and reason, mankind must try to reconcile the two.[34]

Hook, argued Horkheimer, did not seem to understand that a comprehensive concept of reason cannot just be "established by methods of public verification open to all who submit themselves to its disciplines."[35] This narrow definition of reason, according to Horkheimer, is positivism and technological fetishism of the worst sort, in that it confuses science with mere procedure and therefore has nothing to say about the actual nature of truth and why a given goal is being pursued. One can well imagine that Horkheimer had Adorno's critique of Jaensch in mind when he leveled the question of legitimacy at Hook's teacher, Dewey:

> If Dewey means to say that scientific changes usually cause changes in the direction of a better social order, he misinterprets the interaction of economic, technical, political, and ideological forces. The death factories in Europe cast as much significant light on the relations between science and cultural progress as does the manufacture of stockings out of air.[36]

The underlying problem for all of Pragmatism, argued Horkheimer, comes in equating cognition with truth, and both with outcome and survival. In so doing, it allows economic and state organization of society and research to determine "the functions necessary to the organization of material already patterned according to that very commercial culture which intelligence is called upon to criticize."[37] This renders knowledge the servant of production *tout court*. Worse, it extends the cult of action by suggesting that any act is more valid than doing nothing. Such "pragmatic" views, argued Horkheimer, promote either triumphalism or blind submission to the status quo. Showing his proximity to the theory of wounded subjectivity, Horkheimer summarized the debate about the end of theistic rationalism and of Pragmatism alike with a Schopenhauerian gesture informed by the ongoing work on *Studies in Prejudice*: "Although most people never overcome the habit of berating the world for their difficulties, those who are too weak to make a stand against reality have no choice but to obliterate themselves by identifying with it."[38] One can defend objectivity also through non-identity.

This critique of Hook, Dewey, and James as models of American strength through democracy was a variant of Horkheimer's critique of Weber as a German nationalist-democrat; he could have argued the same points in Germany. But the double claim that democracies were always pragmatic, and that Pragmatism was a science of democracy, was even more problematic when combined with the narrative of American exceptionalism: together, these wove a dangerous myth, constituting a magical belief that Americans were immune to subjective irrationalism in the political realm. Horkheimer thus took pains both to attack this myth and to address American alternatives to Pragmatism. Pragmatism was in fact just another variant of subjective reason run amok, and Horkheimer argued that religious pluralism in America was not the only indigenous trace of objective reason. As in Europe, so in America, the mainline subjectivism of value-free science-as-means undercut notions of caste; while this was often liberatory, Horkheimer wished to remind his readers that Southern aristocratic thinking still preserved a sense of the sacral order of the Great Chain of Being and the love of the particular, and that this style of (ideologically compromised) reasoning harbored a splinter of objective reason connecting it to a corporativist defense of the minority. Where subjectivism took no prisoners and tolerated no slavery, objective reason still preserved an awareness, however retrograde, of the prisoner and the slave as part of society. Horkheimer's contrarian criticism of the purity of majority rule and subjective self-possession as a doctrine of truth is announced in the prologue, which describes the struggle to separate a subjective from a sacral objective order as part of Socrates's struggle against Athens, Spinoza's fight with the late Middle Ages, and the American Founders' struggle with the idea of simple majority rule. Though no rational and progressive person could side with objectivist theism over subjective rationalism, or theocracy over democracy, modernists who treated all metaphysical ideas as worthless and eradicated the objective sphere to which they pertained threatened to undermine all notions of the social constitution. Decrying the "neo-liberal" view that deploys the form of universal subjectivity to undercut all notions of objective or social reason, Horkheimer argued that the deification of an abstract social choice enforces the marginalization of any minority concern that does not carry currency in the marketplace of ideas.[39]

These are Weberian thoughts concerned with the relation between the definition of reason and the idea of society. Horkheimer was observing the historical process of the modern period, where first science and religion, and then art, culture, politics, and law, divided into separate value spheres that would be judged no longer by notions of a metaphysical truth, but pragmatistically, by their worldly success, by their power to command allegiance. Modernity, in carving up the world into value spheres, demanded internal contradiction, experientially and logically: the doctrine of values required individuals to hold the same passion for science, economics, politics, and art as they once did for religion, while also demanding that this loyalty be divided. This had the effect of rationalizing and disenchanting the inner and outer world—the world of objectivity and subjectivity—and of rendering everything irrational a matter of personal choice. The idea of objectivity—of an interest outside the self, an allegiance to the preservation of all—became increasingly difficult for individuals to theorize because objectivity appeared to be a matter of weak choice, of division rather than unity, of something dying rather than of vital interest. In the case of the French and American Revolutions and their notion of rights-bearing subjectivity, the concept of subjective reason and self-interest took the upper hand in defining legitimacy, but the notion of objective reason as a kind of benevolent concern for the minority was preserved in both progressive and regressive ways. Citing John Dickinson, James Madison, Noah Webster, John Adams, and George Fitzhugh among others, Horkheimer showed a deep engagement with the question of majority rule in American thought in both the aristocratic and pluralistic dimensions of arguments defending the political and social minority. Notions about human rights in the eighteenth century and Romantic period had a theological component that boiled down to a doctrine of tolerance and an embrace of the concept of nationhood as the "ultimate, supra-individual motive in human life."[40] Ultimately, though, the concept of self-interest, once a subset of an objectivist conception of reason, came to be considered the foundation of all reason. Subjective reason has simultaneously a leveling and dehumanizing effect, breaking down categories of distinction, dissolving hierarchies, and submitting everything to the rule of utility while narrowing the register of moral concern to a calculation of self-interest. Under industrial society, notions of social solidarity are negated along with those of caste and race, and even those of law and minority protection. Increasingly, reason seems to align against any concept of morality or obligation: "there is no longer any rational concept of social cohesion"; so irrational notions of collective duty must be maintained through increasing emotional emphasis on heroic sacrifice.[41] Nowhere is this played out so clearly for Horkheimer as in the tension between liberalism's definitions of the law and of community:

> The idea of national community, first set up as idol, can only be maintained by terror. This explains the tendency of liberalism to tilt over into fascism and of the intellectual and political representatives of liberalism to make their peace with its opposites. This tendency, so often demonstrated in recent European history, can be derived, apart from its economic causes, from the inner contradiction between the subjectivistic principle of self-interest and the idea of reason that it is alleged to express. Originally the political constitution was thought of as an expression of concrete principles founded in objective reason; the ideas of justice, equality, happiness, democracy, property, all were held to correspond to reason, to emanate from reason. Subsequently, the content of reason is reduced arbitrarily to the scope of merely a part of this content, to the frame of only one of its principles; the particular preempts the place of the universal. This tour de force in the realm of the intellectual lays the ground for the rule of force in the domain of the political.[42]

For Horkheimer, a Kantian who reads Kant through Sade and Nietzsche, there is grave danger in basing the concept of lawfulness on the concept of self-interest, as the latter will eventually corrode the former's legitimacy when the majority is asked to make sacrifices for the economic, political, or ethnic minority. People will blame the minority even for reasonable sacrifices made for the common good. And because liberalism as a doctrine tends to attack all idealisms and metaphysical concepts of the higher good in favor of commonsense, majority- and market- based procedures, it will eventually find itself in a position where a popular vote decides the question of the rights of the minority. In the pure liberal scenario, inequality grows to epic proportions, and people have no language for criticizing it beyond chaining themselves further to market forces; in the fascist scenario, a small minority of illiberal activists convince the liberal majority that their survival depends on handing over their self-definition to violent forces bent on eradicating all differences. The defense of democratic pluralism occupies the very dangerous middle ground of trying to defend equality and unity as a majority position that will also be equivalent to success and prosperity.

One might look at this argument and think that Horkheimer has brought himself back around to a position identical to that of Weber in "Science as Vocation." But it is wrong to read *Eclipse* in this way, for Horkheimer thinks that a defense of democracy based on the fundamental leap of faith into the meaning of subjective will is in fact merely a social Darwinistic, arbitrary choice to embrace the winning side, domination, or even terror. To defend liberalism as science or democracy or as a show of will would be to make the subjectivistic mistake for which he attacks Hook. Counterintuitively, it is in the attempt to redeem objective reason's admittedly ideological concern for human weakness, knowledge of the minority, and the need for some sense of order that will relieve suffering, where Horkheimer hopes to rediscover the categories of reason.

It must have puzzled his progressive American audience that Horkheimer, in calling for the recovery of objective rationality and the defense of Socratic *eros*, cited George Fitzhugh, author of the pro-slavery *Cannibals All, or Slaves without Masters*. But the provocation had a purpose: Horkheimer wished his American readers to consider Fitzhugh as not *indifferent* to the needs of slaves but rather (like a good slaveowner) as someone who cultivated a *knowledge and love* of slaves. Fitzhugh's objective rationality was parallel to the social hierarchies of medieval humanism—ideological but nevertheless engaged in real social analysis akin to Marx's recognition that "[a] Negro is a Negro. He only becomes a slave in certain circumstances."[43] *Eros* and knowledge were twinned even in slavery at least to the point that the master's interest in the slave was self-interest. Modern racism did not rise to this level of recognition of human needs: it identified the Others through instrumental projection, defining the self existentially through having an enemy; and modern liberalism, unfortunately, reinforced this negative identity by pretending that by sticking to the majority rule, it was enacting the essence of scientific, democratic modernism. To the contrary, thinking about how to address the problem of the victim, the minority, outcast, and the stranger was, for Horkheimer, the way to recover a rough outline of objective reason and legitimate authority. This was to be achieved not through the assertion of procedure, or the positivity of facts, or markets over churches, but through negativity: by knowing the worst, by thinking of knowledge—and even love—as a form of wound. Though Madison's proceduralism and subjectivism in defense of the minority in "Federalist No. 10" was more democratic and universalist than Fitzhugh's sociologism and ideologized ontology, there did come a point when a transformed version of Fitzhugh's objective interest in the Other could reenter into a dialectic of emancipation. As *Minima Moralia* argued, embracing criticism meant learning to hate things properly—by which it was meant that hate, like its inverse, love, must be appropriate to its object and mode of objectification: "only those who know a tradition hate it properly."[44] The doctrine of majority rule as truth runs afoul of the social constitution of objectivity; forms of knowledge that take into account the detestable minority can, at times, achieve a superior fidelity not just to suffering but also to truth.

In 1945, both Horkheimer and Adorno were rethinking philosophy along the lines of what they conceived to be an irreducible fact of the dialectic—a sense of social-objective analysis accessible to everyone. Subject and object are not concepts but the irreducible poles of knowledge. Everyone living in a society in which exploitation exists always has available the two aspects of knowledge defined by these poles: an understanding that subject can become object and that object can become subject was becoming for Horkheimer and Adorno a new basis on which to rethink objectivity and objective reason. Instead of basing objectivity on a fundamentally irrational will (as had Weber) or seeking to call on *eros* and the pleasure principle as a subjective motivation for sublimation (as had Freud), Horkheimer and Adorno sought to reconstruct the relation to objectivity in terms of woundedness. There are countless versions of this negative ideality developed in *Dialectic of Enlightenment* but then applied to the concept of value. Horkheimer observed in *Eclipse* that though agreement is impossible on "ultimate ends," it can be reached through comparison of negative historical outcomes.[45] We cannot know the good, but we know the worst and can agree to avoid it. Equally, in *Minima Moralia*, Adorno argued that "the unprecedented torture and humiliation of those abducted in cattle-trucks sheds a deathly-livid light on the most distant past, in whose mindless, planless violence the scientifically confected was already teleologically latent. The identity lies in the nonidentity, in what, not having yet come to pass, denounces what has."[46] Thinking about the subject turned object does not solve every problem, but it establishes the legitimacy of forestalling terror, rather than the bad identity of terror deployed as a tool to maintain unity.

This new negative identity ending in objectivity imagined an alternative to the crisis paradigm embedded in theories of purely subjective reason. The great German historian of ideas Reinhart Koselleck, influenced by *Dialectic of Enlightenment*, would in 1956 describe a deep connection between the Enlightenment project of criticizing authority and the anticipation of a cataclysmic crisis that would put an end to all authority. Koselleck's idea was that this "crisis of history" model led to visions of revolutionary redemption that flourished under absolutist regimes where utopian models took the place of real public politics.[47] The underground quality of the critique had the effect of lending an aura of apolitical utopianism to spheres of action that were political by their very nature: religion, education, social planning, even governance. Koselleck was probably at the time commenting not just on the antecedents of the French Revolution, but also on the apparently quiescent critical attitudes of Horkheimer and Adorno; but Koselleck's analysis would have been more complete had he addressed the revolution of negative identity that unfolded in critical theory in the first years of the Cold War. Horkheimer and Adorno's meditations on the not-I in liberalism do just this.

Eclipse argues that the great problem with the line of subjectivist reason that culminated in the subjective irrationalisms of Weberian sociology, Freudian psychology, and existentialist neo-Thomism was that it placed the entire burden of resolving these conflicts on the individual subject as if they were built-in dimensions of merely being human. Though there is some truth in equating the crisis of individual identity with the crisis of social reason, untruth and even damage result when individual identity is required to bear the brunt of this historical conflict. Using Fromm's language of identity for the last time, but in a critical, diagnostic manner, Horkheimer draws a connection between the logical identity of value idealism and aristocratic-clerical identity: Thomism, Horkheimer argues, staved off a critical dualism—the critical social understanding that there was a conflict between the ideal and reality—by upholding "the eternal identity between goodness, perfection, and power" and equating this identity with the self-definition "of groups that held or strove for power."[48] When the power of subjective reason triumphed over objective categories—when philosophy gained the power to criticize the non-identical, antagonistic relations of society through critique—the language of identity gradually turned into a historical but individual concept. Pragmatism and existentialism bore the scars of the latter-day attempt to forge a subjective identity out of the "identity of truth and science,"[49] the identity of "domination with submission," the domination of that which is with that which ought to be, and they provoked the possible response of an absolute negation: a rejection of all forms of mastery, all forms of power, all forms of culture. In the French Revolution, the expansion of critique culminated in a totalizing criticism of all social institutions that dissolved even their legitimate function. But the subjective revolution turned the guns on the self, dissolving it into a subject declared omni-competent subjectivity while being outfitted as the object of mass manipulation. Thus, Horkheimer describes the problem faced by contemporary individuals:

> The crisis of reason is manifested in the crisis of the individual, as whose agency it has developed. The illusion that traditional philosophy has cherished about the individual and about reason—the illusion of their eternity—is being dispelled. The individual once conceived of reason exclusively as an instrument of the self. Now he experiences the reverse of this self-deification. The machine has dropped the driver; it is racing blindly into space. At the moment of consummation, reason has become irrational and stultified. The theme of this time is self-preservation, while there is no self to preserve. In view of this situation, it behooves us to reflect upon the concept of the individual. When we speak of the individual as a historical entity, we mean not merely the space-time and the sense existence of a particular member of the human race, but, in addition, his awareness of his own individuality as a conscious human being, including recognition of his own identity. This perception of the identity of the self is not equally strong in all persons. It is more clearly defined in adults than in children, who must learn to call themselves "I"—the most elementary affirmation of identity.[50]

Horkheimer is arguing that the whole idea of I-pointing and I-calling is acquired and complex. One should not imagine that either selfhood or projective identity is inherently prepared to defend society against the powerful forces of destruction that it unleashes. This notion of the "crisis of the individual" as an expression of and answer to the destructive forces of society was already ridiculous in the era of entrepreneurial capitalism; but in the era of large-scale capitalism, atomic bombs, and widespread social alienation, it was madness, and dangerous. Blurring the distinction between the entrepreneurial self and the realities of subjectivity in industrial society was how neoliberal thinking undercut the ability to conceive of the problems of labor. Echoing *Minima Moralia*, Horkheimer asserted that this imposition of the burdens of society onto the subject—as if the subject caused them—"crushes all vestiges of individuality" and the society it is supposed to defend.[51] Horkheimer proceeds in *Eclipse* to put most of the Institute's cards on the table, arguing in two dimensions at once: first, regarding the need for new forms of engagement in the social science and in politics; and second, regarding the need for a new philosophy that would recover objectivity based on the wounded nature of subjectivity and the incomplete nature of emancipation.

The sociological and psychological rethinking of labor in the age of oligopoly capitalism and huge corporations requires reexamination of the heroic sense of rugged individualism and self-creation myths of (American) liberalism. Promoting these ideals as if they are still the norm for the individual may constitute a good advertising method to spur consumption, but it ultimately cultivates paranoia. Horkheimer was aware, as the negotiations for Taft-Hartley were unfolding, that this ideology of self-made economic individualism—autotelic subjectivity—affects more than just entrepreneurs. It indeed undercuts every profession, because it makes labor neither about the creation of meaning out of objectivity nor about alienation as a form of objectivization but defines both labor and social utility more broadly in terms of compliance with the market. Critical theory conceives of labor in terms of the conflict between dimensions of one's personality and the overall division of labor, and it believes that to abstain from theorizing about how the latter injures the former leaves the individual wounded without a proper explanatory structure. Hook's insistence that one just follow the procedures of the discipline in which one works, with no attention to how its knowledge and labor relate to the broader field of human endeavor, is positivistic, conformist, abject. *Eclipse* equally attacks those (such as Hook) who characterize the unions as monopoly powers or deride as "unproductive" the worker's struggle against capitalist domination. Horkheimer argues for the importance of not allowing union and nonunion workers to be played off one another by the invocation of social and cultural differences and, citing Robert Lynd, characterizes unthinking attacks by social scientists on religious concern as stifling workers' dissatisfaction with the labor system.[52] On the eve of the civil rights era, Horkheimer argues that social analysis would do better to stop contesting the spiritual or material source of beliefs of injustice and focus instead on the objective injustice that drives the sense of wounded belief. Those worried about social alienation should think about how to provide enriching alternatives to the pablum of the culture industry rather than recommend that those suffering from alienation seek to develop their personality or find meaning in science. Social science must combat the widespread problem of exaggerated personalities—as represented by movie stars or strongmen—redefining the nature of wholeness, pleasure, and self-protection. Reciprocally, social knowledge must tear down false essentialisms, notions of exaggerated value claims or heroic action that are merely the obverse forms of conformity or ressentiment. Quoting Huey Long's assertion that "every man can be a king," Horkheimer calls for a thoroughgoing critique of the way media pumps up fake populist personalities like Long, who "are creatures of their own publicity, enlargements of their own photographs," and are therefore mere "functions of social processes."[53] This impulse toward commercialization, fake identities, fake politics must be resisted not because it creates bad culture, but because it mutilates the image of man and prevents ressentiment from being addressed objectively through determinate negation. This deessentialization of personhood and values begins with how one thinks about historical action, about individual being in time. Social science needs to disassemble bogeymen but also recognize how useful belief in bogeymen is to the administration of an atomized society governed by great powers. It must also define the counterheroes, emphasizing the power of struggles undertaken by those who have suffered degradation and loss from systematic oppression. The story of human rights proceeding from this point forward becomes a matter of making palpable the muted heroism of those who struggled against power and lost.

Philosophy has a different role to play than the social sciences. It should analyze social and psychological patterns and turn them toward the objective, working to prevent the modern cults—the cult of facts and the cult of values—from destroying the ability to think about the relation between subject and object. Philosophy must look, as Adorno argued, for the gaps in knowledge and its spheres of power and seek not to fill them but to turn them into tools for social criticism. To do this, one must show how the distorting power of social facts (false positivism) relates to the distorting power of values (false essentialism) and connect both to a larger, self-reflexive history of the becoming of truth out of half-truth. Quoting Hegel's critique of rigid definitions, *Eclipse* challenges philosophy to think about how it participates in, and might overcome, the abuse of language as a tool for creating false essentialism. It argues that all truths are fragments, and that raw public opinion can mislead researchers about the concept at stake. If one can think about concepts in their historical change, one might also be able to think about how societal change occurs: by constantly imperiling individual existence. Failure to turn conceptual non-identity into knowledge allows its rote reproduction to undercut objective social insight and transform it into identity.

The linchpin for this reincorporation of the social and psychological into philosophy comes from recognizing that social and psychological technique cannot be reduced to each other but must mutually criticize each other. Horkheimer argues that from this interdisciplinary approach, a negative anthropology springs—one that observes that science bound to production tends, inherently, to think of something that is essentially "spirit" as if it were raw material out of which to build things. This manifests itself in philosophy's tendency to think itself equivalent to science, to claim that its abstractions are the same as those of science:

> The real difficulty in the problem of the relation between spirit and nature is that hypostatizing the polarity of these two entities is as impermissible as reducing one of them to the other. This difficulty expresses the predicament of all philosophical thinking. It is inevitably driven to abstractions such as "nature" and "spirit," while every such abstraction implies a misrepresentation of concrete existence that ultimately affects the abstraction itself. For this reason, philosophical concepts become inadequate, empty, false, when they are abstracted from the process through which they have been obtained.[54]

Horkheimer argues here for the idea that if philosophy wishes to maintain its legitimacy, it must stop equating truth with the dominant and with survival. Recognizing the fateful course of the world as it is, philosophy should offer resistance not by retreating into a self-identical world of facts or supposedly immanent values but by showing the immanence of truth in everyday life. Reason needs to be thought of as partially wounded, and philosophy needs to look inward so it can recover the principle of truth from being dominated by a distorted notion of self-preservation: "The idea of self-preservation, the principle that is driving subjective reason to madness, is the very idea that can save objective reason from the same fate. Applied to concrete reality, this means that only a definition of the objective goals of society that includes . . . the respect for individual life deserves to be called objective."[55]

Calls for philosophy to respect the dignity of individual life were legion in the immediate postwar period: they were integral to the existentialism of the atomic age. What distinguishes *Eclipse* is its interest in urging the social Darwinistic inheritance of philosophy and the sciences to examine their concept of science and cultivate a critical objectivity. *Eclipse* insists that the "adaptation" paradigm has neither unified the sciences, created a unity in the public discourses of culture, nor rendered discussions about human survival more objective, scientific, or democratic. Rather, it has created fragmentation and subjectivization that needs to be considered critically:

> The task of philosophy is not stubbornly to play the one against the other, but to foster a mutual critique and thus, if possible, to prepare in the intellectual realm the reconciliation of the subjective and objective reason in reality. Kant's maxim, "The critical path alone is still open," which referred to the conflict between the objective reason of rationalistic dogmatism and the subjective reasoning of English empiricism, applies even more pertinently to the present situation. Since isolated subjective reason in our time is triumphing everywhere, with fatal results, the critique must necessarily be carried on with an emphasis on objective reason rather than on the remnants of subjectivistic philosophy, whose genuine traditions, in the light of advanced subjectivization, now in themselves appear as objectivistic and romantic.[56]

In the following pages, Horkheimer restates this abstract philosophical program in interdisciplinary and social terms that emphasize the importance of protecting the public ideals of science, democracy, and critical inquiry from being undercut by notions of relativism, actionism, or decisionism that emphasize effective truth over critical truth and that privilege arbitrary change over the maintenance of objective insight. Thus, Horkheimer argued that philosophy must work not just with the social sciences but also with journalism to help defend the line between truth and propaganda, the line between the measurement of opinion and the social realities of economic and social conditions. He argued that the critique of false essentialism must be cultivated in all spheres, lest even forms of engagement aimed at humanitarian purposes distort and mutilate mankind. Politically, one must not let the subjective rationality of state power turn into a new pragmatism where might makes right, and the perception of action occludes objective understanding. One must cultivate the actual study of oppressed groups as they are and prevent such studies from becoming tools for future exploitation.

All ideas will be occluded by subjectivized reason unless theory intervenes. A philosophy that starts off with the principle that the tools of science distort even as they measure might allow for a more objective analysis of social, cultural, and psychological patterns of thinking, one that actually considers what it means to be a subject in a world of other subjects—a subject who has become more readily exploitable because he has come to view interdependence as a threat, and because he perceives himself, rightly but also wrongly, through this lens of "the antagonistic social forces."[57]

This updated definition of critical theory explicitly intensifies the Institute's commitment to public engagement and does so as a universalist defense of the non-identical minority. *Eclipse* presented an ambitious vision of what theory could do and arguably did do during the next twenty years of its public life. By defining critical theory as an urgent, necessary negation of the world of subjective non-identity, misshapen objects and "loves" masking social relations, *Eclipse* signaled the end of the "message in a bottle" tactic and the start of the need to engage with the new ideology. The idea of defusing the negative identities of liberal thought became as important as the idea of preserving an oppositional sensibility. From this point onward, private philosophical ideas were insufficient unless they engaged the public culture and its ideas of truth, and this meant engagement with a broad range of public disciplines, seeking to stop them from straying into false positivisms, essentialisms, or myth making.

Subjectivity and Universal Homelessness

In 1950, Adorno, in thinking of returning to Germany, wrote what is today the introduction to *Minima Moralia*. Preparing to make public his private notebooks, Adorno engaged in a Marxist-Hegelian meditation on the meaning of ethics and individualism in an age dominated by oligarchical capitalism. Claiming the need to update John Stuart Mill's notion of economics as the "dismal science" into a study of one's private thoughts of exile, or "the melancholy science,"[58] Adorno explained that private reflection was at the moment the true sphere of public action. Drawing on the sense that politics had displaced economics in the 1930s and that the combination of Fordist production methods with the welfare state had created a new permanent war economy, Adorno suggested that the stasis between liberalism and socialism in the West, and the global conflict between Communist and capitalist blocs, left critical thought with little option but to turn inward.

The melancholy science of theoretical-moral reflection on the permanently elevated politics of consumption must, he argued, proceed with an analysis of the thought forms of everyday life. Critical theory, which once focused on the economic base, must realize that the superstructure of individualism had been integrated into the base, subjecting the individual to a constant stimulus to consume and struggle against others for the sake of more consumption. Citing Marcel Proust and Hegel, he argues that in an age of unsatisfactory consumption, those who have the privilege to look beyond survival have a duty to themselves and others to dwell on the negative in order to preserve a sense of the objective sources of their dissatisfaction. With a dash of dandyish negativity, Adorno announced that critical theory, by engaging with the question of inner life and identity, and with its "necessary entanglement in liberalistic thinking," would rethink the forms of what Hegel once called objective spirit, without this time taking for granted the emergence of a liberated subjectivity.[59]

In declaring bourgeois interiority the future of social theory, Adorno was invoking the legacy of divided subjectivity in a personal mode. Preparing to return to Germany, he anticipated a world of political denial, projective negative identity, and Romantic concepts of the good old times and the undamaged German national essence. He also was aware that he would, in returning, need to present himself as a returned exile and make positive use of his objective negative identity. He would need to, as it were, show a positive identity that was capable of negative reflection. Adorno's work in *The Authoritarian Personality* had paved the way for a greater sympathy with the idea that people have no choice but to adopt an identity, and Adorno was in the process of thinking what it would mean to be a German representing not just himself but his fellow exiles, and not just German philosophy but the estranged mixture of Kantian and Marxian universalism, Freudian and Weberian objectivity that he had developed in America.

With its postwar introduction in place, *Minima Moralia* advances the duality of the modern, divided self as a vehicle and object for theory. Developing the antinomy that the self is the last refuge of freedom and the superstructure-cum-base of modern forms of domination, Adorno argues for a new immanent critique of identity, one that takes the inward divided self as its own model for analyzing an antagonistic society. Rejecting every kind of ontology or theory of subjective truth—rejecting notions of the found, given, produced, essential, or irreducible forms of unity, and declaring them as suspect as the concept of the given or natural "I"—Adorno argued for a self that would recover its sense of reason by "giving itself over to the object" not as a kind of surrender but as theory of reconstituted objectivity that could serve a true rather than a sham notion of universal subjectivity. This negative objectivity, the obverse of the idea that "all reification is a forgetting," would be a new way of "tarrying with the negative" that did not abandon the self to face "crisis" alone, insist on being the sole category of legitimacy, or demand that individuals create out of themselves a neoclassical synthesis of harmonious selfhood.[60]

As a matter of theory, the divided self needed to be thought of and modeled in relation not just to a society divided between manual and mental labor along the lines of the social division of labor but also to a reconstituted notion of disciplinarity in knowledge that drove the technical division of labor and mandated the rupture between different emotional, practical, and epistemological dimensions of the self. This project of working from the subjective immanence of "life" to the world of labor and the disciplines and then returning in dialectical form was the stated goal of *Minima Moralia* as described in its introduction. The book indeed traces a path that originates in *Lebensphilosophie* and slowly seeks to unfold the relation among sociology, psychology, and phenomenology. Invoking both Simmel's famous attempt to put a "material basis" under the Kantian subject and his own grappling with Simmel's estranged epistemology as a way of understanding American sociology, Adorno presented his *Minima Moralia* as a kind of Odyssean telling of his own tale and a testament to his awareness that he would, in returning to Germany, be returning to the basic problems of identity, non-identity, and negative identity that he encountered in America.[61]

If *Minima Moralia* tells the story of the movement from the immanence of life to the analysis of the divided self, the experience of living in exile meant that it was the daily work of the philosopher to connect the experience of negative identity to a critique of authority. In the short talk "Questions on the German Emigration" that Adorno gave to the Jewish Club of Los Angeles in 1945, he addressed the issue of his own negative identity as a German exile of Jewish descent. To the question of what it meant to have an identity as an immigrant, Adorno spoke in a counterintuitive and dialectical fashion. With Adorno's gift for saying exactly the thing his audiences least expected or wanted to hear, Adorno turned a speech about what kind of "contribution" German-Jewish immigrants could make into a small lesson in human rights. Adorno knew that the Jewish Club of Los Angeles, like that of New York—which published the journal *Aufbau*—

was dedicated to helping displaced Jews adjust to American life and that it pursued a politics that insisted that postwar efforts at "restitution" should not *require* Jews to return to Germany. A mixture of patriotic duty and the pressure of assimilation comprised a sufficiently sensitive constellation of ideas such that in 1945 the Los Angeles club sent a board member to a B'nai B'rith lodge meeting to announce that

> 99% of the refugees organized in the Jewish Club of 1933 have no other aim and intention than to be or become American citizens, fulfilling the duties and exercising the right this privilege involves. It would be a great mistake to assume—or to conclude from an exceptional single case—that the Jewish refugees from Germany would ever think of returning there. . . . The fact itself cannot be stated clearly enough.[62]

Adorno's talk to this organization spoke to this problem by starting off with a quick discussion of the difference between the immigrant and the *émigré*:

> The immigrant is a person who comes by importing himself, more or less freely, attracted by the unlimited possibilities. The *émigré* is a refugee, someone in flight, who is seeking the kind of protection that we found in America. If we want to call ourselves immigrants, we would do so correctly in the sense of our identity papers, but this would belie our actual situation. We would be announcing a kind of eagerness [to fit in] that our American friends certainly notice, even if they are too polite to say so. If we were in truth immigrants, then we could present ourselves as a spiritually homogenous group, such as the religious sects that settled America. But our connection did not emerge from having a common sensibility. What unifies us is a negative—that we were driven out of Germany—experiencing the hardship that seemed accidental, gratuitous, and personal for all not-politically conscious *émigrés*.[63]

This emphasizes his view that an émigré is in exile from his home, regardless of whether he personally intends to go back to it or not. Adorno demands scrutiny of the category of immigrant, which he argues is wrongly loaded with the expectation that newcomers to any country must somehow find a way to "make a contribution" so that they can "earn" their citizenship. Without denying the personal importance of having citizenship—Adorno had naturalized as a US citizen in the 1930s—Adorno insists on the idea that every refugee should insist that freedom from oppression should never be linked to "performance." It is a public duty to refuse the quid pro quo. If one does not insist, then the language of "making a contribution" turns quickly into "adaptation, making oneself useful, and ultimately, self-sacrifice":

> And speaking in this way becomes an *as if*—that because we escaped the gas chambers—it is *as if* we want to say please accept us, but with "our apologies that we were ever born," so that we may pay the premium for having been left in our skin. Such gestures insult the hospitality that we believe to be due, and scorn democratic ideals. Human rights were never conceived as a reward for compliant behavior.[64]

Adorno rarely spoke in the first-person singular, much less in the collective. But here it is a form of strategic and principled negative Kantianism. Universality must not just be assumed as form; it must be contested and made substantial. The best way to make good on a nation's hospitality and democratic impulses is to never let the neoliberal logic of immigration as a quid pro quo overwhelm the underlying fact that emigration—even inclusive of a contemplation of a return—has duties attached to it, not those of quietly fitting in and being compliant, but rather of contesting in whatever way one can the barbarization of culture that turns citizens into refugees. Difference should not become grist for the mill—part of the "dazzling . . . vast machinery of American life"—but should become, in words that *Minima Moralia* uses to invert the Gospel phrase, "a splinter in the eye of your neighbor" that helps her to see the meaning of her salvation as well as yours.[65] Partly this sense of difference comes from having a memory, from refusing the personal "blank slate" of immigration, and continuously engaging with both one's personal history and its entwinement with negative identity, objective and subjective. To be a citizen of one's adopted country should not require one to cease being a citizen of the world. One will of course live one's life partly always in translation, but daily existence should continue to "transfer exactly that which we are told is not transferable" and to keep alive a sense of meaningful labor on issues of substance, without concern for a contemporary audience.[66] Everyone who can, argues Adorno, should seek to resist the public definition of the category of immigration as a primarily economic category. One must, to the degree that one is able, make one's daily life that of an émigré who teaches the meaning of exile to which even the natural-born are subject.

In the private space of the Los Angeles club, Adorno was willing to speak in the language of personal identity and was willing to speak about his own (half) Jewishness in a language that sought to inject the particular meaning of exile, one of the central narratives of Jewish existence, into the universal language of citizenship. One might wonder if Adorno knew of Hannah Arendt's 1943 "We Refugees," but he is here echoing the same basic left-Kantian formula that viewed emigration as a kind of "vanguard of peoples—if they keep their identity."[67] As was the case with Arendt's expression of a need to rethink citizenship, here Adorno was resisting the salvific belief in democracy as a permanent achievement. Like Arendt, Adorno emphasized that the everyday struggle of immigrant life serves as the best tool to historicize citizenship as a paradigm of universality that had otherwise become abstract, formalistic, and detached from the complex realities of the unstable nation-state. There is indeed in both thinkers a moment of (Western) European pride in having come from the world of *Bildung* and a frankness in acknowledging that not everyone has the freedom to speak and work politically as they do. Both texts even share acknowledgment of a negative definition of Jewishness—an acknowledgment that until the terror of the 1930s, the western and eastern Jews of Europe were very divided and could not be thought a singular "people" with shared beliefs, but were what Bauer described as a "community of fate" connected to each other through the experience of exile. Certainly, Adorno was uncomfortable with Arendt's essentialisms—her existentialist denotation of "man as a political animal"—preferring negative formulations and the epistemology of estrangement that would deem her language too accommodating to the "fact" of the national identity; Arendt would have wished Adorno would speak more concretely about the tension between the educated and uneducated and the institutional nature of politics. But the fact is that these two refugees, who were becoming pivotal theorists of the problem of racism and domination, approximated each other closely at this moment. They theorized not just a negative construction of citizenship but also a daily struggle to uphold the sense of "two souls in one breast" that defined refugee life, turning it toward renewing the concept of citizenship and rescuing the category of immigration from being another tool of internalized self-hatred or marginalization of negative identity.

It may well be true, as many scholars have argued, that Adorno never contemplated anything but returning to Europe once the war was over. But it seems then also true that from 1945 to 1950—in the years between speaking to the Los Angeles club and writing the introduction to *Minima Moralia*—Adorno had rethought the entire notion of identity and being, essentialism and citizenship, in a way that made the émigré and wounded subjectivity part of the story of subjectivity in both its abstract, philosophical and its concrete, everyday dimensions. This was the same interlude in which Adorno wrote *The Authoritarian Personality* and labored to transform the AJC's wish for what Arendt described as "another scholarly tome" titled "The Jews and . . . ." Such titles conjoin two histories, argued Arendt, so as to "anticipate some future harmony."[68] Instead, the book Adorno left behind articulated a general critique of racism and its role in constructing the politics of reaction, and the book he took back with him—*Minima Moralia*—proclaimed the value of the epistemology of estrangement. This was a kind of negativity that Adorno believed was the duty of the émigré as vanguard, as a wounded subject: to articulate the possibilities of what "not having yet come to pass, denounces what has." The dialectic, as always, ran both ways, and the task for his return to Germany was already articulated: making the abstract "solvent" of the dialectic capable of transforming the wounds of the subject into scars of a more universal recognition.

Conclusion

The modern concept of identity was articulated in America, and it was in America that the concept of identity was first negated. The dialectical origin story of this concept has been largely neglected. And more: the concept as a form of implied practice possesses historical and philosophical dynamics that are still not understood. This book has explored the way the material history of the identity concept is bound up with that of critical theory in America, and it has shown that both positive and negative identity came into the world in estranged form. From the beginning, identity and non-identity were conceptual placeholders for thoughts and fears that did not fully understand themselves: they registered the anxiety of being an exile not at home in the world, the hope for the possibility of "being different without fear";[1] they spoke to mystification at how modern society had made subjectivity more perilous and vulnerable even as it had made it more free and universal. The idea of identity still carries within it a utopian longing that the subject will find itself fulfilled in the world or that the subject will be able to remake the world in its own image. The concept of positive identity in particular still carries within it the confusion of its subjective and objective Other: the question of how the search for the security of "having an identity" relates one to the machinery of production and the communities of others whose thought and labors define the cosmopolitan and capitalist world.

Between 1931, when Horkheimer first called for a critical theory to challenge and supplement traditional theory, and 1950, when *The Authoritarian Personality* was published in America, the core aspiration of the Institute for Social Research remained unchanged: it sought to draw on Marxian and Kantian universalism to update the interdisciplinary sciences, and vice versa. The rise of fascism disrupted this research agenda, requiring critical theory to grapple not only with how rationality had unfolded subjectively and objectively but also with how much modern society produced and integrated irrationalism, narcissism, neurosis, and ressentiment into its everyday practices. The key concepts that might seem to bridge between Kant's and Marx's universalism were all wrong. Desiring to create neither a science of applied irrationalism nor a *Kallipolis* of impractical idealism, the Institute's theorists instead came to define their work as developing and defending a universalism that could grapple with the actual, disfigured world of the intrawar period and that could explain why capitalist and social elites would—whether in Germany or elsewhere—throw in with the violent and authoritarian fringe movements of which Hitler's National Socialists seemed merely the most successful example. Critical theory's Marxism demanded an economic and political rationale for the alliance of elites and radicalism, but it also looked to the theory of autonomy, to the ways in which modern conditions of labor and social power frustrated or limited the defense mechanisms of individual and collective subjectivity. As irrationality came to appear less a consequence than a mainspring of fascism's expansionistic notion of the state and foreign policy, the question of whether the Enlightenment or revolutionary—the Kantian or Marxian—"subject of history" would come to the rescue turned from being a tragic hope to a tragic realization: perhaps the mere idea of collective or individual subjectivity was itself a form of ideology or illusion.

Critical theory brought these concerns about collective and universal identity, subjective and systems identity with them to America when they fled European fascism. Their American experience quickly taught them that they had understood only part of the problem. Identity moved to the center of their concerns when one of their members, Erich Fromm, translated critical theory's concept of the antagonistic whole into the language of American cultural and social adaptation. Explicitly invoking the language of identity, Fromm argued that liberal capitalist societies needed to defend individualism from the encroachments of fascist sadism and move toward progressive liberation of the desires, toward the removal of sexual repression, toward a more equal and just society characterized by caring, respect, and connectedness. Fromm's model of social dynamism imagined that cultural assimilation and the cultivation of harmonious personalities were the keys to fending off fascism, but reading his work taught his Institute colleagues something different. It confirmed their growing suspicions about subjective rationalism itself: about the subject-centeredness of Kant's thought, about the way the Kantian subject had been built into nineteenth-century liberal thought, about the Kantian inheritance in Marxian visions of revolutionary progress and autonomy. Fromm, in Adorno's reading, was assuming that a well-formed society could escape social irrationalism and that the scientific-liberal notion of rationality would not be damaged by the violence of the coming war. But if one did not draw the cap over one's own eyes and insist on a specifically German (or Russian, Italian, Croatian, or Japanese) "cultural tendency" toward authoritarianism, then the question of really existing fascism demanded that one explain how neoauthoritarianism could emerge even from democratic liberalism. Adorno and Horkheimer were disturbed by liberalism's naïve faith that the solution to authoritarianism was a cultural model of pluralism that emphasized how communities and individuals could learn to mutually assimilate to one another and that mutual adaptation alone would defeat the subjective impulses toward domination and the social push toward hierarchy, conflict, and distortion. If American Pragmatism had something to teach, it was about the barbarism inherent in all forms of culture. Practice was worse than theory. Most of the American social science apparatus they experienced was so geared toward advertising, marketing, and a stimulus-response model of measurement that anyone proposing to study inequality, conflict, or prejudice was likely either to be sidelined or, worse, to find his interest in the dominated classes interpolated back into pathological pseudo-sciences of differences—racial, sexual, national, or class—masquerading as cultural relativism. Democratic in principle, America was riven by the color line in practice; if it had something to teach critical theory, it was not about how to think about universalism per se, but how to think about universalism negatively.

The Institute's turn toward negativity coincided with its invention and rejection of subjective identity. Adorno's insight that alienation was productive for sociological knowledge and that there was an epistemological value in researching divided selfhood and divided disciplinarity pointed the way toward a revision of the idea of scientific universality grounding the Institute's empirical research and of the Kantian idea, fundamental to its philosophical work, that the forms of subjectivity cast a negative light on the forms and practices of reason. Speculating that modern capitalism cultivated the idea of subjective freedom largely to manipulate individuals into subordination, Adorno inquired into how science made use of the division of labor to forbid topics of social concern from being articulated in empirical research. An examination of the psychology of authoritarian behavior revealed a rationality to the *irrational* choice of one's victims for being symbolically powerful and simultaneously powerless. Critical theory, once focused on developing the notion of an objectively rational subjectivity—on discovering the Marxian "subject of history"—now sought to understand how individual consciousness mediated and reproduced social conflict. This led Adorno and Horkheimer in particular to push toward a thoroughgoing consideration of how even the most progressive subjective universalism could be transformed into a regressive, mass-mediated logic of authoritarian politics. Their experience with the scientific techniques of the social survey and the new media's techniques of mass persuasion led them to ask hard questions about whether anyone participating in wartime research, as they had, might be compromising the ability for an emancipated society to resist the power of top-down control. As they looked forward to the war's end, they feared that the social research system and the culture industry would, by desubstantalizing subjectivity, also proliferate the conditions for the possibility of fascism, reactionary politics, and the horrors of weaponized negative identity. While they did not believe that advertising, the mass media, or applied psycho-social research was inherently fascistic, they feared that the divided subjectivities, divided forms of knowledge, and divided societies of modernity provided sufficient material for turning individuals against society and that the danger of aggressive, institutionalized heteronomy was already deeply embedded in modern life. They developed these ideas of rational and irrational subjectivity into a model of a layered form of conflicting rationality that needed to be studied with an interdisciplinary approach to both knowledge and subject/object relations. Regarding their view of Marx and Freud as "orthodox," in the sense that it recovered a universalized model of object relations, Horkheimer and Adorno were fully aware of the heterodoxy in their application of Kant and Weber as theorists of a negative idealism useful for diagnosing the unstable relation between subject and object.

Critical theory changed American life, and it did so in a very American way: not by transforming theory but by reforming practice. In their collaboration with Americans brought together from many institutions to work on *Studies in Prejudice*, Adorno and his colleagues challenged the postwar world to take race more seriously as a social problem and liberalism more seriously as a political form, and, once finished, the massive project established a new standard for studying the interconnections among racism, anti-Semitism, and other forms of prejudice. The model established by the collaborative work would shape American social science in large ways and small for decades. Yet the centrality of non-identity to the making of *The Authoritarian Personality*, and vice versa, has not been understood. Only a handful of Americans had any sense of the historical reading of Kantian autonomy, the Hegelian reinterpretation of Marx, or the Freudian interpretation of Weber. The problem was simple: they remained Strangers in American sociology. They could not directly assail the shibboleths of American social thought or redress the weakness of social analysis in a country that had experienced authoritarianism primarily in its peripheries. Critical theory had to use the vocabulary of American empiricism—and did so, while deessentializing the race concept, socializing the notion of personality, articulating the social power of narrative, exposing the danger of media manipulation, and introducing the concept of victim blaming into the analysis of ideology. They fought against the misuse of the idea of cultural assimilation as a model for education and the politics of immigration and pointed out that authoritarian politics could be fought only by engaging with how inequality, consumerism, and fantasies of dominance deformed everyday concepts of universalism. Yet they had little effect on their collaborators' basic philosophical assumptions. The core *theoretical* innovations of critical theory had been articulated in private writings in a philosophical language wholly foreign to American ears and minds. In the privacy of their own letters, they despaired whether they had the energy to keep working to smuggle critical theory in from below—acting as galley slaves in the editorial house of large-scale research projects, borrowing concepts from social Darwinistic or psychologistic empiricism and repurposing them for ends radically different from those the Americans contemplated. The decision was made to leave behind *The Authoritarian Personality* (with its critique of race relations) as a calling card. It would make its contribution or not; but it was time to go home.

Germany was, of course, not really home. That Horkheimer had to work with the office of the US Department of War to obtain a special act of Congress to preserve his American citizenship (and the right of a second refuge) testifies to the precarious nature of critical theory and to how firmly his and Adorno's identity as theorists was tied to theory's own experience of negative identity. Adorno returned to Germany without such a guarantee, in pursuit of a negative, unchosen vocation. Seeking to return to Germany in the guise of Simmel's Stranger, he asked what it would mean to update the categories of Kantian autonomy in knowledge, action, and judgment to be adequate to the age of genocide and cheap thrills. The central categories of Adorno's American years would not disappear but would be refigured as he and Horkheimer reclaimed not just their German citizenship but also their right to teach Germans about the consequences of domination and exile, in theory and practice. Working through core themes of his American experience, Adorno would rework the categories of philosophical subjectivity and negative identity as they were embodied in the sciences and social life. Non-identity and the negativity of identity formed the epistemology of return from exile. The idea of divided selfhood, of wounded subjectivity, of universal homelessness, of culture that required criticism to be culture, would be turned on forms of identity and consciousness that Adorno had once known as his own, and they would provide the key to the reconstruction of philosophy, citizenship, and a barbarized social world. As Adorno would put it in *Negative Dialectics*, "autonomy can only be grasped, judged and evaluated in relation to its otherness, the not-I."[2]

Abbreviations

This book uses the German-language edition of Adorno's collected works:
GS   Theodor W. Adorno, *Gesammelte Schriften*, ed. Rolf Tiedemann, 20 vols. (Frankfurt am Main: Suhrkamp, 1970–86).

For English-language translations and scholarly collections of Adorno's writings, I use the following abbreviations:

AT   *Aesthetic Theory*, trans. Robert Hullot-Kentor (Minneapolis: University of Minnesota Press, 1997).

BB   *Briefe und Briefwechsel*, ed. Henri Lonitz (Frankfurt am Main: Suhrkamp, 1994).

CM   *Critical Models: Interventions and Catchwords*, trans. Henry Pickford (New York: Columbia University Press, 2005).

EM   *Essays on Music*, ed. Richard D. Leppert, trans. Susan H. Gillespie (Berkeley: University of California Press, 2002).

HTS   *Hegel: Three Studies*, trans. Shierry Weber Nicholsen (Cambridge, MA: MIT Press, 1993).

LP   *Letters to His Parents, 1939–1951*, ed. Christoph Gödde and Henri Lonitz, trans. Wieland Hoban (Cambridge: Polity, 2006).

MM   *Minima Moralia: Reflections from Damaged Life*, trans. E. F. N. Jephcott (London: Verso, 1974).

NL   *Notes to Literature*, 2 vols., trans. Shierry Weber Nicholsen (New York: Columbia University Press, 1991–92).

Prisms   *Prisms*, trans. Samuel and Shierry Weber (Cambridge, MA: MIT University Press, 1967).

SIK   "Über das Problem der individuellen Kausalität bei Simmel," *Frankfurter Adorno Blätter* 8 (2003): 42–58.

I have used the following abbreviations for frequently cited journals and scholarly monographs:

AP   Theodor W. Adorno, Else Frenkel-Brunswik, Daniel J. Levinson, and R. Nevitt Sanford, *The Authoritarian Personality* (New York: Harper, 1950).

Abbreviations

CS   Erik Erikson, *Childhood and Society* (New York: Norton, 1993).

CT   Max Horkheimer, *Critical Theory: Selected Essays*, trans. Matthew J. O'Connell (New York: Continuum, 1982).

DC   Detlev Claussen, *Theodor W. Adorno: One Last Genius*, trans. Rodney Livingstone (Cambridge, MA: Harvard University Press, 2008).

DE   Theodor W. Adorno and Max Horkheimer, *Dialectic of Enlightenment*, trans. John Cummings (New York: Continuum, 1972).

DEJ   Theodor W. Adorno and Max Horkheimer, *Dialectic of Enlightenment: Philosophical Fragments*, trans. Edmund Jephcott (Stanford, CA: Stanford University Press, 2002).

DI   Martin Jay, *The Dialectical Imagination* (Berkeley: University of California Press, 1996).

EFF   Erich Fromm, *Escape from Freedom* (New York: Farrar and Rinehart, 1941).

ER   Max Horkheimer, *Eclipse of Reason* (New York: Continuum, 1985).

FSE   Thomas Wheatland, *The Frankfurt School in Exile* (Minneapolis: University of Minnesota Press, 2009).

FSSB   Wolfgang Kraushaar, ed., *Frankfurter Schule und Studentenbewegung: Von der Flaschenpost zum Molotowcocktail 1946–1995*, 3 vols. (Frankfurt am Main: Rogner and Bernhard, 1998).

GI   Gerald Izenberg, *Identity: The Necessity of a Modern Idea* (Philadelphia: University of Pennsylvania Press, 2016).

HCC   Georg Lukács, *History and Class Consciousness: Studies in Marxist Dialectics*, trans. Rodney Livingstone (Cambridge, MA: MIT Press, 1972).

HIL   "The Present Situation of Social Philosophy" (Horkheimer inaugural lecture), in *MHGS*, 2:20–35.

IM   Donald Fleming and Bernard Bailyn, eds., *The Intellectual Migration: Europe and America, 1930–1960* (Cambridge, MA: Belknap, 1969).

ISS   Robert Park and Ernest Burgess, eds., *Introduction to the Science of Sociology* (Chicago: University of Chicago Press, 1921).

LK   Leszek Kołakowski, *Main Currents of Marxism*, 3 vols., trans. P. S. Falla (New York: Norton, 2008).

MECW   Karl Marx and Friedrich Engels, *Collected Works*, 50 vols. (London: Lawrence and Wishart, 1988–2004).

MHGS   Max Horkheimer, *Gesammelte Schriften*, ed. Alfred Schmidt and Gunzelin Schmid Noerr, 19 vols. (Frankfurt: S. Fischer, 1988–96).

PDM   Jürgen Habermas, *The Philosophical Discourse of Modernity: Twelve Lectures*, trans. Frederick Lawrence (Cambridge, MA: MIT Press, 1987).

PM   Georg Simmel, *The Philosophy of Money*, trans. David Frisby (New York: Routledge, 2004).
SAF   Max Horkheimer, ed., *Studien über Autorität und Familie* (Paris: F. Alcan, 1936).
SMAP Richard Christie and Marie Jahoda, eds., *Studies in the Scope and Method of "The Authoritarian Personality"* (Glencoe, NY: Free Press, 1954).
TFS   Rolf Wiggershaus, *The Frankfurt School: Its History, Theories, and Political Significance*, trans. Michael Robertson (Cambridge, MA: MIT Press, 1995).
UV   James T. Kloppenberg, *Uncertain Victory: Social Democracy and Progressivism in European and American Thought, 1870–1920* (Oxford: Oxford University Press, 1986).
WBAP Walter Benjamin, *The Arcades Project*, ed. Howard Eiland and Kevin McLaughlin (Cambridge, MA: Belknap Press, 1999).
WBGS Walter Benjamin, *Gesammelte Schriften*, ed. Rolf Tiedemann, 7 vols. (Frankfurt: Suhrkamp, 1977).
WBSW Walter Benjamin, *Selected Writings*, ed. Michael W. Jennings, 4 vols. (Cambridge, MA: Belknap, 1996–2003).
WCWG Erich Fromm, *The Working Class in Weimar Germany: A Psychological and Sociological Study*, ed. Wolfgang Bonss (Warwickshire, UK: Berg, 1984).
WDB   W. E. B. Du Bois, *Writings*, ed. Nathan Huggins (New York: Library of America, 1987).
WM   Max Weber, *On the Methodology of the Social Sciences*, trans. Edward Shils (Glencoe, NY: Free Press, 1949).
ZfS   *Zeitschrift für Socialforschuung / Studies in Philosophy and Social Science* (New York: Institute for Social Research, 1932–41).

I use the following abbreviations for archives and frequently cited documents:

AJCSR   American Jewish Committee Archives, Scientific Research Department, http://ajcarchives.org.
ASFS "Fascism Scenario for America," RPAS, 8–18.
ASP1 Proposal for Anti-Semitism Project, in *ZfS*, 9:124–43.
ASP2 Revised ASP1, MHA 662, Box IX, File 92, Document 7a, October 30, 1942.
ASPN   Notes on ASP2, Document 7b, December 30, 1942.
ASTW Friedrich Pollock,"Total War Memo," RPAS, 62–64.
ASWC "Westcoast Statement," RPAS, 14–16.

MHA   Max Horkheimer Archive, *Universitätsbibliothek*, Goethe Universität, Frankfurt am Main. Now partially available at http://sammlungen.ub.uni-frankfurt.de/horkheimer.

RAP   "Remarks on the Authoritarian Personality," MHA 506, Box VI, File 1D, 71r–101r.

RPAS "Anti-Semitism Project Documents," MHA 664, Box IX.

TL   "Typology Letter," Horkheimer letter to Adorno, October 11, 1945, in AJCSR, http://www.ajcarchives.org/AJC_DATA/Files/5A60.PDF.

Notes

INTRODUCTION

1. *GS*, 6:15.
2. *FSSB*, 1:418.
3. *GS*, 10.2:765–66.
4. For a history of the identity concept, see Gerald Izenberg's excellent survey GI, esp. 1–24.
5. Christine M. Korsgaard, *Self-Constitution: Agency, Identity, and Integrity* (New York: Oxford University Press, 2009), 20.
6. Ibid., 19.
7. See the discussion of the "Eight Ages of Man" with "epigenetic chart" in *CS*, 222–45.
8. NGram Viewer, "identity, freedom, culture," accessed July 12, 2016, https://books.google.com/ngrams/graph?content=identity%2C+freedom%2Cculture&year_start=1800.
9. Bundespräsident Joachim Gauck, "Vorlesung zum Tag des Gedenkens an die Opfer des Nationalsozialismus," Der Bundespräsident, Berlin, January 27, 2015, http://www.bundespraesident.de/SharedDocs/Downloads/DE/Reden/2015/01/150127-Gedenken-Holocaust.pdf. Newspapers running "Identität" in the headline on January 26–27 include *die Süddeutsche Zeitung, die taz, die Welt,* and *Merkur*.
10. *GS*, 10.1:30.
11. "Ideologies of Hate," Southern Poverty Law Center, accessed November 4, 2016, https://www.splcenter.org/fighting-hate/extremist-files/ideology/.
12. Markus Willinger, *Generation Identity* (London: Arktos, 2013).
13. Reinhard Bingener, "Das Wörterbuch der neuesten Rechten," *Frankfurter Allgemeine Zeitung*, April 6, 2016.
14. Isaiah Berlin, *Two Concepts of Liberty* (Oxford: Clarendon Press, 1958), 6.
15. *HTS*, 194. Translation modified.
16. Deborah Cook, *Adorno on Nature* (New York: Routledge, 2014); Jane Bennett, *Vibrant Matter* (Durham, NC: Duke University Press, 2010).
17. Peter E. Gordon, *Adorno and Existence* (Cambridge, MA: Harvard University Press, 2016), 6.
18. *DE*, 200.

CHAPTER 1: "JAZZ, THE WOUND"

Portions of this chapter were previously published in "Jazz, the Wound: Negative Identity, Culture, and the Problem of Weak Subjectivity in Theodor Adorno's Twentieth Century," *Modern Intellectual History* 13, no. 2 (August 2016): 357–86. Reproduced with permission from Cambridge University Press.

1. *GS*, 11:95.
2. The concept of tradition in a sociological sense and repetition in a phenomenological sense was for Adorno a variant of the identity concept. See "Tradition," *GS*, 14:127–42.
3. See *AT*, 20–25; *NL*, 1:37–51.
4. *NL*, 1:83.
5. Ibid., 1:85.
6. Martin Heidegger, "Letter on Humanism," in *Basic Writings*, trans. David Krell (London: Routledge, 1978), 208.
7. *GS*, 6:129.
8. Josef Früchtl, *Mimesis: Konstellation eines Zentralbegriffs bei Adorno* (Würzburg: Königshausen + Neumann, 1986); Martin Jay, "Mimesis and Mimetology: Adorno and Lacoue-Labarthe," in *Cultural Semantics* (Amherst: University of Massachusetts Press, 1998), 120–37.
9. See "Freudian Theory and the Pattern of Fascist Propaganda," *GS*, 8:411–15.
10. I am paraphrasing two passages in *Negative Dialectics*, in ibid., 6:29–39, 225–36.
11. Heinz Steinert, *Die Entdeckung der Kulturindustrie, oder: Warum Professor Adorno Jazz-Musik nicht ausstehen konnte* (Vienna: Verlag für Gesellschaftskritik, 1992), typifies the cultural logic of moralizing attacks on Adorno's jazz articles, arguing that Adorno secretly hated the deep communal basis of great art in Harlem and Vienna. Steinert sees little reason why a German-Jewish émigré in 1937 would be wary of theories of organic, communal authenticity.
12. All dates from *EM*, 682–90. "Zeitlose Mode. Zum Jazz" appears in *GS*, 10.1:123–37, translation in *Prisms*, 119–32.
13. *GS*, 10.2:809.
14. Ibid., 10.2:805–9.
15. The phrase "affirmative character of culture" refers to Herbert Marcuse's essay by the same name, originally in *ZfS*, 6:54–94. The lead essay of *Prisms*, "Cultural Criticism and Society," extended Marcuse's concept.
16. *GS*, 10.1:138–39; *Prisms*, 133–34.
17. *GS*, 10.2:735.
18. Eric Porter, *What Is This Thing Called Jazz? African American Musicians as Artists, Critics, and Activists* (Berkeley: University of California Press, 2002). For an excellent guide to the larger field of research on popular music in the 1930s, see Leppert's commentaries in *EM*, especially 327–72.
19. Adorno's approach was not culturalist or epistemological pluralism but a negative dialectic between the universal and particular. His late essay "On Subject

and Object" elucidates the development of subject/object reciprocality in the negative phenomenological terms of *Negative Dialectics*. *GS*, 10.2:714–58.

20. Ibid., 17:303.

21. See Michael Brenner, *The Renaissance of Jewish Culture in Weimar Germany* (New Haven, CT: Yale University Press, 1996); Paul R. Mendes-Flohr, *German Jews: A Dual Identity* (New Haven, CT: Yale University Press, 1999). See also Hartmut Scheible, *Theodor W. Adorno: Mit Selbstzeugnissen und Bilddokumenten* (Reinbek: Rowohlt, 1989).

22. See DC, 12–38, 365. As Jack Jacobs has observed, Adorno's father did not wish for his son to have a bar mitzvah, and Teddie Wiesengrund was confirmed as a Lutheran. Jacobs argues that neither Adorno's sense of impending disaster for the Jews nor his analysis of anti-Semitism "can be attributed to Jewish identity" in the sense of growing up in an observant household. See Jack Jacobs, *The Frankfurt School, Jewish Lives, and Antisemitism* (Cambridge: Cambridge University Press, 2016), 54. Concurring with Jacobs's conjecture that Adorno's "half-Jewishness" attuned him to the peril of Jews living in Hitler's Europe in the 1930s, I would add that if understood in terms of negative identity, Adorno had a not *not*-Jewish identity by 1937 when he left for America. It is also tragically true that in Central Europe during the 1930s and 1940s, expulsions and violence objectively defined the relation between Jewish identity and negative identity.

23. Leo Lowenthal, *An Unmastered Past: The Autobiographical Reflections of Leo Lowenthal* (Berkeley: University of California Press, 1987), 22–35.

24. In line with the Marxian and Kantian traditions, Adorno resisted dignifying anticapitalist, antimodernist, or anti-Semitic discourses of race with a "concept" thereof. Considering race a suspect classification in legal, philosophical, or ethical thinking, Adorno helped create the research topic of "racism," defined as the study of the relation between prejudice and authoritarianism. On racism within Austro-Marxism, see LK, 2:267–305. For a more recent view, see Tommie Shelby, "Ideology, Racism, and Critical Social Theory," *Philosophical Forum* 34, no. 2 (2003): 153–88. Compare with Adorno, *GS* 9.2:248–63, 20.1:13–45.

25. *GS*, 18:729–76.

26. Benjamin describes a dynamic relation between "wish symbols," material production, and the awakening from commodity fetishism in *WBAP*, 13.

27. *WBSW* 4:109, 396; Samuel Weber, *Benjamin's -abilities* (Cambridge, MA: Harvard University Press, 2010), 242–46.

28. See LK, 3:253–300. Arpad Kadarkay quotes the publisher Wieland Herzfelde's memoirs describing Lukács as a shrewd figure in a horrible situation: "Lukács always knew what to write and whom to attack. He associated with people I considered hangmen, like Zhdanov; but I can forgive his Moscow behavior. After all, we lived in constant fear." *Georg Lukács: Life, Thought, and Politics* (Cambridge: Basil Blackwell, 1991), 303. See also Kees Boterbloem, *The Life and Times of Andrei Zhdanov, 1896–1948* (Montreal: McGill University Press, 2004). On Rjazanov, see Carl-Erich Vollgraf, Richard Sperl, and Rolf Hecker, eds., *David*

Borisovic Rjazanov und die erste MEGA (Berlin: Argument, 1997). On the Frankfurt Institute's earlier relation to the Moscow Institute, see Carl-Erich Vollgraf, Richard Sperl, and Rolf Hecker, eds., *Marx-Engels-Forschung im historischen Spannungsfeld: Zum Schicksal von Rjazanov und von Mitarbeitern des Moskauer Marx-Engels-Instituts in den 20er und 30er Jahren* (Berlin: Argument, 1993).

29. *IM*, 340.

30. *MECW*, 35:81; LK, 3:77–109, as well as discussion of Lenin's "Left-Wing Communism," ibid., 2:381–405.

31. See Albrecht Dümling, *Entartete Musik* (Düsseldorf: Landeshauptstadt Düsseldorf, 1988).

32. *GS*, 18:770–75.

33. *WBGS*, 4:525; Richard Wolin, *Walter Benjamin, An Aesthetic of Redemption*, 2nd ed. (Berkeley: University of California Press, 1994), 139.

34. See Adorno's 1934 review of Herbert Müntzel, *Die Fahne der Verfolgten*, in *GS*, 19:331–33. In response to its reprinting in the student newspaper *Diskus*, Adorno self-critically described this review as a typical "kind of stupidity" that addressed fascism through a strategy of avant-garde politics. *FSSB*, 2:162, 168.

35. See *Prisms*, 129.

36. In *IM*, 340, Adorno acknowledged that his essay "suffered severely" from not knowing the American context. One can imagine the missing musicological exploration of jazz and German universalism by reference to Max Paddison, *Adorno's Aesthetics of Music* (New York: Cambridge University Press, 1993) and Max Paddison, *Adorno, Modernism and Mass Culture: Essays on Critical Theory and Music* (London: Kahn and Averill, 1996), read alongside Carl Dahlhaus, *The Idea of Absolute Music* (Chicago: University of Chicago Press, 1989) and Carl Dahlhaus, *Nineteenth-Century Music* (Berkeley: University of California Press, 1989). For a vibrant assertion that Adorno's Schönbergian affiliation was antipopulist avant-gardism, see Alex Ross, *The Rest Is Noise: Listening to the Twentieth Century* (New York: Farrar, Straus and Giroux, 2007). A fruitful cross-examination would look at Adorno's emphasis on the "machine age" (rather than ethnic or primitivist) quality of jazz's rhythms. See Joel Dinerstein, *Swinging the Machine: Modernity, Technology, and African American Culture between the World Wars* (Amherst: University of Massachusetts Press, 2003).

37. WDB, 365, 842–44.

38. Ibid., 536–46.

39. Both cited in Paul Allen Anderson, *Deep River: Music and Memory in Harlem Renaissance Thought* (Durham, NC: Duke University Press, 2001), 11–25. On Du Bois, see also David L. Lewis, *W. E. B. Du Bois* (New York: H. Holt, 1993); and Aldon Morris, *The Scholar Denied: W. E. B. Du Bois and the Birth of Modern Sociology* (Berkeley: University of California Press, 2015).

40. Anderson, *Deep River*, 16, 21, see also 47.

41. Du Bois probably read Simmel's *Schopenhauer and Nietzsche* (Urbana: University of Illinois Press, 1991), but he was certainly familiar with his Stranger topos.

Du Bois's idea of double consciousness and second sight is profitably read as genealogically related to Nietzsche's discussion of the "free spirit." A helpful exploration of this family resemblance is found in Kathleen Higgins, "Double Consciousness and Second Sight," in *Critical Affinities: Nietzsche and African American Thought*, ed. Jacqueline Scott and A. Todd Franklin (Albany: SUNY Press, 2006), 51–74.

42. Citations in this paragraph from Alain Locke, "Enter the New Negro," *Survey Graphic* 6, no. 6 (1925): 631–34.

43. On the NAACP leadership's cautious, classicist attitude toward jazz, see Mark Schneider, *"We Return Fighting": The Civil Rights Movement in the Jazz Age* (Boston: Northeastern University Press, 2002).

44. A useful overview is provided by Porter, *What Is This Thing Called Jazz?* Representative of the first approach is Grover Sales, *Jazz: America's Classical Music* (Englewood Cliffs, NJ: Prentice-Hall, 1984). Important to the history of the second is LeRoi Jones [Amiri Baraka], *Blues People: Negro Music in White America* (New York: W. Morrow, 1963). Exemplary is Scott Knowles DeVeaux, *The Birth of Bebop: A Social and Musical History* (Berkeley: University of California Press, 1997). A useful corrective to the "Whiggish" avant-garde interpretation is Mark Gridley, "Misconceptions in Linking Free Jazz with the Civil Rights Movement," *College Music Symposium* 47 (2007): 139–55. For jazz as an "official" American export, see Penny Von Eschen, *Satchmo Blows Up the World: Jazz Ambassadors Play the Cold War* (Cambridge, MA: Harvard University Press, 2004).

45. Slaves in a foreign land: *Deuteronomy* 15:15. On sorrow songs: Gunther Schuller's histories of jazz technique and style examine cultural and musicological development in tandem. Gunther Schuller, *Big Band Jazz: From the Beginnings to the Fifties* (Washington, DC: Smithsonian Institution Press, 1983); *Early Jazz: Its Roots and Musical Development* (New York: Oxford University Press, 1986); and *The Swing Era: The Development of Jazz, 1930–1945* (New York: Oxford University Press, 1989). These texts also demonstrate that the meaning of the referent "jazz" has changed considerably since the 1930s.

46. *NL*, 1:84–85.

47. Ibid., 82–83. Translation modified.

48. *GS*, 6:129.

49. George M. Fredrickson, *Racism: A Short History* (Princeton, NJ: Princeton University Press, 2002), 99–125.

50. *GS*, 3:194.

51. Ibid., 3:207–8.

52. WDB, 364. Aldon Morris makes a strong case that Robert Park (and those of the Chicago and Columbia Schools of sociology) knew Du Bois's work in the 1910s and 1920s but systematically avoided citing it. His influence was thus much greater than the record reflects. See *The Scholar Denied*, 141.

53. There is a vast literature on mimesis in the African American tradition, but exemplary is Eric Lott, *Love and Theft: Blackface Minstrelsy and the American Working Class* (London: Oxford University Press, 1993). For an Adornian-inspired ap-

plication of mimesis as an anthropological mode, see Michael T. Taussig, *Mimesis and Alterity: A Particular History of the Senses* (New York: Routledge, 1993), esp. chaps. 11–12.

54. On "incomplete emancipation," see Detlev Claussen, *Grenzen der Aufklärung: Die Gesellschaftliche Genese des modernen Antisemitismus* (Frankfurt: Fischer, 1994), 85–108.

CHAPTER 2: AMERICA; OR, THE STRANGER

1. In addition to *IM*, see Franz L. Neumann, *The Cultural Migration: The European Scholar in America* (New York: Arno Press, 1953). As H. Stuart Hughes's essay in *IM* illuminates, Neumann believed social sciences emerged only out of exile experience. Adorno's first version of the essay was published in the 1964 volume of *Perspectives in American History*.

2. *GS*, 10.2:702.
3. Compare *IM*, 338–39, with *GS* 10.2:702–3.
4. *IM*, 339.
5. Ibid., 270–337.
6. Ibid., 342.
7. Ibid., 350.
8. Ibid., 301.
9. Theodor W. Adorno, *Current of Music: Elements of a Radio Theory*, trans. Robert Hullot-Kentor (Frankfurt: Suhrkamp, 2006), 209–10.
10. *IM*, 288.
11. *GS*, 6:10.
12. *GI*, 1–7.
13. *ISS*, 326. See also *PM*, chap. 3.
14. *ISS*, 326–27.
15. Roger Chickering, *Karl Lamprecht: A German Academic Life (1856–1915)* (Atlantic Highlands, NJ: Humanities Press, 1993).
16. *NL*, 2:213. See also Siegfried Kracauer, *Soziologie als Wissenschaft* (Dresden: Sibyllen, 1922); *DI*, 219–39.
17. SIK, delivered April 19, 1940. Adorno's title played off the lead essay in Georg Simmel, *Das individuelle Gesetz*, ed. Michael Landmann (Frankfurt: Suhrkamp, 1968).
18. *FSE*, 35–81. Martin Jay, *The Dialectical Imagination: A History of the Frankfurt School and the Institute of Social Research, 1923–1950* (Berkeley: University of California Press, 1996), 219–39.
19. On the American Simmel, see Gary D. Jaworski, *Georg Simmel and the American Prospect* (Albany: SUNY Press, 1997).
20. SIK, 54. Compare with 51.
21. On the fin de siècle imperative to "move beyond Kant" that flourished in Pragmatism, see *UV*, 15–40.

22. Elizabeth Goodstein, "Style as Substance: Georg Simmel's Phenomenology of Culture," *Cultural Critique* 52 (2002): 209–34. Kloppenberg observes that a historical notion of "practice as theory" was generative for the notion of immanent critique. See *UV*, 107. On neo-Kantianism, see also Klaus Köhnke, *Der junge Simmel: In Theoriebeziehungen und sozialen Bewegungen* (Frankfurt: Suhrkamp, 1996); and Peter E. Gordon, *Continental Divide: Heidegger, Cassirer, Davos* (Cambridge, MA: Harvard University Press, 2010). On social Darwinism, see Richard Hofstadter, *Social Darwinism in American Thought* (Boston: Beacon Press, 1992).

23. John P. Diggins, *The Promise of Pragmatism: Modernism and the Crisis of Knowledge and Authority* (Chicago: University of Chicago Press, 1994), 415. See also the essays in Mitchell Aboulafia, Myra Bookman, and Cathy Kemp, eds., *Habermas and Pragmatism* (New York: Routledge, 2002).

24. *CT*, 145–46. Translation modified.

25. SIK, 42–47.

26. Ibid., 42.

27. "Veblen's Attack on Culture," in *Prisms*, 73–94; Theodor Adorno, "Kultur and Culture," *Social Text* 27, no. 2 (99) (Summer 2009): 145–58.

28. *CT*, 146–47; see also *PM*, 225.

29. SIK, 59. See also Georg Simmel, "Metropolis and Mental Life," in *The Sociology of Georg Simmel*, ed. K. H. Wolf (New York: Free Press, 1950), 409–24.

30. An example of Simmelian social mathematics then circulating in New York is seen in J. L. Moreno's *Who Shall Survive? A New Approach to the Problem of Human Interrelations*, trans. Helen H. Jennings (Washington, DC: Nervous and Mental Disease Publishing, 1934), a book that uses Simmelian models of "objective group relations" to develop a Spencerian-Darwinian mathematics of existential interaction. Adorno cites the book in the 1956 *Gruppenexperiment*, *GS*, 9.2:355.

31. Simmel's description of the Stranger plays a prominent role in the "Bible" of the Chicago School (*ISS*), which sought an objective "science of sociology" defined as the study of peoples adapting within space and time.

32. SIK, 48.

33. Ibid., 47.

34. Ibid., 42.

35. Ibid., 43. Adorno sees a dialectic within the concept of autonomy in Simmel's thought here that is analogous to that explored by Martin Shuster, *Autonomy after Auschwitz: Adorno, German Idealism, and Modernity* (Chicago: University of Chicago Press, 2014), 29–36.

36. Immanuel Kant, *Critique of Practical Reason*, trans. Werner Pluhar (Indianapolis, IN: Hackett, 2002), 203.

37. SIK, 43.

38. Ibid., 43–44. Emphasis added.

39. Ibid., 43.

40. *WBAP*, 479–80 (*Konvolut* N14:3). Benjamin is citing *PM*, 476–77.

41. HIL, 20–21.

42. "The Work of Art in the Age of Its Technological Reproducibility," *WBSW*, 101–33. See *AT*, 54–56, for an argument for the need to refine Benjamin's schema in terms of the categories of subject/object non-identity.

43. Alfred S. Schütz, "The Stranger: An Essay in Social Psychology," *American Journal of Sociology* 49, no. 6 (1944), 506–7.

44. SIK, 51.

45. Ibid., 47, 53–54.

46. Ibid., 47. See also Marcuse, "Zum Begriff des Wesens," *ZfS*, 5:1–39; and Peter Fenves, *The Messianic Reduction: Walter Benjamin and the Shape of Time* (Stanford, CA: Stanford University Press, 2010), 1–7.

47. Weber's methodological essay on the concept of objectivity and the ideal type also examines the *Vereinswesen* (voluntary associations), asking how their group dynamics modified the individualistic logic of the ideal type. Adorno here is working through Weber's nominalism by defending its universalism, negatively. See *WM*, 1–15, 39–43, 75–83, 92–98.

48. SIK, 54.

49. Ibid., 54.

50. *TFS*, 321.

51. Most notably, *Jargon of Authenticity*—for example, *GS*, 6:130–32.

52. *WM*, 90.

53. *GS*, 4:90–91.

54. SIK, 55.

55. *IM*, 240.

56. Ibid.

57. Ibid., 240–41.

58. Ibid., 225.

CHAPTER 3: NEGATIVE IDENTITIES OF THE SUBJECT IN WARTIME AMERICA

1. *DE*, 3.

2. Ibid., 6.

3. *MM*, 192.

4. Lowenthal, when asked to look for a translator of *Dialectic of Enlightenment*, quipped: "Huxley did not understand dialectics, and Joyce is alas dead." See James Schmidt, "The *Eclipse of Reason* and the End of the Frankfurt School in America," *New German Critique* 100 (Winter 2007): 47–76.

5. *TFS*, 157–59, 279.

6. See for example *MM*, 161.

7. An earlier version of the lecture was given at Boston University on March 23, 1982. See Jürgen Habermas, "The Entwinement of Myth and Enlightenment: Re-reading *Dialectic of Enlightenment*," *New German Critique* 26 (Spring–Summer, 1982): 13–30.

8. *PDM*, 104–8.

9. Compare "Re-reading," 16, to *PDM*, 109. Translation amended. In the 1982 lecture, Habermas's use of the word "identity" was embedded in a discussion that attributed a Frommian notion of psychosociology to Horkheimer and Adorno. In the later version, the same sentence appears in a paragraph asserting that instrumental reason creates an identity between domination and selfhood and therefore renders impossible scientific and ethical analysis. The slippage between these usages in the 1980s, when subjective identity discourse was becoming dominant, shows how the precision of the 1940s critique of identity was flattened out in the 1980s.

10. Habermas, "Entwinement," 16.

11. *PDM*, 110. See Koselleck discussion in Chapter 6.

12. *PDM*, 110.

13. Georg Lukács, *The Theory of the Novel*, trans. Anna Bostock (Cambridge, MA: MIT Press, 1971), 22.

14. Ibid., 18.

15. Compare ibid., 29 to *MM*, 15–16.

16. Horkheimer's letter of May 18, 1942, congratulates Neumann on the publication of *Behemoth*, dialectically praising Neumann for not "sacrificing the decisive concept [as] most emigrants had" but also looking forward to the day when "our individual fates disappear behind the labor for which we have life-long prepared." *MHGS*, 17:288–89. Even Horkheimer's letters mothballing the Institute sought to find a future orientation in the philosophical value of exile.

17. Whereas Jay, Wheatland, and Wiggershaus see the Institute's claims to interdisciplinarity in the 1940s as nostalgic for the 1930s Institute, here the concern for interdisciplinarity is viewed as a way to preserve a universalist, Kantian-Marxian notion of science while seeking broader collaboration. See *ASP1* for the 1941 proposal; and *ASP2* for the revised proposal.

18. *TFS*, 343.

19. *ASP1*, 142–43.

20. *TFS*, 294–95.

21. *LP*, 97.

22. *TFS*, 309–10.

CHAPTER 4: CRITICAL THEORY GOES TO WAR

1. *ZfS*, 9:365.
2. "Veblen's Attack on Culture," in ibid., 389–413.
3. *ZfS*, 9:401.
4. Ibid., 402.
5. *WBAP*, 470–75 (Konvolut N7a:1, N10:3).
6. *MHGS*, 17:208.
7. *ZfS*, 9:402.
8. Ibid., 366–88; here, 370–72; *DI*, 51–64.
9. *ZfS*, 378.

10. Ibid., 384.
11. For analysis of the 1942 moment, see Patrick Hayden, *Camus and the Challenge of Political Thought* (New York: Palgrave, 2016), 14.
12. Marx and Hegel are invoked by reference to Engels's "Feuerbach and the End of Classical German Philosophy." *MECW*, 26:353–98.
13. In the anthropological overview to *Authority and the Family*, Horkheimer uses the word "identity" to refer to the unity of empirical and ontological selfhood conferred by Christian conversion. *SAF*, 54, 166.
14. See GI, 62–86. Though I here challenge Izenberg's dismissal of personal identity's connection to systems and logical identity, my larger argument accords with Izenberg's. Horkheimer and Adorno's initial rejection of identity had everything to do with identity's affinity for the existentialist motifs that Izenberg analyzes so well. Critical theory preferred accounts of divided selfhood similar to those of literary modernism: the individual's multilayered, at once alienated and affective relation to complex social systems, group membership, and systems of knowledge and domination.
15. Josef Chytry, *The Aesthetic State: A Quest in Modern German Thought* (Berkeley: University of California Press, 1989).
16. *MHGS*, 17:171.
17. *BB*, 2:217.
18. *ZfS*, 9:476.
19. Ibid., 477.
20. Ibid., 478.
21. Letter, September 4, 1941, in *MHGS*, 17:161–67.
22. *CT*, 44; compare with *CT*, 211–14.
23. *TFS*, 160–66; also see Neil McLaughlin, "Origin Myths in the Social Sciences: Fromm, the Frankfurt School and the Emergence of Critical Theory," *Canadian Journal of Sociology* 24 (1999): 109–39.
24. *EFF*, 1.
25. Ibid., 10–11, 183.
26. Jacob Burckhardt, *The Civilization of the Renaissance in Italy* (Mineola, NY: Dover, 2010), 119.
27. Berlin, *Two Concepts*, 6; *EFF*, 34, 155.
28. *ZfS*, 9:494.
29. Ibid., 9:494–95.
30. The comparison of false synthesis to reification is here useful: Axel Honneth, *Reification: A New Look at an Old Idea* (Oxford: Oxford University Press, 2012).
31. Horkheimer also had both Marcuse and Adorno respond seminar style to Huxley's *Brave New World*, out of which came Adorno's essay on Huxley in *Prisms*. There Adorno discussed how Huxley transformed the French revolutionary *Liberté, Égalité, Fraternité* to "Community, Identity, Stability."
32. *TP1*.
33. Freud, looking at Gustav Le Bon's concept of "mass hypnotism," declared

group psychology a form of regression. See Sigmund Freud, *Group Psychology and the Analysis of the Ego*, trans. James Strachey (New York: Norton, 1990), 117.

34. "The Method and Function of an Analytical Social Psychology," *ZfS*, 1:28–54.
35. *WCWG*, 22.
36. *TFS*, 266; *DI*, 101–4.
37. *WCWG*, 267–69.
38. Ibid., 268–91.
39. *TFS*, 174.
40. Ibid., 167–69.
41. *RPAS*, 1–12.
42. Carole Fink has shown how the negotiation of peace treaties came to be shaped by international Jewish organizations advocating for minority clauses in the promulgation of constitutions by the Great Powers. Carole Fink, *Defending the Rights of Others: The Great Powers, the Jews, and International Minority Protection, 1878–1938* (Cambridge: Cambridge University Press, 2004). On the analytic of alterity in the discourse of human rights, see Samuel Moyn, *The Last Utopia: Human Rights in History* (Cambridge, MA: Belknap, 2010).
43. *TFS*, 350–82.
44. The 1941 proposal works backward from persecutor to victim, developing a set of ideal types "of present day anti-Semites" while emphasizing the importance of "refusing the race theory" for analyzing who the Jews actually were. *ASP1*, 139.
45. *RPAS*, 14. Cited in *FSE*, 239.
46. *DC*, 251–53.
47. *TFS*, 372.
48. *MM*, 86.
49. *TL*, 3.
50. May 7, 1943, "Joint Meeting AJC. 2. Report on Progress," *ASTW*, 1. Horkheimer is referencing Immanuel Kant, *Practical Philosophy*, ed. Mary J. Gregor (Cambridge: Cambridge University Press, 1996), 273–310.
51. *DEJ*, 64 (*GS*, 3:101–2).
52. Ibid., compare with *DEJ*, 98 (*GS*, 3:146).
53. *DE*, 3–5.
54. *LP*, 128 (March 8, 1943).
55. Bertrand Russell, "Knowledge by Acquaintance and Knowledge by Description," *Proceedings of the Aristotelian Society* 11 (1911): 108–28. See also *ZfS*, 9:483–86. On idem-identity, see GI, 12–28.
56. *MECW*, 37:811.
57. *HCC*,1.
58. Benedict Anderson, *Imagined Communities: Reflections on the Origin and Spread of Nationalism* (London: Verso, 1991), 83–120.
59. Otto Bauer, *The Question of Nationalities and Social Democracy* (Minneapolis: University of Minnesota Press, 2000), 126–27. Translation modified.

60. Kevin Anderson and Peter Hudis, eds., *The Rosa Luxemburg Reader* (New York: NYU Press, 2004), 281–322.
61. *HCC*, 12–14.
62. Ibid., 103–4. Emphasis added.
63. *DE*, 83. Translation modified.
64. For an excellent overview, see Martin Jay, *Marxism and Totality: The Adventures of a Concept from Lukács to Habermas* (Berkeley: University of California Press, 1984), esp. 80–88. Jay's focus is on the concept of totality for Western Marxism's reception of Lukács, while the focus here is on how non-identity inherently transformed the totality concept: the critique of culture and being, the idea of the division of labor, the dialectic of the universal and particular, and interdisciplinarity all became part of the divided self and whole.
65. *DE*, 86–87.
66. *GS*, 3:107.
67. *DE*, 82. Translation modified.
68. Ibid., 83–84.
69. Immanuel Kant, *The Critique of Pure Reason*, ed. and trans. Paul Guyer and Allen Wood (Cambridge: Cambridge University Press, 1999), 204–14.
70. Edmund Husserl's defense of the Kantian categories subjectivized Kant's schematism concept by embracing a procedure he called "phenomenological reduction." Husserl argued that epistemology had to start with complex perceptions and systematically reduce them to their epistemological essences.
71. *GS*, 3:336–37, 299.
72. July 17, 1943, *FSE*, 244, MHA Box VI, File 27a, 12–13.
73. *GS*, 12:122–25.
74. *MHGS*, 17:146; *TFS*, 302.
75. September 14, 1941, *MHGS*, 17:171.
76. August 28, 1941, ibid., 17:148.
77. Ibid., 150.
78. *DE*, 155. See also *TFS*, 302.
79. *DE*, 167.
80. Carl Schmitt, *The Concept of the Political* (Chicago: University of Chicago Press, 2007), 26.
81. *ASTW*, 4.
82. *GS*, 3:212–14.
83. *EFF*, 274.
84. *GS*, 3:64–66, consulting *DE*, 47, and *DEJ*, 38.
85. *GS*, 9.1:12–14.
86. *DE*, 168.
87. Ibid., 183.
88. Ibid., 184.
89. Ibid., 202.
90. Ibid., 171–73.

91. Ibid., 170–71.
92. Ibid., 205.
93. Ibid., 207.
94. *MM*, 131.
95. *CS*, 36.
96. Erik H. Erikson, *Identity: Youth and Crisis* (New York: Norton, 1968), 88.
97. *CS*, 413.
98. Ibid., 221. In his attempt to use the concept of identity to address, Spengler-like, the Russian and American Cold War conflict, Erikson shows the severe limits of the psycho-social model. In his analysis, two forms of Protestant identity—Western antiauthoritarian and Eastern "proletarian and industrial"— need to learn to embrace and incorporate one another. See also ibid., 361–62.
99. Lawrence Friedman, *Identity's Architect: A Biography of Erik H. Erikson* (Cambridge, MA: Harvard University Press, 2000), 186.
100. *CS*, 416.
101. Ibid., 374.
102. Herbert Aptheker, *The Negro People in America: A Critique of Gunnar Myrdal's "An American Dilemma"* (New York: International Publishers, 1946).
103. RAP, 25.
104. Erikson fleetingly describes "pseudo-identities" as a "new individuality" based on imagined origins. *CS*, 371.
105. RAP, 3.
106. Gunnar Myrdal, *An American Dilemma: The Negro Problem and Modern Democracy* (New York: Harper, 1944), 110.
107. The review was rejected for publication by the *New Republic*. See Ralph Ellison, *The Collected Essays of Ralph Ellison*, ed. John F. Callahan (New York: Modern Library, 1995), 335. On Fromm, see Arnold Rampersad, *Ralph Ellison: A Biography* (New York: Vintage, 2008), 200–204.
108. Through Aptheker's influence, Du Bois may well have read some Frankfurt work. See his celebrated "Apologia" to *The Suppression of the African Slave-Trade to the United States of America, 1638–1870* (New York: Social Science Press, 1954), 327–29.
109. Robert LeVine, "Culture and Personality Studies, 1918–1960: Myth and History," *Journal of Personality* 69, no. 6 (2001): 803–18.
110. John P. Robinson, Phillip R. Shaver, and Lawrence S. Wrightsman, eds., *Measures of Personality and Social Psychological Attitudes* (San Diego, CA: Academic Press, 1991), 504.
111. "Little History of Photography," *WBSW*, 2:507.
112. James Anderson, "An Interview with Henry A. Murray on His Meeting with Sigmund Freud," *Psychoanalytic Psychology* 34, no. 3 (2017): 322–31.
113. Henry A. Murray, *Explorations in Personality* (Oxford: Oxford University Press, 1938), 148.
114. *AP*, 466.
115. Ibid., 747.

CHAPTER 5: NEGATIVE MODELING

1. *ER*, 164–67.
2. *AP*, 1.
3. William Graham Sumner, *Folkways and Mores* (New York: Schocken, 1987).
4. On law: *AP*, 33–38, 47–49, 170–71; on Stranger hatred: RAP, 17. See the discussion of Jaensch and Schmitt and the problem of agonistic and dyadic ontologies in Chapter 6.
5. *AP*, 3.
6. Ibid., 228.
7. Ibid., 229.
8. Ibid., 230.
9. Ibid.
10. Ibid., 12–14, 607.
11. Ibid., 607.
12. Ibid., 606.
13. Ibid., 607.
14. Ibid., 612.
15. Ibid.
16. Ibid., 614.
17. Ibid., 746; on technique and method: ibid., 13–18.
18. Ibid., 745–48.
19. Ibid., 609.
20. Ibid., 610.
21. Ibid., 618.
22. Ibid., 619.
23. Ibid., 619–20.
24. Ibid., 617.
25. Ibid., 615.
26. Ibid., 617.
27. Ibid.
28. Ibid.
29. Ibid.
30. Hannah Arendt, *The Origins of Totalitarianism* (New York: Harcourt, Brace, Jovanovich, 1973), 269–85.
31. *AP*, 613.
32. Ibid., 2.
33. Ibid.
34. Ibid., 612–14.
35. Ibid., 612.
36. Ibid., 722–23.
37. Ibid., 726.
38. TL, 3.
39. *AP*, 726.

40. Richard Hofstadter, *The Paranoid Style in American Politics* (New York: Vintage, 2008); Daniel J Boorstin, *The Image: A Guide to Pseudo-events in America* (New York: Atheneum, 1987).
41. *AP*, 698.
42. *SMAP*, 27–28.
43. Ibid., 33.
44. Ibid., 33, 39.
45. Ibid., 45.
46. *GS*, 8:42–45.
47. Adorno, letter to Marie Jahoda, June 22, 1953, MHA Shelf VI, Box 1E, 178. See also "Zum Verhältnis Psychologie und Soziologie," *GS*, 8:42–85.

CHAPTER 6: SUBJECT/OBJECT AND DISCIPLINARITY

1. RAP, 7.
2. *MM*, 35–49.
3. Ibid., 60.
4. Ibid., 60–61.
5. Ibid., 44.
6. Ibid., 67.
7. Ibid., 63–64.
8. *EFF*, 186.
9. *GS*, 408–32.
10. Anna Freud, "Aggression in Relation to Emotional Development: Normal and Pathological," *Psychoanalytic Study of the Child* 3, no. 1 (1947): 37–42.
11. *GS*, 9.1:201.
12. A. H. Maslow, "A Theory of Human Motivation," *Psychological Review* 50, no. 4 (1943): 370–96.
13. Herbert Marcuse, *Eros and Civilization: A Philosophical Inquiry into Freud* (Boston: Beacon, 1974), 56.
14. *AP*, 232–33.
15. Catalogued in ibid., 921.
16. Franz Neumann, *Behemoth: The Structure and Practice of National Socialism* (Oxford: Oxford University Press, 1942), 468–69.
17. RAP, 9–10.
18. Neumann, *Behemoth*, 46–51. See also Kirchheimer, ZFS, 9:456–58.
19. *AP*, 456.
20. Ibid., 454–58.
21. *GS*, 6:269–72, cites this passage in analogy to Kant.
22. Ibid., 8:24. The English original remains unpublished; see *DI*, 102–3.
23. *GS* 8:40; compare to *MM*, 63.
24. *MM*, 53. I am indebted here to Detlev Claussen. See DC, 149–60.
25. *MM*, 56. Translation modified.

26. *ER*, vii.
27. Ibid., 3.
28. Ibid., 6.
29. Ibid.
30. Ibid., 11.
31. Adorno's *Metakritik* surveys the Platonic *logoi* as objectivities constitutive of the Husserlian form of intuition. See *GS*, 5:35–38.
32. Schmidt, "The *Eclipse of Reason*," 13–15; Neil Jumonville, *The New York Intellectuals Reader* (New York: Routledge, 2007), 73.
33. *ER*, 184.
34. Ibid., 126.
35. Ibid., 73.
36. Ibid., 75.
37. Ibid., 82.
38. Ibid., 113.
39. Ibid.
40. Ibid., 19.
41. Ibid., 20.
42. Ibid., 20–21.
43. *HCC*, 1.
44. *MM*, 53.
45. *ER*, 234.
46. *MM*, 234–35.
47. Michael Schwartz, "Leviathan oder Lucifer: Reinhart Kosellecks *Kritik Und Krise* Revisited," *Zeitschrift für Religions- und Geistesgeschichte* 45, no. 1 (1993): 33–35.
48. *ER*, 69.
49. Ibid., 72.
50. Ibid., 128.
51. Ibid., 148, 135.
52. Ibid., 148, 185–87.
53. Ibid., 159.
54. Ibid., 171.
55. Ibid., 174.
56. Ibid.
57. Ibid., 139, 170.
58. *MM*, 15.
59. Ibid., 16–17.
60. *DEJ*, 191.
61. *MM*, 15; *PM*, 54.
62. Anne Clara Schenderlein, "'Germany on Their Minds?': German Jewish Refugees in the United States and Their Relationships to Germany" (PhD diss., University of California, San Diego, 2014), 277.

63. *GS*, 20.1:353.
64. Ibid.
65. *MM*, 50.
66. *GS*, 20.1:355.
67. Hannah Arendt, "We Refugees," in *Altogether Elsewhere: Writers on Exile*, ed. Marc Robinson (San Diego, CA: Harcourt Brace, 1996), 119. Following the pattern of the 1940s, Arendt uses the word "identity" to signify the disruption of intellectual continuity caused by exile: "Our identity is changed so frequently that nobody can find out who we actually are" (116).
68. Ibid., 118.

CONCLUSION

1. *MM*, 101.
2. *GS* 6:222.

Index

Abraham, Karl, 146
Ackerman, Nathan, 201; *Anti-Semitism and Emotional Disorder*, 150
action: American Pragmatism and, 268–71; in American sociology, 238; collapse of thought/theory into, 2–4, 7, 89, 270; culture in relation to, 89, 92, 99–101, 135; fascism and, 234, 259; Frankfurt School critique of, 2–4, 13, 89–90, 100–101, 265
Adams, John, 272
adaptation/assimilation: autonomy vs., 73–81, 91–93, 110; cultural role of, 94–95; identity in relation to, 32; immigrants' experience of, 74, 285–86; non-identity linked to, 40–43, 81; positive contributions of, 110–11; resistance to, 26, 72, 80, 285–86; Simmel and, 88–89, 91; as social science paradigm, 82, 102–3
Adler, Alfred, 146
Adorno, Gretel, 127, 138
Adorno, Theodor: death of, 2; Du Bois compared to, 58–62; early philosophical experience 84–85; Erikson's relationship to, 197; father of (*see* Wiesengrund, Oskar); German identity of, as wartime hazard, 127; *Habilitation* of, 139; Horkheimer's working relationship with, 127, 138; Jewish heritage of, 20, 34–35, 37–38, 42–44, 284–87, 301n22; in Los Angeles, 126–27; music in the life of, 42–43; negative identity personally experienced by, 80, 127–28, 283–87; in Oxford, 52; philosophical universalism of, 21–22, 27–28, 151; and politics, 43–44, 50, 235–39; reception of, 1–2; relation to Institute for Social Research 1–2, 15, 151–52; return of, to Germany, 30, 34, 65, 288, 293–94; sociological music research conducted by, 75–79; in the United States, 20, 22, 49, 53–55, 71–112
Adorno, Theodor, works by: "Abschied vom Jazz" (Farewell to jazz), 37, 52; "Far from the Line of Fire," 265; "Freudian Theory and the Pattern of Fascist Propaganda," 250; "Gaps," 108; "Heine, the Wound," 29–32, 34, 41, 63–65, 67; *The Intellectual Migration*, 72, 76; "Jazz," 37; jazz writings, 36–41; "Marginalia on Theory and Practice," 2, 3; *Minima Moralia*, 27, 71, 73, 108, 116, 123, 125, 154, 173, 205, 242, 244, 246–48, 265, 275, 277, 282–88; *Negative Dialectics*, 1–3, 32, 65, 68–69, 89–101, 294; "On the Problem of Individual Causality in Simmel's Thought," 86–109; "On the Relation between Sociology and Psychology," 238;

The Philosophy of Modern Music, 71, 182–84; *Prisms*, 37–40, 131–8; *Psychological Technique of Martin Luther Thomas's Radio Addresses*, 191–92; "Questions on the German Emigration," 284–87; "Remarks on *The Authoritarian Personality*," 241, 253, 257–58; "Schema of Mass Culture," 179; "Social Science and Sociological Tendencies in Psychoanalysis," 260; "Theses on Antisemitism," 187; "Über den Fetischcharakter der Musik und die Regression des Hörens" (On the fetish character of music and the regression of listening), 37; "Über Jazz" (On Jazz), 37, 40, 53–54, 68, 168; "Veblen's Attack on Culture," 131–33, 138, 184, 260; "Vierhändig, noch mal" (Four-handed, once again), 41–43, 45; "Wissenschaftliche Erfahrungen in Amerika" (Scientific experiences in America), 71–74, 79–81, 86, 110–11, 113; "Zeitlose Mode. Zum Jazz" (Timeless fashion: jazz), 37–39; "Zur gesellschaftlichen Lage der Musik" (On the social situation of music), 37, 45–48, 50–51, 53, 68. See also *The Authoritarian Personality* (Adorno et. al); *Dialectic of Enlightenment* (Adorno and Horkheimer)

advertising, 78–79, 179, 185, 292

aggressivity, fascist manipulation of, 12, 250, 253–57

AJC. See American Jewish Committee

Alberti, Leon Battista, 143

alienation: Adorno's experience of, 81–82; knowledge's origin in, 32, 80–81, 112, 291; in modern context, 31; negative identity in relation to, 4; Simmel and, 81–84; socioeconomic, as source of aggression, 223, 256, 258, 263, 278–79. See also otherness; stranger

Allport, Gordon, 241

American Jewish Committee (AJC), 109, 128, 145–46, 148–49, 202, 288

American Pragmatism, 71, 72, 87, 88, 89, 132, 141, 158, 208, 244, 268–71, 291

American Revolution, 272

American sociology, 26; and adaptation, 102–3; Adorno's disapproval of, 71–72, 82, 238, 291; Adorno's engagement with, 72, 109, 123, 131–32, 207–8; concept of culture in, 92, 94; and music research, 75–79; politics of, 87; Simmel's thought in relation to, 87–88, 93–94

Anderson, Benedict, 161

antipolitics, 234

anti-Semitism: *The Authoritarian Personality* on, 199, 212; bourgeois identity and, 193–94; emotional expressivity of, 191–94; enemy creation as manifestation of, 187; Enlightenment in relation to, 117; eroticism of, 223–24; Frankfurt School study of, 128, 149–55; German, 29, 44; Heine and, 29; Jewish identity and, 193; Jewish traits identified with, 218–19; limits to reform of, 224–25; methodology of studying, 151; Nazi Germany and, 187, 258–59; as pattern of negative identity, 256; principles of modern, 23–24; racism in relation to, 24, 200; socialization into, 227–29; in Thomas's radio addresses, 191–92. See also minorities; prejudice

Apollonian principle, 55, 117–18
Apteker, Herbert, 199
Arbeiter und Angestellte (*Blue- and White-Collar Workers*) (Frankfurt School project), 147–48
Arendt, Hannah, 225, 287–88; "We Refugees," 287
Aristotle, 6–7, 105, 137, 177, 268
Armstrong, Louis, 40, 61
Army-McCarthy hearings, 235
art: Adorno's theory of, 40; Benjamin's theory of, 31; critical function of, 67; folk culture in relation to, 57–58, 63–65; freedom in relation to, 46–47; negative identity and, 56–62; non-identity and, 13, 30, 64–65. *See also* culture; music
assimilation. *See* adaptation/assimilation
Aufbau (journal), 284
Auschwitz, 10–12, 34. *See also* Holocaust
authenticity, 6
authoritarianism: left-wing, 236; liberalism and, 291; as psychological problem, 210; racism linked to, 199; and the superego, 250; techniques of, 192
The Authoritarian Personality (Adorno et al.), 20, 27, 123, 288; Adorno's afterword to, 241, 253, 257–58; anti-Semitism as topic of, 199, 212; assumptions underlying, 214–15; as capstone of *Studies in Prejudice*, 149–50; conduct of project resulting in, 201–5, 207–8; criticisms of, 221, 235–38; divided self in, 214; Erikson's relationship to, 197–99; ethical concerns of, 220–21; and Freud, 252–53, 260; goals of, 59, 217; on identity thinking, 194–95; individual-society relationship in, 204; influence of, 73, 79, 109, 198–99, 234–35, 293; ingroup/outgroup concept in, 211–12, 222, 232, 236–37; interdisciplinarity in, 199–200, 211–12, 214; interpretation of results in, 221–22; methodology of, 150, 152–54, 207, 211–21, 232, 235, 243; and non-identity, 219, 293; notion of personality in, 210; place of, in Adorno's oeuvre, 151–52, 154, 207; potential fascists as category for, 210, 212, 215, 216, 226–27, 235, 254–55; psychological tests used for, 203; subject of, 212–13; use of "pseudo" in, 229–36
autonomy: adaptation vs., 81, 91–93, 110; in capitalist society, 24; and epistemology, 97–98, 108; of the individual, 34; individual causality and, 106–7; non-identity linked to, 81; Simmel and, 91. *See also* individuals and individualism, orthodox Marxism, universality
avant-garde art and music, 40

Bach, Johann Sebastian, 39
Bacon, Francis, 157, 188; *The New Organon*, 157
Barendt, Joachim-Ernst, 37–38
Bartók, Béla, 38
Baudelaire, Charles, 31
Bauer, Otto, 180, 222, 287; *The Nationalities Question in Social Democracy*, 160–63
Bebel, August, 45
Bechet, Sidney, 50–51, 61
Benedict, Ruth, 95, 201
Benjamin, Walter, 31, 48, 52, 53, 84–85, 100–101, 107, 133, 138, 203
Berg, Alban, 75
Bergson, Henri, 90–92
Berlin, Isaiah, 14, 17, 143

Bettelheim, Bruno, *The Dynamics of Prejudice*, 149, 236
Bloch, Ernst, 48, 85
Boas, Franz, 94, 95
bourgeoisie: Adorno and, 43; art and, 42, 47; critical theory and the crisis of, 101; Jews in relation to, 193; Nazi threat to, 45; Odysseus as model for, 117–19, 172, 263–64; science associated with, 157; and selfhood, 18, 46; socialism and, 44
Bradley, F. H., 173
Brahms, Johannes, 38
Brecht, Bertolt, 52, 127
The Broadway Melody (musical), 50
Brunswik, Egon, 202
Bühler, Karl, 202
Burckhardt, Jacob, 143
Bureau of Applied Social Research, 109

Camus, Albert, *Myth of Sisyphus*, 136
Camus, Renaud, 14
Cantril, Hadley, 241
capitalism, 23–24, 168, 180, 190, 246, 257, 277–78, 291
Carnap, Rudolf, 89
causality, 94–95, 103–8
Chicago School, 211, 236, 305n31
Christian identity, 13
citizenship, 287
civil rights, 61–62
clowning, 68
Cold War, 73, 85, 235, 237–38
collective identity: dissolution of self into, 4; personal identity in relation to, 7–8, 10, 18, 211; right-wing versions of, 13–14; subjective universality in relation to, 209. *See also* national identity
Columbia University, 86, 95, 108–9, 141, 201
Cominternation, 48–49
commodification, 46–47
Communism, 47–48, 233, 237
consciousness: capitalism's effect on, 168, 180, 190; class, 147–48, 162–64, 180; *Dialectic of Enlightenment* on, 175; epistemological role of, 175–78; Fromm's notion of, 167–68; historical, 41, 51, 165; identity of, 135–37; Lukács on, 162–69, 180; racism as path to developing, 56, 57, 60; society's mediation of, 129, 145. *See also* false consciousness
contradiction, 96–97
cosmopolitanism, 83–84
critical theory: American Pragmatism in relation to, 89; and the crisis of the bourgeoisie, 101; divided self as ground of, 283–84; Frankfurt School and, 150, 290–91; goal of, in 1940s, 184, 209; Habermas's critique of, 120–22; and immanent critique, 164–65; influence of, on American life, 292–93; negative identity as basis of, 190, 276; philosophy and, 279–82; race as subject of, 59; Simmel's relation to, 85, 86; subject/object reflexivity of, 22–25, 64, 188–90, 279–80
cultural criticism, 39, 196–97
culture: action in relation to, 89, 92, 99–101, 135; affirmative character of, 38–39, 55; American sociology's concept of, 92, 94; as analytic of fascism 257–61; causality and, 94–95; critics in relation to, 39; identity in relation to, 9–10; *Kultur* compared to, 92; in modern context, 9; Simmel and, 92–96; as totality, 132, 135; universality of, 92. *See also* art; culture industry; music
culture and personality movement, 201–2, 205, 210, 220

culture industry: dangers of, 235, 278–79, 292; *Dialectic of Enlightenment* on, 117, 173, 177–79; and the divided self, 186–87; Frankfurt study of, 126–27, 235; narrative psychology of, 185–86; and reason, 177; and subjectivity, 178–79. *See also* entertainment; mass media

Damrosch, Walter, 77
Darwinism, 89, 269
death drive, 251, 254
democracy, 110, 194, 199, 219–20, 226, 231, 268–71, 274, 286–87
Dewey, John, 89, 95, 269, 270
dialectical image, 133
Dialectic of Enlightenment (Adorno and Horkheimer), 23–24, 27, 71, 115–27, 205; characteristics of, 115–16; on the culture industry, 117, 173, 177–79; and Freud, 184; genesis of, 126–27, 131, 144; Habermas's critique of, 119–22; and identity, 120–22; inverted universality in, 191–95; on Kant, 117, 173–77; and negative identity, 122–27, 172–77; Odysseus in, 117–19, 172, 189, 263–64; planned sequel to, 116; psychologisms of, 185–88; and science, 155–58, 164–71; as speculative work, 242; on subjectivity, 119–20, 172–73, 180, 186–87; topics of, 117
Dickinson, John, 272
Diderot, Denis, *Letter on the Blind*, 115
difference, 193, 286
Dilthey, Wilhelm, 138
Dionysian principle, 55, 117–18
disciplinarity, 183–84. *See also* interdisciplinarity
divided self: *The Authoritarian Personality* and, 214; critical theory grounded in, 283–84; the culture industry and, 186–87; disciplinary extremism and, 188–9; epistemological value of, 110; Frankfurt School's analysis of, 172–73, 186–87; Freud's notion of, 242, 251; kitsch as manifestation of, 132; Lukács on, 168–69; Marxian notion of, 163; modern problem of, 101–2, 108, 123–24, 135–38, 172–73; Simmel's notion of, 96, 101–2; wholeness sought as remedy for, 137–38, 186. *See also* subjectivity: wounded
domination: in American culture, 62, 82; *Dialectic of Enlightenment* on, 174; and formation of the individual, 103, 105, 107, 120, 135–36, 140, 167, 170–73, 180–81, 184, 226–28, 247–49, 283; identity in relation to, 11–18, 180–191; kitsch and, 133; objectivity shaped by, 22–23; racism as instance of, 60–62; socioeconomic, 96, 103, 105, 107, 165, 167–68, 170–72, 175, 200; subjectivity shaped by, 22–23
double consciousness, 83, 303n41
Du Bois, W. E. B., 56–60, 62, 64, 66–67, 302n41, 303n52; *The Souls of Black Folk*, 56–58
Durkheim, Émile, 8

Echternach hermeneutic, 152, 158, 178, 184, 242
ego psychology, 252, 261, 263
Eisler, Hans, 127
Ellington, Duke, 40, 61
Ellison, Ralph, 200
emancipation. *See* incomplete emancipation
emotional expressivity, 42–44, 149–150, 158, 160–61, 175, 182–86, 191–92, 223–25, 244–49, 256–58

empiricism, 72, 123, 207–218, 281
enemies, political/dialogical creation of, 187–88, 194–95, 211. *See also* otherness
Engels, Friedrich, 66, 116
Enlightenment: Adorno and, 21, 30; Adorno's and Horkheimer's critique of, 115–27; *Dialectic of Enlightenment* on, 173; and epistemology, 65; individual autonomy as characteristic of, 34; modern rival to, 66; Romanticism vs., 31; and the Stranger type, 83
entertainment, 74, 79, 116, 173, 235. *See also* culture industry
Erikson, Erik, 5, 7–8, 15, 195–202, 205, 249, 257, 260; *Childhood and Society*, 195–98
Eros, 268, 274, 275
eroticism, of stereotypy, 223–24
exile: academic and legal outcomes of, 73; Adorno's experience of, 30, 71–82, 85, 110, 113, 284–87; epistemological value of 78–80, 287–8; identity and, 80; as philosophical problem, 30; Simmel and, 85
existentialism, 5–7, 59, 136–38, 140, 158–59
experience, commodification of, 46
extraception, 203

false consciousness, 19, 25, 164–67, 172–73, 203
falsity: in aesthetics, 63–65, 181–84; in identity, 2, 25, 56, 59, 65; in universality, 34, 68–69
fascism: creation of enemies by, 187, 194; Frankfurt School and, 290–91; fraternal vs. paternal underpinning of, 249; Fromm on psychology of, 142; individuals' potential for, 210,
212, 215, 216, 226–27, 235, 254–55; liberalism's relation to, 254–55, 257–58, 273; non-identity as opposition to, 102; political methods of, 234, 249–50, 259; as return to myth, 116; and the self, 136, 142; techniques of, 192–93
Fenichel, Otto, 241, 251–52
Ferenczi, Sandor, 261, 262
fetishization, 45, 50
Fichte, Johann Gottlieb, 33, 68
Fisk University Choir, 57
Fitzhugh, George, 272, 274–75
Flowerman, Samuel, 241
folk culture: African-American, 60; art in relation to, 57–58, 63–65; commercialized, 50; German, 31; Heine and, 30, 31, 63; jazz and, 68; Nazi Germany and, 52
Frankfurt School (Institute for Social Research): Adorno at, 1–2, 15, 48; American research proposals of, 145–46, 148–51; anti-Semitism study by, 128, 149–55; Columbia's negotiations with, 86–87, 108–9; divergence of, from Soviet Union, 49; Erikson's relationship to, 197–98; Fromm's association with, 140–41, 146–49; goals of, 289–90; *Gruppenexperiment* of, 11; history of, 53, 125–26, 131; and identity, 124; Lukács as influence on, 124–25; and negative identity, 62, 144–45; and Pragmatism, 89; and race, 58–59, 66; and universality, 161–62, 290
freedom: art in relation to, 46–47; Fromm and, 143–44; identity in relation to, 6–10; particularity and, 60–61; positive vs. negative, 17, 142–43. *See also* incomplete emancipation
French Revolution, 272, 277

Frenkel-Brunswik, Else, 197, 202, 220, 241, 260; *Mechanisms of Self-Defense*, 202
Freud, Anna, 146, 252
Freud, Sigmund, 202, 203, 275; Adorno's critique of, 247–49; *Beyond the Pleasure Principle*, 251; *Civilization and Its Discontents*, 142, 251; *Dialectic of Enlightenment*'s elision of, 184; and the divided self, 242, 251; *The Ego and the Id*, 251; Frankfurt School's linking of Marx with, 141, 143, 146; Frankfurt School's use of, 54, 136, 205, 241–57, 260, 266; Fromm's criticism of, 245–46; *Group Psychology and the Analysis of the Ego*, 250, 251; and identity, 197; Kant in relation to, 261; revisionists of, 260–64; and social Darwinism, 211; and subjectivity, 7, 32–34, 67, 74; *Totem and Taboo*, 184. *See also* orthodox Freudianism; psychoanalysis
Freudian Left, 252
Friedman, Lawrence, 197
Fromm, Erich, 15, 17, 140–49, 151, 155–60, 163–65, 167–68, 171, 176, 184, 197, 201, 205, 211, 244–45, 260, 262, 268, 276, 290–91; *Escape from Freedom*, 131, 140–45, 155–56, 187–88, 200

Gauck, Joachim, 10–13
gender, and prejudice, 227–30
Génération Identitaire, 13–14
genre, 45–46, 48
German Nationalist Party, 2
Germany: anti-Semitism in, 29, 44; identity questions in, 10–13; music in the culture of, 40, 42; race in, 34–35; self-identity of, 29, 34. *See also* Nazi Germany

Goethe, Johann Wolfgang, 56, 110
Goethe University, 1
golden age, 142–43, 169, 171–72, 178
Gordon, Peter, 18
Gorky, Maxim, 196
Green Party, 2
group identity. *See* collective identity; national identity
Grünberg, Carl, 146, 160
Gruppenexperiment, 11
Guterman, Norbert, *Prophets of Deceit*, 149

Habermas, Jürgen, 119–22, 267; "Entwinement of Myth and Enlightenment," 120; *The Philosophical Discourse of Modernity*, 120–21; *Theory of Communicative Action*, 120
Harlem Renaissance, 58–60, 62, 200
Hartmann, Heinz, 252
Hegel, G. W. F., 17, 18, 56, 68, 110–11, 139–40, 144–45, 196, 260, 265, 266, 279, 283; *Differenzschrift*, 136; *Logic*, 136
Hegelianism, 25, 61, 250–51. *See also* neo-Hegelianism
Heidegger, Martin, 17, 32, 33, 68, 136, 141, 189
Heine, Heinrich, 29–32, 41, 63–64; "Die Heimkehr" (The homecoming), 63–64; "Die Lorelei," 30
Helvétius, Claude Adrien, *De l'ésprit*, 115
Hitler, Adolf, 196, 265
Hitler Youth, 196, 197, 249
Hofstadter, Richard, 234, 235
Holocaust, 11, 32, 34, 69. *See also* Auschwitz
homelessness, 32, 63–64
Homer, *Odyssey*, 117–19, 172, 185, 264

Hook, Sidney, 269–70, 274, 278

Horkheimer, Max, 73, 101, 220; on Adorno's essay on Veblen, 133; Adorno's working relationship with, 127, 138; and American sociology, 109; and anti-Semitism, 23, 233; and *The Authoritarian Personality*, 152–53; citizenship of, 293; *Eclipse of Reason*, 27, 123, 154, 208–9, 244, 266–82; "The End of Reason," 131, 134–38, 140, 157, 186, 266; Fromm's relationship with, 141, 147; and genre, 48; German identity of, as wartime hazard, 127; *Habilitation* of, 138; on identity, 135–38, 144; "The Latest Attack on Metaphysics," 89; in Los Angeles, 126–27; "Materialism and Metaphysics," 89; and metaphysics, 89–90; negative identity personally experienced by, 127–28; philosophy of, 27–28; on prejudice, 226–28; and psychology, 181; as supervisor of Frankfurt research projects, 150–55, 182, 207; "Traditional and Critical Theory," 27, 141; and universality, 160. See also *Dialectic of Enlightenment* (Adorno and Horkheimer)

Horney, Karen, 201, 205, 244, 262; *New Ways in Psychoanalysis*, 260

House Un-American Activities Committee, 237

Humboldt, Wilhelm von, 137, 140

Hume, David, *Dialogues Concerning Natural Religion*, 115

Husserl, Edmund, 90, 138, 177

Idealism, 32–33, 55, 64, 88–90, 136, 139, 169–70, 174

ideal types, 83, 86, 105, 107, 150, 209–212, 220

identification, 246–47

identity: aspects and connotations of, 5; in capitalist society, 24; concept of, 5–6, 159, 195–96, 289; critique of, 3–4, 15–16; culture in relation to, 9–10; dialectical analysis of, 24–25; *Dialectic of Enlightenment* and, 120–22; domination in relation to, 11–12; dual nature of, 5, 183–84; Erikson's notion of, 195–202, 205; exile and, 80–82, 285–87; false, 2, 25, 56, 59, 65; Frankfurt School and, 124, 155–59; freedom in relation to, 6–10; Fromm's notion of, 143–45, 163–65, 167, 171, 176, 184, 195, 197, 205, 276, 290; history of concept of, 4–10, 15, 137–45, 195 –205; Horkheimer and, 135–38, 144; formation of, 11–12; as metaphysics, 91, 119–24, 143–45, 158–64; in modern context, 8, 135; negativity as precursor to, 4, 66, 111; non-identity's relation to, 189–90; objectivity in relation to, 19; popularity of concept of, 195–96; selfhood in relation to, 5–6; survival of, 24, 170–71, 193. See also collective identity; national identity; negative identity; non-identity; personal identity; positive identity

identity thinking, 13, 37, 91, 195, 233, 250

idiographic categories, 95

immanent critique, 111, 133, 164–67, 175–76, 260, 283

immigrants, 13–14, 74, 284–86

incomplete emancipation, 61, 65, 69, 108, 193, 207, 244

individuals and individualism: American ideal of, 278; causality and, 94–95, 103–8; groups in relation to, 147; Odysseus as model of, 117–19, 123, 172, 204, 263–64; as resistance to totalitarianism, 103. *See also* autonomy; particularity; self and selfhood

ingroup/outgroup concept, 211–12, 222, 232, 236–37

Institute for Marxism-Leninism, 49

Institute of Child Welfare, Berkeley, 197, 202

integration (psychology), 252–53

interdisciplinarity: Adorno and, 242–43, 264–65; in *The Authoritarian Personality*, 199–200, 211–12, 214; culture and, 95–96; Erikson's opposition to, 198; Frankfurt School and, 27, 146–48, 150–51. *See also* disciplinarity

intraception, 203–4

intelligible objectivity, 76, 166–68, 176, 275–76

introjection, 251

Izenberg, Gerald, 299n4, 308n14

Jacobs, Jack, 301n22

Jaensch, Erich Rudolph, *Der Gegentypus* (The type of the antagonist), 220–21, 270

Jahoda, Marie, 79, 202, 220, 237; *Anti-Semitism and Emotional Disorder*, 150

James, William, 89, 269

Janowitz, Morris, *The Dynamics of Prejudice*, 149

jazz, 26, 50; civil rights in relation to, 61–62; controversy over, 37–41, 49–55; failures in Adorno's writings on, 35–36, 54–55; and negative identity, 62, 68; race and, 51–52, 54, 68; scholarship on, 61–62; as ticket to America, 53

Jewish Club of Los Angeles, 284–87

Jews. *See* anti-Semitism

Jim Crow, 19, 68, 256

Jonny spielt auf (Jonny starts to play) [jazz opera], 51

judgment, 96, 137–38

Jung, C. G., 220, 252–53

Kant, Immanuel, and Kantianism: Adorno and, 21, 23, 68, 286; *Critique of Pure Reason*, 175, 177; and culture, 95; *Dialectic of Enlightenment* on, 117, 173–77; and epistemology, 17, 89–90, 231; Freud in relation to, 261; Horkheimer and, 266; and metaphysics, 90; modernity and, 24; and reason, 175, 177–79, 261; and science, 88–89; Simmel and, 85, 88–89, 97; and subjectivity, 21, 32–34, 54, 65, 69, 97–98, 134, 168–69, 174–76, 291; and theory-practice distinction, 6–7; and universality, 26, 71, 80, 81. *See also* neo-Kantianism

Kardiner, Abram, 201

Kautsky, Karl, 163

Kierkegaard, Søren, 48, 136, 139, 141

Kirchheimer, Otto, 149; "The Legal Order of National Socialism," 131

kitsch, 132–33

knowledge: alienation as source of, 32, 80–81; alterity as source of, 83–84; Kantian notion of, 231; pseudo-, 230–31; relativism as source of, 80; wound as origin of, 32–33, 263–64

Kołokowski, Leszek, 47

Korsch, Karl, 48

Korsgaard, Christine, 6–7, 8

Koselleck, Reinhart, 276

Kracauer, Siegfried, 84–85, 100

Krenek, Ernst, 51–52

Ku Klux Klan, 233–34

Kultur, 92

labor unions, 278
Lamprecht, Karl, 84
Lang, Fritz, 127
Laski, Harold, 128
Lazarsfeld, Paul, 75–79, 87, 109, 148, 181, 185, 202; *Marienthal*, 79
Lebensphilosophie, 59, 85, 88, 96, 137, 284
Lenin, Vladimir, 116, 163, 236
Levinson, Daniel, 201, 202, 241
liberalism, 192, 254–55, 257–58, 273–74, 291
liberty. *See* freedom
Locke, Alain, 59–60
Locke, John, 80, 134
logical positivism, 89, 159
Long, Huey, 279
Lotze, Hermann, 84
Lowenthal, Leo, 27, 266; *Prophets of Deceit*, 149
Lukács, Georg, 32, 48–50, 85, 124, 173; *History and Class Consciousness*, 160, 162–71; *The Theory of the Novel*, 124–25
Luther, Martin, 44
Luxemburg, Rosa, 162–63
Lynd, Robert, 87, 109, 278

Mach, Ernst, 89
MacIver, Robert, 87, 109, 241
Madison, James, 272, 275
Mahler, Gustav, 31, 63–65
majority rule, 9, 194, 269, 271–75
Mann, Thomas, 127
Marcuse, Herbert, 53, 126, 146, 149, 181, 238, 253; *Eros and Civilization*, 253–54; *Reason and Revolution*, 131, 139–40, 144–45; "Some Social Implications of Modern Technology," 131
Maritain, Jacques, 269
Marx, Karl, 48, 66, 68, 116, 146, 159, 165–66, 266; *Theses on Feuerbach*, 1, 2. *See also* Marxism
Marxism: Adorno and, 21, 23, 26, 44, 48, 69, 85; Lukács and, 162–71; and music criticism, 45–47; orthodox, 28, 160, 163, 171–72, 175, 181, 292; and science, 160; and universality, 21, 80
Maslow, Abraham, 253
Massing, Paul, *Rehearsal for Destruction*, 150
mass media: popular appeal of, 180; research on, 20, 50, 149, 185–86; as source of popular information, 231; as threat to democracy, 233. *See also* culture industry
McCarthy, Joseph, and McCarthyism, 235, 237
Mead, George Herbert, 89
Mead, Margaret, 201
meaning, crisis of, 135–36
mechanical solidarity, 8
media psychology. *See* narrative, psychology of
Melville, Herman, *Moby-Dick*, 203
metaphysics, 89
Militant League for German Culture, 220
Mill, John Stuart, 282
mimesis, 33, 67
Mingus, Charles, 61
minorities: ameliorating behaviors toward, 193; hatred of, 194; interests of, 270–75; objective reason and, 274–75; othering of, 192. *See also* anti-Semitism; otherness; prejudice; race and racism
modernity: alienation in, 31; culture in, 9; fear of, 52; identity in, 8, 135; positive identity in context of, 61; self and subjectivity in, 18, 98–99; truth in, 134; value spheres in, 272

More, Thomas, 157
multiculturalism, 54
Murray, Henry, 197, 202–4, 210, 252
music: Adorno on technique in, 182–84; avant-garde, 40; fetishization in, 45; in German culture, 40, 42; Nietzsche and, 55–56, 58; particularity and, 55; psychoanalytic approach to, 53–54; social theory of, 45–48, 50–51, 53–54; sociological research on, 75–79; sociology of, 40; universality and, 42–46, 55–58. *See also* art; culture; jazz
The Music Appreciation Hour (radio show), 77–78
Myrdal, Gunnar, *An American Dilemma*, 199, 200
myth, fascism as return to, 116

narcissism, 33
narrative: analysis of, as form of empiricism, 191–92, 201–4, 214–16; psychology of, 185–86, 188–92, 202–3, 262, 264–65; theory of, 23–25, 106–7, 117–20, 137–38, 172–73
national identity: American, 191; Bauer on, 160–62; politics and, 195; reemergence of, 13–14; supposed postwar eclipse of, 20
Nazi Germany: and anti-Semitism, 187, 258–59; character of, as a state, 258–59; and cultural degeneracy, 51–52; modern Germany in relation to, 10–12; self-identity of, 30; social typologies employed by, 220; subjectivity of, 51–52
negative identity: Adorno's personal experience of, 80, 127–28, 283–87; alienation in relation to, 4; art and, 56–62; in capitalist society, 23–24; concept and origins of, 4, 13, 69, 72, 82; critical theory based on, 190, 276; dialectic involving, 25, 61; *Dialectic of Enlightenment* and, 122–27, 172–77; Du Bois and, 56–60; enemy creation as means to, 187; examples of critical application of, 64–65, 152–53; exile and, 80; features of, 23, 62; Frankfurt School and, 62, 144–45; Horkheimer's personal experience of, 127–28; jazz and, 62, 68; Locke and, 60; personal identity as, 35; positive vs., 17–18; priority of, to identity, 4, 66, 111, 251; projectivity of, 230–39, 255–56; race and, 60–62, 66; as reciprocal subject/object relation, 245; societal impositions of, 19–20. *See also* non-identity
neoconservatism, 235
neo-Hegelianism, 33
neo-Kantianism, 84, 87, 89, 95, 97, 105
neoliberalism, 8, 271–72
Neumann, Franz, 126, 149, 258–59; *Behemoth*, 258; *The Cultural Migration: The European Scholar in America*, 72–73, 75
Neurath, Otto, 89
New School for Social Research, 103
New York Times (newspaper), 57
Niebuhr, Reinhold, 269
Nietzsche, Friedrich, 55–56, 58, 59, 62, 84, 118, 121, 141, 171, 187, 204, 266, 269, 303n41; *Beyond Good and Evil*, 56; *The Birth of Tragedy*, 55
Nietzscheanism, 21, 26
nomothetic categories, 95
non-identity: art and, 13, 30, 64–65; *The Authoritarian Personality* and, 219, 293; concept of, 3, 16–17, 32, 110; conceptual prehistory of, 158–71; epistemological role of, 17; Frankfurt School's concept of, 184; identification and, 246–47; identity

dependent on, 189–90; kitsch as instance of, 132–33; of reason, 118; scholarly inattention to, 17; of subjectivity, 118; theories of, 55–62. *See also* negative identity
not-I, 15–16, 254
Nuremberg Laws, 19

objectivity: critique of, 16; damaged by prejudice, 225–30; domination's effect on, 22–23; identity in relation to, 19; negative identity and, 245; of reason, 267–68, 274–75; subjectivity in relation to, 257, 275–76
Odysseus, as model of the individual, 117–19, 123, 172, 189, 204, 263–64
Oedipal complex, 204, 246, 263
Office of Radio Research, 109
Order 9066, US Federal, 127
orthodox Freudianism, 241–57, 264, 292
orthodox Marxism, as universality, 28, 160, 163, 171–72, 175, 181, 292
otherness: framed as a problem, 223, 234; political uses of, 192–93, 209–10; psychological uses of, 209, 222–23; race and, 67. *See also* alienation; anti-Semitism; enemies, political/dialogical creation of; minorities; prejudice; race and racism; stranger

paranoid style, in American politics, 234
Park, Robert, 236
Parker, Charlie, 61
Parsons, Talcott, 238
particularity: Adorno and, 34, 133; as false universality, 34; Fromm and, 60–61; music and, 55; science and, 87–89; universality in relation to, 82–83, 97–99, 133. *See also* individuals and individualism

personal identity: collective identity in relation to, 7–8, 10, 18, 211; as negative identity, 35; politics in relation to, 3, 9
personology, 210
phenomenology, 90, 137
philosophy, postwar role of, 279–82
Plato, 223, 268
poetry, 12–13
politics: Adorno and, 43–44, 50; and antipolitics, 234; creation of enemies in, 187–88, 194–95, 211; fascist use of, 234, 249–50, 259; national identity and, 195; paranoid style in American, 234; personal identity in relation to, 3, 9; uses of otherness in, 192–93, 209–10
Polla, W. C., "The Dancing Tambourine," 50
Pollock, Friedrich, 126–28, 148, 154; "Is National Socialism a New Order?," 131
positive identity: attractions of, 61; characteristics of, 11–12; concept of, 289; dialectic involving, 25, 61; enemy creation as means to, 187–88; Erikson and, 196–97; exclusion linked to, 19; Frankfurt School's objection to, 142–45, 200, 244–45; Fromm's notion of, 140–45, 155–60, 200, 244–45; in modern context, 61; negative vs., 17–18
positivism, 86
Pragmatism. *See* American Pragmatism
praxis, theory in relation to, 2, 6–7, 96, 99–100
prejudice: *The Authoritarian Personality* as study of, 59, 198–200, 217; gender and, 227–30; limits to reform of, 224–25; mass media's role in, 233; neurosis associated with, 150, 153, 212, 222, 226–27;

psychological approach to, 200–202, 222–23; psychological factors in, 216–17; reason in relation to, 177–79. *See also* anti-Semitism; minorities; otherness; race and racism; *Studies in Prejudice*
primitivism, 52, 54, 57–58
Princeton Radio Project, 37, 75–76, 113, 213
projective psychological tests, 202–3
Proust, Marcel, 283
pseudo-conservatism, 234, 236
psychoanalysis: Adorno and, 249, 260–62; Frankfurt School and, 146–47; in music criticism, 53–54; neo-Freudian, 213. *See also* Freud, Sigmund
psychologisms, as disciplinary fusions, 185–88, 190–91, 242–44
psychometrics, 202

race and racism: Adorno and, 37–38, 45; anti-Semitism in relation to, 24, 200; authoritarianism linked to, 199; *The Authoritarian Personality* on, 199; as distorted universality, 231; Du Bois's notions of, 56–60, 66; Frankfurt School study of, 58–59, 66, 190, 301n24; in Germany, 35; jazz and, 51–52, 54, 68; Locke's notion of, 60; Nazi Germany and, 51–52; negative identity and, 60–62, 66; and otherness, 67; in United States, 34–35, 292–93. *See also* minorities; prejudice
Radio City Music Hall, 74
Reagan, Ronald, 238
reason: Bacon's classical conception of, 157; *Dialectic of Enlightenment* on, 169–70, 173–74; Horkheimer on, 266–77; Kant's notions of, 175, 177–79, 261; objective, 267–68, 274–75; subjective, 168, 268–77, 291; technical application of, 177–78
reductionism, 90, 238
regression, 116
Reichmann, Frieda, 141
relativism: cultural, 22, 81, 94, 141, 201; knowledge arising from, 80; as weapon against racism, 94
religion, 7, 23–24, 58–60, 140–41, 174–76, 233–34, 246, 272
Renaissance, 135, 142–43, 157–58, 163, 167–68, 170–71, 172, 196
ressentiment, 14, 123, 150, 187, 257, 279, 290
Ricardo, David, 167
Rickert, Heinrich, 95
right Hegelianism, 140, 144
Rjazanov, David, 49
Rolland, Romain, 246
Romanticism: Enlightenment vs., 31; and epistemology, 65; Heine and, 63; and the Stranger type, 83
Roosevelt, Franklin, 127
Rorschach Test, 202
Rosenberg, Alfred, 220
Rousseau, Jean-Jacques, *Discourse on Inequality*, 115
Russell, Bertrand, 159
Russian Machians, 163

Sachs, Hans, 141
Sade, Marquis de, 117, 121, 173–74, 177–78
Sanford, Nevitt, 201–4, 210, 241
San Francisco Psychoanalytic Society, 197, 260
Sartre, Jean-Paul, 136
Schachtel, Ernst, 131, 140–41, 143–44
Schiller, Friedrich, *Letters on the Aesthetic Education of Man*, 137
Schmidt, James, 269

Schmitt, Carl, 187, 194–95, 211
Schönberg, Arnold, 40, 50, 52, 75
Schopenhauer, Arthur, 73, 84, 121, 269, 271
Schütz, Alfred, "The Stranger," 102–3
science: bourgeois, 157; *Dialectic of Enlightenment* and, 155–58, 164–71; divisions of, 168–69; Idealist approach to, 89–90; Kant and, 88–89; Simmel and, 87–91; subjectivity and, 90, 158–59; systematization as threat to, 156–57; universality and particularity in, 87–89; utility of, 156–57
second sight, 56, 64, 67, 69, 303n41
self and selfhood: autonomy of, 34; in capitalist society, 24; dissolution of, 4; fascism and, 136, 142; Heine and, 31; Horkheimer on, 136–38; identity in relation to, 5–6; in modern context, 98–99; rationality as grounded in, 156; in the Renaissance, 142–43; Simmel and, 98–99; the wound in, 29–30. *See also* divided self; individuals and individualism; subjectivity
self-interest, 272–74
Shils, Edward, 221, 235–38
Show Trials (Moscow), 49, 85
Simmel, Ernst, 241
Simmel, Georg, 26, 56, 81–113, 138, 150, 163, 171, 186, 212, 236, 284; academic career of, 84; Adorno lecture on, 86–109; and culture, 92–96; support for World War I, 85; influence of, 84–85; *Kant*, 85, 97; *Philosophy of Money*, 93; *Problems of Historical Philosophy*, 94; and science, 87–91; "Tragedy of Culture," 93
Simpson, George, 113
Small, Albion, 87, 94

Smith, Adam, 167
social Darwinism, 27, 81, 103, 112, 144, 188, 211, 232, 236, 269–70, 274
socialism, 43–45, 162, 179–80
social typologies, 220–21
sociology and social science: causality in, 104–6; Frankfurt School's projected transformation of, 157–58; the Stranger as ideal type of, 83. *See also* American sociology
sociometrics, 107
sociopsychology, applied, 185–88
Socrates, 267, 268, 271, 274
Soviet Union, 46, 48–49, 232–33, 237
speculative philosophy, 152–54, 242–43
Spencer, Herbert, 88–89, 89, 94
Spinoza, Baruch, 271
spirituals, 57, 60
Stalin, Joseph, 49, 85, 236
stereotypes, 179, 217, 223
stranger, 81–83, 86, 102–3, 212, 223, 294, 305n31. *See also* alienation; otherness
Strasser, Gregor, 258
Studien über Autorität und Familie (Frankfurt School project), 146, 148
Studies in Philosophy and Social Science (journal), 37, 125, 129, 131, 139, 144–45. See also *Zeitschrift für Sozialforschung* (journal)
Studies in Prejudice (Frankfurt School project), 109, 123, 126, 131–46, 149–55, 201–5, 208–9, 227, 235, 241, 271, 292–93
subjective universality, 43, 122–23, 175, 190–91, 209, 292
subjectivity: critique of, 15; the culture industry and, 178–79; *Dialectic of Enlightenment* on, 119–20, 172–73, 180, 186–87; domination's effect on, 22–23; Kantian, 21, 32–34, 54, 65, 69, 97–98, 168–69,

174–76; modern, 18; of Nazis, 51–52; negative identity and, 245; objectivity in relation to, 257, 275–76; and reason, 268–82, 291; Sadean, 174–75; science and, 90, 158–59; wounded, 32–34, 64–68, 108, 123, 187, 220, 225, 251, 260–63, 288 (*see also* divided self). *See also* self and selfhood

suffering: art/music linked to, 30, 55–58, 182; narrative as means of relief from, 270, 274; negativity associated with, 17, 81, 113; subjectivity associated with, 33, 117–18, 263; truth in relation to, 65, 73

Sumner, William Graham, 211, 226, 236, 237

superego, 250–51, 253–55, 257, 261–62

Taft-Hartley Act, 278
Tagore, Rabindranath, 245
TAT. *See* Thematic Apperception Test
technique, 182–85, 191–92, 214
terror, 181, 273, 274, 276
Thematic Apperception Test (TAT), 197, 203
theory, praxis in relation to, 2, 6–7, 96, 99–100
Thomas, Martin Luther, 179, 191–92
Thomas Aquinas, 268
Thomism, 276
ticket mentality, 194, 215, 219, 235
Tillich, Paul, 131, 139–40
Tocqueville, Alexis de, 8
totality: analyses of, 162–70; anti-Semitism as, 151, 225; culture/society as, 123, 132, 135, 138, 151, 217, 258; state as, 129, 162, 258; subjective identity as, 164, 167
"Trink, Brüderlein, Trink" (Drink, little brother, drink), 50
Troeltsch, Ernst, 143

truth: American Pragmatism and, 269–70; margins as the source of, 73; in modern context, 134; Nietzschean notion of, 56; suffering in relation to, 65, 73

United States: Adorno in, 20, 22, 49, 53–55, 71–112; critical theory's influence in, 292–93; race in, 34–35, 292–93; relativism in, 22; susceptibility of, to fascism, 225–26

universality: Adorno and, 21–22, 34, 133; cultural, 39–40; culture and, 92; false, 34, 68–69; Frankfurt School and, 161–62, 290; immigrants and, 286–87; inverted, 191–95; Kantian, 21, 71, 80, 81; Marxian, 21, 80; music and, 42–46, 55–58; particularity in relation to, 82–83, 97–99, 133; positive sense of, 244–46; in post-Hegelian thought, 25; racism as distorted, 231; science and, 87–89; subjective, 43, 122–23, 175, 190–91, 209, 292

US Department of State, 126, 149
US Department of War, 293
utopianism, 10, 21, 64, 174–76, 276, 289

values, 95–97, 105–7
value spheres, 100–101, 272
Veblen, Thorstein, 131–33
vitalism, 59, 85. See also *Lebensphilosophie*

Wagner, Richard, 38
Weber, Alfred, 141, 143
Weber, Max, 83, 84, 107, 121, 125, 150, 162, 232, 236–38, 259, 266, 267, 271, 275; "Science as Vocation," 274
Webster, Noah, 272
"The Wedding of the Painted Doll" (song), 50

Werfel, Franz, 245
"Wer hat denn den Käse zum Bahnhof gerollt?" (song), 50
Wesensnotwendigkeit, 105–6, 112, 192, 195
Western Marxism, 48
Whiteman, Paul, "Valencia," 50
Wiesengrund, Oskar (Adorno's father), 43–44, 301n22
Wiggershaus, Rolf, 148
Wilders, Geert, 14
Windelband, Wilhelm, 95
Wirth, Louis, 236
Wittgenstein, Ludwig, 89
World War II, 127–29, 265
woundedness: art's manifestation of, 30; critical theory resulting from, 32; in German self-identity, 29; Heine as, 29–32, 63–64; individual paths to healing of, 32; jazz writings as, 36–41; of Odysseus's cunning, 117–19, 262–64; of self and subjectivity, 30, 32–34, 64–68; as source of knowledge, 32–33, 263–64. *See also* subjectivity: wounded

Young, Lester, 61

Zeitschrift für Sozialforschung (journal), 37, 131, 142, 144, 146, 151, 185, 202. See also *Studies in Philosophy and Social Science* (journal)
Zhdanov, Andrei, 49

Cultural Memory | *in the Present*

David Marriott, *Whither Fanon? Studies in the Blackness of Being*

Reinhart Koselleck, *Sediments of Time: On Possible Histories*, translated and edited by Sean Franzel and Stefan-Ludwig Hoffmann

Devin Singh, *Divine Currency: The Theological Power of Money in the West*

Stefanos Geroulanos, *Transparency in Postwar France: A Critical History of the Present*

Sari Nusseibeh, *The Story of Reason in Islam*

Olivia C. Harrison, *Transcolonial Maghreb: Imagining Palestine in the Era of Decolonialization*

Barbara Vinken, *Flaubert Postsecular: Modernity Crossed Out*

Aishwary Kumar, *Radical Equality: Ambedkar, Gandhi, and the Problem of Democracy*

Simona Forti, *New Demons: Rethinking Power and Evil Today*

Joseph Vogl, *The Specter of Capital*

Hans Joas, *Faith as an Option*

Michael Gubser, *The Far Reaches: Ethics, Phenomenology, and the Call for Social Renewal in Twentieth-Century Central Europe*

Françoise Davoine, *Mother Folly: A Tale*

Knox Peden, *Spinoza contra Phenomenology: French Rationalism from Cavaillès to Deleuze*

Elizabeth A. Pritchard, *Locke's Political Theology: Public Religion and Sacred Rights*

Ankhi Mukherjee, *What Is a Classic? Postcolonial Rewriting and Invention of the Canon*

Jean-Pierre Dupuy, *The Mark of the Sacred*

Henri Atlan, *Fraud: The World of* Ona'ah

Niklas Luhmann, *Theory of Society, Volume 2*

Ilit Ferber, *Philosophy and Melancholy: Benjamin's Early Reflections on Theater and Language*

Alexandre Lefebvre, *Human Rights as a Way of Life: On Bergson's Political Philosophy*

Theodore W. Jennings, Jr., *Outlaw Justice: The Messianic Politics of Paul*

Alexander Etkind, *Warped Mourning: Stories of the Undead in the Land of the Unburied*

Denis Guénoun, *About Europe: Philosophical Hypotheses*

Maria Boletsi, *Barbarism and Its Discontents*

Sigrid Weigel, *Walter Benjamin: Images, the Creaturely, and the Holy*

Roberto Esposito, *Living Thought: The Origins and Actuality of Italian Philosophy*

Henri Atlan, *The Sparks of Randomness, Volume 2: The Atheism of Scripture*

Rüdiger Campe, *The Game of Probability: Literature and Calculation from Pascal to Kleist*

Niklas Luhmann, *A Systems Theory of Religion*

Jean-Luc Marion, *In the Self's Place: The Approach of Saint Augustine*

Rodolphe Gasché, *Georges Bataille: Phenomenology and Phantasmatology*

Niklas Luhmann, *Theory of Society, Volume 1*

Alessia Ricciardi, *After* La Dolce Vita: *A Cultural Prehistory of Berlusconi's Italy*

Daniel Innerarity, *The Future and Its Enemies: In Defense of Political Hope*

Patricia Pisters, *The Neuro-image: A Deleuzian Film-Philosophy of Digital Screen Culture*

François-David Sebbah, *Testing the Limit: Derrida, Henry, Levinas, and the Phenomenological Tradition*

Erik Peterson, *Theological Tractates*, edited by Michael J. Hollerich

Feisal G. Mohamed, *Milton and the Post-secular Present: Ethics, Politics, Terrorism*

Pierre Hadot, *The Present Alone Is Our Happiness, Second Edition: Conversations with Jeannie Carlier and Arnold I. Davidson*

Yasco Horsman, *Theaters of Justice: Judging, Staging, and Working through in Arendt, Brecht, and Delbo*

Jacques Derrida, *Parages*, edited by John P. Leavey

Henri Atlan, *The Sparks of Randomness, Volume 1: Spermatic Knowledge*

Rebecca Comay, *Mourning Sickness: Hegel and the French Revolution*

Djelal Kadir, *Memos from the Besieged City: Lifelines for Cultural Sustainability*

Stanley Cavell, *Little Did I Know: Excerpts from Memory*

Jeffrey Mehlman, *Adventures in the French Trade: Fragments toward a Life*

Jacob Rogozinski, *The Ego and the Flesh: An Introduction to Egoanalysis*
Marcel Hénaff, *The Price of Truth: Gift, Money, and Philosophy*
Paul Patton, *Deleuzian Concepts: Philosophy, Colonialization, Politics*
Michael Fagenblat, *A Covenant of Creatures: Levinas's Philosophy of Judaism*
Stefanos Geroulanos, *An Atheism That Is Not Humanist Emerges in French Thought*
Andrew Herscher, *Violence Taking Place: The Architecture of the Kosovo Conflict*
Hans-Jörg Rheinberger, *On Historicizing Epistemology: An Essay*
Jacob Taubes, *From Cult to Culture*, edited by Charlotte Fonrobert and Amir Engel
Peter Hitchcock, *The Long Space: Transnationalism and Postcolonial Form*
Lambert Wiesing, *Artificial Presence: Philosophical Studies in Image Theory*
Jacob Taubes, *Occidental Eschatology*
Freddie Rokem, *Philosophers and Thespians: Thinking Performance*
Roberto Esposito, *Communitas: The Origin and Destiny of Community*
Vilashini Cooppan, *Worlds Within: National Narratives and Global Connections in Postcolonial Writing*
Josef Früchtl, *The Impertinent Self: A Heroic History of Modernity*
Frank Ankersmit, Ewa Domanska, and Hans Kellner, eds., *Re-figuring Hayden White*
Michael Rothberg, *Multidirectional Memory: Remembering the Holocaust in the Age of Decolonization*
Jean-François Lyotard, *Enthusiasm: The Kantian Critique of History*
Ernst van Alphen, Mieke Bal, and Carel Smith, eds., *The Rhetoric of Sincerity*
Stéphane Mosès, *The Angel of History: Rosenzweig, Benjamin, Scholem*
Pierre Hadot, *The Present Alone Is Our Happiness: Conversations with Jeannie Carlier and Arnold I. Davidson*
Alexandre Lefebvre, *The Image of the Law: Deleuze, Bergson, Spinoza*
Samira Haj, *Reconfiguring Islamic Tradition: Reform, Rationality, and Modernity*
Diane Perpich, *The Ethics of Emmanuel Levinas*
Marcel Detienne, *Comparing the Incomparable*
François Delaporte, *Anatomy of the Passions*
René Girard, *Mimesis and Theory: Essays on Literature and Criticism, 1959–2005*
Richard Baxstrom, *Houses in Motion: The Experience of Place and the Problem of Belief in Urban Malaysia*

Jennifer L. Culbert, *Dead Certainty: The Death Penalty and the Problem of Judgment*

Samantha Frost, *Lessons from a Materialist Thinker: Hobbesian Reflections on Ethics and Politics*

Regina Mara Schwartz, *Sacramental Poetics at the Dawn of Secularism: When God Left the World*

Gil Anidjar, *Semites: Race, Religion, Literature*

Ranjana Khanna, *Algeria Cuts: Women and Representation, 1830 to the Present*

Esther Peeren, *Intersubjectivities and Popular Culture: Bakhtin and Beyond*

Eyal Peretz, *Becoming Visionary: Brian De Palma's Cinematic Education of the Senses*

Diana Sorensen, *A Turbulent Decade Remembered: Scenes from the Latin American Sixties*

Hubert Damisch, *A Childhood Memory by Piero della Francesca*

José van Dijck, *Mediated Memories in the Digital Age*

Dana Hollander, *Exemplarity and Chosenness: Rosenzweig and Derrida on the Nation of Philosophy*

Asja Szafraniec, *Beckett, Derrida, and the Event of Literature*

Sara Guyer, *Romanticism after Auschwitz*

Alison Ross, *The Aesthetic Paths of Philosophy: Presentation in Kant, Heidegger, Lacoue-Labarthe, and Nancy*

Gerhard Richter, *Thought-Images: Frankfurt School Writers' Reflections from Damaged Life*

Bella Brodzki, *Can These Bones Live? Translation, Survival, and Cultural Memory*

Rodolphe Gasché, *The Honor of Thinking: Critique, Theory, Philosophy*

Brigitte Peucker, *The Material Image: Art and the Real in Film*

Natalie Melas, *All the Difference in the World: Postcoloniality and the Ends of Comparison*

Jonathan Culler, *The Literary in Theory*

Michael G. Levine, *The Belated Witness: Literature, Testimony, and the Question of Holocaust Survival*

Jennifer A. Jordan, *Structures of Memory: Understanding German Change in Berlin and Beyond*

Christoph Menke, *Reflections of Equality*

Marlène Zarader, *The Unthought Debt: Heidegger and the Hebraic Heritage*

Jan Assmann, *Religion and Cultural Memory: Ten Studies*

David Scott and Charles Hirschkind, *Powers of the Secular Modern: Talal Asad and His Interlocutors*

Gyanendra Pandey, *Routine Violence: Nations, Fragments, Histories*

James Siegel, *Naming the Witch*

J. M. Bernstein, *Against Voluptuous Bodies: Late Modernism and the Meaning of Painting*

Theodore W. Jennings, Jr., *Reading Derrida / Thinking Paul: On Justice*

Richard Rorty and Eduardo Mendieta, *Take Care of Freedom and Truth Will Take Care of Itself: Interviews with Richard Rorty*

Jacques Derrida, *Paper Machine*

Renaud Barbaras, *Desire and Distance: Introduction to a Phenomenology of Perception*

Jill Bennett, *Empathic Vision: Affect, Trauma, and Contemporary Art*

Ban Wang, *Illuminations from the Past: Trauma, Memory, and History in Modern China*

James Phillips, *Heidegger's* Volk: *Between National Socialism and Poetry*

Frank Ankersmit, *Sublime Historical Experience*

István Rév, *Retroactive Justice: Prehistory of Post-communism*

Paola Marrati, *Genesis and Trace: Derrida Reading Husserl and Heidegger*

Krzysztof Ziarek, *The Force of Art*

Marie-José Mondzain, *Image, Icon, Economy: The Byzantine Origins of the Contemporary Imaginary*

Cecilia Sjöholm, *The Antigone Complex: Ethics and the Invention of Feminine Desire*

Jacques Derrida and Elisabeth Roudinesco, *For What Tomorrow . . . A Dialogue*

Elisabeth Weber, *Questioning Judaism: Interviews by Elisabeth Weber*

Jacques Derrida and Catherine Malabou, *Counterpath: Traveling with Jacques Derrida*

Martin Seel, *Aesthetics of Appearing*

Nanette Salomon, *Shifting Priorities: Gender and Genre in Seventeenth-Century Dutch Painting*

Jacob Taubes, *The Political Theology of Paul*

Jean-Luc Marion, *The Crossing of the Visible*

Eric Michaud, *The Cult of Art in Nazi Germany*

Anne Freadman, *The Machinery of Talk: Charles Peirce and the Sign Hypothesis*

Stanley Cavell, *Emerson's Transcendental Etudes*

Stuart McLean, *The Event and Its Terrors: Ireland, Famine, Modernity*

Beate Rössler, ed., *Privacies: Philosophical Evaluations*

Bernard Faure, *Double Exposure: Cutting across Buddhist and Western Discourses*

Alessia Ricciardi, *The Ends of Mourning: Psychoanalysis, Literature, Film*

Alain Badiou, *Saint Paul: The Foundation of Universalism*

Gil Anidjar, *The Jew, the Arab: A History of the Enemy*

Jonathan Culler and Kevin Lamb, eds., *Just Being Difficult? Academic Writing in the Public Arena*

Jean-Luc Nancy, *A Finite Thinking*, edited by Simon Sparks

Theodor W. Adorno, *Can One Live after Auschwitz? A Philosophical Reader*, edited by Rolf Tiedemann

Patricia Pisters, *The Matrix of Visual Culture: Working with Deleuze in Film Theory*

Andreas Huyssen, *Present Pasts: Urban Palimpsests and the Politics of Memory*

Talal Asad, *Formations of the Secular: Christianity, Islam, Modernity*

Dorothea von Mücke, *The Rise of the Fantastic Tale*

Marc Redfield, *The Politics of Aesthetics: Nationalism, Gender, Romanticism*

Emmanuel Levinas, *On Escape*

Dan Zahavi, *Husserl's Phenomenology*

Rodolphe Gasché, *The Idea of Form: Rethinking Kant's Aesthetics*

Michael Naas, *Taking on the Tradition: Jacques Derrida and the Legacies of Deconstruction*

Herlinde Pauer-Studer, ed., *Constructions of Practical Reason: Interviews on Moral and Political Philosophy*

Jean-Luc Marion, *Being Given That: Toward a Phenomenology of Givenness*

Theodor W. Adorno and Max Horkheimer, *Dialectic of Enlightenment*

Ian Balfour, *The Rhetoric of Romantic Prophecy*

Martin Stokhof, *World and Life as One: Ethics and Ontology in Wittgenstein's Early Thought*

Gianni Vattimo, *Nietzsche: An Introduction*

Jacques Derrida, *Negotiations: Interventions and Interviews, 1971–1998*, edited by Elizabeth Rottenberg

Brett Levinson, *The Ends of Literature: The Latin American "Boom" in the Neoliberal Marketplace*

Timothy J. Reiss, *Against Autonomy: Cultural Instruments, Mutualities, and the Fictive Imagination*

Hent de Vries and Samuel Weber, eds., *Religion and Media*

Niklas Luhmann, *Theories of Distinction: Re-describing the Descriptions of Modernity*, edited and introduction by William Rasch

Johannes Fabian, *Anthropology with an Attitude: Critical Essays*

Michel Henry, *I Am the Truth: Toward a Philosophy of Christianity*

Gil Anidjar, *"Our Place in Al-Andalus": Kabbalah, Philosophy, Literature in Arab-Jewish Letters*

Hélène Cixous and Jacques Derrida, *Veils*

F. R. Ankersmit, *Historical Representation*

F. R. Ankersmit, *Political Representation*

Elissa Marder, *Dead Time: Temporal Disorders in the Wake of Modernity (Baudelaire and Flaubert)*

Reinhart Koselleck, *The Practice of Conceptual History: Timing History, Spacing Concepts*

Niklas Luhmann, *The Reality of the Mass Media*

Hubert Damisch, *A Theory of /Cloud/: Toward a History of Painting*

Jean-Luc Nancy, *The Speculative Remark: (One of Hegel's Bon Mots)*

Jean-François Lyotard, *Soundproof Room: Malraux's Anti-aesthetics*

Jan Patočka, *Plato and Europe*

Hubert Damisch, *Skyline: The Narcissistic City*

Isabel Hoving, *In Praise of New Travelers: Reading Caribbean Migrant Women Writers*

Richard Rand, ed., *Futures: Of Jacques Derrida*

William Rasch, *Niklas Luhmann's Modernity: The Paradoxes of Differentiation*

Jacques Derrida and Anne Dufourmantelle, *Of Hospitality*

Jean-François Lyotard, *The Confession of Augustine*

Kaja Silverman, *World Spectators*

Samuel Weber, *Institution and Interpretation: Expanded Edition*

Jeffrey S. Librett, *The Rhetoric of Cultural Dialogue: Jews and Germans in the Epoch of Emancipation*

Ulrich Baer, *Remnants of Song: Trauma and the Experience of Modernity in Charles Baudelaire and Paul Celan*

Samuel C. Wheeler III, *Deconstruction as Analytic Philosophy*

David S. Ferris, *Silent Urns: Romanticism, Hellenism, Modernity*

Rodolphe Gasché, *Of Minimal Things: Studies on the Notion of Relation*

Sarah Winter, *Freud and the Institution of Psychoanalytic Knowledge*

Samuel Weber, *The Legend of Freud: Expanded Edition*
Aris Fioretos, ed., *The Solid Letter: Readings of Friedrich Hölderlin*
J. Hillis Miller / Manuel Asensi, *Black Holes / J. Hillis Miller; or, Boustrophedonic Reading*
Miryam Sas, *Fault Lines: Cultural Memory and Japanese Surrealism*
Peter Schwenger, *Fantasm and Fiction: On Textual Envisioning*
Didier Maleuvre, *Museum Memories: History, Technology, Art*
Jacques Derrida, *Monolingualism of the Other; or, The Prosthesis of Origin*
Andrew Baruch Wachtel, *Making a Nation, Breaking a Nation: Literature and Cultural Politics in Yugoslavia*
Niklas Luhmann, *Love as Passion: The Codification of Intimacy*
Mieke Bal, ed., *The Practice of Cultural Analysis: Exposing Interdisciplinary Interpretation*
Jacques Derrida and Gianni Vattimo, eds., *Religion*

The authorized representative in the EU for product safety and compliance is:
Mare Nostrum Group
B.V Doelen 72
4831 GR Breda
The Netherlands

www.ingramcontent.com/pod-product-compliance
Lightning Source LLC
Chambersburg PA
CBHW031754220426
43662CB00007B/398